Leeds

GW00721930

The Complete Handbook to Life in Leeds

Totally revised and updated, and radically redesigned to provide many new features and illustrations, this is the second edition of the best-selling Leeds Fax. It is an indispensable guide for everyone who lives in or visits the Leeds metropolitan area.

Edited by Roger Ratcliffe

Front Cover—*lower centre, Sarah Payne in the title role of "Sugar" at West Yorkshire Playhouse; anti-clockwise from top, Leeds Town Hall; fine food at a Leeds restaurant; exhibit from the new Royal Armouries Museum being built in Leeds; the Huntsman symbol of Tetleys beer; an Edwardian poster from the famous City Varieties; a colourful scene from Leeds Market; the Metro logo.*

Back Cover—*top, members of the Leeds-based Phoenix Dance Company; below, Harewood House; left, Calendar newsreader Gaynor Barnes; right, Leeds United manager Howard Wilkinson with the English League Championship cup in 1992; bottom, a baby being examined with the latest computer equipment at Killingbeck Hospital's highly acclaimed heart unit.*

Leeds Fax

2nd Edition published by
Aire Press & Publishing
PO Box HP36
Leeds LS6 3RN

© Aire Press & Publishing 1992

ISBN 1 871774 02 0

Cover reproduction by Intone Graphics, Morley.

Printed and bound by Staples Printers, St. Albans.

Important

The editor and publisher accept no responsibility
whatsoever for loss occasioned to any person or
business acting or refraining from acting as a result
of information contained in this book. It is the user's
responsibility to check details, which are subject to
change.

Editor's Note

Restaurants, pubs, shops, sports facilities and other
businesses and services have not paid to be included
in this book. There is no advertising. Those
establishments described in the following pages
were selected in order to give a balance of styles
and price-ranges, within the space limitations of a
handbook that is easily portable. If readers/owners
would like any omissions considered for the next
edition, please write to the above address.

About this book

Leeds Fax was produced almost entirely by desktop
publishing technology. All text was typeset by the
editor on an Apple Macintosh PowerBook 140 4/40
using Acta 7 version 1.0.3 outline processor and
exported to Nisus version 3.06 Br. word processor
for editing. This text was proof-read in Thunder 7
spell-checker and placed in Aldus PageMaker
version 4.01. Pages were composed on an Apple
Macintosh SEHD20 and Viking two-page display
monitor, and print-proofing was done on an Apple
LaserWriter IINT. The completed book was copied
onto a series of nine floppy disks and the page
masters were output on bromide by Autograph,
Bradford. Whilst the editor has done all this
typesetting and on-screen page make-up himself and
impressed you to death, he may have failed to splot
the oddy typing mistukk. Please be understanding.

Also available

The Bradford Book

Sales of Leeds Fax

Small businesses can share in the success of Leeds
Fax by selling it to generate an additional source of
income. Or local clubs & charities can sell it as part
of their fund-raising efforts. Conference organisers
might consider giving Leeds Fax to delegates. And
employers/personnel officers will find it a useful
gift with which to welcome new employees or
trainees to the Leeds area. Whatever your needs, if
you would like more information drop a line to Aire
Press & Publishing, PO Box HP36, Leeds LS6 3RN.

Introduction

By now, Leeds Fax is an established part of the Leeds scene. The first edition was an enormous success, but became obsolete very quickly and after a year I decided to let it go out of print. This new edition has been written to have a much longer life. But don't throw away the old one—it is already a collector's item.

The amount of change in Leeds in the last few years has been enormous. That meant we had to start from scratch, making the revised edition into virtually a new book. Some things—like the name chosen by Leeds Polytechnic to reflect its elevation to University status, and the new-look Yorkshire Television resulting from its merger with Tyne Tees—were not available as we went to press but most of what you read in this book should require little alteration for some considerable time.

This edition covers the most exciting developments in the 1990s, like the Royal Armouries Museum, new nature reserves, new waterfront walks and facilities, new theatres and rock venues, the proposed Supertram system, new sports and fitness facilities, and new places to go on days out from the Leeds area.

Most of the best pubs and restaurants of Leeds are included, plus the amazing new retail areas which have made Leeds one of the top shopping centres in the UK. And there is a completely redesigned history of Leeds, so that the growth of the city is properly explained rather than rattling off—machine gun-style—a cold list of dates and facts. That was perhaps a shortcoming in the last edition.

And there is a revised list of local clubs and organizations.

The book addresses the complete range of leisure and survival aspects of life in Leeds, with contacts given for those who require further details. Within the space limitations of a handbook, I am sure you will agree that there is a good balance of information for everyone.

With many more photographs and new features, there is plenty to satisfy those people who bought the first Leeds Fax. For old and new readers alike, I hope this book comes close to their ideal guidebook for the city.

In order to save vital space, I have not included an index but the contents should help you find your way around the book, together with the references at the top of each page.

If you have any suggestions for the next edition, please don't hesitate to write.

Roger Ratcliffe
Editor

Contents

Central Leeds Map 6
Metropolitan Leeds Map 7
Credits & Acknowledgements 8

Part One:
Surviving in Leeds
Leeds in the 1990s 10
Population Profile 11
Climate 11
General Help & Advice 12
Help for Visitors 13
Leeds Housing 14
Transport 16
Health 20
Addiction 23
Disability Help 23
Counselling Services 23
Women's Help 24
Student Survival 25
Education 25
Further & Higher
   Education 27
Adult Education 28
Libraries/Archives 29
Employment 30
Green Issues 31
Leeds Media 32
Leeds Politics 34
Religion 36

Part Two:
Exploring Leeds
Tourist Information Centres 38
A Year in the Life of Leeds 38
Star Attractions 40
Museums 46
Galleries 50
Parks & Gardens 54
Wild Leeds 57
Architectural/
   Historical Features 62
Conducted Walks/Tours 62

Part Three:
Leeds Night Life
Listings sources 72
Cinemas 72
Theatres 75
Music & Opera 79
Ballet & Dance 82
Jazz 84
Folk 85
Rock & Pop 86
Rock Venues 87
Nighclubs 89
Gay & Lesbian Scene 90

Part Four:
Pubs & Restaurants
Central Bars & Pubs 92
Suburban/Country
   Bars & Pubs 98
Bistros 104
English Restaurants 105
Fish & Chips 106
French 107
Greek 107
Italian 108
Polish 109
Vegetarian 109
American 109
Caribbean 109
Asian 109
Thai 111
Vietnamese 111
Chinese 112
Cafés & Tea Rooms 113

Part Five:
Shopping
Leeds Lights 116
Central Leeds shopping 116
Leeds Markets 117
Corn Exchange 119
Outer Leeds shopping 120

Contents

Part Six:
Sports & Fitness

Spectator Sports 122
Soccer 122
Cricket 122
Rugby 123
Horse Racing 124
Other Sports 125
Recreational Sports 126
Sports Development 127
Sports & Fitness Centres 129

Part Seven:
Clubs & Organizations

Voluntary Action Leeds 132
Leeds Volunteer Bureau 132
Activities 132
Arts/Entertainment 134
Campaigns/Interest Groups 135
Charities/Voluntary Groups 136
Ex-Service & Retired 136
Health & Parental Groups 136
Housing/Homelessness 138
Local/Community Groups 138
Miscellaneous Help & Advice 138
National & Ethnic Groups 139
Religious Organizations 139
Social Organizations 139
Sports: Regional Contacts 139
Women's Groups 141
Youth/Children 142

Part Eight:
Leeds History

To 1066 144
Leeds Population Growth 145
The Middle Ages 145
The 17th Century 146
The 18th Century 147
The 19th Century 148
The 20th Century 152
Ten Famous Leeds Residents 153

Part Nine:
Beyond Leeds

Leeds & Northern
   England Map 156
The Bradford Area 157
Bradford 157
Haworth 159
Ilkley 160
Keighley 161
Saltaire 161
Shipley 162
The Harrogate Area 163
Knaresborough 164
Ripon 164
Nidderdale 165
Masham 165
Calderdale & Kirklees 166
Calderdale 166
Kirklees 167
The Wakefield Area 169
The Yorkshire Dales 170
Airedale & Wharfedale 170
Western Dales 171
Wensleydale 173
Swaledale 173
The York Area 174
York 174
The Selby Area 176
Ryedale 177
North York Moors 178
The East Coast 180
North Yorkshire Coast 180
North Humberside Coast 181
County Humberside 182
The North Bank 182
The South Bank 184
South Yorkshire 185
Further Afield 187
Going South 187
Going West 188
Going North 190

Leeds Lifelines 192

REGENT STREET
BYRON STREET
GOWER ST
BRIDGE ST
EASTGATE
WEST YORKSHIRE PLAYHOUSE
ST. PETER'S STREET
YORK STREET
EAST STREET
CROWN POINT ROAD
LEEDS PARISH CHURCH
MARSH LANE
KIRKGATE
THE CALLS
MAUDE ST
HIGH COURT
TRAFALGAR ST
GRAFTON STREET
NORTH STREET
PARK ROAD
LOVELL
TEMPLAR ST
TEMPLAR PL
BRIDGE STREET
EDWARD ST
TEMPLAR LA
UNION ST
GEORGE ST
DYER ST
HARPER ST
CENTRAL BUS STATION
HARWOOD ST
VICAR LANE
NEW YORK STREET
CROSS YORK ST
CROWN ST
CORN EXCHANGE
MARKETS
MARKET ST
GALL LANE
LEEDS BRIDGE
BEGRAVE ST
GRAND THEATRE
HARRISON ST
MERRION STREET
CITY VARIETIES
KING EDWARD
KIRKGATE
DUNCAN ST
BRIGGATE
SWINE GATE
MERRION WAY
WADE LANE
MERRION CENTRE
WOODHOUSE LANE
ST JOHN'S CENTRE
DORTMUND SQ
SCHOFIELDS CENTRE
LANDS LANE
KING CHARLES ST
ALBION PLACE
COMMERCIAL ST
BOAR LANE
STATION ST
NEW STATION ST
SOVEREIGN STREET
SOVEREIGN
VICTORIA BRIDGE
QUEEN SQUARE
SAYPIL LANE
CIVIC THEATRE
ROSSINGTON ST
ST ANNE ST
ALBION ST
BOND ST
BOND STREET CENTRE
MILL HILL
ALBION ST
LEEDS CITY STATION
NEVILLE STREET
CR
PORTLAND ST
PORTLAND
LEEDS CIVIC HALL
CALVERLEY STREET
GREAT GEORGE STREET
COOKRIDGE ST
CENTRAL LIBRARY ART GALLERY
LEEDS TOWN HALL
SOUTH PAR
BEDFORD ST
GREEK ST
RUSSELL ST
PARK ROW
INFIRMARY ST
CITY SQ
QUEBEC ST
AIRE STREET
CANAL BASIN
LEEDS-LIVERPOOL CANAL
A653 DEWSBURY ROAD
LEEDS GENERAL INFIRMARY
OXFORD PLACE
OXFORD ROW
PARK STREET
COURTS
WESTGATE
THE HEADROW
EAST PARADE
PARK CROSS ST
PARK SQUARE
ST PAUL'S STREET
KING ST
PARK PLACE
YORK PLACE
WELLINGTON STREET
COACH STATION
NORTHERN ST
WHITEHALL ROAD
RIVER AIRE
INNER RING ROAD
LISBON ST
LITTLE QUEEN STREET
QUEEN STREET

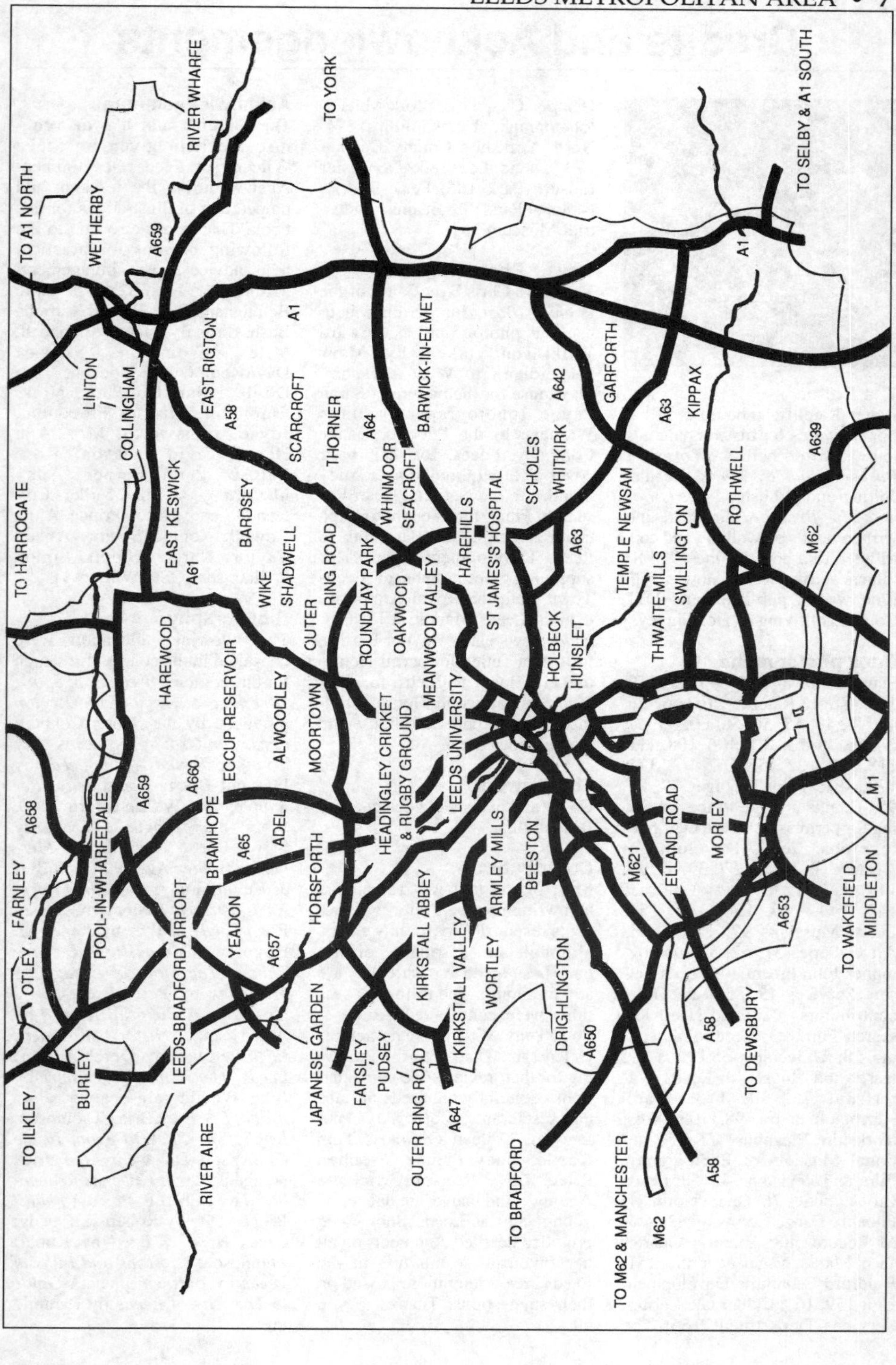
TO A1 NORTH
WETHERBY
A659
RIVER WHARFE
TO YORK
A1
TO SELBY & A1 SOUTH
LINTON
COLLINGHAM
EAST RIGTON
SCARCROFT
THORNER
A64
BARWICK-IN-ELMET
A642
GARFORTH
A63
KIPPAX
A1
TO HARROGATE
EAST KESWICK
A58
BARDSEY
A61
WIKE
SHADWELL
OUTER RING ROAD
ROUNDHAY PARK
WHINMOOR
SEACROFT
HAREHILLS
ST JAMES'S HOSPITAL
SCHOLES
WHITKIRK
A63
TEMPLE NEWSAM
THWAITE MILLS
SWILLINGTON
ROTHWELL
A639
M62
HAREWOOD
ECCUP RESERVOIR
ALWOODLEY
MOORTOWN
OAKWOOD
MEANWOOD VALLEY
HOLBECK
HUNSLET
A658
FARNLEY
POOL-IN-WHARFEDALE
A659
A660
BRAMHOPE
A65
ADEL
HORSFORTH
HEADINGLEY CRICKET & RUGBY GROUND
LEEDS UNIVERSITY
ARMLEY MILLS
BEESTON
M621
ELLAND ROAD
MORLEY
MIDDLETON
M1
OTLEY
LEEDS-BRADFORD AIRPORT
YEADON
A657
JAPANESE GARDEN
KIRKSTALL ABBEY
KIRKSTALL VALLEY
WORTLEY
DRIGHLINGTON
A650
A58
TO DEWSBURY
A653
TO WAKEFIELD
TO ILKLEY
BURLEY
RIVER AIRE
FARSLEY
PUDSEY
OUTER RING ROAD
A647
TO BRADFORD
TO M62 & MANCHESTER
M62
A58

Credits and Acknowledgements

The Editor

Roger Ratcliffe (above) won national awards for his campaigning journalism on both the *Yorkshire Post* and *Sunday Times*. Besides editing and publishing *Leeds Fax* and *The Bradford Book* he has written books on walking and contributed to a book on the 1984-85 miners' strike. He is now a full-time writer, publisher and DTP Consultant living in Headingley.

Book photographs

Paula Solloway 9, 13, 91, 97, 110, 131; Roger Ratcliffe 10, 15, 26, 42, 44, 48, 55, 56, 58, 60, 63, 64, 65, 66, 68, 73, 101, 106, 108, 112, 118, 119, 122, 155, 162, 163, 171, 177, 181; Tony Woolgar 77, 86, 95. Thanks are due to the following for permission to use their photographs: Leeds Development Agency 16, 19, 30, 37, 39, 67, 93, 117, 121, 123; Leeds Libraries 143, 144, 149, 150, 152, 154; Leeds Museums 47, 147; Leeds Art Galleries 51, 52, 53 (photographer John Freeman); Leeds Leisure Services 45, 80, 129. Other contributors—National Heart Research Fund 23; Leeds Polytechnic 28; University of Leeds 29; Harewood House 40; Leeds Waterfront 46, 50, 113; Frank Herrmann 8, 69, 98, 103; West Yorkshire Playhouse 71, 75; National Museum of Photography, Film & Television 74, 158; Leeds City Varieties 76; Opera North 81; Phoenix Dance Company 83; A & M Records 88; Victoria Quarter 115; Marks & Spencer plc 151; Bradford Economic Development Unit 159, 160; Calderdale Leisure Services Department 166; The Dean & Chapter of York Minster (photographer Derek Phillips) 174; North Yorkshire County Council 179; David Lee 183; Doncaster Leisure Park 186; Peak District National Park 188; Beamish Industrial Museum 191.

Cover Photographs

Thanks to Chris Bye, Editor of the *Evening Post*, for permission to use the photograph of Howard Wilkinson (taken by Mark Bickerdike); to West Yorkshire Playhouse for the picture of Sarah Payne (photographer: Simon Warner); to the Phoenix Dance Company, Leeds, for their back cover picture (photographer Andy Snaith); to the National Heart Research Fund for the photograph taken at Killingbeck Hospital; to Leeds Development Agency for supplying photographs of Leeds Town Hall, the Royal Armouries exhibit, Leeds Market, YTV *Calendar* newsreader Gaynor Barnes; to Joshua Tetley for permission to use their logo; to Metro for their logo; to Harewood House for illustrations of both their house and the delicious meal.

The Artwork

Cover and maps were designed by Bill Rudling.

Contributors

Most of the text was researched and written by the Editor, who accepts responsibility for any errors, although all reasonable efforts have been made to ensure they are at a minimum. The following sections were contributed—Rock & Pop, Tony Woolgar; Nightclubs, Helen Fox. Thanks to the following for their reviews/recommendations of literally hundreds of pubs and restaurants: Helen Fox, Paul Drewitt, Colleen O'Grady, Tom Keene, Lucy Prince, Stephen Price, Dave Ronson, Michelle Andrew. And thanks are due to the young lady at Leeds Show who provided detailed comments on all her favourite restaurants in the Leeds area. Many more passed on their suggestions. Thanks to you all.

Acknowledgements

The Editor would like to recognise the help given by Steve Wilcock of Leeds Development Agency during the research and preparation of illustrations for this book. Thanks are also due to the following persons for practical help, advice and encouragement: Michelle Andrew, Jane Bellingham, Peter Brears, Katriona Bush, Chris Bye, Janice Campbell, Miles Crompton, Stewart Davidson, Owen Dodson, Tom Doyle, Alan Dorward, Nicki Embleton, Murray Freedman, Joyce Hainsworth, Mrs. Ann Heap, David Jackson, Rose Lapish, Peter Larner, Andy McCartney, Corinne Miller, Colleen O'Grady, Lucy Prince, Anita Rowell, Ronnie Senior, Alison Taylor, Chris Tebbutt, Simon Williamson, Olha Wilnyckyj.

Bibliography

The following publications were consulted in the course of research for this edition. *Directory of Sport: Yorkshire & Humberside Region* produced by the Sports Council; *Leeds for Groups* by Leeds City Tourism; *Round About Leeds* by Edmund Bogg; *Leeds & Its Region* by M. W. Beresford & G. Jones; *War, Plague & Trade* by Steven Burt & Kevin Grady; *Merchants Golden Age* by Steven Burt & Kevin Grady; *Roundhay Park: An Illustrated History* by Steven Burt; *Leeds at War* by James M. Hagerty; *Curiosities & Rare Things: The Story of Leeds City Museums* by Peter Brears; *The Headrow: A Pictorial Record* by Ann Heap; *A History of Modern Leeds* edited by Derek Fraser; *Leeds: The Heart of Yorkshire* by John Waddington-Feather; *Portrait of Leeds* by Brian Thompson; *Leeds: The Back to Front Inside Out Upside Down City* by Patrick Nuttgens; *Leeds Cinemas Remembered* by Robert E. Preedy; *That'll Be The Day* by Robert E. Preedy; *Leeds Born & Bred* by Robert Thompson; *Old Inns and Pubs of Leeds* by Barrie Pepper; *A Guide to The City of Leeds* by Pyramid Press.

PART ONE:
Surviving in Leeds

The pace of life in a modern city creates many pressures, especially for the poor and the sick. Those in good health and with money in the bank have different choices to make about their quality of life. But for all sections of the community the range of services is vast. Where do you start?

This first section of Leeds Fax provides an up-to-date, near comprehensive description of the facilities—public and private—serving a resident population of 706,000 people and thousands more visitors.

Beginning with an overview of Leeds in the 1990s, "Surviving in Leeds" continues through basic sources of help and advice on things like legal services, housing, transport, health and counselling. There's also a detailed appraisal of the area's education establishments, an employment profile, and review of local green issues, the media and political life. And a complete list of church and religious organizations.

The laughing butcher. A scene from the everyday life of Leeds.

Leeds in the 1990s

Now the undisputed Capital of Yorkshire and Humberside, Leeds is Britain's fastest changing city and a growing name in Europe.

In the end, you can attribute most things to the weather. But right from the first glimmers of 1990, the sun has shone on Leeds just as momentous events were taking place. Like the day work started on building the huge new office complex at Quarry Hill to house around 2,000 NHS and DSS civil servants, a major boost to the city's economy and prestige. Or like the day Leeds United celebrated its winning of the English League Football Championship (see the photograph below). And Leeds's fortunes continue to look sunny. As cities like Liverpool, Glasgow and neighbouring Bradford see their main sources of income virtually wiped out in just a few years and embark on self-marketing campaigns to attract new industries and tourists alike, Leeds is quietly prospering. But in the 1990s Leeds will dramatically raise its public profile.

European Leeds

One of the city's declared objectives for the decade is to be recognised as one of the major, progressive non-capital cities of Europe, rubbing shoulders with the likes of Milan and Munich, Barcelona and Lyon. In its endeavours to achieve this ambition, the quality of life in Leeds will improve, and everyone will benefit. The central shopping area, already renovated by the Landmark Leeds project, will become even cleaner and "greener". Public transport systems, including the introduction of a pollution-free Supertram—a pre-requisite for any self-respecting European city—will be improved. Already, the city is the 20th largest in the European Community, a major international sports and cultural centre, and home to many people of European origin. And among other European cities, only Vienna has more parks and open spaces.

Future Leeds

Already it is possible to glimpse how Leeds will look in the year 2001. In ambitious proposals set out in Leeds City Council's Unitary Development Plan, Leeds becomes one of the most modern cities in Britain. But it will not be wholesale transformation: another watchword is conservation. The area's essential architectural heritage and wildlife will be safeguarded from the following—

❑ **Roads**. *A £250m. programme to improve the area's roads, including the A1-M1 link, a Leeds eastern bypass; East Leeds Radial to improve links with the A1-M1; completion of the Inner Ring Road; improvements to the Outer Ring Road in North Leeds.*

❑ **Public Transport**. *An electric Supertram (see page 18), guided busways, a new Coach Station, major expansion of Leeds City Station, more suburban stations and park-and-ride schemes, further growth of Leeds-Bradford Airport.*

❑ **Shopping**. *Pedestrianisation of Briggate, completing an "outdoor shopping and leisure mall" stretching from Vicar Lane to Park Row, from Boar Lane to The Headrow.*

❑ **Sports**. *Elland Road becomes an all-seater 40,000 capacity sheltered football stadium; staging of more international sports events.*

❑ **The Leeds Arena**. *A huge £40m. indoor arena is proposed for South Leeds, near Elland Road. This would become a major venue for rock concerts and events like ice spectaculars.*

❑ **Leeds Town Hall**. *As the courts withdraw into the new Court House, the best-known civic building in Britain will be available for increased cultural, exhibition and entertainment uses.*

❑ **Museums**. *The Royal Armouries and an international Medical Museum are earmarked for Leeds in the second half of the 1990s.*

❑ **Office Expansion**. *Leeds's rise as a British commercial centre is illustrated by the quantity of office floorspace under construction. At the time of writing, 824,000 square feet was going up. Significantly, planning permission had been granted for a further 2 million square feet of office accommodation in Leeds.*

❑ **The Waterfront**. *Nowhere is the regeneration of Leeds more apparent than beside the River Aire and the canal basin. Further leisure and housing developments are planned, especially on the south side.*

❑ **Science Park**. *The University, Polytechnic, city council and other agencies are pooling resources to explore the potential for a major Science Park in the city.*

The Leeds renaissance was mirrored by Leeds United—Football League Champions.

Population

The Leeds Metropolitan District, which includes the city and its myriad satellite towns and villages, has a total population of approximately 706,000. Leeds is at the centre of a large conurbation, with more than 2,200,000 living within a half-hour drive. At the turn of the 1990s, the following was the estimated analysis of the city's population age groups: **0-14** 68,100 male, 64,700 female; **15-29** 82,800 male, 80,000 female; **30-44** 73,400 male, 72,100 female; **45-59** 76,000 male, 57,700 female; **60-plus** 44,600 male, 87,200 female.

Ethnic Structure
A survey of the population's ethnic origins stated that this comprised: 643,500 White British; 10,500 Black ; 7,900 British Asian; 7,800 Indian; 5,800 Irish; 5,500 Pakistani; 2,600 Bangladeshi; 1,600 Chinese/Vietnamese; and 6,800 others.
White British. In the 1990s, the trend is for predominantly white middle-class workers from the south-east to move to Leeds, living in the suburbs or satellite towns and commuting to work in the city centre's growing number of high-rise offices.
Irish. Besides smaller number of recent immigrants, there are many descendents of 19th century settlers, accounting for the significant Roman Catholic population.
Jewish. Around 10,000 Jewish people, many descended from immigrants who escaped Tsar Alexander II's programs in the 1880s, live in the north-east suburbs of Alwoodley, Chapel Allerton, Moortown and Roundhay.
Black. There are around 11,000 Afro-Caribbeans in the Chapeltown and Harehills areas. Most first generation arrived in the late-1950s in response to a British government drive for workers in public transport and health service.
Asian. Of the 25,000 population, most came in the 1950-65 period, settling in the Chapeltown, Harehills, Burley, Brudenell and Holbeck areas. Includes a significant Sikh population.

Village Leeds
Leeds is a vast network of districts, villages and small towns. The table below analyses the city's total population (excluding scattered houses).
Aberford: 990
Armley: 21,520
Arthington Village: 270
Bardsey cum Rigton: 2,410
Barwick-in-Elmet: 2,490
Beeston: 17,890
Bramhope: 3,520
Bramley: 21,560
Boston Spa: 4,660
Burmantofts: 21,520
Clifford: 1,500
Chapel Allerton: 23,780
Collingham Village: 2,120
Cookridge: 22,260
East Keswick: 1,180
Great & Little Preston: 1,510
Guiseley: 13,800
Halton: 21,720
Harehills: 22,640
Harewood: 3,260
Headingley: 21,310
Horsforth: 22,170
Hunslet: 15,600
Kirkstall: 19,800
Ledsham: 180
Ledston: 370
Leeds Centre & Holbeck: 21,180
Lotherton-cum-Aberford: 180
Methley & Mickletown: 2,820
Micklefield: 1,620
Middleton: 18,500
Moortown: 20,400
Morley: 20,700
Otley: 13,440
Oulton: 3,590
Pool: 1,680
Pudsey: 44,890
Rawdon: 6,270
Richmond Hill: 20,420
Robin Hood: 1,000
Rodley: 2,250
Rothwell: 11,920
Roundhay: 20,700
Scarcroft: 970
Scholes: 2,710
Seacroft: 19,600
Swillington: 3,680
Thorner: 1,430
Thorp Arch: 1,010
Tingley: 4,110
University Area: 19,460
Weetwood: 20,360
West Ardsley: 4,800
Whinmoor: 20,620
Woodlesford: 3,130
Wortley: 23,040
Yeadon: 11,870.

Climate

Compared with many other parts of Northern England, Leeds has an equable climate, escaping the high rainfall and low temperatures of the north-west and the Pennines and Dales, the dense fog of the Vale of York, and the blustery winds and occasionally severe snowstorms of the east coast. And because the city's location is more or less equidistant between the Irish and North Seas, Leeds often manages to achieve temperatures on a par with London and the south of England during mild weather, thanks to the absence of cooling sea breezes. When this happens in summer, Leeds has an advantage over southern areas—there are noticeably longer hours of daylight in which to enjoy the fine weather. In 1985, the National Meteorological Office at Bracknell opened the Leeds Weather Centre, with a staff of 22 operating a 24-hour forecast service. Besides providing weathermen like Alan Dorward and Bob Rust for the region's television stations, it issues forecasts to local councils for road gritting, to electricity and gas companies for possible sudden increases in energy demands, and to supermarkets whose buyers can decide which products will sell best depending on expected weather conditions. The centre has a waiting list for schools and organisations wishing to see how it receives and makes use of satellite photographs and constructs the colour graphics you see in TV bulletins. There is an education liaison officer.
☛ *For information about commercial services contact Leeds Weather Centre, Oak House, Park Lane, Leeds LS3 1EL.*
☎ *Leeds 457703.*

Leeds Weather
Our local climate is governed by two physical characteristics—the Pennines and the North Sea. Rainfall is largely dictated by the chain of hills and moors to the west of the city, which pushes air upwards. While rainfall is enhanced in the upland areas, to the east of the Pennines is a phenomenon known

as a "rain shadow" area. In this zone the air dries out as it comes off the hills. This progressive lowering of rainfall eastward is demonstrated by average rainfall figures for the region. Bradford receives an average 826mm. of rain annually, Leeds 655mm, Harrogate (which is higher than Leeds) 735mm, York 631mm, Scarborough 649mm. The other driver of the Leeds weather, the North Sea, can often decide the sort of temperatures we get 60 miles inland. If, for example, the sea is cold and the winds are easterly or north easterly then Leeds will have a cold spell. In recent years, there has been a cycle of these winds being virtually absent, and the North Sea has remained warm well into the winter. Thus, there has been little snow in Leeds, just one factor in a complex weather pattern which has led to several new records being established for the city. The highest temperature (34.4 Celsius) was achieved on 2 August, 1990; the sunniest day (15.9 hours) was on 19 June, 1989; and the wettest day (62mm of rain) was on 25 August, 1986. Average daily temperatures (Celsius) for the Leeds area are as follows: Jan 5.6, Feb 5.8, Mar 8.5, Apr 11.4, May 15.0, Jun 18.3, Jul 19.9, Aug 19.8, Sep 17.3, Oct 13.4, Nov 8.8, Dec 6.6.

Local Weather Forecasts

A 24-hour telephone service, updated three times daily, is operated for West and South Yorkshire. ☎ 0898-500417.

Barometer Setting

If you have a barometer you will need to set it to achieve an accurate atmospheric pressure reading. Leeds City Museum's Enquiry Service will provide the correct setting by telephone, office hours. ☎ Leeds 478275.

General Help & Advice

There is a vast amount of free information available in the Leeds area. If you need to know your rights regarding a wide range of aspects of living in Leeds, the appropriate service below should be able to help. See also separate sections in the following pages dealing with Counselling, Housing, Employment, Health and Education. A detailed list of Leeds Helplines appears on the last page of this book.

Leeds Citizens Advice Bureau

A wide range of legal/financial/ welfare/housing/employment and other problems can be taken to a Citizens Advice Bureau (CAB). The confidential service is free of charge and is open to all sections of the community. It is especially useful to low-income people who cannot express their needs/rights effectively themselves. There is no appointment required. Simply walk in off the street. The CABs also run a Telephone Advice Service. Each centre has different specialists available to give advice on such things as how to deal with debt, welfare rights (they will take up your case with the Department of Social Security), employment rights (will represent you at an Industrial Tribunal if you feel you have been unfairly dismissed or harassed at work), and housing case workers will help with landlord/tenant, disrepair problems. Will also represent you at County Court in cases involving debt and housing/eviction. The CABs below are listed with their "extensions" in which the CAB staff hold regular sessions at a variety of halls/centres in their area.

Leeds Citizens Advice Bureau, *Westminster Buildings, 31 New York Street, Leeds LS2 7DT. (Moving to new city centre base in 1993—ring first).*
☎ *Leeds 457679.Open Mon-Fri 9.30am-3.30pm (Thur 12 noon-6.15pm).*
Also holds sessions at (ring Leeds for times): **Armley Library,** *Stock Hill, LS12;* **Morley Town Hall,** *Queen St.;* **Hall Lane Community Centre,** *65 Hall Lane, Armley, Leeds LS12;* **Burley Lodge Community Centre,** *Burley Lodge Road, Leeds LS6;* **Crossgates Methodist School Hall,** *Austhorpe Road, Leeds LS15;* **Welfare Hall,** *Main Street, Garforth;* **Compton Road Library,** *Harehills Lane, Harehills,*

Leeds LS9; **High Royds Hospital,** *Menston;* **Richmond Hill Community Centre,** *Long Close Lane, Leeds LS9;* **Alston Lane Community Centre,** *South Seacroft, Leeds LS14;* **Micklefield Fire Station,** *Micklefield.*
Chapeltown Citizens Advice Bureau, *Willow House, New Roscoe Buildings, Cross Francis Street, Leeds LS7 4BZ.* ☎ *Leeds 629479. Open Mon, Tue, Thur & Fri 9.30am-12 & 1pm-3.30pm, Wed 9.30am-12 & 2pm-3.30pm. Plus 6pm-9pm by appointment.*
Also holds sessions at **Chapeltown Community Centre,** *Reginald Terrace, Leeds LS7 3EY.* **Leafield Clinic,** *109 King Lane, Leeds LS17 5BP.* **Prince Philip Centre,** *Scott Hall Avenue, Leeds LS7 2HL.*
Pudsey Citizens Advice Bureau, *The Manor Hall, Robin Lane, Pudsey.* ☎ *578000. Open Mon-Fri 10am-3pm, Sat 10am-12 noon.*
Also holds sessions at **Bramley Community Centre,** *Waterloo Lane, Leeds LS13.*
Otley Citizens Advice Bureau, *North Parade, Otley, LS21 1BA.* ☎ *0943-466976. Open Mon, Tue & Thur 9.30am-3pm, Wed & Fri 9.30am-12.30pm. Also at* **Yeadon Town Hall,** *High Street, Yeadon.*

Leeds City Council Information

If you have a query about any of the hundreds of Leeds City Council services, consult the Leeds Information Centre at the Civic Hall. Everything from Community Charge/Council Tax to dustbin emptying enquiries are dealt with by this office. Usually, they will find someone in the right department to sort out your problem. All council papers are also available for inspection here, including minutes of sub-committees, committees and full council meetings, and agendas for future meetings.
☛ Leeds Information Centre, Leeds Civic Hall, Portland Crescent, Leeds LS1 1UR. Open: Mon-Thur 8.30am-5pm, Fri 8.30am-4.30pm. Closed Sat & Sun.
☎ Leeds 474024.

Racial Discrimination

Leeds is a multi-racial city with few tensions. Most problems concern racial discrimination at work, or in housing. Any complaints will be dealt with by the following. Cases may even be pursued as far as Industrial Tribunals in employment situations. Also, the implementation locally of the 1976 Race Relations Act is monitored.
Commission for Racial Equality.
☛ *Yorkshire Bank Chambers 1st Floor, Infirmary St., LS1 2JP.*
☎ *Leeds 434413.*
Leeds Racial Equality Council.
☛ *Centenary House, North Street, Leeds LS2 8JS.*
☎ *Leeds 430696.*

Harehills & Chapeltown Law Centre

All kinds of free legal advice is available here for anyone in Leeds from a full-time staff of advisers and qualified lawyers, who may represent clients in courts and tribunals. Although it will take on legal aid cases, the centre is useful when there is no legal aid available. While juvenile and some adult crime cases are accepted, much of the centre's work involves immigration and nationality problems, welfare tribunals, landlord/tenant disputes, employment disputes like dismissal and redundancy, and Community Charge/Council Tax problems. Although the centre will always try and help new visitors, it is best to make an appointment.

A consultation at Harehills & Chapeltown Law Centre.

☛ *263 Roundhay Road, Leeds LS8 4HS. Open 10am-12 noon & 2pm-4pm Mon-Fri (but closed Wed).*
☎ *Leeds 491100. Line staffed 9am-1pm & 2pm-5pm Mon-Fri (9am-1pm only on Wed). Other times, ansaphone gives contacts for anyone seeking legal help/advice regarding crime, immigration, domestic violence, childcare and landlord/tenant disputes.*

West Yorkshire Trading Standards Service

If you feel you have a legitimate complaint about something you've bought, a poor service, a bad holiday, goods that don't live up to the maker's claims, or you have been given short measure, this service may be able to help. Will take complaints from any local resident but the service being complained of can be in another part of the UK, or even another country.
☛ *West Yorkshire Trading Standards Service, PO Box 5, Morley, Leeds LS27 0QP.*
☎ *Leeds 536111. Open Mon-Fri 9am-4.45pm.*

Help for Visitors

An increasing number of tourists visit Leeds, often as part of a carefully planned itinary that includes York, the Yorkshire Dales, the Lake District and Scotland. There is a highly efficient Tourist Information Centre which handles everything from finding you a bed for the night to fixing up accommo-

dation at your next destination. Staffed by local people, it is a useful source of advice and information on all aspects of staying in Leeds. There are also TICs at Otley and Wetherby (see page 38).
☛ *Leeds TIC is in Wellington Street, 100 yards west out of City Square, between the railway and coach stations. Open: Mon-Fri 9.30am-5pm, Sat 9.30am-12.30pm & 1.30pm-4pm.*
☎ *Leeds 478301/2/3.*

Hotels & Guest Houses

There is a growing number of hotels and guest houses at both ends of the market. New luxury hotels in the Leeds area have been opening at the rate of about one a year in recent times, while new medium and budget-priced establishments seem likewise to be on the increase. The Tourist Information Centres (see above) publish a free updated Accommodation Guide every year. It lists all the hotels, guest houses, bed & breakfast and self-catering establishments in the Leeds area (including Rothwell, Morley, Pudsey, Horsforth, Menston, Otley, Harewood, Wetherby and Garforth) which meet the standards required by the English Tourist Board.

Hostels

The main hostel accommodation in Leeds is the **YWCA**, for both sexes. One YWCA is near the city centre at *Lovell Park Road* (☎ *457840*). The other is on the west side of the city centre at *St. Ann's Lane, between Burley Road and Kirstall Lane* (☎ *758864*). Usually booked up by students in term time, but from late-July to late-September the bedrooms provide good, very low-priced accommodation for touring backpackers, etc. There are no **Youth Hostels** in Leeds. The nearest are at Haworth (☎ *0535-642234*) and York (☎ *0904-653147*).

Camping and Caravan Sites

Leeds is a popular stop on north-south touring holidays. There are two large sites in the Leeds area. The most convenient for the city centre and Leeds attractions is the **Roundhay Park Touring Site,** *Elmete Lane, Roundhay, Leeds*

LS8 2LG. ☎ *652354.* It has 60 pitches for tents/caravans/motorvans. Open late-Mar to late-Oct. The other is the **St. Helena's Caravan Site,** *None-go-Bye Farm, Horsforth, Leeds LS18 5HZ.* ☎ *582621.*

Survival for Foreign Visitors

Few visitors from abroad use Leeds-Bradford Airport as their point of entry. However, the city does get a substantial number of foreign tourists, especially in summer. And a growing number of students from outside the UK come straight to Leeds to take up university or college courses. The following is some basic information they will find useful.

Money. Decimal coins are easily understood, there being 100 pence to one pound. Most coins are 1p, 2p, 5p, 10p, 20p, 50p and £1 (or 100 pence). A £2 was proposed at the time of writing. Banknote denominations are £5, £10, £20 and £50. You may occasionally find a £1 banknote from Scotland, which is legal tender, though they are rare in Leeds.

Banks. There are well over 100 branches of the main banks throughout the Leeds area. These, as well as the popular local Yorkshire Bank, are mostly open 9.30am-3.30pm Monday-Friday, although some have later opening on Thursdays and Fridays and 9am-12 noon opening on Saturdays. All will change travellers's cheques and foreign currency. They are closed on public holidays—see right.

Electricity. In Leeds, as the rest of the UK, there is a 220 volt electricity supply. The normal plug has three-pins and adapters for Continental plugs can be bought in most local electrical shops.

Postal Service. Post Offices are open from 9am-30pm Mon-Fri and 9am-1pm on Saturdays (except public holidays—see right). The Leeds Sorting Office handles 15 million letters a week. Stamps can be bought from Post Offices and many shops and newsagents. All post boxes are painted cherry red.

Telephones. Public kiosks accept all coins except 1p, 2p & 5p, and many take Phonecards only (ob-tainable at Post Offices, Tourist Information Centres and many newsagents). Cheapest times to make calls are between 8pm and 8am Mon-Fri and all day Sat & Sun. The International Operator is on 155; International Directory Enquiries on 153.

Public Holidays. There are eight statutory public holidays in England: New Year's Day (Jan 1), Good Friday (Fri before Easter), Easter Monday, May Day (1st Mon of May), Spring Bank Holiday (last Mon in May), August Bank Holiday (last Mon in August), Christmas Day (Dec 25), Boxing Day (Dec 26).

Medical. All healthcare in the UK is free if you are a citizen. If you are a visitor from abroad, it is free if your country has a reciprocal agreement (all EEC and Commonwealth countries do). Visitors from the United States will have to pay for treatment, although emergency treatment is free.

Pharmacists. Medication is available on prescription. The doctor you visit will advise which one is the nearest. There is also a list in the local Yellow Pages telephone supplement. And a useful list of late-night and weekend chemists is published every night in Leeds's *Evening Post* newspaper, available at newsagents, city centre street corners, the railway station and many petrol stations.

Emergencies. See the list of services and telephone numbers on page 192 of this book.

Leeds Housing

While most other regions of England and Wales were experiencing a house price slump in the early 1990s, the Leeds area managed to mark up a modest rise in prices. This said a lot about the city's economy, which continues to be one of the most buoyant in the UK. Meanwhile, in the rented/part-ownership sector the growth of Housing Associations and the new Leeds Partnership Homes venture have made much new low-cost accommodation available. Also, Leeds has the biggest stock of low-cost furnished lets outside London in the sprawling flat and bedsit land of Woodhouse, Burley and

Headingley. And with good quality houses within half an hour's drive of Leeds, thousands enjoy the benefits of both country living and big city life.

Buying and Selling Property

There are hundreds of Estate Agents in the Leeds area, most of them now part of large regional or even national chains. Generally speaking, prices are lower in South and West Leeds, in East Leeds areas like Richmond Hill, Osmondthorpe, Halton and Whitkirk, and North Leeds areas like Burley, Chapeltown, Harehills, Kirkstall, Potternewton and Woodhouse. Much medium-priced housing is in Chapel Allerton, Headingley, Cross Gates, Bramley, Calverley, Farsley, Pudsey, Roundhay, Oakwood, Moortown, Alwoodley, Horsforth, Yeadon, Otley, Garforth and Kippax. Prices seem to be higher in some parts of Headingley and Roundhay and outlying areas such as Bramhope, Rawdon, Guiseley, Thorner, Shadwell, Bramham. Apart from the Estate Agents' own property newspapers, the best windows on the local property market are the Friday edition of the *Evening Post* and—for mostly upmarket property—the Saturday edition of the *Yorkshire Post.*

Renting Private Accommodation

One of the biggest areas of private rented accommodation in the UK is in the adjoining postal districts of Leeds 3, 4 and 6. Centre of this flat and bedsitland in Leeds is Headingley, with literally thousands of properties. An estimated one-in-three residents here live in private, fully furnished rented accommodation. Standards range from dodgy to luxurious. The predominantly under-30s residents are well catered for with an abundance of fast-food takeaways, coin-op laundries video stores, cinemas, pubs and bargain clothes shops. Elsewhere in Leeds, the main areas are Chapel Allerton, Harehills and—increasingly—Beeston. Numerous newsagent windows in these areas carry advertisements for properties, and there is a good classifieds section in the *Evening*

Post every night. Below are some of the agencies with good reputations.

Inter-City Accommodation Agency. Well established with a friendly service. Handles few bedsits but mainly self-contained flats, semi's and detached houses of between 1-5 bedrooms and will give advice on best areas of the city.

☛ *47 New Briggate, Leeds LS2 8JD. Open Mon-Fri 10am-6pm, Sat 10am-2pm.*

☎ *Leeds 445342.*

Albion Accommodation Agency. Deals in rented bedsits, flats and houses throughout Leeds. Also offers a property management service, maintaining houses while owners abroad or handling rental of a property.

☛ *168 Lower Briggate, Leeds LS1 6LY.*

☎ *Leeds 421679.*

UNIPOL Accommodation Bureau. A well-established charity that helps find rented accommodation for students in Leeds. Most houses/flats/bedsits are in the Leeds 6 (Headingley) area but increasingly there are properties in Chapel Allerton, Burley, Harehills and Beeston.

☛ *8 Fenton Street (opposite the BBC), Leeds LS1 3EA. Opening times vary according to season (ring first). In the busiest house-hunting time, June to early October, the office is open weekends and Bank Holidays.*

☎ *Leeds 430074. Information line 0426-981107.*

Council Accommodation

There are some 80,000 properties in council ownership in the Leeds area, ranging from flats in 17-storey blocks to two/three/four/-bedroomed houses on estates. The waiting list is divided into four bands and properties are allocated according to the applicant's priority needs. Application forms can be obtained at any of the 38 Local Housing Offices (listed in the Leeds and District Phone Book) or from the address below.

☛ *Department of Housing Services, Dudley House, 133 Albion Street, Leeds LS2 8PX.*

☎ *Leeds 348080.*

Housing Associations

Thousands of properties are provided by Housing Associations in the Leeds area. Most provide specialist accommodation, such as for the elderly, family housing, single people/parents, disabled, flats & bedsits and shared ownership (half buying, half renting). To find one that caters for your needs, an up-to-date list and advice can be obtained from the address below

☛ *The Housing Corporation, St. Paul's House, 23 Park Square, Leeds LS1 2ND.*

☎ *Leeds 469601.*

Leeds Partnership Homes

This £100m. initiative will provide over 2,000 properties in Leeds, Otley, Pudsey, Rothwell, Kippax and Bramham. A partnership between five major Housing Associations and Leeds City Council, the LPH aims to build some 1,800 rented houses and 300-500 low-cost homes for sale by the late 1990s. They are suitable for families, extended families, single persons, the elderly, people in wheelchairs or in need of special care. Three-quarters of the properties will be let to people already on the council housing list, and your first contact should be the city's housing department (left). An information pack is also available from—

☛ *Leeds Partnership Homes are at Tennant Hall, Blackman Lane, Leeds LS2 9ET.*

☎ *Leeds 343009.*

Housing Advice Centre

This council-run centre offers free help/advice on landlord harassment, what to do about poor quality of rented accommodation, homelessness, council housing allocation, benefits, how to find Housing Association properties, etc. Friendly counter service, but experts will listen to your problem in a private consultation room if necessary.

☛ *Leeds Housing Advice Centre is at 21-27 The Headrow, Leeds LS1 6PU. Open Mon-Fri 9am-4pm. Closed Sat & Sun & Bank Hols.*

☎ *Leeds 476919.*

Homelessness

Like every major city, Leeds has a homelessness problem, especially amongst single persons aged 17-25. Thankfully, there are a number of good hostels and organizations for the homeless in the Leeds area (a list is in Part Seven of *Leeds Fax*, on page 138). The following is some basic advice for anyone who finds themselves without a bed for the night.

Housing Advice Centre. This one-stop centre *(see address and opening times above)* will assess your need, suggest a solution.

Social Services Emergency Duty Team. Outside office hours, call this number for emergency advice.

☎ *Leeds 696198.*

Shaftesbury House *(Beeston Road, Leeds LS11* ☎ *705212).* A large, last-resort hostel run by council. Unsuitable for young or elderly.

A classic Headingley terrace—the area is the largest flat & bedsitland outside London.

St. George's Crypt *(Great George Street, Leeds LS2 ☎ 459061)*. An emergency church shelter often used by persons who have been sleeping rough. The last admission for first-time residents is 9.30pm.

Leeds Benefits Service

If you are on a low income, you may be entitled to help with your Community Charge/Council Tax or rent. The Leeds Benefit Service will tell you if you qualify for such assistance.
☛ *Selectapost 15, Dudley House, 133 Albion Street, Leeds LS2 8PX. Open 8.30am-4pm Mon-Fri. Closed Sat & Sun.*
☎ *For people living in hostels or board and lodging accommodation, the telephone enquiries number is 476123. Other numbers relate to the first letters of surnames. A-Ba 476015; Be-Br 476016; Bu-Ch 476020; Ci-Da 476021; De-E 476024; F-Gl 476023; Go-Ha 476027; He-Hy 476028; I-Kh 476030; Ki-McC (inc. Mac) 476034; Mad-Mk 476033; Mo-O 476032; P-Ra 476131; Re-Sc 476132; Se-Sr 476130; St-To 476126; Tr-We 476127; Wh-Z 476125.*

Transport

The crossroads of Northern England is just a few miles down the M1 from Leeds, while train, coach and air services from the city reach all the main centres in the UK. Within Leeds itself, there is a vast network of bus services. And a Transport Strategy into the 21st Century plans an electric Supertram system between the city and suburbs. Providing pollution-free travel for commuters and shopper, it will alleviate city centre traffic, as will more cycle routes, more lorry bans, the completion of the Leeds Inner Ring Road, an improved outer ring-road in North Leeds and the long-overdue M1-A1 link which will effectively mean a Leeds Eastern Bypass. With more park and ride schemes and more suburban railways stations being considered Leeds is set to avoid the chronic congestion that afflicts cities like London, Sheffield and York. The result will be more pedestrianisation in the city centre, yet free-moving traffic on the edge. If you are flying to Europe on holiday or business, taking the train to London or the bus to Temple Newsam, the Leeds transport system provides the minimum of fuss.

Rail Travel

Leeds City Station is one of the largest railway interchanges in Britain. On an average day 850 trains carry up to 40,000 passengers in and out. The station itself dates to 1859, but recent modernisation of the main concourse has created the atmosphere of a modern airport terminal, with improved buffet, bar and waiting facilities. Services from the city fall into four main categories.

Metro. Trains in West Yorkshire are part of the huge Metro network, an integrated rail-bus system of travel that reaches to every corner of the county. There are nine different regional railway Metro lines connected to Leeds, serving stations as follows. The Airedale Line: *Shipley, Frizinghall, Bradford Forster Square, Saltaire, Bingley, Crossflatts, Keighley, and connects also to Steeton, Silsden and Skipton*. Caldervale Line: *Bramley, New Pudsey, Bradford Interchange, Halifax, Sowerby Bridge, Mytholmroyd, Hebden Bridge, Todmorden, Walsden, Rochdale, Manchester Victoria (also to Burnley, Blackburn, Preston, Blackpool)*. Goole & Hallam Lines: *Woodlesford, Castleford, Normanton, Wakefield Kirkgate, Darton, Pontefract, Knottingley, Goole (also to Barnsley, Meadowhall, Sheffield)*. Harrogate Line: *Burley Park, Headingley, Horsforth, Harrogate, Starbeck,*

"The train now standing . . . " Leeds City Station's main concourse.

Knaresborough, York. Huddersfield Line: *Cottingley, Morley, Batley, Dewsbury, Ravensthorpe, Mirfield, Deighton, Huddersfield, Slaithwaite, Marsden, Stalybridge, Manchester Victoria, Manchester Oxford Road, Manchester Piccadilly.* The Penistone Line (joined at Huddersfield): *Lockwood, Berry Brow, Honley, Brockholes, Stocksmoor, Shepley, Denby Dale, Penistone, Barnsley, Meadowhall, Sheffield.* The Wakefield Line: *Outwood, Wakefield Westgate, Sandal & Agbrigg, Fitzwilliam, South Elmsall, Doncaster, Moorthorpe, Rotherham, Meadowhall, Sheffield.* The Wharfedale Line: *Guiseley, Baildon, Shipley, Fizinghall, Bradford Forster Square, Menston, Burley-in-Wharfedale, Ben Rhydding, Ilkley.* York & Selby Lines: *Cross Gates, Garforth, East Garforth, Micklefield, Selby, Hull, York, Scarborough.*

Leeds-London. The showpiece service to and from Leeds has been greatly improved since the introduction of full electrification. This has brought the fastest journey time to the capital down to below

---

two hours (services which stop only at Wakefield Westgate). Trains are hourly for most of the day in each direction. Now fitted with public telephones.

UK Rail Network. Other main through services from Leeds are to Newcastle & Edinburgh, Cardiff, Birmingham & Plymouth; Torquay & Paignton; and Manchester & Liverpool (a half-hourly service to Manchester during the day), Lancaster and Morecambe.

Settle-Carlisle Line. Leeds is the main starting point for many of the trains along this famous scenic line (see also page 172). The timetable is especially suited to walkers from April to October, with remote stations like Horton-in-Ribblesdale, Ribblehead, Dent, Garsdale and others within reach for a day's walking. There's also an annual programme of Nostalgic Steam Days Out. Cumbrian Mountain Limited use several famous locomotives, including the 4771 Green Arrow, on journeys from Leeds to Carlisle. Carlisle is also where you change for Glasgow and Fort William. Pick up a leaflet at Leeds City Station.

☛ *Leeds City Station is off City Square (road access from Boar Lane), Leeds LS1.*

☎ *For timetable enquiries: Leeds 448133. To book seats by telephone (MasterCard Visa, Amex or Switch), Leeds 411674.*

National Express Coaches

Britain's coach travel in the 1990s emulates airline-style standards of service and efficiency. On-the-road comfort by National Express and other long-distance carriers has greatly improved, while baggage handling and transfers are slick. There are departures from the busy coach station in Wellington Street, Leeds, at most times of day or night. (A new coach station, incidentally, is proposed for the mid-late 1990s). Many are direct services, hundreds of other destinations are accessible by changing *en route*.

Direct. The city is linked with an astonishing number of UK mainland centres, many of them difficult to reach by train. Services from Leeds depend on whether the winter timetable (late-October to

---

late-April) or summer timetable (late-April to late-October) is in operation. But the range includes: Aberdeen, Banbury, Barnstaple, Basingstoke, Birmingham, Blackburn, Blackpool, Bournemouth, Brighton, Bristol, Burnley, Cambridge, Cardiff, Carlisle, Cheltenham, Corby, Coventry, Darlington, Derby, Doncaster, Dundee, Durham, Edinburgh, Glasgow, Gloucester, Hartlepool, Hull, Ilfracombe, Kendal, Keswick, Lancaster, Leamington Spa, Leicester, Lichfield, Lincoln, Liverpool, London, Luton, Manchester, Middlesbrough, Milton Keynes, Morecambe, Newcastle-upon-Tyne, Nottingham, Oldham, Oxford, Perth, Peterborough, Portsmouth, Preston, Reading, Sheffield, Southampton, Stockton-on-Tees, Sunderland, Swansea, Swindon, Taunton, York.

Leeds-London. There are nine coaches daily. The journey takes approximately 3 hours 40 minutes. Airport services also link Leeds with Manchester Airport (10 daily), Heathrow (9 daily), Luton Airport (9 daily) and Gatwick Airport (9 daily).

Booking. You can choose between a Reserved Ticket or a Standby Ticket (the former allows travel at any time subject to space availability). You must buy Reserved tickets at least 30 mins. before scheduled departure time. Standby fares are up to 20% cheaper than reserved fairs. Other good deals include day returns and economy returns. Seniors aged 60 or over and young people (16-23 inc) can buy a Discount Coach Card giving a discount of approximately 30% off normal fares. Children aged 5-15 also get this discount. There are group discounts and season tickets for daily travellers. All tickets are bookable at many Travel Agents throughout the Leeds area, in the Coach Station or by phone with Credit Card to the number below.

☛ *The Coach Station is on the north side of Wellington Street (west exit out of City Square) in Central Leeds.*

☎ *Leeds 460011 for National Express timetable/fare enquiries and credit card bookings (Access & Visa).*

Railcards

Family Railcard. Allows at least 25% off most leisure fares and very low rate for accompanying children.

Young Persons Railcard. Available to anyone aged 16-23 or students over 23 studying in UK more than 15 hours a week. Benefits include one-third off savers, SuperSavers, Network Away-Breaks, Cheap Day Returns, Standard Single, Standard and Open Return fares.

Senior Railcard. Half-price rail fares for persons aged 60 or over.

Disabled Persons Railcard. Benefits include one-third off most tickets, including Savers, SuperSavers, Network Away-Breaks, Cheap Day Returns, Standard Single and Open Returns.

☛ For full details of how to obtain the above passes, call at Leeds City Station or any Travel Agent showing the BR sign.

Bus Travel in Leeds and Yorkshire

Vast—that's the only word to describe the bus service network in the Leeds area. It comes under the West Yorkshire-wide umbrella of Metro, and involves almost 700 bus services by some two dozen operators, including Yorkshire Rider, Yorkshire, West Riding, Keighley & District, Harrogate & District, Selby & District, South Yorkshire, Yorkshire Traction and Don Valley Buses. Metro produce leaflets/timetables galore, which can be picked up at libraries and information centres, or the Metro Travel Centre below.

Central Bus Station. The hub of all bus travel activity in Leeds is this sprawling terminus situated between the Leeds markets area to the east of Vicar Lane and West Yorkshire Playhouse. There is a Metro Travel Centre, which is open 8.30am-5.30pm Mon-Fri; 9am-4.30pm Sat. Closed Sundays and Bank Holidays.

☎ *Metro timetable enquiries (services in Leeds and to other parts of West Yorkshire) Leeds 457676.*
Yorkshire Rider (Leeds Area) service enquiries Leeds 429614.

Yorkshire Rider

By far the biggest bus operator in Leeds, with routes reaching into most parts of the city and Bradford. Timetables can be picked up at the Yorkshire Rider Enquiry Office in Briggate (near junction with Boar Lane), or at the Metro Travel Centre (see above).

Leeds Ridercard. If you are a regular user of Yorkshire Rider services in the city, this season ticket will save you money. Cards are weekly or monthly and can be bought from most Post Offices, or from the offices above. You need to fill in an application form first, and require a passport photograph.

☛ *For further details, contact Yorkshire Rider, 1 Swinegate, Leeds LS1 4DQ.*
☎ *Ridercard and Timetable enquiries, Leeds 429614.*

Saving Money on Metro

Regular travellers on Metro trains & buses outside Leeds area benefit from pre-paid tickets.

Metrocard. There are two types: City and District Metrocards. You need a permanent PhotoCard, with the holder's photograph, name and address. Weekly, monthly, quarterly & annually.

Student Metrocard. You need a special Student PhotoCard and a renewable Student monthly ticket. Only full-time students attending a recognised educational establishment are eligible.

Metro Travel Concessions. For the elderly, disabled and blind people. Blind Persons (free travel at all times) require a certificate from their Social Services Dept. Elderly and disabled persons (concessionary travel) require proof of identity & age, a photograph, and a small fee. Disabled also require certificate as for blind person.

Metro Dayrover. One-day leisure ticket. Unlimited trips by bus/train in West Yorkshire on one day.

Metro Saverstrip. Twelve rides for price of 10. No time limit on when you make your journeys. (Available at Travel Centres, bus & railway stations, post offices and many newsagents.)

☎ *Further details of all passes & permits available by ringing Metro's Telephone Bureau on Leeds 457676. Open 8am-7pm Mon-Sat and 9am-5pm on Sun and Bank Holidays.*

Accessbus

This expanding fleet of buses (16 at the time of writing) pick up disabled persons from their homes and drop them off in Leeds city centre—or other parts of the city—for shopping, visiting friends or relatives, etc. Pick-up points and times for the return journey are also arranged. Each bus has nine seats and four wheelchair places. The services operates seven days a week. Those wishing to use Accessbus must first register (a small annual fee is payable) by completing an application form, which is available from the address below. The whole of West Yorkshire is now covered by Accessbus.

☛ *Accessbus, Metrochange House, 61 Hall Ings, Bradford BD1 5SQ.*
☎ *Bradford (0274) 304297. The line is Minicom-compatible.*

Taxis

Leeds has no shortage of taxis. There are two classes operating throughout the city: approximately 280 Hackney Carriages, the black and white taxis you see on the streets, which are allowed to ply for hire and stand on the ranks; and some 1,600 Private Hire taxis, which have to be booked, usually by telephone. Most of the latter are small one-man set-ups operating in particular localities and advertise in the *Yellow Pages*. Some of the major taxi firms are:
Telecabs ☎ *630404 (Hackney Carriage).*
Speedline ☎ *441444 (Hackney Carriage & Private Hire).*
Streamline ☎ *443322 (Hackney Carriage).*
Unicab ☎ *443355 (Hackney Carriage & Private Hire).*

The Supertram

Like all Victorian cities, Leeds developed its own tram system. Horse-drawn at first, then steam and electric-driven, they ran continuously from 1871 until their withdrawal in 1959. The 1990s will see a return of this popular form of environment friendly transport. A totally modern version, based on an electric system already working in 300 cities around the world, will cover those suburbs not served by existing commuter railways. It starts with a route into the city centre from South Leeds. Later stages include East Leeds, North-East Leeds and North-West Leeds. They will mostly run on special tracks at ground level, on verges or central reservations, causing little inconvenience to traffic. Their timetables and routes will link up with buses, coaches and trains in the city centre. And at the outer end of the Supertram lines, there will be special parking facilities to encourage Park and Ride.

Leeds-Bradford Airport

Over 700,000 passengers a year now fly in and out of Leeds's own international airport. The range of domestic and Continental destinations increases annually and it is worthwhile checking with one of the local travel agents to find out about new services, which in future years may expand to include more holiday flights to Greece in particular. Among the Scheduled Services are flights to Amsterdam, Belfast City, Belfast International, Brussels, Dublin, Edinburgh, Glasgow, London Heathrow, London Gatwick (from September, 1992), Paris Charles de Gaulle and—in summer only—Jersey, Guernsey and Isle of Man. The principal scheduled service is to London-Heathrow, operated by British Midland, and is a popular alternative to the train for businessmen travelling to the capital, with early morning departures and mid-evening returns. In total, there are five flights a day in each direction. Flying time is 50 minutes. Charter Services are operated by 12 holiday companies to over 100 resorts on the Continent and in the Mediterranean area. Summer destinations include Alicante, Malaga, Bulgaria, Corfu, Gerona, Ibiza, Cyprus, Malta, Palma, Rhodes, Salzburg, Toronto and Zante. Winter destinations include Lyon, Salzburg, Innsbruck Malaga, Las Palmas, Tenerife, Alicante, Palma and Malta. There are more than 50 Austrian ski resorts accessible each winter from Leeds-Bradford. All Leeds travel agents have up-to-date details of Summer and Winter charter flights, including package deals with accommodation and transfers.

☛ *The Airport is about 8 miles from the centre of Leeds. By car, travel from Leeds centre via A65 to traffic lights at Rawdon, then right on A658 to airport. Alternatively, drive via Leeds Outer Ring Road A6120 to Otley Road junction, then A660 to traffic lights at Dyneley Arms, then left on A658 to airport. Taxi from Leeds can cost in region of £10-£15. By bus from Leeds City Square (next to the railway station), Service 37 operates hourly in the daytime, Monday to Saturday.*

☎ **Information** *Leeds 509696*
Open Car Park *Leeds 507892*
Covered Car Store *Leeds 843620*
Aer Lingus *0345-010101 (Res)*
Leeds   508194   (Enq)
Air UK *0345-666777 (Res)*
Leeds   503251   (Enq)
B. Midland *Leeds 451991 (Res)*
Leeds   508194   (Enq)

CityFlyer. *0345-222111 (Res)*
Leeds   508194   (Enq)
Dan Air *0345-100200 (Res)*
Leeds   503251   (Enq)
Jersey Euro *0345-676676 (Res)*
Leeds   503251   (Enq)
Loganair *Leeds 343434 (Res)*
Leeds   508194   (Enq)
Manx Air *061-436-1010 (Res)*
Leeds   508194   (Enq)
Sabena *Leeds 503366 (Res)*
Leeds   503251   (Enq)

Leeds Community Transport

An excellent, cheap mini-bus hire service for the city's community groups. It has seven 15-seater mini-buses plus two "access" mini-buses with tail-lifts for wheelchairs. They are self-drive, but where no driver is available LCT may be able to supply a voluntary driver. The organisation is keen to encourage voluntary groups and companies who are under-using their own vehicles to allow LCT temporary use of them.
☎ *Leeds 342563.*

Cycling In Leeds

Cheapest and healthiest of all modes of transport, cycling is popular in Leeds despite the slopes that have to be negotiated on the north side. Numerous new facilities for Leeds cyclists are appearing as the 1990s progress. The first fruits of this were the cycle lanes to help cyclists through the complex Sheepscar Interchange, and a shared pedestrian/cyclist provision on Dewsbury Road. This is followed by a dedicated Cycle Route

which links the city centre with Headingley and Burley. The first stage begins at the Clarendon Road-Woodhouse Lane junction and runs to the Kirkstall Lane-Queenswood Road junction. Another Cycle Route has been built into the Inner Ring Road Stages 6 & 7 (South Accommodation Road, Crown Point Roundabout to Marsh Lane) planned for the second half of the 1990s. Many more secure cycle racks are proposed for the city centre, especially near city square (for Leeds City Station). New office developers have said they will make more provision for bicycles in their parking plans.

Cycle Hire. The most centrally located cycle hirer is Watson Cairns, who have a huge pool of bikes for rent on a daily or weekly basis.
☛ *Watson Cairns are at 157 Lower Briggate, Leeds LS1.*
☎ *458081.*

Road Travel

Leeds is one of the crossroads of England. The London-Leeds M1 motorway is a mile from the city centre, while the M62 is a five-minute drive south. It is a 3-4 hour drive to London, two hours to Birmingham, 90 minutes to Newcastle or Leicester, an hour to Hull or Manchester. Later in the 1990s, the up-grading of the entire A1 to motorway status from London to Edinburgh and the new M1-A1 link road to the east of Leeds will make it one of the best-situated cities in the country for road communications.

Leeds's "gate" to the British motorway network—the start of the M1 and M621.

Road Distances from Leeds to other parts of the UK—

Aberdeen 327
Birmingham 114
Blackpool 72
Brighton 240
Cardiff 220
Carlisle 119
Doncaster 29
Dover 260
Edinburgh 202
Glasgow 215
Grimsby 78
Gt. Yarmouth 196
Harrogate 17
Harwich 223
Holyhead 164
Hull 55
John o' Groats 487
Land's End 394
Liverpool 75
London 189
Manchester 40
Newcastle 92
Norwich 176
Nottingham 70
Oban 307
Plymouth 316
Scarborough 62
Sheffield 33
Southampton 232
Whitby 69
York 24

Car Hire

There are scores of car hire firms in the Leeds area, from the big names like Hertz to small operations. Pricing is extremely competitive, especially among the minnows, and unless you intend leaving the car at your intended destination it would be worthwhile telephoning round the lesser-known hirers for a quote. Peak times like Easter and Christmas are busy, so it would be as well to book in advance. There is no better routine than drawing up a list from the *Yellow Pages* and hitting the phone. Remember to ask if the price includes free delivery and collection.

Hitch-hiking from Leeds

You can hitch to just about anywhere in Britain from Leeds, but it helps to know the best thumbing points. Most require a bus-ride from the city centre. Check numbers and times by telephoning the Yorkshire Rider enquiries desk on Leeds 429614.

London, Hull, A1 (South), Manchester, Wales & South-West: At the start of the main motorway system from Leeds, on Dewsbury Road. The M1 is for London and points south (and M62 drop for Hull & A1 South). The M621 is for Manchester, the west and south-west.

The West Dales, Lakes, Glasgow & West Highlands: You need the A65 to the M6 and A74 for Scotland. Try thumbing from the start of Kirkstall Road ((other side of flyover from *Yorkshire Post*) or at the A65 and outer ring road roundabout, New Road Side, Horsforth.

Harrogate, East Dales: Hitch from the bottom of Scott Hall Road, near the large Sheepscar intersection, or from the outer ring road's roundabout with Harrogate Road, Moortown.

Newcastle, Edinburgh & East Highlands. You need the A1 north. Try the Roundhay Road/Easterly Road junction, or the A58/ring road junction.

York & East Coast. Try the York Road/Wykebeck Valley Road junction.

Health

Although preventive medicine has had a huge impact in the last decade, the Leeds area still has some bad health problems. The rate of

---

Giving Blood

Around 2,800 pints of blood a week are required in the region and donations vary between 140,000-150,000 annually. There are two main blood donor centres in Leeds. No appointment is necessary for the simple 30-45 minute session. Donors should be aged 18-60, not less than eight stone in weight and be in good health.
☛ Leeds Blood Donor Centre, 9 St. Paul's Street (off East Parade) Leeds LS1. Open Mon-Thur 9.30am-1pm & 2.45pm-6.30pm. Away from the city centre is The Clinical Blood Transfusion Unit, Seacroft Hospital, York Road, Leeds LS15. Times as above.
☎ Leeds 645091 for both units.

---

heart disease, although not nearly as high as England's blackspot of neighbouring Dewsbury, shows that there is still considerable room for improvement in the city's diet and lifestyle. And an estimated one in eight deaths are thought to be associated with smoking. Strokes are a cause for concern, and there is a study in progress to identify factors linked with their incidence in Leeds (and thus hopefully prevent them) and to improve services for stroke sufferers. Fortunately, the Leeds area has very good health service provision across the whole range of needs, from the biggest community health programme in England to top hospitals offering the main east-of-Pennine specialist care in a number of important treatments. The NHS reforms of the early 1990s have been widely embraced in Leeds, and the planning of services to meet the needs of most of the Leeds Metropolitan area have been brought under the umbrella of a single Leeds Health Authority, Leeds Healthcare.

United Leeds Teaching Hospitals NHS Trust. A group of hospitals of which the biggest is Leeds General Infirmary, a large district teaching hospital offering virtually all services. Specialities include cardiothoracic surgery, neurosurgery, neurology, paediatric neurology, poisons bureau, genito-urinary medicine, artificial limbs, wheelchair services and a Dental Hospital. Other hospitals in the Trust are Chapel Allerton (small acute hospital) and Newton Green Wing (rehabilitation) which are combining on the Newton Green site; Cookridge Hospital, the regional radiotherapy and cancer care hospital; and the small Ida & Robert Arthington Hospital (rehabilitation).

St. James's NHS Trust. Centred on the St. James's Hospital of YTV's *Jimmies* programme. Even before reorganisation was one of the biggest teaching hospitals in Europe. Regional specialities include: bone marrow transplant, cystic fibrosis, haemophilia, plastic surgery, all renal treatments including transplants, liver transplants, paediatric oncology, nephrology.

Community Health

Leeds has one of the widest-ranging and most comprehensive networks of community health services in England. The table below lists most of the main centres from which community health care is dispensed.
KEY— **V** Health Visitor Base; **N** District Nurse Base; **C** Child Health; **S** Speech Therapy; **Ch** Chiropody; **D** Dietetics; **W** Cytology/Well Womens Clinic; **F** Family Planning; **De** Dental Services.

CLINIC/HEALTH CENTRE	ADDRESS	PHONE	SERVICES
Alston Lane Clinic	Community Centre, Alston Lane, LS14	731991	CF
Alwoodley Clinic	Community Centre, The Avenue, LS17	671331	C
Ardsley Health Centre	Bradford Road, East Ardsley	537627	VNCSChDF
Armley Clinic	2 Theaker Lane, LS12	637036	VNCSChWFDe
Beechwood Clinic	Beechwood Nursery, Seacroft LS14		C
Beeston Hill Health Centre	134 Beeston Road, LS11	709721	VNCSChDWFDe
Belle Isle Clinic	2 Aberfield Rise, LS10	713384	VCChWF
Boston Spa Clinic	West End, Boston Spa	0937-842068	VCCh
Bramhope Health Centre	Tredgold Crescent, Bramhope	676539	VC
Bramley Clinic	255 Town Street, LS13	552444	VNCSChDWF
Burmantofts Health Centre	1 Cromwell Mount, LS9	484330	VNCSChF
Calverley Clinic	11 Chapel Street, Calverley	574407	VCCh
Community Health Clinic	Chapel Allerton Hospital, LS7	620714	VC
Chapeltown Health Centre	Spencer Place, LS7	485522	VNCSChWFDe
Cottingley Clinic	115 Cottingley Approach, LS11	718471	C
Cringleber Clinic	415 Bradford Road, Pudsey, LS28	571686	VC
Crossgates	St. Theresa's School, Crossgates, LS15		C
East Keswick	Methodist School Room, Main Street		C
East Leeds Clinic	Harehills Lane, Off York Road, LS9	480006	VNCSChFDe
Farsley Clinic	Farfield House, Farfield Avenue, Pudsey	564859	VCChF
Garforth Clinic	Lidgett Lane, Garforth, LS25	863429	VCSDe
Gildersome Health Centre	Finkle Lane, Gildersome	520611	VCChD
Gipton Clinic	60 Coldcotes Drive, LS9	492207	VC
Guiseley Clinc	Oxford Road, Guiseley	0943-870114	VCSChWFDe
Halton Clinic	25 Primrose Lane, Ls15	602281	VNCSChWF
Holt Park Health Centre	Holt Road, LS16	679741	VNCSChDW
Horsforth Clinic	Church Lane, Horsforth	585151	VNCSChWDe
Hunslet Health Centre	24 Church Street, LS10	771811	VNCSChWFDe
Firthfield Clinic	Community Centre, East Garforth		C
Leafield Clinic	King Lane, Moortown	693161	VNCSCh
Kippax Health Centre	Moorgate Drive, Kippax	868551	VNCSCh
Kirkstall Clinic	15 Morris Lane, LS5	759954	VNCSChFDe
Meanwood Health Centre	548 Meanwood Road, LS6	741313	VNCSChWFDe
Methley Clinic	Main Street, Methley	515230	VC
Middleton Clinic	Middleton Park Avenue, LS10	700773	VCSChWFDe
Morley Health Centre	Corporation Street, Morley	522051	VNCSChDWFDe
New Wortley Health Centre	15 Green Lane, LS12	792411	VNCChD
Osmondthorpe Clinic	Middle School, Neville Road, LS9	482803	CWF
Otley Clinic	Manor Square	0943-850182	VNCSChWF
Oulton Health Centre	Quarry Hill, Oulton	821149	VCS
Pudsey Health Centre	18 Mulberry Street, Pudsey	550141	VNCSChDWF
Rawdon Clinic	Greenacre Hall, New Road Side	505292	VCS
Rothwell Health Centre	Stone Brig Lane, Rothwell	820520	VNCSChFDe
Roundhay Clinic	12 Devonshire Avenue, LS8	664733	VC
Scholes Clinic	Village Hall, Scholes		C
Seacroft Clinic	The Green, Seacroft Avenue, LS14	731991	VCSChFDe
Swillington Clinic	Hillcrest Close, Swillington	861395	VCCh
Swinnow Clinic	Swinnow School, Swinnow Lane, LS13	578604	C
West Park Clinic	North Parade, Off Arncliffe Road, LS16	789409	CS
Wetherby Health Centre	St. James Street, Wetherby	0937-582738	VNCSChDF
Wigton Moor Clinic	Church Hall, Wigton Moor, LS17		C
Woodhouse Health Centre	Off Woodhouse Street, LS6	431281	VNCChDWF
Woodsley Road Health Centre	Woodsley Road, LS6	444831	VNCSChDWFDe
Yeadon Health Centre	17 Southview Road, Yeadon	509292	VNCChDW

Seacroft-Killingbeck. Still directly managed by Leeds Healthcare. Killingbeck is the regional cardiothoracic (heart) surgery unit. This is expected to move to a new wing at the LGI site in the mid to late-1990s. Seacroft has several functions, including hosting the breast screening service for Leeds, Wakefield and Pontefract and the regional infectious diseases unit. Also provides several treatment areas for the elderly. The third hospital in the group is the excellent Wharfedale General Hospital at Otley.

Leeds Community and Mental Health Services. Applied to become a Trust from 1993. Covers mostly mental health services (especially at the huge High Royds Hospital), learning disabilities (Meanwood Park) acute psychiatric (Roundhay Wing at St. James's) and geriatrics (St. Mary's Hospital).

Leeds Family Health Services Authority

Administers services provided by family doctors, dentists, chemists and opticians in the Leeds area.

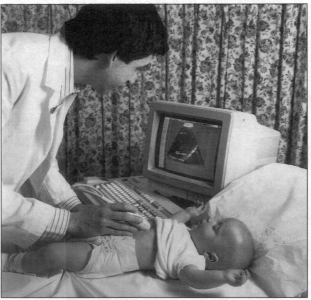

*Leeds is justly proud of its Cardiac Research Unit at Killingbeck Hospital, one of the top centres in Europe for pioneering new ways of treating heart disease. Supported by the Leeds-based **National Heart Research Fund**, the unit is currently active in 35 heart research projects. These include training skeletal muscle from the back to become more "heart like". When wrapped around the diseased heart, the trained muscle contracts to assist the failing heart to eject more blood. This effectively means that a heart transplant is not required. Other work at Killingbeck includes the growing of artificial tissue outside the body to become "test tube arteries" in by-pass surgery, and laser welding to replace stitches, thus making heart by-passes and transplants quicker and safer. The NHRF needs more than £500,000 a year to keep this amazing research unit going, and raises money by engaging in everything from flag days and concerts to sponsored walks and golf tournaments. If you would like to make a donation or help organise a fund-raising event, get in touch.*
☛ *National Heart Research Fund, Concord House, Park Lane, Leeds LS3 1EQ.*
☎ *Leeds 347474.*

This is the place to come if you require advice on exemption certificates for prescription charges, purchase of prescription-pre-payment certificates, loss of medical card, or advice on all services. It also deals with complaints about the service provided by doctors, dentists, chemists or opticians.
☛ *Brunswick Court, Bridge Street, Leeds LS2 7RJ.*
☎ *Leeds 450271.*

Leeds Community Health Council

Commonly known as the patient's voice in the NHS, the Council represents the views of the consumer to the local health authority, Leeds Healthcare, and Leeds Family Health Services Authority. The council also tries to assist patients with any complaints they may have, helping them through the correct complaints procedures. A lot of information on health services is produced, including a regularly updated directory of self-help & support groups in Leeds and the Yorkshire Region, covering many condition-specific areas, a guide to elderly person's homes, consumer surveys on the health service to identify areas of unmet need, and. The council also produces an information sheet explaining how you go about obtaining access to your medical records.
☛ *Leeds Community Health Council, 3-4 Vicar Lane House, Templar Street, Leeds LS2 7NU. Public meetings are held at 7.15pm on the fourth Tuesday of every month. Ring for venue.*
☎ *Leeds 457461.*

Private Healthcare

Paying a monthly subscription for private medical treatment for individuals, families and employees became very popular in the 1980s, and there are two well established schemes in Leeds.
BUPA. With its own 85-bed hospital at Roundhay, and a Medical Centre for full body "MOT's" (well woman screening, heart-risk assessment for men, etc). Subscriptions vary according to age.
☛ *BUPA Membership, Trafalgar House, 29 Park Place, Leeds LS1 2PT.*
☎ *Leeds 444041.*

Private Patients Plan. Also offers medical insurance, using a variety of hospital facilities, and provides health screen etc. for private and corporate subscribers.

☛ *PPP, 11 Belgrave Street, Leeds LS2 8DD.*

☎ *Leeds 432893.*

Alternative Healing

Leeds has an exceptionally large number of alternative medicine and therapy practitioners. The range includes aromatherapy, homeopathy, acupuncture, hypnotherapy, massage, reflexology, shiatsu, stress management and "neuro-linguistics". The list of practitioners and services often changes and anyone interested should consult the updated edition of the excellent *Leeds Healing Directory*, available at all city bookshops, wholefood shops or by post from 10 Bracken Edge, Leeds LS8 4EE. Costs £1.50 plus .60p p & p. Cheques payable to "Leeds Healing Directory".

Sexual Hygiene

The city's centre for treatment of sexually transmitted diseases is the Department of Genito-Urinary Medicine at Leeds General Infirmary. Telephone first for an appointment, and specify whether you would prefer to be examined by a male or female doctor. Open 9am-4.30pm Mon-Fri (closed 11.30am-1.30pm Thurs).

☎ *Male appointments—437124; Female appointments—437125.*

Addiction

All major cities have a drug addiction problem and Leeds is no exception. In the 1990s, there has been a development in usage of so-called Rave Scene designer drugs like Ecstasy. The psychedelic drug LSD has even made a comeback in Yorkshire, while widespread amphetamine usage has continued. There is evidence of the cocaine-derivative Crack being used in the inner city area, as well as other Class A drugs such as heroin and opium. If you feel unable to discuss your own (or your friend or loved-one's) problem with your GP, the following may be able to help:

Leeds Addiction Unit

Part of the local health authority, Leeds Healthcare, the Unit offers counselling and treatment for persons with any addiction/substance misuse problem with legal or illegal drugs, including tranquillisers, solvents, alcohol, heroin, ecstasy, LSD, etc. User or relative/friend can make appointment without going through GP. Also runs a Needle Exchange, a network of 15 chemists offering pack of new syringes, needles and condoms to drug users in order to help prevent the spread of HIV and hepatitis.

☛ *19 Springfield Mount, Leeds LS2 9NG. Open every day of the year (inc. Xmas) 9am-8.30pm Mon-Tue-Thur-Fri, 9am-12 noon Wed. Sat & Sun 9am-4.30pm.*

☎ *Leeds 316920 (reception); Leeds 316940 (information and counselling, and names of chemists participating in Needle Exchange).*

Leeds Drugs Project

In the first instance, a confidential telephone helpline/counselling service for all addicts. Also runs a Tranquilliser Support Group for anyone who has become addicted to tranquillisers.

☛ *Telephone staffed 10am-5pm Mon-Fri. Then ansaphone.*

☎ *Leeds 423182.*

Disability Help

Numerous council-run and voluntary services exist in Leeds for anyone who has a mobility problem, blind and partially sighted people, and deaf/hard-of-hearing people. The following are well-established sources of help and information. See also Railcards (p. 17), Travel Concessions and Accessbus (p. 18), Libraries (p 29)

DIAL

DIAL stands for the Disablement Information and Advice Line, which has been going since the late-seventies. It is a voluntary telephone helpline for all people with disabilities of all kinds in Leeds and the surrounding area. Everything from advice on wheelchair acquisition/repair to receiving financial aid from charities, answering transport, housing & education

queries, access and mobility information, advising on special (and sometimes free disabled holidays, fighting benefits appeals at DSS tribunals, etc. Will also advise you on your nearest Resource Centre in Leeds.

☛ *The William Merritt Centre, St. Mary's Hospital, Green Hill Road, Leeds LS12 3QE.*

☎ *Leeds 795583. Staffed 10.30am-3.30pm Mon-Fri.*

Leeds Centre for the Deaf

An excellent drop-in centre, social club and source of help and advice on such things as aids and adaptations. Licensed club is open pub hours.

☛ *Centenary House, North Street, Leeds LS2 8AY. Centre open 9am-5pm Mon-Fri.*

☎ *Leeds 438328. Weekend emergencies: 0459-106595.*

Centres for the Blind

There are several such centres, providing social contact and means of receiving help and advice. Within Leeds itself, these are provided by Leeds Social Services Department. In the old West Riding, they are run by the Leeds Incorporated Institute for Blind and Deaf People. Centres at Horsforth, Morley, Kippax, Otley and Wetherby.

☛ *Leeds IIBD, Centenary House, North Street, Leeds LS2 8AY.*

☎ *Leeds Social Services Blind Welfare, Leeds 348080. Leeds IIBD, Leeds 433250.*

Counselling Services

Leeds has many long-established voluntary organisations offering free, sympathetic and confidential counselling on all emotional problems. Most are staffed by trained counsellors or by persons who have direct experience of specific emotional/health problems. See also Addiction (left), Women's Help on page 24 and Student Survival on page 25.

Samaritans

The Samaritans offer 24-hour confidential support for the suicidal, distressed or anyone who wants to discuss a problem. Callers are encouraged to review their situation and options and to arrive at their own choice. Telephone or call in personally.

☛ *93 Clarendon Road (road running at back of Leeds University, between Park Lane and Woodhouse Lane), Leeds LS2 9LY.* ☎ *Leeds 456789.*

Relate

Formerly known as the Marriage Guidance Council, Relate has widened its brief to include counselling for boyfriend/girlfriend and family relationship difficulties. The service operates on an appointments system. The first 20-minute session can usually be fitted in within seven days; then counselling is in weekly one-hour sessions.

☛ *Relate is at 38 Call Lane, Leeds LS1 6DT. Counselling is between 9am-5pm and 9pm-9pm weekdays, and 9.30am-12.30pm Saturdays.* ☎ *Leeds 452595.*

Victims Support Schemes

As any victim knows, crime is a traumatic experience. The biggest current scandal in Leeds is that the police have lost the battle against burglaries and thefts from cars in some areas, especially Headingley and Woodhouse. They don't even bother to visit many victims to investigate theft of their property! The Victims Support Schemes exist to help those who find themselves affected by crime. This free and confidential service includes counselling, or even practical help with repairs or security, advice about compensation claims and help in replacing stolen documents.

☛ *North East Leeds VSS, 2 Vinery Avenue, Leeds LS9 9LX* ☎ *Leeds 485028; North West Leeds VSS, 28 The Turnways, Leeds LS6 3DU* ☎ *Leeds 756928; South Leeds VSS, 199 Dewsbury Road, Leeds LS11 5EG* ☎ *Leeds 713558.*

West Indian Family Counselling Service

This walk-in service, open 10am-1pm Monday to Friday, offers counselling on many problems, including mixed marriages.

☛ *Roscoe Methodist Church, Francis Street, Leeds LS7 4BY.* ☎ *Leeds 625131.*

Oxford Place Centre

A free, confidential person-to-person counselling service is available at the Oxford Place Centre. No appointment is necessary.

☛ *The Centre is in Oxford Place (on the west side of Leeds Town Hall), off The Headrow. Open 12 noon-2pm Monday to Friday.*

NCH Touchline

A special telephone helpline for children & adults with problems of sexual abuse, either now or in the past. Also welcomes calls from anyone who suspects cases of sexual abuse. Has therapeutic groups for victims and can offer face-to-face counselling.

☎ *Leeds 457777 Mon-Fri 10am-9.30pm (ansaphone outside hours).*

NCH Careline

Emotional worries, stress, family & sexual problems experienced by children, young people and their families are among the areas covered by this sympathetic, confidential telephone service. Face-to-face counselling or therapy can be arranged, if desired.

☎ *Leeds 456456 Mon-Fri 10am-9.30pm (ansaphone outside hours).*

Gay & Lesbian Counselling

There are several good support and counselling services in the Leeds area. The best-established are—
Leeds Gay Switchboard. Offers confidential help, advice and information on local gay scene, being gay and about safe sex. Also holds regular monthly social night.

☛ *Letters can be sent to Box HH29, Leeds LS8 2UA.* ☎ *Leeds 453588 7pm-10pm every night except Tuesday.*
Leeds Lesbian Line. Help/support for anyone in Leeds who is Lesbian, whether resident or a visitor. Besides telephone helpline, has regular monthly meetings.

☛ *Letters to PO Box HP4, Leeds LS6 2HJ.* ☎ *Leeds 453588 7.30pm-9.30pm every Tuesday.*
Lesbian & Gay Christian Group. Provides support to lesbian and gay Christians (interdenominational), working both within and outside the church.

☎ *Leeds 741037 (Andrew).*
Parents Friend. Support group and helpline for the parents, relatives and close friends of gay men and lesbian women who find it difficult to understand/accept their offspring/friends' homosexuality.

☛ *c/o 36 Newmarket, Otley, LS21 3AE.* ☎ *Leeds 674627 (Joy).*

HIV and AIDS

After London and the south-east, West Yorkshire is one of the regions hardest hit by HIV. The following groups offer counselling—
Leeds Aids Advice. The city's main support/advice service. Offers a wide range of services, including talks to schools and groups, prevention advice, welfare rights advice, support/counselling for anyone contemplating HIV test, etc.

☛ *Drop-in centre at 50 The Calls, Leeds LS2.* ☎ *Leeds 423204.*
Body Positive Yorkshire. Helpline, support/companionship group, counselling service, hospital and home visiting for anyone who is HIV antibody positive, or who is suffering from HIV-related illnesses (and discrimination and prejudice as a result) and AIDS, and their partners, friends and carers.

☛ *PO Box CR15, Leeds LS7 4TP.* ☎ *0924-456667 (Helpline open Tues 7pm-9pm. Or ansaphone, checked regularly).*

Women's Help

Leeds is well served by women's advice, help and information sources. The following offer free, confidential counselling—

Women's Counselling & Therapy Service

Women in distress may call the service for help and support. There are drop-in sessions on Tues, 2.30pm-6.30pm; on Thurs, 10am-2pm; and since October 1992 sessions for black women on Fri from 10am-2pm. Please ring for information on other services.

☛ *Oxford Chambers, Oxford Place, Leeds LS1 3AX.* ☎ *Leeds 455725.*

Widows Advisory Service

Offers counselling on coping with bereavement and loneliness and will generally assist with getting back into the mainstream of life for women of all ages and backgrounds. Advice on widows' pensions & benefits, income tax, housing, etc. Runs meetings once a fortnight on Sundays and organises talks, socials, parties, day-trips etc. Ring for details.

☛ *At 14 Great George Street, Leeds LS1 3DW. Open Mon-Thur 10.30am-3pm.*
☎ *Leeds 450553.*

British Pregnancy Advisory Service

All aspects of pregnancy can be discussed, including abortion. Has a fast pregnancy testing service. For an immediate result, call with an early-morning urine sample.

☛ *2nd Floor, 8 The Headrow, Leeds LS1 6NG. Open 9am-5pm Mon-Thur.*
☎ *Leeds 443861.*

Leeds Rape Crisis

Women and girls who have been raped, sexually assaulted, harassed or sexually abused as a child can use this free confidential service.

☎ *Leeds 440058. Open Mon-Fri 12-4pm and 7pm-9pm.*
☛ *Letters to PO Box 27, Wellington Street, Leeds LS2 7EG.*

Student Survival

So you're one of 40,000-plus full-time students in Leeds? Who cares! Actually, lots of people. You're a solid gold VIP in this city, part of a huge growth area in the Leeds economy. That puts you in a position of strength. Hundreds of businesses out there are *desperate* for your custom. Lots of shops/restaurants/hairdressers/nightclubs etc. advertise student discounts. Usually, your NUS card is all they need to see. The West Yorkshire NUS publishes a list of many businesses offering discounts, in a free diary available each September. If you can't obtain a copy, contact your college NUS official or—

☛ *The West Yorkshire NUS Office, c/o Leeds Poly, Brunswick Terrace, Leeds LS2 8BU.*
☎ *452312.*

Help & Advice

Your time in Leeds should be reasonably trouble-free. At the end of their degrees, many students who'd never been to Leeds before decide they enjoyed the place so much they want to live here. For those who do experience problems, or who simply need advice, there are numerous sources—

Leeds University. The Welfare Services section helps with matters such as financial, housing, immigration and personal problems. Open 9.30am-4.30pm Mon-Fri (not Thur).

☎ *Leeds 314244.*

Leeds Poly Union. Has full-time workers at the City site and Beckett Park, ready to help with everything from debt to tenancy, academic and personal problems. Usually open Mon-Fri 10am-3pm (not Thur).

☎ *Leeds 430171 (City); 823116 (Becket Park).*

Nightline. A confidential service, staffed by student volunteers, which is available to all students in Leeds. All kinds of help, including emotional, counselling, student gay/lesbian group contacts, or a sympathetic voice.

☎ *Leeds 442602. Open 8pm-8am, seven days in term time.*

Legal Problems. Specialist free and confidential help is available from the Leeds Citizens Advice Bureau (see page 12) and the Harehills & Chapeltown Law Centre (page 13).

☎ *Leeds CAB, 457679; H & C Law Centre, 491100.*

Drugs. Only a small proportion of students are users. Jogger's high is a more likely experience. Hard-drugs are rare among students but in recent years there's been an increase in "rave scene" pharmaceuticals like Ecstasy and LSD in Leeds. Both can do serious and lasting damage.

☛ *Volunteers staff a friendly counselling and information service called Leeds Drugs Line.*

☎ *Leeds 423182. Staffed 10am-5pm Mon-Fri then ansaphone.*

Gay/lesbian scene. College or University is possibly the place for lesbians and gay men to "come out". There are societies at the University and "Poly" (ask at your union office).

☛ *See also the support groups listed on the opposite page. Or ring Nightline on Leeds 442602.*

Safe Sex. This has been taken to new heights in Leeds with a shop in the Corn Exchange elevating the humble condom to Cult Object. On a serious note, there *are* AIDS casualties in Leeds.

☛ *If you want professional advice, make an appointment at your university Health Centre or nearest clinic (there's a list on page 21).*

Flat/House Hunting. The Students Unions provide useful advice. For freelance efforts, there's UNIPOL Student Homes. It has a Landlord Index in which students have passed judgment on landlords/properties. See also the windows of newsagents and supermarkets in Headingley and Harehills. Or the *Evening Post* classifieds, especially Friday night.

☛ *UNIPOL, 8 Fenton Street, opposite the BBC, Woodhouse Lane.*
☎ *430074; Info Line 0426-981107.*

Travel. For most students, Young People's Railcards and other discount passes for long distance and local coach/bus journeys are vital. They are detailed on pages 17 & 18. Sea also hitch-hiking advice on page 20.

Overseas Students. The thousands from abroad who come to Leeds for courses at college and university are particularly well provided with information and advice. The Leeds Council For Overseas Student Affairs is there to help. It also organizes a varied social programme, including sightseeing trips, visits to Opera North, etc.

☛ *c/o Leeds Polytechnic, Brunswick Terrace, Leeds LS2 8BU.*
☎ *460999.*

Education

Like health, the whole subject of education provision is in a state of flux in the 1990s. With "opt-out" and "independent" the buzz-words of both headlines and headmasters' studies, any picture of the current level of state education looks like an express train captured in freeze-frame. Just as Leeds Polytechnic became an independent institution in the late-1980s, the Leeds City Council education department's nine colleges (see opposite) were achieving their independence in 1993. Less easy to predict is the direction of many of the city's fine schools, which have the choice of remaining under the umbrella of Leeds Department of Education, or receiving funds direct from Whitehall. What can be said is that, both in state and private schools, expanding college courses and in part-time adult courses, Leeds covers every conceivable need in modern education.

State Education in Leeds

On the threshold of the education reforms, Leeds City Council's Department of Education had some 100,930 pupils in its primary schools, high schools and special schools (the middle-school tier was removed in 1992).

Nursery Education. There is a major commitment to this in Leeds. Since 1980, when the policy of increased provision was adopted, the total number of places

in the Leeds area has steadily risen from 450 to nearly 8,500, and it is still growing month by month. There are ambitious plans to provide a nursery place for every three and four-year-old child whose parents want one. There are 154 education nursery centres, mostly at primary schools, but with over 30 of them attached to Community Centres.

☛ *If you want to know your nearest nursery education unit or have a query, contact the Under-8 Unit, Civic Hall Annex, Leeds LS1 1UR.* ☎ *Leeds 474335.*

Primary Schools and High Schools. Before any decided on taking the "opt-out" route, there were 47 high schools, 117 primary schools and 21 special schools under the control of the Department of Education. There has been a particular effort to integrate pupils with learning difficulties in mainstream schools. And Leeds is one of the few local education authorities to be building new schools. In

the last decade more than 20 ultra-modern replacement schools have been put up across the city— a record envied by many. Another notable achievement is the Technical and Vocational Education Initiative (TVEI) which aims to make education more relevant to the world outside the classroom.

☛ *If you have any query about your child's education in Leeds, contact the Education Advisory Division, Department of Education, 9th Floor East, Merrion House, Leeds LS2 8DT.* ☎ *Leeds 475678.*

Independent Schools

For those parents who wish to educate their children independently, there is no lack of choice of both day and boarding schools in the Leeds area. Write or ring for latest term fees. Besides Leeds Grammar School (see left) there are—

Leeds Girls' High School, *Headingley Lane, LS6 1BN.* ☎ *744000.* Approx. 350 girls 3-11, 600 girls 11-18, all Day. Some assisted places. Founded in 1876, the school stands in its own 10-acre grounds.

Froebelian School, *Clarence Road, Horsforth, LS18 4LB.* ☎ *583047.* Small prep school for 4-11 years with 90 boys and 95 girls, all Day.

Fulneck Boys' School, *Pudsey, LS28 8DT.* ☎ *571864.* One of the schools in the Moravian Settlement, founded nearly 250 years ago. Boys 8-18, 55 boarding and 270 Day.

Fulneck Girls' School, *Pudsey, LS28 8DS.* ☎ *570235.* Another Moravian school, founded in 1753 on the outskirts of Pudsey. Boys 4-8, Girls 4-18. Pupils: 382 Day, 64 boarding.

Gateways School, *Harewood, LS17 9LE.* ☎ *Leeds 886345.* Girls' day school founded in 1941, with 380 pupils.

Moorlands School, *Foxhill Drive, Weetwood Lane, LS16 5PF.* ☎ *Leeds 785286.* Founded in 1898, all boys & girls aged 4-13.

North Leeds & St. Edmund's Hall Preparatory School, *Gledhow Lane, LS8 1RT.* ☎ *Leeds 668005.* Boys 3-11 (104), girls 3-11 (76), all Day.

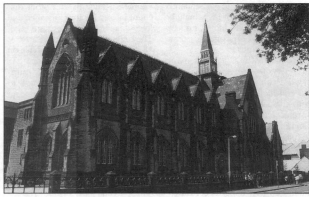

The oldest educational establishment in the area is **Leeds Grammar School.** *Founded in 1552 with a bequest from Sir William Sheafield, it was first in a Chantry Chapel near Leeds Bridge, then for over two centuries off Vicar Lane, behind the Grand Theatre. In 1857 the all-boy school moved into the Gothic building above, designed by E. M. Barry, son of the architect of the Houses of Parliament, Sir Charles Barry. There have been further extensions: a chapel, assembly hall, classrooms, music and art rooms, sixth form centre, music centre, language laboratories, sports hall, technology and economics centres, a beautiful library, computer laboratory, theatre and a new science block. It is run closely with Leeds Girls' High School (see above). There are approximately 150 boys in the Junior School (8-10 years) and over 1,000 in the senior school (11-18 years). Although fee paying, there are some 30 free and assisted places per year group.*

☛ *On Moorland Road (facing Woodhouse Moor), Leeds LS6 1AN. Write or ring for prospectus.*
☎ *Leeds 433417/8.*

Richmond House School and Far Headingley Preparatory School, *LS16 5LG*. ☎ *752670*. 200 boys and 100 girls, all 3-11.

St. Agnes PNEU School, *25 Burton Crescent, Headingley, LS6*. ☎ *786722*. The only Parents National Education Union school in the area. Not run by Governors but by a parents/teachers management committee. 55 mixed pupils, 3-8.

Brontë House School, *Apperley Bridge, Rawdon, BD10*. ☎ *Leeds 502811*. The Prep school for Woodhouse Grove. Has 170 mixed pupils, aged 7-11.

Woodhouse Grove School, *Apperley Bridge, Rawdon, BD10*. ☎ *502477*. Founded in 1812. Day/boarding school on the Leeds/Bradford border. 570 mixed pupils aged 11-18, of which 150 are boarders.

Further & Higher Education

Leeds has one of the highest student populations in the UK. There are nearly 50,000 students in full-time education and almost as many again on part-time courses throughout the city. The following are the main centres. Write or call for the latest prospectus.

Leeds Polytechnic

Now with University status, the word "University" was being adopted in 1993-94. It was established in 1970 by bringing together a number of local colleges, and today the number of students is heading for 20,000. Many, particularly those on part-time courses linked to their jobs, are from the Leeds area but a growing number come from the south-east and overseas. The University is spread at numerous sites around the city. Among its major faculties are Leeds Business School, one of the largest in Europe; Cultural & Education Studies, for teaching and management in such areas as food, tourism and leisure (including the famous Carnegie physical education college at Beckett Park and the new Northern School of Film & Television); Leeds School of the Environment; Health & Social Care; and Information & Engineering Systems.

☛ *Course Enquiries Office, Calverley Street, Leeds LS1 3HE. For 16-plus pupils wishing to study in higher education, there is an annual open day.*

☎ *Course enquiries: Leeds 832600 ext. 3027. Open day details: ext. 3018.*

Further Education Colleges

There are 9 main centres of Further Education in Leeds, with a total of well over 50,000 full and part-time students. From April, 1993, they were independent of Leeds City Council.

Airedale & Wharfedale College. *Calverley Lane, Horsforth, LS18 4RQ*. ☎ *581723*. Courses range from business & commercial subjects to GCSEs, A levels, BTEC computing, health & leisure courses. Engineering, micro-electronics, etc.

Joseph Priestly College, *71 Queen Street, Morley, LS27 8DZ*. ☎ *533749*. This South Leeds (Morley & Rothwell) business/industrial college covers courses in Business Studies, Computing, Office Skills, General and Adult Education.

Park Lane College, *Park Lane, Leeds LS3 1AA*. ☎ *443011*. Offers a wide range of courses from GCSE & A-levels, business & computer studies, secretarial, travel & tourism, etc. Also good "study at home" courses and much Adult Education. See libraries for leaflets.

Thomas Danby College, *Roundhay Road, LS7 3BG*. ☎ **494912**. Food Technology (baking, meat, confectionery); Community Services (social care, nursery nursing and hairdressing & beauty therapy); Hospitality Services (catering). Courses for ethnic groups, mature students, retraining, etc.

Kitson College, *Cookridge Street, Leeds LS2 8BL*. ☎ *430381*. Mechanical/electrical engineering & scientific college, with 6,000 students, mostly part-time. Also motor/ computer/ photography & printing, dental technicians. Has database on all Further Ed course in Leeds & UK and offers guidance/counselling.

Leeds College of Building, *North Street, Leeds LS2 7QT*. ☎ *430765*. Full range of construction industry courses, from carpentry to computing, plumbing & town planning. Many students go on to Poly/University degree courses.

Jacob Kramer College, *Vernon St., Leeds LS2 8BH*. ☎ *439931*. The city's main pre-degree art college, offering many courses in art, design and crafts. Around 350 students, most on a two-year or one-year course. Levels are from part-time "leisure" classes to HND.

City of Leeds College of Music, *43a Woodhouse Lane, Leeds LS2 8JT*. ☎ *452069*. Full-time courses, including Jazz & Contemporary Music and Musical Instrument Technology. Also has many part-time courses (orchestral instruments, piano & guitar; opera, instrument repair, etc).

Northern School of Contemporary Dance, *98 Chapeltown Road, Leeds LS7 4BH*. ☎ *625359*. Three-

Now with University status—Leeds "Poly".

year course in contemporary dance; also training in classical ballet, choreography, allied arts music, lighting and costume design. Large programme of part-time classes for adults and children.

South Leeds Further Education Centre

Part of a Leeds City Council initiative to improve South Leeds, this centres has full and part-time courses for thousands of adults and young people living on the south side of the city. Courses include GCSEs, A levels, secretarial, medical, receptionist, information technology, travel, tourism, business and finance. Courses are tutored by staff from several of the colleges listed on page 27.
☛ *Burton Avenue, Leeds LS11 5ER.*
☎ *Leeds 711994.*

Adult Education

There is a massive choice of adult/community education in Leeds. Many courses provide qualifications for jobs or routes to further and higher education, or are on subjects of recreational interest. Most enrollments are in early-mid September, early January and after Easter, although lots—especially examination and certificate courses—run the whole academic year. The commonest is one consisting of one two-hour session a week. Literature outlining new courses are available each summer in the reception at Leeds Central Library and at branch libraries. Most of the colleges listed on page 27 offer courses, and their literature can also be picked up.

Community Education

Leeds City Council's massive range of courses in all areas of Leeds are explained in brochures, available each summer. For information about courses in your area, contact the following—
West Leeds: Armley, Bramley, Pudsey & Wortley ☎ *559582;* Brudenell, Kirkstall, Little London and Woodhouse ☎ *780982.*
North West Leeds: Aireborough, Cookridge Horsforth, Otley, West Park & Bramhope ☎ *477616 or*

The University of Leeds *is among the five largest in Britain, with over 14,000 students, 1,000 academic staff and a choice of over 300 undergraduate courses. These include rare subjects such as Food Science, Textiles, Chinese, Japanese, Biophysics, Ceramics and Colour Chemistry (unique in Europe). It is highly thought of by its students: it emerged as the most popular English university in a national newspaper survey. It received its Charter in 1904, but its earliest origins can be traced back to 1831 when the Leeds School of Medicine was founded. The famous Parkinson Building (above) was completed in 1951. The University is a major Leeds employer with nearly 4,600 staff. Services to the local community include adult education courses, part-time degrees, public lectures, concerts and exhibitions. Business services include professional and industrial updating courses, technology consultancy, contract research, conference and exhibition facilities.*
☛ *The University of Leeds, Woodhouse Lane, Leeds LS2 9JT.*
☎ *Information Office—Leeds 336699.*

0943-851098.
South Leeds: Belle Isle, Hunslet & Middleton ☎ 706449; Beeston, Holbeck & Cottingley ☎ 778224; Osmondthorpe, Halton Moor & Richmond Hill ☎ 402895.
East Leeds: Allerton Bywater, Garforth, Scholes, Methley, Micklefield, Swillington, Great and Little Preston ☎ 868061; Burmantofts, Seacroft, Whinmoor, Cross Gates & Halton ☎ 362555; Chapeltown, Harehills, Gipton & Chapel Allerton ☎ 495069.
North East Leeds: Roundhay, Moortown & Wetherby ☎ 692555.

Swarthmore Centre

A famous independent community education establishment close to the city centre. It is a charity, grant-aided by the council. Course include computing, most creative arts, dance, movement, self-defence, psychic studies, health & food issues, foreign languages and many more.

☛ *Brochure from Swarthmore Centre, 3-7 Woodhouse Square, Leeds LS3 1AD.*
☎ *Leeds 436327.*

University of Leeds

The Department of Adult Continuing Education offers courses which cover many subjects, from archaeology to astronomy, from renaissance art to the world of the microscope, from the music of Schubert to how to survive stress.
☛ *Leeds LS2 9JT.*
☎ *Leeds 333221.*

Workers Educational Association.

Courses aimed at people who left school at the minimum age. Range of subjects includes history, literature, creative writing and local wildlife studies.
☛ *Philip Ralph, WEA, 39 Newton Garth, Newton Road, Leeds LS7 4HG.*
☎ *Leeds 622441.*

Open University

Leeds is the Open University's Yorkshire Region base. Many thousands in the city have taken their degrees on part-time courses with the OU. Courses do not require entry qualifications. Most study is at home, a typical full-credit course taking 12-14 hours of work a week for between four and six years. There are two local study centres, which OU Students attend for tutorials—weekly in the first year.

☛ *At Fairfax House, Merrion Street, Leeds LS2 8JU. You can pop in and look at the course material before committing yourself.*
☎ *Leeds 444431.*

Library & Archive Facilities

The main provider of library services in the area is Leeds City Council's Department of Leisure Services. Altogether, it has a total stock of 1.7 million books, spread through 62 branch libraries, eight mobile libraries, and the various departments of Leeds Central Library (see below).

Local Libraries. If you want to know your nearest branch and its opening times contact:
☛ *Library Headquarters, 32 York Road, Leeds LS9 8DT.*
☎ *Leeds 482026.*

Mobile Libraries. There are eight vehicles, plus a van specially serving the housebound (there is a waiting list for its use). Mobiles visit those parts of Leeds that do not have a local library.
☎ *For details call 401317.*

Leeds Central Library

A Victorian building of great character, it houses most of the library service's specialist departments.

Central Lending Library *(Ground floor.* ☎ *Leeds 478270/ 478271).* Fiction and non-fiction, plus books in foreign languages, language learning cassettes.

Library of Commerce, Science & Technology *(Ground floor.* ☎ *478265, 478266 or for renewals 478264).* Joining with Central Lending in 1993 to create a Business Information Services section. Has company data, trade names,

market research consumer info, medicine, natural history, transport, DIY, photography.

Reference Library *(Third floor.* ☎ *478282).* Has books, encyclopaedias and journals on the humanities and social sciences. Also, a comprehensive collection of government papers, local and national newspapers, maps, educational prospectuses and exam papers. The St. Catherine's House indexes to the records of births, deaths and marriages in England and Wales 1837-1980 are available on microfilm. Booking advisable on Leeds 478283.

Local History Library *(Third floor, access through Reference Library.* ☎ *478290).* Contains almost everything ever published on the city and Yorkshire. It has many old photographs/prints of Leeds, maps, directories, electoral rolls, parish registers and the census returns 1841-1891 for the whole of Yorkshire.

Art Library *(Ground floor of Leeds City Art Gallery next door.* ☎ *478247).* Books and periodicals on all aspects of visual art and design. Many of the books are available for loan.

Music and Audio Library *(Ground floor, through Central Lending Library.* ☎ *478273).* Large collection of books on music and musicians, and music scores. LPs, compact discs and cassettes can also be borrowed (there is a modest loan charge).

Braille and Large Print Services *(Ground floor, by entrance from Headrow.* ☎ *477999).* Kurzweil reading machine; electronic magnifying aid (CCTV) for which there is a modest charge; but free tactile photocopying of maps, plans, diagrams and sketches, large printing (18pt or 24pt) and Braille transcription of reports, articles, instruction leaflets etc.
☛ *Central Library is in Municipal Buildings, Calverley Street, Leeds LS1 3AB (between Art Gallery and Town Hall). Open Mon-Sat, including some evenings. Phone to check with each department, as times change. There is continuing work to improve access for the disabled.*
☎ *Reception desk/membership enquiries Leeds 478274.*

Other Libraries/Archives

Leeds has some first class independent library and research facilities. They are—

The Leeds Library. Founded in 1768, it is Britain's oldest surviving proprietary subscription library. It contains over 120,000 books and periodicals dating mainly from the 19th and 20th centuries, but with earlier items including Reformation pamphlets, Civil War tracts and late-18th century imprints. Some 800 volumes are added annually. Use is restricted to 500 Proprietors, their spouses and children, 150 Associates, staff and postgraduate students of the University of Leeds, and other bona fide researchers. There is a waiting list to join.
☛ *18 Commercial Street, Leeds LS1 6AL.*
☎ *Leeds 453071.*

Law Library. English Law only. Open to members of the public for reference use only, but appointment advisable.
☛ *The Court House, Oxford Row, Leeds LS1. Open Mon-Fri 9am-5.30pm (closed 1pm-2pm). Photocopy service.*
☎ *Leeds 830040 ext. 433.*

Leeds District Archives. Three miles of shelves containing business/municipal/church/family/property/trades union/natural history records and much more going back to the 12th century. Many use the Archives to trace the histories of families and homes.
☛ *Part of the West Yorkshire Archive Service, Chapeltown Road, Sheepscar, Leeds LS7 3AP. Appointment is essential. Open Mon-Fri 9.30am-5pm with restricted service noon to 2pm. Last order for documents 4pm.*
☎ *Leeds 628339.*

University of Leeds Library. Is open to non-members of the University but written requests should first be sent to the Librarian—casual visitors are not admitted. Its strengths include fine historical and literary sections (including many original manuscripts), and medical/scientific/technical papers from around the world.
☛ *All enquiries to the Librarian, University of Leeds, Leeds LS2 9JT.*
☎ *Leeds 335513.*

Employment

Unlike most other major cities in Britain, Leeds has not suffered crushing unemployment. For while its original wealth was built on the cloth manufacturing, ready-made clothing and engineering industries, in the last 50 years Leeds has established itself as the capital of Yorkshire and Humberside with a greatly diversified economy. The following are the main areas of employment—

Service Sector. Since the early 1960s, this has emerged as the main strength in the Leeds economy. It employs 225,000 people, mostly in white-collar jobs in banking, building societies, insurance, accountancy, law firms, retailing, television, hotels and catering, central and local government, the health service and further education. The largest employer is Leeds City Council, with 30,000 employees, and there are 14,000 workers in the health service. The biggest private employers are ASDA, Yorkshire Bank, Yorkshire Post Newspapers, Yorkshire Television, Yorkshire Water and Leeds Permanent Building Society. All the High Street Banks, British Gas, Yorkshire Electricity and British Telecom have their regional offices here, as do the main Government departments. Newcomers to the city include the national headquarters of the Department of Health's NHS Management Executive and Department of Social Security Benefits Agency, based at those dramatic new offices at Quarry Hill; British Telecom Mobile; and the National Audit Office (Northern England and Scotland office). There are 27 UK, international and foreign banks with offices in Leeds, over 120 insurance companies, 230 accountancy firms, and 31 major law firms. Leeds is now the biggest legal centre in the UK outside London. National banking services run from the city include First Direct Bank, NatWest Switchcard Customer Services, and Barclays Bank Direct Mortgage Service.

Manufacturing. There are around 75,000 people employed by over 4,500 manufacturing firms in Leeds. The secret of Leeds's success is in the enormous range of products made, so that the city is not dependent on one single employer or market for its jobs. They include electronic components, battle tanks, board games, surgical equipment, jet turbine blades, newspapers, glassware, buses, beer, chemicals, pharmaceuticals and toiletries. Among the household names with a major presence in Leeds are Waddingtons Games, Joshua Tetley, Vickers Defence Systems and Elida Gibbs.

Unemployment

Figures change monthly but one "snap-shot" survey in the 1990s compared Leeds's unemployment rates with those of the other 15 major UK cities. Leeds had the second-lowest jobless total. The comparative unemployment rates (%) were as follows: Edinburgh 7.6; Leeds 8.2; Leicester 8.4; Southampton 8.8; Bristol 9.3; Cardiff 9.5; London 9.5; Bradford 9.6; Manchester 9.9; Nottingham 10.0; Newcastle 11.2; Sheffield 11.4; Glasgow 11.5; Birmingham 11.6; Belfast 13.0; Liverpool 15.2.

Finding Work

Away from Job Centres, wider opportunities are to be found in the Thursday editions of the *Evening Post* and *Yorkshire Post* job vacancy sections.

Leeds City Council is the city's biggest employer. A list of current vacancies is updated regularly and can be obtained by sending a large sae to Personnel & Training Division, Civic Hall, Leeds LS1 1UR.

Employment Agencies. There are over 100 Employment/Recruitment Agencies listed in the Leeds Area *Yellow Pages*. Among the most common are office temps. and catering staff but there are also agencies dealing in executive recruitment, skilled workers, computer operators, accountants, legal services, nursing staff, drivers, cleaning staff, sales & insurance reps, translators, and many more.

Starting Your Own Business

There is no shortage of help for new businesses in the Leeds area. The following will provide all the information you require on the road becoming a business tycoon.

Leeds Business Venture. The essential first call. Completely free help for new and existing small businesses in Leeds. Advice on accounting, business plan preparation, finding premises, cash flow, raising finance, taxation, hiring staff, marketing, etc.

☛ *Commerce House, 2 St. Albans Place, Wade Lane, Leeds LS2 8HZ.*

☎ *Leeds 446474.*

Leeds TEC. Advises all the way from setting up your business, to streamlining an existing one. Free consultations initially. Also has a complete training advice service for Leeds area.

☛ *Leeds TEC Limited, Fairfax House, Merrion Street, Leeds LS2 8JU.*

☎ *Leeds 446181.*

Westgate House—first of a new generation of Leeds office developments.

Leeds Development Agency. Has start-up grants for people who live in or will start a business in the Leeds inner-city area. You require some finance yourself and must demonstrate a need for grant assistance. The range of grants is wide. And the LDA can also provide information and contacts for loans offered by the following: Leeds & Bradford Enterprise Loan Scheme; European Coal and Steel Community Loans; British Coal Enterprise; West Yorkshire Small Firms Fund. For further information call the number below and ask for the Business Development Officer.
☎ *Leeds 477893.*

Green Issues

Few European cities have such a mix of dense population, central shopping/office areas, and vast acreages of factories and warehouses that are so closely integrated with parks, gardens and natural wildlife habitats. For, thankfully, Leeds escaped many of the appalling ravages that afflicted cities like Manchester, Birmingham and Sheffield before environmental awareness was raised in the 1970s. But there are still many problems to solve if Green Leeds is to be preserved and enhanced. Below are listed the main challenges of the 1990s. If you wish to get involved, there are numerous conservation campaigns and direct action groups (they are listed in the Clubs & Organisations section, from page 131). The Leeds Green Strategy, produced by the city council, highlights a framework for action in Leeds and can be consulted at libraries.
☞ *If you have any queries about Green Strategy in Leeds, contact the Project Implementation Unit, Department of Administration, Civic Hall, Leeds LS1 1UR.*
☎ *Leeds 474482.*

Traffic
Although we are still some distance from gridlock, the internal combustion engine poses the greatest long-term threat to the quality of life in Leeds, as it does in every other city in the UK. It is the biggest source of air pollution and noise, and road accidents cause many deaths and injuries. The Leeds Transport Strategy proposes more pedestrianisation of city centre streets, a more efficient and pollution-free public transport system (see Supertram on page 18), restricted traffic access and parking in the city and residential areas, more cycle routes, more lorry bans and bypasses. Extensive public consultation by the city council will produce further specific courses of action to limit the impact of what is both a necessity and a menace.
☞ *The Leeds Transport Strategy, a 15-year-plan for Leeds, can be consulted at libraries. Or contact the Leeds Development Agency, Civic Hall, Leeds LS1 1UR.*
☎ *Leeds 474455.*

Leeds Buildings
Leeds has many fine Georgian, Victorian and Edwardian buildings still intact. With the growth of Leeds in the 1990s, developments could sweep away many gems. As some of the aberrations of the 1960s come, thankfully, to the end of their lives, there is now a strict planning policy of renovating old buildings rather than allowing their demolition, making new buildings fit in with their neighbours, and making sure their construction is with quality materials for a long life (like Westgate House, pictured opposite). The most active group supporting the city's built environment is Leeds Civic Trust.
☞ *Leeds Civic Trust is at Claremont, 23 Clarendon Road, Leeds LS2 9NZ.*
☎ *Leeds 439594.*

The River Aire
Leeds's earlier prosperity was based on the Aire, especially when it began carrying its produce to the North Sea. But sewage and industrial pollution is still a problem. Yorkshire Water is investing in huge sludge incinerators to clean the Aire, and there are several conservation projects in the Aire Valley itself (see Kirstall Valley, page 59). EYE on the AIRE is an umbrella organisation of groups campaigning for the river and its valley to be improved, and to increase awareness of its wildlife.
☞ *EYE on the AIRE, Claremont, 23 Clarendon Road, Leeds LS2 9NZ.*
☎ *Leeds 439594.*

Nature Conservation
With so many green pockets spread throughout the city, there is keen public interest in Leeds's urban wildlife. But there are still regular challenges to its survival in the form of proposed developments, pollution and neglect. The council's response to these challenges has been a Nature Conservation Strategy for Leeds, which puts the interests of wildlife first by improving sites, providing nature reserves and access, and promoting enjoyment. An excellent Countryside Service exists to put many of these objectives into action through management, education projects and special events.
☞ *The Strategy can be seen at libraries. The Countryside Service is based at Temple Newsam, Leeds LS1 0BJ.*
☎ *Leeds 326871.*

Recycling
Leeds has been at the forefront of reusing valuable resources, and contiues to set trends with a number of experimental and established schemes.
SWAP. One of Britain's most successful waste recycling schemes was set up here in the 1970s. Today, Save Waste and Prosper is now at the leading edge of recycling. Swap runs recycling centres through Leeds, coordinated by the council's environment department. Surplus income from the sale of materials goes to community and charity organisations in Leeds. Collections are of paper, glass, cans, plastic bottles, textiles and waste oil.
☎ *For your nearest SWAP collection site, ring Leeds 622588.*
SORT. A council scheme which allows householders to separate recyclable materials and organic waste for recycling using split wheeled dustbins.
☎ *For further information, ring Leeds 622020.*
ALCAN. Sell your empty aluminium drinks cans. Approx. 1p a can, for yourself or charity.
☎ *For details, ring Leeds 450602.*

Leeds Media

Some of the biggest names in regional newspapers, radio and television are based in Leeds. And some of the smallest too. The range is vast—from huge commercial operations like Yorkshire Television to flighty "pirate" radio stations in Chapeltown, from England's top regional daily morning paper the *Yorkshire Post* to the excellent alternative/listings paper *Northern Star*.

BBC Radio Leeds
Local radio at its very best. If you never buy a newspaper, you'll find all you need to know about what's going on in Leeds, West Yorkshire and the world by frequent listening to this splendid BBC station. Radio Leeds strikes up at 6am with its popular breakfast show, a vital feature being regular traffic reports at 29 mins and 59 mins past each hour, which continue throughout the day and total 30. There are also 20 weather forecasts a day, provided by Leeds Weather Centre. And there is a first-class bulletin of local, national and international news on the hour, every hour. The programmes themselves are a lively mix of features, celebrity interviews, phone-ins, quizzes, news inserts and music. Community service is a particular strength, with frequent What's On events listings each day and a Helpline to assist listeners with problems of all kinds (see below). But perhaps Radio Leeds's area of excellence is its sports coverage. For everyone interested in sports in West Yorkshire, whether live coverage of Leeds United at Elland Road or elsewhere, or cricket from Headingley or wherever Yorkshire are playing in England, or rugby league, or rugby union, speedway, hockey, golf, and all the rest, Radio Leeds is an essential part of life.

☛ *Broadcasts on 92.4 FM stereo and 774 KHz/388m. Medium Wave. Also 95.3 FM in Wharfedale and 103.9 FM in West Leeds and the Aire Valley. Address: BBC Radio Leeds, Woodhouse Lane, Leeds LS2 9PN.*
☎ *Leeds 442131. Phone-in/quiz: Leeds 443222. What's On Guide: 0274-730150. (Local clubs and non-commercial organisations can publicize their events by ringing the above number). Helpline: 0422-349407. Ring if you have a problem—big or small.*

Radio Aire FM & Magic 828
After a decade of broadcasting, Leeds's commercial radio station has split its output in two, catering for distinctly different audiences. But both are still on the air 24 hours a day. **Radio Aire FM** is the modern side, broadcasting chart records and anything else that appeals to its youngish target listeners of sub-35. Its most popular show is the 6-9.30am slot hosted by Mark Page, who won the national Sony Award for best music-based breakfast show. **Magic 828** is pure nostalgia—a habit-forming diet of golden oldies. Top show is the morning slot hosted by Ray Stroud, of the "What Have I Got in my Hand?" quiz fame. Magic also carries sports programmes, with extensive coverage of Leeds sports, especially at weekends. Both channels share hourly news, traffic and weather reports.

☛ *Aire FM broadcasts on 96.3 FM. Magic 828 broadcasts on 828m medium wave. Address: PO Box 362, 51 Burley Road, Leeds LS3 1LR.*
☎ *Leeds 452299. Phone-in/competition lines: Aire FM Leeds 344963; Magic 828 Leeds 344828.*

Some Radio Leeds presenters (l-r): Jon Hammond, Ian Timms (back), Rory Morrison, Alvin Blossom, Peter Levy and Steve Merike.

Community Radio

Unlike mainstream radio stations these are unpredictable, lively little outfits. Names and numbers change from month to month but some of the best-established are three Afro-Caribbean stations. **Supreme** (104 FM), **RCR** (105.3 FM) and **People's** (105.6 FM) can be heard throughout Leeds. They play a mix of soul, reggae, ragga, house and hip-hop with other specialist shows for jazz, world music, and gospel. Because of the popularity of house (or "rave") in recent years there is **Dream FM** (100.05 FM), on 24 hours a day with a set of DJs playing the full range of house—techno to ambient to garage and so on.

☛ *The stations have no addresses, but if you want to get in touch listen out for their mobile phone numbers for requests, dedications and information.*

BBC Television

Since 1968 BBC Television has had a Yorkshire base in Leeds. The output consists mainly of its weekday nightly news and magazine programme *Look North* and a small number of weekly opt-out political and current affairs programmes on BBC 2. Although occasionally top-heavy with sport for some tastes, *Look North's* news operation is very good. A range of specialist correspondents provide real depth to many local stories.

☛ *BBC North, Broadcasting House, Woodhouse Lane, Leeds LS2 9PN.*
☎ *Leeds 441188.*

Yorkshire Television

A top provider of network programmes on the ITV commercial channels, YTV also has a strong local output. Based at studios on Kirkstall Road since 1968, the station has a licence until the end of the decade to broadcast to six million viewers in a region stretching from the Pennines to the East Coast, from North Yorkshire to North Norfolk. Nationally, its reputation rests on output like the award-winning *First Tuesday* current affairs programme, the Yorkshire Dales soap *Emmerdale* and flashes of brilliance like *The Darling Buds of May*. Locally, its flag-

ship is the nightly magazine *Calendar*, a lively mix of news, features, sport, music, trivia and fun.
☛ *Kirkstall Road, Leeds LS3 1JS.*
☎ *Leeds 438283.*

Evening Post

The biggest-selling evening newspaper in Yorkshire, with around 140,000 copies sold a day, the *EP* provides unrivalled coverage of Leeds area news. Its style is bright and it makes great use of colour photographs. The *EP* is also a swashbuckling campaigner of the old school, pursuing many investigations and crusades of local and national interest. The sports coverage, including a Saturday edition with instant results and match reports, is awesome. Still the region's premier classified and display advertising medium, the appearance of the *EP* is eagerly awaited on Thursdays for its jobs pages and on Fridays for its property market section.
☛ *Wellington Street, Leeds LS1 1RF.*
☎ *Leeds 432701.*

Yorkshire Post

This highly respected morning paper looks like a regional *Independent* with a style of reporting not dissimilar to the *Daily Mail's* and is required reading for everyone interested in the wider Yorkshire scene. Years ago it claimed to sell "twixt Tweed and Trent" but the *YP's* daily circulation of 90,000 is now largely in the Broad Acres. Its feature pages are especially good. Talented writers produce articles on arts and entertainments, women's interests, sports, the Yorkshire countryside, travel and eating out.
☛ *Wellington Street, Leeds LS1 1RF.*
☎ *Leeds 432701.*

Northern Star

The alternative voice of the region, and essential listings guide to arts, entertainments, talks & events. Named after the Leeds Chartist newspaper published by Feargus O'Connor in the 19th century, the *Northern Star*, as you would expect, is left-wing in its outlook. Formerly *Leeds Other Paper* (born out of the 1974 miners' strike) the

name change has broadened its appeal in West Yorkshire. Run by a cooperative, the papers sells approximately 5,000 copies a week.
☛ *52 Call Lane, Leeds LS1 6DT.*
☎ *News desk 440069; listings 343121; advertising 440060.*

Weekly newspapers

A number of weekly newspapers circulate in localised areas of Leeds.
Leeds Weekly News *(PO Box 49, Wellington Street, Leeds LS1 1LW.* ☎ *Editorial—388966; Advertising—439872).* Yorkshire's biggest freesheet. Approximately 190,000 copies delivered each week, covering over 90% of Leeds homes.
Skyrack Express *(31 Austhorpe Road, Cross Gates, Leeds LS15 8BA.* ☎ *Leeds 644278).* One of the oldest weekly papers in the region, it is delivered free to homes in the postal districts of Leeds 8, 9, 14, 15, parts of 17, and 25.
Rothwell Advertiser *(Lamberts yard, Rothwell, Leeds LS26 0DA.* ☎ *Leeds 828282).* A small (5,000) paid-for weekly selling in and around Rothwell & Oulton.
Morley Advertiser *(7 Commercial Street, Morley, LS27 8HX.* ☎ *Leeds 524020).* One of two weeklies in Morley. a paid-for tabloid with 4.200 weekly sale.
Morley Observer *(35a-37 Queen Street, Morley, LS27 8EE.* ☎ *523456).* Broadsheet selling 4,500 copies weekly.
Jewish Gazette *(1 Shaftesbury Avenue, Leeds LS8 1DR.* ☎ *Leeds 668273).* The larger of Leeds's two Jewish weeklies. Sells 4,000-4,500 weekly.
Jewish Telegraph *(4a Roman View, Leeds LS8.* ☎ *Leeds 695044).* Smaller circulation than the above, but "meatier".
Pudsey Times *(6a Lowtown, Pudsey, LS28 7AA.* ☎ *Leeds 565695).* A freesheet with 28,000 letterbox deliveries.
Wetherby News *(28 High Street, Wetherby, LS22 4LT.* ☎ *0937-582663).* Traditional country weekly paper, with a circulation around 6,000.
Wharfedale & Airedale Observer *(45 Boroughgate, Otley, LS21 1AG.* ☎ *0943-465555).* Sells around 24,000 copies weekly in Guiseley, Menston and Otley.

Leeds Politics

Leeds defies all models of British politics. Since 1980, Labour has been the dominant party on the City Council and it would now take a landslide for it to lose control. And yet when it comes to General Elections, four of the city's eight seats are won by the Conservatives. At Westminster, moderation has been the hallmark of Leeds's politicians for decades (eg Hugh Gaitskell, Denis Healey and Merlyn Rees). And in recent years, while the Labour councils of Sheffield, Manchester and Liverpool became notorious for confrontation and high spending, the Labour-controlled Leeds City Council quietly managed to steer an impressive course, engendering business confidence while maintaining and increasing a remarkable level of public services.

Council Meetings. Open to the public, they are held every six weeks on Wednesdays at 2pm with a break for tea at 5.30pm.

☛ *Held at Leeds Civic Hall, Portland Crescent, Leeds LS1 1UR.*

☎ *Leeds 474024 for date of the next meeting.*

Councillors. If you want to get in touch with one of your local councillors, you can contact them at:

☛ *Leeds Civic Hall, Portland Crescent, Leeds LS1 1UR.*

☎ *Labour Councillors 474470; Conservative Councillors 474551; Liberal Democrat Councillors 474580.*

Members of Parliament. You can contact your MP at the following address and phone number. Some also have local offices (see the constituencies below). Ring to find out times and places of their regular surgeries.

☛ *The House of Commons, London SW1A 0AA.*

☎ *071-219-3000.*

Elmet

On the east side of Leeds, it ranges from the Leeds council estates of Swarcliffe & Whinmoor and the mining area south of Garforth, where one would expect Labour to predominate, to affluent commuter villages like Collingham, Boston Spa, Barwick and Thorner. Wetherby is also safe Conservative ground. Considered a Conservative marginal, Elmet's MP since 1983 has been Spencer Batiste. His majority shrank from 7,856, to 5,356 in 1987, and to 3,261 last time round. Batiste was a former solicitor and sprang from the ranks of the Federation of Conservative Students. He is married with one son and one daughter.

Election Result. *Spencer Batiste Con 27,677 (47.5%); Colin Burgon Lab 24,416 (41.9%); Ann Beck Lib Dem 6,144 (10.5%). Con majority 3,261, a 2.10% swing to Lab. Of 70,558 electorate 58,237 voted, a turnout of 82.53.*

Contacts. *Spencer Batiste—c/o J. Duckworth Ridgeland House, 5 The Shambles, Wetherby, LS22 4NR.* ☎ *0937-580109; Labour—Paul Howden, 34 Willow Garth Avenue, Leeds LS14 2DY.* ☎ *Leeds 733527.; Liberal Democrats—Bob Hutchinson, 6 Naburn Road, Leeds LS14 2DD.* ☎ *Leeds 892797; Green—David Corry, Hulen, Becca, LS25 3BQ.* ☎ *813376.*

Leeds Central

Classic inner city Labour territory, with a notoriously low turnout by its electorate (65% in 1987, 61% in 1992). Electorally, Leeds Central comprises the following wards: Beeston; City & Holbeck; Richmond Hill; University. The Labour MP since 1987 has been Derek Fatchett, a university lecturer on industrial relations and a former Wakefield councillor. Born in August, 1945, he is married with two teenage sons. He has served as a Labour front-bench spokesman on Education.

Election Result. *Derek Fatchett Lab 23,673 (62.2%); Tessa Holdroyd Con 8,653(22.7%); David Pratt Lib Dem 5,713 (15.0%). Lab majority 15,020, a 4.69% swing to Lab. Over 62,058 electorate 38,039 voted, a turnout of 61.29%.*

Contacts. *Derek Fatchett—Dudley House, Albion Street, Leeds LS2 8PX.* ☎ Leeds *441097; Conservative—D. Boynton, 17 Royal Place, Leeds LS10 2RS.* ☎ *Leeds 770922. Liberal Democrats—Richard Bradney, 2 Chantrel Court, Leeds LS2 7HA. Green—Ruth Young, 15 Noster Place, Leeds LS11 8QH.* ☎ *Leeds 762373.*

Leeds East

From 1952 to 1992, Denis Healey was MP for this constituency. On Healey's retirement (he is now Lord Healey), long-time Leeds councillor and trade union official George Mudie took his place and, despite the bushy-eyebrowed one's personal popularity, managed to obtain a healthy increase in the Labour vote. Leeds East is classic Labour territory, with council estates and inner city streets, plus some suburban wards. Mudie is a diligent moderate politician who did much to shape the style and direction of today's city council. Born in Dundee, he moved to Leeds in 1968 to work for NUPE and was first elected to the city council for Seacroft ward in 1971. He became Labour group leader while the Conservatives were running the city in the 1970s and Leader of the Council when Labour took control in 1980. He stood down from the leadership in 1989. He is married with two sons.

Election Result. *George Mudie Lab 24,929 (57.7%); Neil Carmichael Con 12,232 (28.3%); Peter Wrigley Lib Dem 6,040 (14.0%). Lab majority 12,697, a 3.61% swing to Lab. Of 61,695 electorate 43,201 voted, a turnout of 70.02%.*

Contacts. *George Mudie—Seacroft Library, Seacroft Cresecent, Leeds LS14.* ☎ *Leeds 323266. Conservative—C. Booth, 19 The Drive, Leeds LS15 8ER.* ☎ *Leeds 648398; Liberal Democrats—David Hollingsworth, 77 Templegate Avenue, Leeds LS15 0HL.* ☎ *603538; Green—as Leeds North West.*

Leeds North East

Timothy Kirkhope has held Leeds North East for the Tories in two General Elections, with a steadily reduced majority. Safely home by 4,244 votes in 1992, the seat is regarded as a marginal. The constituency is a wide mix of comfortable suburbia welded to inner city areas such as Chapeltown, with above-average unemployment. Born in 1945, Timothy Kirkhope was a member of Northumberland

County Council between 1981 and 1985 and unsuccessfully fought two previous parliamentary seats: Durham in February 1974 and Darlington in 1979. He is married with four sons. Special interests include defence, foreign affairs, broadcasting, health and aviation (he holds a pilot's license).

Election Result. *Timothy Kirkhope Con 22,462 (45.4%); Fabian Hamilton Lab 18,218 (36.8%); Christopher Walmsley Lib Dem 8,274 (16.7%); John Noble Green 546 (1.1%). Con majority 4,244, a 5.88% swing to Lab. Of 64,372 electorate 49,500 voted, a turnout of 76.89%.*

Contacts. *Timothy Kirkhope— New Leeds Constitutional Club, 205 Roundhay Road, Leeds LS8 4JP. ☎ Leeds 492502; Liberal Democrats—Mrs. Susan Bentley, 51 Alwoodley Lane, Leeds LS17 7PU. ☎ Leeds 675036; Labour— Lorraine Hardy, 1b Bentcliffe Mount, Leeds LS17 6QW. Green— Andrew Tear, 96 Bankside Street, Leeds LS8 5AD. ☎ Leeds 496808.*

Leeds North West

The most diverse constituency in Leeds, it ranges from student Headingley, through suburban Weetwood, Adel, Cookridge and Bramhope to the market town of Otley. The MP is Dr. Keith Hampson, who entered the Commons in 1974 as MP for Ripon, but switched to Leeds North West in 1983, winning with a majority of 8,537. This was cut to 5,201 in 1987 but against the local trend rose to 7,671 in 1992 despite polling 730 fewer votes. Dr. Hampson was a history lecturer at Edinburgh University, and Sir Edward Heath's personal assistant for a time. His posts have included opposition Education spokesman and Michael Heseltine's Parliamentary Private Secretary. He is married to TV current affairs presenter, Sue Cameron.

Election Result. *Keith Hampson Con 21,750 (43.0%); Barbara Pearce Lib Dem 14,079 (27.8%); Sue Egan Lab 13,782 (27.3%); David Webb Green 519 (1.0%); Noel Nowosielski Lib 427. Con majority: 7,671, a 2.55% swing to Con. Of 69,406 electorate 50,557 voted, a turnout of 72.84%.*

Contacts. *Keith Hampson—Otley Conservative Office, 90 Boroughgate, Otley, Leeds LS21 1AE. ☎ 0943-462462; Labour—M. Miller, 10 Northwood Road, Leeds LS6 1DZ. ☎ Leeds 782045. Liberal Democrats—Andrew Davies, 3 Glebe Terrace, Leeds LS16 5NA. ☎ Leeds 757193; Green—D. Webb, 2 Grove Lane, Leeds LS6 2AP. ☎ Leeds 741011.*

Leeds West

Thanks to a split in Liberal Democrat and the "old" Liberal vote, Labour has managed to turn this seat from a Liberal marginal to a safe seat. Former Leeds City Councillor, John Battle won it in 1987 from the Liberal Michael Meadowcroft with a majority of 4,692. By 1992, this had become a Labour majority of 13,828. Leeds West has always seemed safe from the Conservatives, with large council estates and much lower-end owner occupier housing. Battle's special interests are poverty, housing, inner cities and development issues.

Election Result. *John Battle Lab 26,310 (55.1%); Paul Bartlett Con 12,482 (26.2%); George Howard Lib Dem 4,252 (8.9%); Michael Meadowcroft Lib 3,980 (8.3%); Alison Mander Green 569 (1.2%); Robert Tenny NF 132. Lab majority 13,828, a 4.46% wing to Lab. Of 67,084 electorate 47,725 voted, a turnout of 71.14%.*

Contacts. *John Battle—18 Branch Road, Leeds LS12 3AQ. ☎ 310258; Conservative—Bramley Conservative Club, Upper Town Street, Leeds LS13 3JX. ☎ Leeds 565206; Liberal Democrats—as Leeds Central; Liberal Party—see panel on right; Green—G. Branch-flower, 6 Park Crescent, Leeds LS12 3NL. ☎ Leeds 790264.*

Morley and Leeds South

On the retirement of former Home Secretary and Northern Ireland Secretary Merlyn Rees (now Lord Rees), John Gunnell comfortably held this large seat for Labour with an increased majority on the 1987 result. Gunnell is a stalwart of the region's political scene. He twice (unsuccessfully) contested Leeds North East for Labour, spent five years as leader of the West York-

shire Metropolitan County Council until its abolition in 1986 and was a member of the West Yorkshire Passenger Transport Authority until 1990. Current positions include membership of the board of Opera North, and Yorkshire and Humberside Development Association. A former lecturer in science education at the University of Leeds, he is married with two sons and one daughter.

Election Result. *John Gunnell Lab 23,896 (52.2%); Richard Booth Con 16,524 (36.1%); Joan Walmsley Lib Dem 5,062 (11.1%); Robert Thurston NLP 327. Lab majority 7,372, a 0.33% swing to Lab. Of 63,107 electorate 45,809 voted, a turnout of 72.58%.*

Contacts. *John Gunnell—Morley Town Hall, Queen Street, Morley, LS27 9DY. ☎ Leeds 477138; Conservative—Morley Conservative Club, Chapel Hill, Morley, LS27 9JH. ☎ Leeds 535342; Liberal Democrats—Tom Leadley, 181 Haigh Moor Road, West Ardsley, WF3 1EN. ☎ Leeds 535677.*

Pudsey

One of those constituencies where the name causes resentment. The residents of Horsforth wonder why they should be lumped under the heading of Pudsey, which lies across the Aire Valley. Electorally, besides Pudsey and Horsforth, the constituency consists of Yeadon,

Rawdon, Guiseley and Menston. Thanks to a divided opposition, the Conservatives have ruled supreme in this area since 1945, with over 70 per cent of houses owner-occupied. The MP since 1974 is Sir Giles Shaw, born in 1931 and a former President of the Cambridge Union. He was Parliamentary Under-Secretary for the Environment in 1981-83; and for Energy 1983-4; Minister of State at the Home Office, 1984-86; and Minister of State, Department of Trade & Industry in 1986-87.

Election Result. *Sir Giles Shaw Con 25,067 (44.1%); Arthur Giles Lab 16,095 (28.3%); David Shutt Lib Dem 15,153 (26.7); Jean Wynne Green 466 (0.8%). Con majority 8,972, a 4.61% swing Lab. Of 61,914 electorate 56,781 voted, a turnout of 80.14%.*

Contacts. *Sir Giles Shaw—Primrose Rooms, 83 Town Street, Horsforth, LS18 5BP.* ☎ *Leeds 587296; Labour—Bernie Haynes, 205 Low Lane, Horsforth, LS18 5QW.* ☎ *Leeds 589159. Liberal Democrats—Mrs. Bernice Brock, 49 Tennyson Street, Guiseley, LS20 9LN.* ☎ *0943-79412; Greens—G. Williamson, 42 Rose Terrace, Leeds LS18 4QA.*

Religion

The Church of England, Roman Catholic Church and Methodism predominate in Leeds, but the area also has literally dozens of other religious communities, from Jewish and Muslim to Polish and Greek Orthodox, to Quakers, Pentecostal and Buddhists. There are so many Christian and other groups that a couple of Directories are published with contacts for each one.

Aslan publishes the Leeds Christian Directory, a list of all groups and much more.

☛ *36 Basinghall Street, Leeds LS1 5ED.*

☎ *Leeds 444767.*

Leeds Metropolitan Council of Churches publishes an annual Directory of all Churches in the area.

☛ *Available for £2.00 post free from Rev. W. T. Snelson, Bardsey Vicarage, Woodacre Lane, Leeds LS17 9DG.*

☎ *0937-572243.*

Religious Organisations & Churches

The following are the main contacts for religious groups in the Leeds area. Ring for times and places of worship.

Church of England. The Bishop of Ripon, Bishop Mount, Ripon HG4 5DP. ☎ 0756-2045; The Bishop of Knaresborough, 16 Shaftsbury Avenue, Leeds LS8 1DT. ☎ 664800; The Archdeacon of Leeds, 712 Foundry Lane, Leeds LS14 8BL. ☎ 602069; Ripon Diocesan Secretary, Diocesan Office, St. Mary's Street, Leeds LS9 7DP. ☎ 487487; Ripon Diocesan Registrar, York House, York Place, Knaresborough, HG5 0AD. ☎ 0423-862266.

Roman Catholic Church. The Bishop of Leeds, 13 North Grange Road, Leeds LS6 2BR. ☎ 304533; The Administrator of St. Anne's Cathedral, Cathedral House, Leeds LS2 8BE. ☎ 454545; Curial Office, 7 St. Mark's Avenue, Leeds LS2 9BN. ☎ 444788.

The Methodist Church. Chairman of the District, 281 Otley Road, Leeds LS16 5LN. ☎ 785546.

United Reformed Church. Lidgett Lane, Leeds LS8 1PQ. ☎ 666627; Secretary of the Leeds District, 2 Park Crescent, Leeds LS8 1DH; Provincial Office, 43 Hunslet Lane, Leeds LS10 1JW.

Baptist Churches. Superintendent of the North East Region, 26 Weetwood Road, Leeds LS16 5LT. ☎ 785946.

Leeds Jewish Representative Council, 151 Shadwell Lane, Leeds LS17. ☎ 697520.

Church of Jesus Christ of Latter Day Saints, Kingswear Parade, Leeds LS15. ☎ 646874.

Muslim. Muslim Community of Metropolitan Leeds. 168 Beeston Road, Leeds LS11; Muslim Cultural Centre, Harehills Place, Leeds LS8. ☎ 480711.

Sikh. Ramgarhia Board, 8/10 Chapeltown Road, Leeds LS7 ☎ 624027; Sikh Temple, 281 Chapeltown Road, Leeds LS7. ☎ 691686.

Hindu Temple, 36 Alexandra Road, Leeds LS6. ☎ 757024.

Leeds Buddhist Centre, 148 Harehills Avenue, Leeds LS8 4EU. ☎ Leeds 405880.

Lutheran Church. 105 Otley Old Road, Leeds LS16 6HH. ☎ 676360.

Latvian Lutheran. 10a Calverley Lane, Leeds LS13 1HE. ☎ 568710.

Moravian Church. 38 Fulneck, Leeds LS28 8NT. ☎ 564828.

Polish Orthodox. 13 Newlay Wood Drive, Leeds LS18 4LL. ☎ 583298.

Greek Orthodox. 19 Whinmoor Gardens, Leeds LS14. ☎ 654255.

Leeds Free Church. 21 Moor Drive, Leeds LS6 4BY. ☎ 752428.

Society of Friends. Call for details of Meetings—Leeds ☎ 507093; Adel 670289; Carlton Hill ☎ 422208; Gildersome ☎ 523632; Otley ☎ 0943-467888; Rawdon ☎ 507093; Roundhay ☎ 667246.

Salvation Army. Divisional Headquarters, Waterloo Road, Leeds LS10 2NS. ☎ 771700.

Pentecostal. Bridge Street ☎ 668060; Horsforth, The Manse, Parkside, Horsforth ☎ 582722.

Leeds Assembly of God Pentecostal Church, 232 Cardigan Road, Leeds LS6. ☎ 788259.

Mount Zion Pentecostal Mission. 2 Avenue Hill, Leeds LS8. ☎ 621675.

Church of God of Prophecy. 378 Meanwood Road, Leeds LS7. ☎ 621271.

First United Church of Jesus Christ (Apostolic) 43/45 Victoria Road, Leeds LS6. ☎ 628744.

New Testament Church of God. 3 Easterly Road, Leeds LS8. ☎ 629089.

Wesleyan Holiness Church. Hustler Grove, Leeds LS7. ☎ 629572.

United Church of Jesus Christ. Gledhow Grove, Leeds LS8. ☎ 468865.

International City Mission. Harehills Avenue, Leeds LS7. ☎ 623209.

City Evangelical Church. Cemetery Road, Elland Road, Leeds LS11.

Church of the Nazarene. 236 Cross Flatts Grove, Leeds LS11. ☎ 709275.

First Church of Christ Scientist, 4 Alma Road, Leeds LS6.

Christian Science Reading Room, 30 Headingley Lane, Leeds LS6. ☎ 785211.

Kingdom Hall of Jehovah's Witness, Stainbeck Road, Leeds LS7.

PART TWO:
Exploring Leeds

Leeds has become a marvellous place to have time on your hands. New things to see and do are being added all the time, like the Kirkstall Valley Nature Reserve, the Nocturnal House at Tropical World and the Henry Moore Sculpture Centre on The Headrow. And not too far in the future loom even bigger developments of international importance—the Royal Armories and the Medical Museum.

But many of the area's amenities are not purpose-built. They are the architectural gems which made Leeds one of the greatest cities of the Industrial Revolution, and the parks and open spaces that have given it a reputation for being one of Europe's greenest cities.

This section describes all the principal attractions—and many of the lesser-known ones—in the 217 square miles of the Leeds Metropolitan District.

Left: Leeds Town Hall dominates the view west along The Headrow.

What Shall We Do Today?

Heritage and great architecture, nature reserves and fine arts, steam trains and working farms— Leeds is a self-contained leisure haven.

Only London, Edinburgh and York can match the number of major attractions that Leeds has to offer in its 217 square miles. But unlike some other northern cities, Leeds does not claim to have metamorphosed as a "tourist" centre. There is not the sense of grim determination that pervades neighbouring Bradford's pursuit of the tourism market. For Leeds has a diverse economy that has not suffered like Bradford's, and the great success of visitor attractions in the Leeds area is the icing on the cake. Most of the organised attractions described in the following pages are busy all year round because the local population makes good use of them. But quietly, Leeds *has* become an important centre for outside visitors. The use of the word "tourism" usually conjures up images of people coming to spend their fortnight's holiday, exploring a new attraction every day with several hundreds of pounds of Japanese optical equipment round their necks. But it is not like that here. Most outsiders arriving in Leeds usually come to visit friends or relatives, to study or train, or on short-term work. They quickly realize that there is an awful lot going on, with major facilities like Tropical World or Temple Newsam Home Farm, famous restaurants like Harry Ramsden's, and a multitude of historic sites to visit, from the Leeds-Liverpool Canal to Kirkstall Abbey and Temple Mill, and galleries of international importance like the Henry Moore Sculpture Centre. There is so much to do in such a compact area, and those who came here for what they thought was a one-off visit keep returning. They also use Leeds as a central base for exploring the North of England, because no other city in Britain is so ideally situated for visiting such a large number of major attractions (*see Beyond Leeds, pages 155-191*). Of course, Leeds gets some itinerant tourists and backpacking students, especially in summer. Interestingly, of those visitors from the UK who come to Leeds for a weekend break, most appear to be from East Anglia, the London area and Kent. While such visitors will find the following section invaluable, its primary audience is the people who live right here in the Leeds area.

What's On? Ask the Information Centres

Special events, guided tours, conducted walks, new attractions, travel and accommodation advice, useful contacts, leaflets and brochures.

Leeds Tourist Information Centre. The Basement, 19 Wellington Street, Leeds LS1 1DG. Open Mon-Fri 9.30am-5pm, Sat 9.30am-12.30pm & 1.30pm-4pm. ☎ Leeds 478301/2/3.

Otley Tourist Information Centre. 8 Boroughgate, Otley, Leeds LS21 3AH. Open Mon-Thur 9am-4.30pm, Fri 9am-4pm. Also Sat & Sun, May Bank Holiday to September, 10am-3pm. ☎ Leeds 477705.

Wetherby Tourist Information Centre. Council Offices, 24 Westgate, Wetherby, LS22 4NL. Open Mon-Thur 8.30am-5pm, Fri 8.30am-4.30pm. ☎ Leeds 477253.

For news of forthcoming events, see the free **What's On in Leeds** guide, the listings sections of **Northern Star** & **Art Scene** for exhibitions, and the Friday edition of the **Evening Post.**

NB. Addresses and opening times may be subject to change. If possible, check by telephone first before making a personal visit.

Events Listings. Besides numerous leaflets, there are two sources of free printed information about special events. A council-backed *What's On* guide, regularly updated, is available at tourist information centres, libraries, galleries and theatres throughout the area and gives details of the constantly changing programme of talks, walks, countryside events and other attractions. The other is *Artscene*, a free monthly magazine about arts in Yorkshire & Humberside, with much information about craft & design, sculpture, photography and painting exhibitions. It is available from libraries, TICs and galleries.

A Year in the Life of Leeds

Even the smallest village usually has some kind of annual event, whether it be a flower show or a folk custom like cheese rolling or pancake racing. Leeds has a programme of literally scores of activities which have been held around the same weekend or date for years. Some are relatively small affairs which appeal mainly to residents of a particular neighbourhood or members and friends of a club or organisation. But many have truly regional appeal and attract thousands of visitors. The following is a list of the main events.

Spring

❏ *Thursday before Good Friday. The* **Woodhouse Easter Funfair** *on Woodhouse Moor. By an agreement with the Showmen's Guild which goes back many years, this fair remains open for 11 consecutive days, including Sunday.*

❏ *Saturday before the Spring Bank Hol. The popular* **Otley Show** *at a permanent ground near the River Wharfe. An old fashioned country show, with show jumping, dogs, livestock, handicrafts, trade stands. On the same date is* **Wetherby Show**, *another agricultural show, at Grange Park, Wetherby.*

❏ **Chapeltown Spring Fair.** *Another long-established funfair, runs from Friday to Sunday, "the*

Sunday of which shall fall 15 days before Whit Monday".

Summer

❑ **The Temple Newsam Rhododendron Display.** A sudden burst of colour among the massive number of rhododendrons. Begins in the first week of June and lasts for several weeks.

❑ Second Saturday in June. The annual **Otley Carnival**. Decorated floats procession ending at Otley Showground.

❑ The last Saturday in June is the **Leeds Lord Mayor's Parade.** A procession of decorated floats winds through the streets of the city centre.

❑ In late June is held the **Otley Triathlon**, a 1.5 kilometre swim in the Wharfe, 40k. cycle ride and 10k. cross country run.

❑ On the 2nd Tuesday of July each year begins the three-day **Great Yorkshire Show**. One of the great country shows of the year, at Hookstone Oval, (off Wetherby Road) Harrogate.

❑ The annual **Leeds Show** is held on the 1st or 2nd weekend of August at Soldier's Field, Roundhay Park. Horticultural with handicraft and trade stands, entertainments, refreshment marquees and much more.

❑ Friday before the August Bank Hol is the **Roundhay Bank Holiday Funfair**, Roundhay Park. Commences on the Friday, and continues for five consecutive days including Sunday.

❑ August Bank Holiday Sunday. As a prelude to the Carnival, there is a **Caribbean Concert** in Potternewton Park, Chapeltown, Leeds, featuring mainly West Indian and World Music.

❑ August Bank Holiday Monday is the **Caribbean Carnival** in Chapeltown, the biggest such event outside London, with steel bands, decorated floats and street tableaux, street snacks, etc. etc.

Autumn & Winter

❑ **Chapeltown September Fair.** Commences "on the Fri. prior to the 3rd Mon. in September and continues to the following Sun. except when the first Sun. of the month falls on the seventh day of September, in which event the Fair commences on the Fri. following the closing of the Woodhouse September Fair." Got that?

❑ **Woodhouse September Fair.** "Commences on the Thurs. prior to the 4th Mon. in September and remains for 10 consecutive days, or at the option of the Showmen's Guild, for four consecutive days."

❑ On the last Saturday of September/1st Sat. of October begins The **Leeds International Concert Season**, over 20 orchestral and choral concerts at Leeds Town Hall until early June.

❑ In mid-October begins the **Leeds International Film Festival**, first held in 1987. Held at cinemas throughout the Leeds area.

❑ Last Sunday of October. The **Leeds Marathon and half-Marathon**. The region's premier running events take place through the city.

❑ November 5th. Huge free **Fireworks Displays and Bonfires** at Woodhouse Moor, Bramley Fall, East End Park, Middleton Park, Springhead Park (Rothwell) and the arena at Roundhay Park. Hot food stands and some live entertainment.

❑ Third week of November. **Leeds Swimming Marathon** at the International Pool over 8 days. Swim 100 lengths or 50 lengths.

❑ Mid-November. The famous **Leeds Christmas Lights** are switched on in Mid-November and can be seen until Twelfth Night. Eight miles of Christmas lighting in Leeds and surrounding towns, the biggest festive lights display in the country (even London has fewer). Seven days a week, they are switched on between 3.30-4pm and off at 12 midnight.

❑ On the second Friday in December, Otley has its annual **Victorian Fair**, a colourful street market where stallholders dress in period costume and traditional snacks and entertainments are on offer. After 5.30pm traffic is banned from the central area and charity stalls take over.

Lining up for the August Bank Holiday Caribbean Carnival in Chapeltown.

Star Attractions

Most of the attractions in this section would qualify for inclusion in the Great Days Out chapter of a similar guide to Manchester or Newcastle. For few cities can claim such diverse facilities as the world's first railway line, major indoor tropical environments, the best preserved Cistercian abbey, a famous TV "soap" location, huge working farm museum, and miles of rejuvinated waterfront area. But that is what Leeds has to offer—and they are all within half an hour's ride from any point in the city. Combined with great galleries and museums, locals are never short of things to do.

Abbey Light Railway

This excellent small railway was built from scratch by a band of enthusiasts and carries passengers every Sunday, rain or shine. It runs on a 2ft. gauge track just a quarter of a mile long, between Bridge Road, Kirkstall, and the grounds of Kirkstall Abbey There are three 12-seater carriages converted from ammunition wagons and of the 12 diesel and petrol locomotives owned by the railway, those used most often are from the 1930's and 1940s. Having built the line themselves, including the excavation of a 20ft cutting and building of a 20ft. bridge across the Aire mill race near Clough House, the enthusiasts (principally Peter Lowe, an engineering lecturer at Kitson College, and his family) are currently tooling up to build a steam locomotive similar to Peter Pan, the "visiting" engine they have every summer. Prospective passengers arriving in cars are encouraged to use the Abbey car park and take the ride down to Bridge Road, returning by train or walking back. An excellent longer Sunday is Peter Lowe's "Best of Leeds" trail. Walk west along the canal from Granary Wharf, behind Leeds City Station, and visit Armley Mills, then cross to the Aire and to his railway, riding on it to Kirkstall Abbey and the Abbey House Museum.

☛ *Off Bridge Road, Kirkstall. Regular Yorkshire Rider buses from outside Lloyds Bank, Park Row. Get off at Bridge Road/Kirkstall Lane traffic lights. The railway operates on Sundays only, running a shuttle service beginning at 12 noon in summer and on Bank Hols and 1pm in winter. The train is also available for party bookings at other times. It is developing a good reputation with narrow-gauge railway enthusiasts from Britain and abroad. There is a small ticket fare, single or return.*

☎ *Information from Peter Lowe on Leeds 675087.*

Bramham House

Known as "The Versailles of Yorkshire." Built in the early 1700s as a Florentine-style villa, Bramham was gutted by fire in 1826 and remained a blackened shell right through the Victorian years. Its restoration was in 1906 and although the exterior is the original, everything inside is a copy. One of the most interesting internal features is the horseshoe-shaped staircase, modelled on one at Fontainebleau. However, it is the park that most people come to see, an astonishing landscape tapestry of beech-hedged rides and avenues of copper beech, cedar, spanish chestnut and lime. Formal pools, fountains and cascades give it that Versailles feel. Famous for daffodils, roses and rhododendrons. Best time is mid-week outside school holidays. The park gets busy during the four-day Bramham Horse Trials, on the weekend following the Spring Bank Holiday.

☛ *Nine miles east from Leeds centre. Take A64 York road to A1 and turn north 2 miles to Bramham village. Can also be reached by quieter route through the village of Thorner. Good bus connection: the regular West Yorks service to Wetherby runs nearby there from Vicar Lane. Closed Sept-Easter then complex opening times.*

☎ *Boston Spa 844265.*

Harewood House *is the house with everything. Designed in 1759 by the brilliant York architect, John Carr, the gardens were landscaped in 1772 by "Capability" Brown, the interior by Robert Adam and the furniture by Thomas Chippendale. Although many alterations were made in Victorian times, it is still a treasurehouse of the Georgian period, with paintings by "El Greco", Bellini and Turner. The home of the Earl and Countess of Harewood, the house is open to the public. Among the attractions are the famous bird garden, four acres of aviaries housing over 150 species, including the emu, penguins, kookaburras, cranes, flamingoes and toucans. The grounds also have a lake and adventure playground; and there's an indoor simulated tropical rainforest.*

☛ *On A61 Leeds-Harrogate road at junction with A659. Frequent bus service (Harrogate route) from Central Bus Station. Open daily April-October, grounds 10am, house 11am, closing at 5.15pm in season. Open Suns. only in Feb, mar. and Nov. if weather suitable. Disabled facilities, dogs must be on lead. Free parking. Admission charge.*

☎ *Leeds 886225.*

Esholt

Esholt's famous sewage works had a plant which extracted lanolin from the water used to wash sheep fleeces at nearby mills. The lanolin was then sold to soap manufacturers. Today, the small village upstream on the River Aire from Leeds is in the "soap" business more than ever, being the outdoor location of the fictitious Beckindale in Yorkshire Television's long-running soap-opera *Emmerdale*. Esholt (derived from "Ashwood") is mostly a pleasant village in a sleepy hollow between Guiseley and Shipley, officially just across the Leeds city boundary. Visitors can go into the Woolpack for a drink, though its interior is disappointingly unlike the TV set, and look at Demdyke Row. Other Emmerdale landmarks can be traced with the use of a map, purchased at the village sub-post office, where key fobs, place mats, postcards and other souvenirs are on sale. The village has a good tearoom and gallery at the Old Hall, and an interesting church, St. Paul's. Nature-lovers will enjoy the walk down the Aire through the Esholt Estate to Apperley Bridge.

☛ *Esholt is off the A6038 Guiseley-Shipley Road (down the hill from Harry Ramsden's, and signposted left turn). Coaches must use the coach park.*

Lotherton Hall & Bird Garden

Rare for a country house dripping with works of art and antiques, Lotherton Hall, right on the Leeds eastern boundary, has an unpompous atmosphere. The secret of its charm is that it is comparatively young: Edwardian in design although there is a Georgian core. It belonged to the Gascoigne family, great colliery owners and collectors of fine art. The house and grounds were given to Leeds in 1968 and the displays have been enhanced by crafts, costume and contemporary decorative arts collections and a famous Oriental Gallery, full of Chinese ceramics from the neolithic period to the beginning of the Ming Dynasty. Outside, there is one of the best Bird Gardens in Britain. The aviaries and ponds have been landscaped to create realistic surroundings for over 200 different species of birds from around the world. Some of them are rare or endangered species and Lotherton is doing its bit for conservation by encouraging them to breed in captivity. Like Temple Newsam, Lotherton also has a large estate. Rangers from Leeds Countryside Service have waymarked nature trails with red arrows and have a useful leaflet.

☛ *13 miles east from Leeds city centre, near Aberford, one mile beyond the A1 trunk road on the B1217 to Towton. Hall open daily Tues-Sun 10.30am-5.30pm (dusk in winter). Closed Mondays except Bank Holiday Mondays. Bird Garden open weekdays 10-5pm, Sun and Bank Hol Mon 11-6pm, Easter to October; Sat & Sun 11-5pm or dusk Nov & Dec. Closed Jan-Easter.*

☎ *Leeds 813259. Countryside Ranger, Leeds 813068 (Wednesdays preferred).*

Meanwood Valley Urban Farm

Among the best urban farms in Britain, these 13 acres of former inner-city wasteland in the Meanwood Valley bustle with activity and must be how labour-intensive farms were a century ago. The farm is run by a charity, with a grant from Leeds City Council and the help of many volunteers, fund-raisers, etc. Unusual breeds are kept, which modern high-intensive farming doe not consider profitable. Pigs are the Gloucester Old Spot, a very old English breed; sheep tend to be Jacob, Whitefaced Woodland and Suffolks; goats include Anglo-Nubian, Toggenberg and Saanen; and there are around 250 poultry, ducks and geese ranging freely around the farm. there's always something new happening, from lambing time to a new litter of pigs or a calf. Staff and numerous trainees work on the land or feed livestock, watched by a constant stream of visitors (around 45,000 annually). All produce in the market garden is grown organically with compost from farm manure, vegetable wastes, etc., and visitors can buy produce at the shop. As well as eggs, goatsmilk, goats yogurt and cheese, this includes, in season: potatoes, peas, beans, cauliflowers, cabbages, broccoli, onions, beetroot, swedes and others. Alternative energy sources are being developed, such as a wind power generator, and solar heating panels. There is a shop, café and an educational centre, with environmental projects geared to needs of the National Curriculum. The farm now has a modern tarmac surface, with good access for the disabled, and car parking.

☛ *The Farm is just over a mile north of Leeds city centre, on Meanwood Road. Regular Yorkshire Rider bus services. Well signposted off Sugarwell Road. Open 9am to 8pm or dusk, seven days a week all year.*

☎ *Leeds 629759.*

Rugby League Hall of Fame

The Rugby Football League and Whitbread Trophy put their heads together to open this splendid tribute to the illustrious history of the 13-a-side code. Much memorabilia is packed into the restaurant and bar of the Bentley Arms Roast Inn at Oulton, on the south side of Leeds. The main purpose is to pay tribute to the greatest British players in the century since the Rugby League was formed as the Northern Rugby Union in Huddersfield on 29th August, 1895. At the time of writing, 10 men had been accepted into this elite group: Jonty Parkin, Jim Sullivan, Harold Wagstaff, Billy Boston, Neil Fox, Gus Risman, Brian Bevan, Billy Batten, Alex Murphy and Albert Rosenfield. Others will be added in future—they must have played mostly for British Clubs and have been retired for at least 10 years. The rest of the exhibits include many famous trophies, such as the John Player Trophy, the European Club Championship Trophy, The BBC Floodlit Trophy, and the Yorkshire League Championship Cup, first won by Hunslet in 1908 and last won by Leeds in 1910. There are caps, badges, medals, old kits, posters, programmes, famous headlines, and much more.

☛ *Bentley Arms Roast Inn, 3 Wakefield Road, Oulton. No ad-*

mission charge and open Mon-Sat 11am to 11pm, Sun 12-3pm, 7pm-10.30pm. Restrictions at lunchtime (12-2pm) and evening (6.30-10pm) in the restaurant.
☎ *Leeds 820202.*

Kirkstall Abbey

The most important old building in Leeds, if not exactly the best-preserved, is Kirkstall Abbey **(pictured left)**. Constructed between 1152 and 1182 on the north bank of the River Aire, for 357 years it was a great community of hundreds of Cistercian monks and lay brothers. Wandering around its great shell and nubbly foundations today, it is still possible to imag-ine the hive of activity it once was, with the early forge, fields of live-stock and early wool and fulling mills which formed the basis of the great Leeds cloth industry and market of the later Middle Ages. Those who founded Kirkstall had originally been at Fountains Abbey, near Ripon, but had moved south to the Aire where they found an ideal location with plenty of building materials for a sister Abbey. After the dissolution of 1539, the Abbey was steadily stripped of its windows, roofs and much of its stonework by local builders for cottages and roads. This didn't stop the great artist, J. M. W. Turner, and the poet, Robert Southey, ad-miring it. Before Leeds sprawled westward to absorb the out-town-ships along the Aire, the Abbey must have had the same haunting atmosphere that the more remote Cistercian ruins like Fountains and Rievaulx have today. But even with a major city on its doorstep, Kirkstall Abbey has managed to retain a "green" location and is at the centre of a Country Park with good walks signposted along the valley. The Abbey's structure is actually preferred by many histo-rians to Fountains and Rievaulx. Lesser experts will find that the principal features are well signposted. Unfortunately, not every part of it is open for public inspection but there is access to most of the important areas for a visit to be well worthwhile. Look for the following -

The Church. Beginning at the west end, the view along the church's entire 200ft. length is un-broken, with eight huge columned arches. At services, there was a strict order from back to front. Closest to the west door is the nave, where lay brothers and lay visitors sat. Closer to the front were aged and infirm monks, then monks and novices in the choir.

The Tower. Not the original 12th century structure, which only at-tained the same height as the church roof. In 1509-27 a new tower was built. The north-west side collapsed in 1779.

The Transepts. On either side of the tower, providing the impor-tant crucifix shape to the church. The north transept doorway gave access to the cemetery after funeral services. A fascinating feature of the south transept is the "night stairs" used by monks to reach the choir from their dormitory for night vigils.

The Cloisters & Chapter House. The Cloisters form one of the most tranquil corners of Leeds, a grass square where monks would sit reading and writing in good weather. The Chapter House has many carved arches and pillars and some old stone coffins.

☞ *In Abbey Road, past Kirkstall traffic lights. Open from dawn to dusk, every day. Regular Yorkshire Rider buses from outside Lloyds Bank, Park Row.*

The world's first railway was the Middleton line in South Leeds, built in 1758. Its coal wagons were drawn by horses until 1812, when its first steam engine was put into service, still one year ahead of George Stephenson's first locomotive. But **Middleton Railway** *(above) has been ignored by history because it was purely a mining railway, carrying no passengers. Today, the railway is still running (now carrying passengers and no freight) thanks to a small but dedicated band of enthusiasts. It transports a steady 15,000-20,000 passengers a year on a line that is just over a mile long, from Moor Road, Hunslet, to the south end of Middleton Park. The two carriages, converted from mail vans, can take a total of 90 on the 10-minute steam or diesel rides. The line is a full standard gauge and has 21 engines—11 steam and 10 die-sel, most of them built by famous Leeds loco builders, such as Hunslet Engine Co., and Hudswell Clarke & Co. Passengers are encouraged to ride from Moor Road, spending a few hours (nature trails, picnics) at Middleton Park before returning.*
☞ *At The Station, Moor Road., Leeds LS11 2JQ. Yorks Rider bus services pass nearby from the Town Hall, the Corn Exchange and Park Row. Clearly signposted off A653 Dewsbury Rd or ex. 45 from M1. Runs week-ends and Bank Hols. Easter to end Sept. Also Wed. in August only & Santa Specials at Xmas. On Sat. diesel service every 45 min. from Moor Rd 1.30-4.30pm; Suns. steam engine every 30min. 1pm-4.30pm. Bank Hol. steam specials, trains at 11, 12 & 1pm then every 30 min. to 4.30pm.*
☎ *Talking timetable Leeds 710320. Other info Leeds 711089 after 6pm.*

Temple Newsam, Home Farm & Estate

A splendid Tudor-Jacobean residence and art gallery, a fascinating traditional farmyard that is a living museum of British agriculture over the last 200 years, and an 1,000 acre estate for walks, nature study and picnics. A family can spend the entire day here, making use of the wide range of facilities and attractions. Begin inside **Temple Newsam House** (pictured below). There was a house here before the Norman Conquest, and a previous building was associated with the Knights Templar religious order of the 12th century, from which part of the name is derived. Historically, it is renowned as the birthplace of Henry, Lord Darnley, second husband of Mary Queen of Scots and father of James I (James VI of Scotland). Being roughly half-way between London and Edinburgh, the house was the scene of much intrigue in Elizabethan times. The building that visitors see today was begun by Thomas, Lord Darcy, before 1521. Sir Arthur Ingram, who bought the house in 1622, commissioned extensive remodelling, and further enlargements were made in the late 18th century. Af-

ter many years in the ownership of the Viscounts Irwin, it descended to the Earl of Halifax, and was bought by the former Leeds Corporation in 1922. Since the War, Temple Newsam has become an internationally famous country house museum of decorative art, having the finest municipally owned collection outside London (it now belongs to Leeds City Council). See the remarkable Georgian long gallery, Chinese drawing room and Elizabethan-style staircase. Impressive silver, porcelain and paintings by Reynolds, Mercier and others (see also page 50). And there is a fine collection of Chippendale furniture. **Temple Newsam Home Farm** is where "All Creatures Great and Small" is brought to life in a huge working farmyard. The accent is on traditional animal rearing—no cooped up battery hens or intensive dairy units here—and squealing piglets scatter across the cobblestones amongst the clucking poultry. There is no admission charge but leave a donation in the bull's head box and there are few restrictions on where you can walk. However, you should respect gates and fences. All the traditional British

farm animals are here. The emphasis is on rare breeds of cattle, sheep, goats, pigs, hens, geese, etc. There is even a dovecote for white fan-tailed pigeons. Many good exhibitions interpret old-fashioned farming methods. Especially good is the collection of harvesting machines. **Temple Newsam Estate** forms one of the biggest parks in Europe and is especially worth a visit in summer, with spectacular displays of rhododendrons, roses and azaleas. Nature trails are well laid-out through a network of woodland and parkland paths, and visitors can expect to see (in season) birds like cuckoo, blackcap, bullfinch, great-spotted woodpecker, nuthatch and jay. Rangers from Leeds Countryside Service are on hand.

☛ *Five miles east from the city centre, signposted off Selby Road (A63) at Halton and Whitkirk. Yorkshire Rider bus from Boar Lane and the Market. House open Tues-Sun and Bank Hol Mons 10.30-5.30pm (dusk in winter). Home Farm open daily, Summer 10am-5pm, winter 10am-4pm. Shop, restaurant (seasonal) and ample free parking.*
☎ *Leeds 647321. Countryside Ranger, Leeds 645535.*

The south-facing aspect of Temple Newsam.

Tetleys Brewery

Tetleys is to Leeds what Guinness is to Dublin. Since 1822, Joshua Tetley & Son have been brewing beer on or near this site off the Hunslet Road in South Leeds, absorbing smaller concerns like Whitakers of Bradford and the late-lamented Melbourne Brewery of Leeds. Today the beer is as highly prized as ever with real ale connoisseurs. In 1994 a special £6m. Visitor Centre was opening next to the brewery, to which the public can walk in and learn about brewing (ring for opening times). Until then, for pre-booked parties of 30 there are twice-daily tours of the brewery, and the stables for the shire horses used in city centre deliveries. They are at 12 noon and 7pm, and include a meal and sample of the product in the Huntsman Bar. There is a long waiting list.

☛ *Joshua Tetley & Son are on Hunslet Road, Leeds LS10. Visitor Centre in Dock St. from 1994.* ☎ *Leeds 435282.*

Tropical World

One of the most popular attractions in the country, with over a million visitors each year and rising, Tropical World (below) is a steamy jungle of banana, coffee, citrus, pineapple and other exotic trees piquant with the sounds and atmosphere of the tropics. Its home is the Coronation House, a vast 1911 conservatory next to Canal Gardens, Roundhay Park. Visitors follow a wooden path through a jungle which is kept at a constant 75-80F and expect to see Tarzan swinging through the lush jungle as they walk deeper into the interior. An impressive waterfall spills 1,000 gallons a minute into a rock pool. There is a pond full of terrapins, another with huge carp lurking in its depths, and there are numerous displays of live reptiles like lizards and tree frogs, insects such as the hairy tarantula, and the Amazon Tank, full of exotic water life. The Butterfly House has more than 30 different species feeding off the plants. Open in the summer 1993 is a Nocturnal House, containing Egyptian fruit bats and other anmials and plants of the night; an orchid house; a cacti and succulent desert; and a huge free-flying bird aviary.

☛ *At Canal Gardens, Princes Avenue, Leeds LS8. Open from 10am till dusk, seven days a week (ex. Xmas Day). Admission is free.* ☎ *Leeds 661850.*

The Waterfront

Right through the heart of Leeds, extending for over 15 miles, cuts the River Aire. To the east, it runs as the Aire-Calder Navigation. And westward it meanders almost parallel to the Leeds-Liverpool Canal. It was along here that the city was founded. The earliest settlement was at Leeds Bridge and in the Middle Ages the genesis of the city was in a cloth market that spread right across the original bridge and extended north up Lower Briggate. The present cast-iron structure was built in 1873. Today, most of the buildings stem from the 18th and 19th Centuries, but many of these historic warehouses had become derelict and for decades these areas were not on many visitors' itineraries. But in the late 1980s, huge environmental improvement schemes got under way and in the Nineties the Leeds Waterfront is fast becoming the liveliest part of town.

Granary Wharf: This area below Leeds City Station, leading outside to the Canal Basin, is at the forefront of the revitalised waterfront. Numerous speciality shops have been built in a totally unique arcade, while arts and crafts stalls spill out across the cobblestoned

Inside the amazing Tropical World at Roundhay Park.

canalside. At weekends there is street theatre, buskers, magicians, puppeteers and jugglers. On Sundays, the area becomes the Camden Market of the north, and the first Sunday of every month is "Funday", with children's entertainers, games with prizes. Visitors can see the Aire running through a tunnel below Leeds City Station, bypassing the Canal Basin.

☛ *Easiest entrance is under the railway bridge in Neville Street, just before the Hilton Hotel. Shops open Tue-Sun 10am-5.30pm.*

☎ *Leeds 446570 for information about latest events.*

Leeds & Liverpool Canal: Beginning at the Canal Basin on the west side of Victoria Bridge, work this famous waterway commenced in 1770 and finished in 1816. It runs for 130 miles to Liverpool, and linked Leeds woollen cloth manufacturers to the growing North American market. An easy walk of about an hour is from the Canal Basin west as far as Gotts Bridge behind the Yorkshire Post building.

☛ *The canal begins at Victoria Bridge, beside the Leeds Hilton Hotel, Neville Street.*

Aire and Calder Navigation: From the east side of Victoria Bridge, the River Aire runs as the Aire & Calder Navigation., opened in November 1700. The river had been deepened, canalised and even bypassed to take Leeds woollens to the Humber and the outside world. The most interesting area is the Leeds Dam & Lock. You can walk east from here along the towpath for several miles.

☛ *Access is from the east side of Crown Point Bridge, a 5 min. walk east from Leeds Parish Church.*

River & Canal Cruises: The Kirkstall Flyboat operates on the Leeds-Liverpool Canal and the Aire-Calder Navigation and is the best way to see the Leeds waterfront area. Beginning from the Canal Basin, its timetable depends on the season and intending passengers should ring in advance. The barge has many double-glazed windows, takes up to 52 passengers and serves refreshments.

☛ *Operates from Canal Wharfe, off Neville Street. Ring for times.*

☎ *Leeds 456195.*

Nowhere in Yorkshire is there a more rejuvinated inner city area than the banks of the River Aire. The various **Waterfront Developments** *can be seen from several footpaths. The most high profile is Asda House (on the south side, between Leeds Bridge and Victoria Bridge) designed by Leeds architects John Brunton and built with traditional materials to fit in with is riverside environment. Continuing east of Leeds Bridge, on the north side is 42 The Calls, a hotel and Brasserie in what was once known as Fletland Mill, dating from the 18th century. The Leeds Design Innovation Centre (eastwards again) was converted from a flour warehouse into offices and studios. Two superb residential developments are Victorian Quays (on the south side) which is a mixture of Aire & Calder Navigation warehouses, and new dwellings; and The Chandlers (on the north side, behind Leeds Parish Church), built around another disused warehouse. All this redevelopment is just the start. Through the 1990s, redevelopment of riverside properties will spread east well away from the city centre, including the £35 million Royal Armouries at Clarence Dock, and many more leisure facilities.*

Museums

Abbey House Museum

This is where the social and domestic life of the Leeds area is recorded, with superb "as it was" displays like three streets of shops, cottages, workshops and other buildings authentically reconstructed from the originals. They are 18th and 19th Century representations of Leeds, built from gritstone, and the streets like Abbey Fold, Harewood Square and Stephen Harding Gate, paved with original "setts". Among 17 shops and workshops is a superb Victorian chemists shop, its beautiful mahogany drawers and ornamental glass jars all well preserved. There is the "Hark to Rover Inn" from Kirkstall, complete with sawdust and spitoons. Other premises include a haberdasher; a barber's shop; grocer; ironmonger, claypipe maker; saddler; blacksmith, wheelwright, musical instrument maker, clock and watchmaker, tobacconist and printer. A collection of toys includes jigsaws, boardgames, dolls' houses, Ninja Turtles and miniature soldiers, as well as Regency, Victorian and Edwardian dolls. The folk galleries are what Abbey House is famous for nationally, with relics from leisure and social activities next to a whole range of items illustrating the peculiarly local customs and beliefs of the West Riding. The museum is in the well-preserved 12th Century gatehouse of Kirkstall Abbey, which is across a busy main road (use the pelican crossing) from the famous Cistercian ruin.

☛ *In Abbey Road, Kirkstall, Leeds 5, three miles west of the city centre. Open Mon-Sat 10am-5pm and Sundays 2pm-5pm. Closed Dec 25-26 & Jan 1. Regular Yorkshire Rider buses run past here from outside Lloyds Bank, Park Row. Admission charge. Disabled facilities.*

☎ *Leeds 755821.*

Armley Mills Museum

It could be said that the story of Armley Mills, pictured below standing on an "island" between the Leeds-Liverpool Canal and a long curve in the River Aire, is pretty close to the story of Leeds industry. Mills were built there in the 17th century, using water power from a mill race (or "goyt") to drive a huge wheel used in the "fulling" process in which cloth was finished. In the late-18th Century the mills were rebuild as a huge woollen mill and corn mill but in 1805 they were almost entirely reduced to cinders by a major fire. The buildings you can see today were quickly rebuilt on the same site, with noticeably less timbers and more fire-resistant stone, brick and cast iron. Inside, the work was still mainly fulling, although other work like carding was done and later yarn and worsted cloth, even bootmaking, was undertaken. It became one of the world's largest woollen mills. More than 400 years of cloth making at the mills ended in 1969, when Leeds City Council took them over to house a constantly improving collection that reflects both the mill's and the city's industrial past. The exhibits, mostly

from the 18th and 19th centuries, concentrate on textile, clothing, engine and locomotive manufacture and many have taped commentaries. See how the woollen cloth trade built Leeds, and trace the fleece from sheep's back to the human back. The collection is so vast that not all of it is always on display, which means you have to keep returning to see things like a model of the 1812 Middleton Colliery loco. The intimate Armley Palace Picture Hall, a reconstruction of a 1920s cinema, illustrates the history of cinema with silent projectors and a pianist (check in advance for performances). Another display tells the story of the world's first moving pictures, taken in Leeds by Louis Le Prince in 1888. There is also a display of underground haulage systems. A good interactive display is "Electrifying Leeds" in which visitors can pedal to generate kilowatts of electricity. Some exhibits are operated during "working weekends", usually Bank Holidays. Working machinery includes the water wheels, a steam engine and the great spinning "mules". Details of these are available from the Tourist Information Centre, in the local press and broadcast on BBC

Radio Leeds. There is a picnic area outside, surrounded by a number of old steam engines, locomotives and small railway rolling stock.

☛ *Off Canal Road (car park), which runs between Kirkstall Road and Armley, just over a mile from the city centre. Open: Tuesday to Saturday, 10am-5pm; Sunday 2pm-5pm. Closed Monday except Bank Hol Mondays. Yorkshire Rider bus services from Corn Exchange.*

☎ *Leeds 637861.*

Horsforth Village Museum of Local History

One of the smallest museums in Yorkshire is housed in the old Horsforth Urban District Council chamber. The authority ceased to exist when Horsforth was absorbed into Leeds on 1st April, 1974, and among the most prized exhibits are the chains of office worn by Horsforth UDC's chairman and chairman's lady. Many displays chronicle 2000 years of history in what to many residents is still a village rather than a town, much less a Leeds suburb. Compare today's scenes with old photographs and postcards (copies for sale). Among several reconstructions of Horsforth life are a village shop

Armely Mills, on a "goyt" or mill race of the River Aire.

window showing beautifully preserved merchandise, and a typical Victorian kitchen. There is a cabinet full of old cameras, and an impressive collection of wireless sets, including the Radiosetz, a cable radio system which an enterprising Horsforth firm once supplied to mostly council houses in the area. Other displays give fascinating facts and figures on modern Horsforth. It is not a "shush" museum. Visitors are encouraged to talk to each other and discuss the exhibits with the curator, or other visitors. At least two major displays are brand new each year. If you live in Horsforth, this is the place to come for books and leaflets on local walks and history, old and new postcards, photographs, notelets, pencils and paperweights.

☛ *Off The Green, Horsforth. Open April-December inclusive. Saturdays 10am-4pm, Sundays 2pm-5pm. Other times open by arrangement.*
☎ *Leeds 589411.*

Leeds City Museum
A traditional museum, displaying subjects as diverse as natural history, coins and medals, pre-historic settlements in Yorkshire, Roman remains and ethnography (artifacts from human societies around the world). What you see—around 10,000 items imaginatively presented in what is quite a compact museum—is just the tip of the iceberg. There are a further 990,000 pieces in reserve, which allows fascinating new displays to be presented to the public regularly. Much of it was collected in the 19th century by the Leeds Philosophical and Literary Society, whose museum received a direct hit from a German bomb in 1941, and some what you see today was salvaged from the rubble. Among the best exhibits is the 124,000-year-old remains of the famous hippopotamus found at Armley in 1852, plus a stuffed hippo (c.1932) to flesh out the bones. The natural history collection, especially the butterflies, is among the top ten in Britain. There are regular exhibitions by local societies, on such things as heraldry, photography, medieval tiles, and Leeds Jewry. There is a very active Friends of

Leeds City Museums organisation, and an excellent Saturday Morning Club for middle-school pupils.
☛ *In Leeds City Centre, on the 1st floor of the Central Library, The Headrow, (east side of the Town Hall). Access for disabled: 15 steps to lift at entrance but ramps and assistance if requested in advance. Open, Tues-Fri all year 9.30am-5.30pm; Saturday 9.30am-4pm. Closed Sun, Mon, Bank Holiday Mon and Tuesdays following Bank Hols. Admission free.*
☎ *Leeds 478275.*

The Medical Museum
This new Leeds museum, appropriately based at Europe's largest teaching hospital, St. James's, will develop throughout the 1990s into a huge collection of international importance. It has been assembled over almost a century, based on the private collection of the long-established Leeds surgical instrument makers Chas F. Thackray Ltd. Around the spring/summer of 1993 it changes from being a restricted exhibition of surgical instruments, pharmaceutical equipment, operating theatre hardware, etc., open only to pre-booked parties, to being accessible to the public on a regular basis. This is a temporary home (signposted from the main entrance on Beckett Street). In 1996, it moves into the former workhouse, from which St. James's Hospital was originally created. In 55,000 square feet of exhibition space, conference and

Virtually unchanged since the time of its construction in the mid-18th Century, the **Fulneck Moravian Settlement** *(which contains a fine museum) has a solid tranquility that it well worth experiencing. The Moravians were Protestant-Episcopals who came to Pudsey from East Germany and built this settlement on the steep hillside below Pudsey, a long terrace of dark Yorkshire stone buildings. The simple Moravian Church and the two schools, both fee paying, dominate the scene (the actress Diana Rigg was a pupil of the girls' school). Many visitors stop outside number 5 Fulneck, the birthplace of the legendary Yorkshire and England cricketer, Len Hutton, who was a Moravian. Today, there are about 75 residents in the settlement, but you won't find any German names. During World War 1, there was an anti-German backlash and English names were adopted. The museum, run by volunteers, is one of the best of its size in Britain. See the recently restored Victorian fire engine; souvenirs brought back by Moravian missionaries from Tibet, Newfoundland, West Indies & Africa; the Moravian sisters' Haubes (bonnets with pink ribbons for single women, blue ribbons for married & white for widows) and a perfectly preserved Victorian scullery.*
☛ *The Moravian Settlement is off Fartown, Pudsey. The Museum is at No. 55 Fulneck, open from Easter to end of October, Wed & Sat. only, 2pm-5pm. Guided tours of the settlement last over two hours and must be booked in advance (parties of 20-plus only). Small charge.*
☎ *Leeds 575474.*

lecture facilities, where will be a vast collection—at least 10,000 items—reflecting the history of medicine, from Greco-Roman times to the present day. Included are a fully equipped state-of-the-art operating theatre, displays showing modern pharmaceutical production, veterinary instruments, old trade catalogues, and everything else concerned with health care down the ages.
☛ *The Medical Museum is at 131 Beckett Street, Leeds LS9 7LP. Ring in advance for bookings, opening times.*
☎ *Leeds 444343.*

Morley Heritage Centre
On a fine day, Morley is a good place to wander, especially for those who are interested in Victorian architecture. The Town Hall, seemingly a little brother of the famous Leeds landmark, was built in 1895 and towers over the main shopping street. Morley does not have a formal museum but this Heritage Centre, in the reception area of South Leeds Groundwork Trust, does a good job illustrating the town's past with a series of display boards, complete with push-button audio commentaries. One recalls old Morley customs, such as The Pancake Bell that rings every Shrove Tuesday to tell apprentices and schoolchildren that it's time to get out their whips & tops and other street games. Morley was one of the first coal-mining areas of Yorkshire, with five pit, and there is a sad reminder of the disaster at Morley Main Colliery which killed 34 men and boys on 7th October, 1872. The history of Morley Cloth is told, including the little-known fact that much of it ended up on the backs of the Yankees and Confederates during the American Civil War. The town's contribution to wars nearer home, such as the 51st (Leeds Rifles) Royal Tank Regiment which was formed in Morley in 1939, is also explained. Lovers of adventure stories will like the display about Will Nevison, better known as Swift Nick, companion of the notorious highwayman Dick Turpin, who was hanged at York after committing a murder in Scotchman Lane, Morley.

☛ *The Morley Heritage Centre is at the South Leeds Groundwork Trust's Environment & Business Centre, Wesley Street, Morley, LS27 9ED. Open Mon-Fri, 8.30am-4.30pm.*
☎ *Leeds 380601.*

Museum of Georgian Leeds
Leeds is famous as one of the great Victorian cities of England, but this permanent exhibition proves there was previously an elegant Georgian townscape. Through maps and drawings, some of them from the original architectural plans, a picture emerges of streets filled with many fine buildings. Most of them disappeared in the rapid growth of Leeds in the second half of the 19th century, but one of the few survivors is the building in which the museum is housed—the Assembly Room of the White Cloth Hall, now used as the Waterloo Antiques Centre. Here, you can trace the history of the great Cloth Halls which made Leeds the woollen cloth capital of the world, and see how the city's gentry lived in the 18th and early 19th century. Among items on show is the shell of a 99 lb. turtle which was served at a Mayor's banquet in 1812, numerous theatre and music programmes from the period, and an excellent display of the famous cream-coloured earthenware made at the Leeds Pottery between 1770 and 1881.
☛ *The Museum of Georgian Leeds is a free-admission display on the 2nd floor of Waterloo Antiques, Crown Street (behind the Corn Exchange), at the foot of Vicar Lane, Leeds. Open during the centre's shopping hours: Tues-Sat 10am-5pm, Sun 11am-5pm.*

Otley Museum
Housed in two rooms of what was once the Mechanics' Institute, now the Civic Centre, Otley Museum is run by volunteers who have compiled fascinating displays on this part of Wharfedale's history. They include objects, artifacts and documentary material drawn from a radius of five miles, beginning with flints from the Mesolithic period to the area's development in the 20th century. Among the most interesting collections is that which

illustrates the market town's prominence in the manufacture of printing machinery. Founded by William Dawson in the 1830s, by 1900 there were seven Otley firms making his "Wharfedale" stop-cylinder press, employing over 2,000 local men. But the industry finally ceased in the 1980s. The museum runs WEA courses, has classes for the disabled, publishes many useful books and leaflets on local history, organises guided walks to explain local history and architecture, and has a large documentary and photographic collection for research purposes.
☛ *Otley is 10 miles north of Leeds, along the A660. Otley Museum is on the ground floor (wheelchair access) of Otley Civic Centre, Cross Green (at start of Pool Road), Otley, Leeds LS21. Open Mon, Tue & Fri mornings 10am-12.30pm, or other times by appointment.*
☎ *Otley (0943) 461052.*

Printing Museum
Opened by a printing enthusiast on the first floor of his antiques shop, this small collection offers a rare chance to see a technology that is fast disappearing as more and more printing works, newspapers, and printing and stationary shops move over to computerised desktop publishing (*Leeds Fax* is a classic offender). A number of Victorian printing pressses have been rescued from probable extinction, such as a treadle-operated Arab press and an Albion Press which can still be used for printing posters with the peculiarly Victorian impression that today's processes cannot copy. There are also some typefaces that have gone out of existence.
☛ *The Museum is above Memorabilia, in Booths Yard, off Lowtown, Pudsey. Open Tues/Thur/Fri/Sat 9.30-5pm or by appointment.*
☎ *Leeds 563653.*

Royal Armouries Museum
In the spring of 1996, this massive collection of armour and weaponry is set to open to the public in a major museum of international importance. Housed in a purpose-built £35 million complex

at Clarence Dock, within a short walk of Leeds city centre, many of the exhibits will be shown in state-of-the-art, themed interactive displays. An expected 1.3 million visitors a year will also be treated to such "live" events as jousting tournaments in a medieval tilt yard (a landscaped park and arena along the south side of the River Aire). Heart of the Royal Armouries will be the Tower of London's famous National Museum of Arms and Armour. Hitherto, only 30% of the 40,000 items were on display. Now many exhibits that could not be seen by the public will be on permanent show. The plans include a cinema, shops, a pub, restaurant and creche.

☛ *The Royal Armouries Museum will be on a promontory between Clarence Dock and the River Aire, next to the river lock. It will be well signposted east from the markets and Boar Lane areas of Leeds city centre, and a short walk from Crown point Bridge.*

Telephone Museum

This small but expanding museum at Pudsey illustrates the history of what is arguably man's single most important piece of technology. There are early telephones from the candlesticks to the "trimphone" (remember them?) and old switchboards, including one that was in the telephone exchange at Worksop in Nottinghamshire for many years. The fast disappearing red telephone box, known to engineers as "K6", is there. And special displays give an insight into the vast network of underground and overhead cabling systems in the country. The collection, put together by Institution of British Telecommunications Engineers members, was originally at BT's training school in Otley. After years lying in boxes, it is on display in a building next to Pudsey Telephone Exchange.

☛ *In Vernon Place, Stanningley, Pudsey. Open to school parties and local societies only. For more information, write to Graham Norton, PCE455, Post Point MH43, Telephone House, 11 Broadway, Bradford BD1 1BA.*
☎ *Answering machine at museum: Leeds 360963.*

Thwaite Mills *is a working industrial museum standing on an "island" between the River Aire and the Aire and Calder Navigation and began life in 1641 as a fulling mill. In 1823 its owners had the original mills demolished and the present building was constructed by the famous millwright, Thomas Hewes. This time it crushed rapeseed for lubricating oils, and among those supplied was George Stephenson, for his famous "Rocket" steam engine. Water turned the two wheels—both 18 feet in diameter—until 1976, when the weir was washed away and the mills closed. At that time the machinery ground flint and china stone for the pottery industry, barytes for paint and whiting for distemper and putty (the latter was also manufactured there). Now the waters of the Aire are turning the wheels once more, but for demonstration purposes only. The two great wheels are continually in operation. There are three floors of interesting exhibits, a gift shop, toilets and picnic area. The Georgian mill owner's house has been restored and houses displays exploring the history of the mill. Or watch the story on video.*

☛ *Look for the brown-and-white sign off Hunslet Road, at its junction with Wakefield Road, Stourton, Leeds LS10. The mills are half a mile down Thwaite Lane. Regular Yorkshire Rider bus service from Central Bus Station travel along Hunslet Road. Open Tue-Sun all year, 10am-5pm.. Closed Mondays. Admission charge.*
☎ *Leeds 496453.*

Galleries

The Craft Centre and Design Gallery

Run by a registered charity, this gallery specialises in contemporary applied arts. Although it also functions as an up-market shop, many of the 150,000-plus visitors it receives annually come to see the regularly changing, free exhibitions and showcase displays of ceramics and jewellery, textiles and metalwork, glassware and fine wood carving. Often, there is a special theme to a particular exhibition. Everything on show is for sale, at prices ranging from £6.95 for small items to over £1,000 for some of the lavish pots. The exhibits are produced all over Britain.

☛ *The gallery is located below Leeds City Art Gallery, in Victoria Gardens, facing The Headrow. Open Tues-Sat 10am-5.30pm. Late opening to 7pm on Thursdays.*
☎ *Leeds 478240.*

Opposite: Chris Drury's "Medicine Wheel" in the Leeds City Art Gallery Henry Moore Collection (see next page).

Leeds City Art Gallery's Henry Moore Collection

Born the seventh child of a coal-miner and his wife at Castleford in 1898, Henry Moore discovered he was a gifted artist while at school. After a year on the Western Front near Arras in the First World War, he came home to spend two years at Leeds School of Art, and won a scholarship to the Royal College of Art. By the time of his death in 1986 he was hailed as the greatest humanist sculptor of the 20th century, and some of his finest work is on display in this major annex to the Leeds City Art Gallery. At the entrance, visitors are immediately confronted by his 1980 recumbent woman in bronze, one of the dominant motifs of his work from as far back as 1926, and inside several other exhibits show its development, including original sketches, maquettes and "working models". Another of Moore's recurring subjects, mother and child, is well represented in his own work and that of his friend Sir Jacob Epstein. Other exhibits are by his fellow student at Leeds School of Art, Barbara Hepworth (1903-75) from Wakefield. Her Phira (1955) in scented guarea wood (specially sent to her from Nigeria) is perhaps the most fascinating, since it requires the use of both nose and eyes for appreciation. Of the contemporary works, visitors linger longest over Stephen Cox's Tanmatras, a kind of identikit picture outfit in five ovals of black granite, and the amazing Medicine Wheel by Chris Drury (born 1948), a great circle of natural objects (bones, feathers, rabbit droppings, hedgehog quills, pussy willow, blackbird's egg, seashells, etc.) each one collected on a different day of the year. (See photograph on previous page). Those interested in contemporary sculpture need to return several times a year to see those items which appear on temporary loan. Immediately next door is the new headquarters and gallery of the Henry Moore Sculpture Trust.

☛ *The collection is on the right inside the front entrance of Leeds City Art Gallery, on The Headrow (next to the Town Hall). Open, Mon-Fri 10-5.30pm (9pm close on Wed), Sat 10-4pm. Closed Sun, Bank Hols and Tues. following Bank Hols. Admission is free.*
☎ *Leeds 478248.*

The Henry Moore Sculpture Centre

Open in the spring of 1993, this major gallery and study centre adjoins the Leeds City Art Gallery through a covered bridge, with its own entrance opposite the War Memorial. The Henry Moore Sculpture Trust adapted an early Victorian merchant's building to provide four floors of space (totalling 20,000 square feet) for sculpture exhibitions, technical facilities, the Henry Moore Centre for the Study of Sculpture and headquarters for the Trust itself. Designed by Jeremy Dixon, who is also responsible for the redeveloped Royal Opera House in Covent Garden, the Institute will show three or four different exhibitions of sculptures a year on its ground floor, covering all periods, styles and nationalities. The Study Centre is located on the first floor. Besides providing space for students, The Centre organises exhibitions and conferences, advertised in leaflets obtainable at information points around Leeds.

☛ *At 11-15 Cookridge Street, Leeds LS1 3AA. Exhibition opening times as Leeds City Art Gallery (left). Free admission.*

A student sketches Henry Moore's famous Reclining Figure (1929).

The Pavilion
Visual Arts Centre

Established in the derelict pavilion on Woodhouse Moor in 1982, this centre has become a unique resource for the city of Leeds. The emphasis is on visual arts created by woman, and on women's issues, and a large part of the work concerns training in all levels of photographic skills for women. The exhibitions are 50-50 photography and other visual arts like mixed-media and silkscreen printing, and change regularly, from one about the life of women in Belfast to the preparations for the West Indian Carnival in Chapeltown. To find out what's on, telephone first or check listings section of *Northern Star* or *Artscene*. The photographic courses run on Wednesdays between 1pm-8.30pm (there is no longer a creche facility but help with child care payments may be given). Other courses, complementary to the exhibitions, run throughout the year. There is a membership scheme, which allows access to darkroom facilities, and hire of cameras, flashguns, tripods etc. Visitors can buy posters, books and postcards.

☛ *The Pavilion is at 235 Woodhouse Lane, Woodhouse Moor (a five min. walk north of Leeds University), Leeds LS2 3AP. Exhibitions are open Mon-Thurs, 10am-4.30pm, and Sat 12-4pm.*
☎ *Leeds 431749.*

The Cookridge
Street Gallery

This two-roomed Gallery on the edge of the city centre is part of the Jacob Kramer College, the main art, crafts and design pre-degree college in Leeds. The annual programme, linked to the academic year, has two distinct halves. The first, between September and late-January, is shows by outside artists and designers, and can be painting, sculture, photography or other fine arts. The second, from February to mid-June, is a programme of different exhibitions mounted by students.

☛ *Access is off Cookridge Street (on left up the hill from the Civic Theatre), Leeds LS2. Opening times are same as college: 9am-* 4.30pm, Mon-Fri. Closed at half-term and during college vacations. Admission is free.
☎ *Leeds 439931.*

Leeds Polytechnic Gallery

This spacious, bright gallery presents a year-round programme of temporary exhibitions. Do not be misled by the venue—rather than being a showcase for Polytechnic students to show their work (although some is displayed) the gallery is primarily a public art venue with non-academic shows. The gallery commissions many of its exhibitions; others are national touring exhibitions of painting, sculpture, crafts, photography, mixed and multi-media. They are accompanied by some educational events, seminars and workshops. Members of the public are offered the opportunity to meet with artists, gain practical skills and explore exhibitions critically.

☛ *Leeds Polytechnic Gallery is on the City Campus, facing*

The best collection of 20th century art outside London is at **Leeds City Art Gallery***. (Above, a couple study "Autumn" by Mark Fisher). The exhibits, spread over three floors, mostly start from around 1820. On the ground floor, the entrance hall contains a variety of different schools of art, but don't miss "Reflections on The Thames; Westminster" by Leeds's greatest contribution to landscape art, Atkinson Grimshaw. Several more of his works are on show in the Ziff Gallery, including one of his best, "Autumn Glory: The Old Mill" and a moody scene of Park Row, Leeds, in 1882. Most of the 20th century collection is upstairs. Works on loan can include "Nude Seated in an Armchair" (1913) by the brilliant French Impressionist, Renoir. Among the permanent highlights is a large collection by the most important British Impressionist and founder of the Camden Town group, Walter Richard Sickert; works by two of his followers, Harold Gilman and Charles Ginner; and by the founder of the abstract Vorticist movement, Percy Wyndham Lewis. Among later paintings of interest are the sinister "The Day of Atonement" by Jacob Kramer, and Paul Nash's "The Shore". At peak times, there's often a crowd around L. S. Lowry's "The Canal". Some of the best contemporary paintings and sculptures are in the galleries facing The Headrow. Major exhibitions in the ground floor and basement make regular visits essential.*

☛ *The Headrow, Leeds. Open, Mon-Fri 10-5.30pm (9pm close on Wed), Sat 10-4pm. Closed Sun, Bank Hols and Tues. following Bank Hols.*
☎ *Leeds 478248.*

Woodhouse Lane (clearly visible on left, just before the BBC), Leeds LS1 3HE. Open, Mon-Fri 10am-5pm, Sat 10am-3pm.
☎ *Leeds 832600 ext. 3499.*

University Gallery Leeds

Leeds University has its own well-established three-roomed gallery which is open to the general public. There are displays of the University's own permanent collection, which is rich in 19th and 20th century British paintings, drawings and prints. It includes drawings from *avant-garde* schools like Camden Town and Bloomsbury, and paintings and sculture by a number of Gregory Fellows. There is a programme of short-term exhibitions of external work, usually by Yorkshire artists or others building a national reputation. Photography, sculpture, textiles, ceramics, drawings, prints and painting are covered.
☛ *The University Gallery is in the prominent Parkinson Building, Woodhouse Lane, Leeds LS2 9JT. Open term time only, Mon-Fri 10am-5pm. There is wheelchair access on the north side of the Parkinson Building.*
☎ *Leeds 332777.*

Country House Galleries

Many of the pre-19th century works of art in Leeds are found at the two grand houses owned by the city council. Temple Newsam, in the eastern suburbs of Leeds, contains one of the most important collections of decorative arts in Britain, including splendid furniture (it is the home of The Chippendale Society), ceramics and silver. Among several interesting portraits are works by Reynolds and Mercier. And there is a series of paintings from the Marco Ricci school, bought in Venice in 1706 when the house's then-occupants were on the Grand Tour. A notable exhibit is an etching by Rembrandt, "Christ returning from athe Temple with His Parents" (1654). Temple Newsam holds several different exhibitions each year, often featuring rarely-seen items of Georgian decorative art from the city's vast permanent collection. At Lotherton Hall, right on the city's eastern boundary, there

is more of a Victorian and Edwardian flavour to the permanent displays and exhibitions. Some of the Oriental porcelain is considerably older, and there is also a fine collection of contemporary ceramics. One of Lotherton's growth areas is its permanent display of fashion, supplemented with changing exhibitions of costume.
☛ *Temple Newsam is five miles east of the city centre, signposted off the A63 Selby road. Lotherton Hall is 13 miles east of the city centre, near Aberford, one mile beyond the A1 trunk road on the B1217 to Towton. Both houses open, Tues-Sun & Bank Hol Mons 10.30am-5.30pm (or dusk in winter).*
☎ *Temple Newsam Leeds 647321; Lotherton Hall Leeds 813259.*

Dixon Bate

This is a commercial fine arts gallery in the elegant Victoria Quarter, running between Briggate and Vicar Lane. Above the shop area new exhibitions are mounted every two or three months. They are split between good local artists earning reputations for themselves, and established national and international figures (there was an exhibition of some of Henry Moore's lesser known etchings). The policy is to strike a balance between what will sell and what is interesting from an art point of view. Dixon Bate shows mostly two-dimensional art but sculpture exhibitions are planned.
☛ *Victoria Quarter, 34-36 Queen Victoria Street, Leeds LS1. Open Mon-Sat 9.30am-5.30pm. Admission free.*
☎ *Leeds 445822.*

Parks & Gardens

It is one of they city's proudest claims that among European cities only Vienna has more public parks and gardens. Everywhere one goes in Leeds, there are well maintained pockets of grass and flower beds, expanses of playing fields and important botanic gardens. To describe them all would take a book in itself. But the following are the floral jewels in the crown of Leeds, and most are open daily from dawn to dusk.

Canal Gardens

Once the vegetable garden for the Mansion House, for which much of Roundhay Park was the estate, Canal Gardens is without doubt one of the most pleasant corners of Leeds. Surrounded by a high wall, it is a sheltered sun trap, and the perfect environment for several major flower collections, including the North of England National Rose Society trial grounds, the National Collection of Dahlias and the National Collection of Violas. There are literally thousands of rose trees and many bedding plants provide additional colour. The canal was never a working waterway but built as a linear pond, and contains numerous ornamental wildfowl, including two splendid and much-photographed black swans from Australia. There is a café, easy access to the vast Tropical World conservatory and a display of Christmas lights (beginning two weeks before Xmas and continuing for a fortnight afterwards).
☛ *The Gardens are on Princes Avenue, Leeds LS8. Regular Yorkshire Rider bus services from Briggate. Open 7.30am-dusk seven days.*
☎ *Leeds 661850.*

Golden Acre Park

Botanic gardens and woodland of some 137 acres beyond the northern fringe of the Leeds built-up area, Golden Acre has a fascinating history. It started as an amusement park, a kind of land-locked Scarborough, complete with a large lake, donkey rides, miniature railway, paddling pool, Winter Gardens Dance Hall and something called a "mountain glide". But the whole thing closed in 1938 and after a period of dereliction, the gardens were landscaped anew, with an unusually large range of plants, bushes and trees. Among its floral features are masses of rhododendrons and azaleas, rose gardens, limestone and sandstone rock gardens, an arboretum (trees and shrubs nursery), and a pinetum (conifer nursery). A new additions is Britain's largest Heather Garden, a collection of moorland plants which will eventually number up to 900 varieties, flowering at different times of the year.

It is sponsored by the famous Harry Ramsden's fish restaurant. One of the most popular features is the Demonstration Garden, a kind of "live" Gardeners' Question Time where all aspects of fruit, vegetable and flower growing are demonstrated to visitors. This is held on one Sunday every month, 2pm-4pm (ring for dates). Other ornamental features include mountain streams, alpine plants and a fine lake with wildfowl to feed. A new development is the Cherry Orchard, in which different varieties of Japanese cherry trees are being planted. You can "buy" a tree as a memorial to a friend or relative (ask at the information centre). Golden Acre is a good place to go for a short walk, for longer rambles via the Leeds Country Way, or to follow the Meanwood Valley Trail south to Leeds, if you arrived by bus.
☛ *Off A660 Otley road at Bramhope. Ample car parking across the road. Frequent bus services from Central Bus Station.*

Information Centre and Café open Mon-Fri 10.34.30pm (4.15pm close in winter), Sat & Sun 10.30am-5pm.
☎ *Leeds 673729.*

The Hollies
This superb botanic garden was once the grounds of a large private house and was given to the city of Leeds in 1921. Since then it has spread down into the upper Meanwood Valley to include some fine mature woodland and totals 90 acres. Today, The Hollies receives visitors from all over the country because of several national collections of flowers, including Philadelpus (of which there are over 100 varieties) and Hemerocallis, which are held for the National Council for the Conservation of Plants and Gardens. There are also large collections of dahlias, rhododendrons, magnolias and rare trees, including several varieties of oak in the arboretum beside the stream. And, of course, there are holly trees—eight different types. Tucked away off the beaten track, The Hollies is less crowded than Golden Acre or Canal Gardens and is particularly charming in summer.
☛ *The Hollies is off Weetwood Lane (fork right off the A660 Otley Road at The Three Horseshoes Pub), Far Headingley.*
☎ *Leeds 782030.*

Middleton Park
Known as "the green jewel of south Leeds", there is a municipal golf course, football, cricket and rugby pitches, tennis and bowling. A lake has boating and a café with local and natural history displays, and there is a good rose garden. The park is often a picnic destination for people using Middleton Railway and there is easy access to Middleton Woods. The park is managed by Leeds Countryside Service, and events include kite-flying for children and guided walks. Tarmac paths make Middleton suitable for prams and wheelchairs.
☛ *Main entrance is on Town Street, off the Ring Road, Beeston Park, which in turn is off Dewsbury Road. Countryside Ranger is at 218 Town Street, Middleton LS10 3TN. Open dawn to dusk daily. Lakeside café open 11am-3pm ex. Thurs in winter, 10.30am-4pm ex. Thurs in summer.*
☎ *Countryside Ranger, Leeds 715811. Café Leeds 719977.*

Pudsey Park
In a heavily built-up area, this seven acre park is a well laid out pocket of greenery. A splendid Conservatory is divided into two sections, one containing a highly fragrant collection of English garden and house flowers, which changes according to the season. The second area has been developed as a humid, spicy mix of tropical plants and trees such as banana, pineapple, fig, palm, rubber, yucca. Next door is an aviary/aquarium and small menagerie recently restocked. The piranha fish are safely in tanks. Star attractions are the 4ft. long Bengali monitor lizard, several marmosets and tamarins (small monkeys). The park itself is a mix of

*A **Japanese Garden** has been imaginatively laid out at Horsforth Hall Park, complete with ornamental bridges, waterfalls, temples, pagodas, lanterns and bamboo water-leaps. Many items have great significance to Buddhists, such as a group of rocks (next to stone bridge) representing the sacred Mount Fuji. There are many plants not found elsewhere in the region, and gardeners can obtain a detailed leaflet on request. The greenery includes the obvious azaleas, bamboos, cherries and Japanese Maples. The lake contains large carp but the single most fascinating feature of the garden is the scale-version of a "Deer Scarer". Water runs out of spouts into three hollow bamboos, making them spin with the weight of water until they hit rocks with a resounding thwack!*
☛ *Horsforth Japanese Garden is at Hall Park, off Hall Lane (off The Green) Horsforth.Open 9am-3.30pm every day. Admission Free.*
☎ *Leeds 581511.*

flowerbeds, herbaceous borders and shrubbery, with much good seating, especially around the bowling green. There is an "old man's" shelter, a large children's playground and café.

☛ *Pudsey Park is off Church Lane, Pudsey.*
☎ *Leeds 551334.*

Roundhay Park

One of the biggest public spaces in Britain, Roundhay Park is 700 acres of greenery and lakes within easy reach of most Leeds districts. It is said to have been named by England's medieval hunting nobility, who established a round enclosure or "hay" to keep the deer in and poachers out. When the park, then a country estate, was put up for sale in 1871, it was bought by the Major of Leeds, John Barran, the founder of Leeds's (indeed, the world's) off-the-peg clothing industry, for a total of £127,000. The following year he sold it for the purchase price plus interest to Leeds Corporation. This act is commemorated by the magnificent Barran's Fountain, pictured below. Even today it is possible to feel lost in the park. It is a good place for wildlife, with woodpeckers, all the common warblers in spring and summer, mute swans, visiting whooper swans, great-crested grebes and herons. There are good crops of crocus in spring, followed by daffodils, bluebells and orchids, and gorse is present in the northern side of the park. Mammals include foxes, roe deer, voles, moles, rabbits and grey squirrels. Voles, especially on the slopes near Ivy Castle, provide a regular diet for tawny owls. Modern facilities include 23 football pitches, 18 cricket squares, 2 rugby pitches, tennis courts, a funfair, a Lakeside café, old and new rose gardens, disabled and blind gardens, and bowling green. On Waterloo Lake, which has suffered from a leak and is being returned to boating after several years of reduced level, there is fishing. Permits are available at the café. The Upper Lake has neither boating nor fishing and is maintained as a wildlife area. A natural amphitheatre, the scene of many military tattoos and Bank Holiday gala days, now hosts huge open-air rock concerts by acts like The Rolling Stones and Michael Jackson. It also has a big bonfire and fireworks displays on November 5th.

☛ *Roundhay Park is best reached from Princes Avenue, Leeds LS8, where there is a large car park. Regular Yorkshire Rider buses travel there from Briggate. The park is open from dawn to dusk every day of the year. Disabled facilities.*
☎ *Leeds 661850.*

Wharfemeadows

Being 60-odd miles from the sea, Leeds has to make do with its rivers and canals for waterfront leisure areas. Fortunately, this superb spot is a lovely riverside park, straddling the broad Wharfe as it cuts through the pleasant town of Otley (see page 68). It is actually three adjoining parks. On the south side (east of the bridge) is Manor Park, known locally as "Tittybottle Park" because more than 60 years ago this is where nannies brought infants in prams, and sat feeding them on pleasant summer days. Today, there is a grass area, flower beds and shrubberies. There is a similar park on the west side of the bridge, known as Manor Garth. Wharfemeadows itself is a linear park spreading along the north side of the Wharfe, from the road bridge to a footbridge which car-

The magnificent Barran's Drinking Fountain in Roundhay Park.

ries a path to Gallows Hill. There are rowing boats for hire in summer, tennis courts, a bowling green, café, open-air swimming poo, a children's paddling pool and playground.

☛ *On the north side of Otley, off the B6451. There is a small car park behind the park.*

☎ *Otley (0943) 466400.*

Wild Leeds

Few cities can boast the variety of wildlife and walking areas which Leeds has within its boundaries. Some, like Middleton Woods and Adel Moor, have long been recognised as superb strongholds of ancient habitats in an increasingly built-up world. Others, like the Leeds-Liverpool Canal and Fairburn Ings, are man-made habitats colonised by flora and fauna after over a century of industrial activity. And there are "new" wildlife sites, such as the wildflower garden planted at Kirkstall and, nearby, the specially created wildlife sanctuary on the River Aire. In total, there are more than 100 separate sites in Leeds that could have been included here, if we had the space. You can spot them for yourself by looking at the Ordnance Survey Landranger Sheet 104, and find the nearest public access. Those appearing in the following pages are either designated as local nature reserves or country parks, or specially managed bird of wildlife reserves, or have been given official recognition as being among the most outstanding areas in the Leeds Nature Conservation Strategy. If you want to know more about the natural world in Leeds, get involved in the various events organised by the Leeds Countryside Service (see details in *What's On* and their own leaflets).

Astley Lake

Not the prettiest place to spend a few hours communing with nature, but often this site can be very productive for birdwatchers in particular. The Lower Aire Valley is a classic environmental eyesore, a vast area of opencast mining schemes. From these workings has developed this new lake, around the margins of which can be found an astonishing list of rare or unusual birds. Among those to turn up here are little-ringed plover and greenshank, some nesting terns, ringed plover, oystercatcher and most species of duck. A hide has been provided by British Coal, but you need binoculars/telescope.

☛ *Access is from Fleet Lane, Oulton (turn left at roundabout near Oulton Church, join Aberford Road and take first right.)*

Breary Marsh

This splendid wildlife area, with well organised public access, is recognised as a Local Nature Reserve and also listed as a Site of Special Scientific Interest. Extending between Golden Acre Park and Otley Old Road, on the Leeds side of Bramhope, it is one of the few remaining areas of Alder Carr in the region, an unspoilt marshland covered with alder trees and great tussock sedge. You have to be something of an expert to find the rare weevils that are to be found here, but lesser naturalists and the public in general will find they can identify many of the area's flowers and birds, especially with the use of the excellent interpretive display boards that have been provided. Among the wetland plants to spot are marsh marigold, angelica, marsh forgetmenot and the beautiful blue bugle. The woodland is good for birds like siskins and long-tailed tits in winter, willow and sedge warblers in summer, and the haunting Pauls Pond regularly attracts great-crested grebe, dabchick and herons. A good boardwalk is provided for visitors, but care is needed when it is wet or under a veneer of frost.

☛ *Breary Marsh is accessible from the car park at Golden Acre Park. Turn right at southern corner, instead of using underpass to park on left. Regular Yorkshire Rider buses from Central Bus Station pass on main road. The best seasons are spring and summer.*

Central Leeds Wildlife Park

A triangle of ground behind Leeds City Station and bordering the River Aire and the Leeds-Liverpool Canal, it has been turned into an astonishing nature area by the South Leeds Groundwork Trust. Even as a piece of urban wasteland, it supported bracken and heather and its lime-rich soil was found to contain numerous wildflower species which in turn attracted the common blue butterfly to name but one. Now it has been cleaned up and replanted. Birds already seen here include moorhen, coot and sedge warbler. There is a new footpath and some display boards to help visitors identify plant, bird and butterfly life.

☛ *Access is from the canal towpath or via some new steps from Whitehall Road. Volunteers are required to help manage the site. For further information contact South Leeds Groundwork Trust.*

☎ *Leeds 380601.*

The Chevin Forest Park

Known locally as Otley Chevin, these 700 acres of woodland, heath and crags form the nearest area of wild ground to Leeds, an easy bus, car or cycle ride from anywhere in the city or even a pleasant walk from the northern suburbs. A Local Nature Reserve, it is managed by full-time rangers from Leeds Countryside Service. Facilities include a permanent three-mile orienteering course, other self-guided trails, a Field Studies Centre, café and the White House Visitor Centre with displays on local history, fossils and wildlife. Most people come to walk on the extensive network of footpaths and bridleways and to enjoy fine views north and west over Wharfedale on summer evenings. A favourite spot is Caley Crags, an impressive outcrop of millstone grit. On the bridleway behind them is a large expanse of bilberry bushes which produce a huge crop of berries every summer. (Note: picking *flowers* is forbidden). The roe deer one finds here are indigenous, and there is the occasional fallow deer. Grey squirrels, stoats, foxes, weasels, rabbits, hares, hedgehogs and three species of vole make up the mammal kingdom. Bird rarities such as goshawks make the occasional appearance, and there is sometimes a party of crossbills. Residents include sparrowhawks, kestrels, all three woodpeckers, goldcrests and woodcock.

☛ *The Park lies on either side of East Chevin Road, and there is ample car parking. To reach it, take the A660 Otley Road from Leeds, turning left at the A658 traffic lights, then right on top of the hill. Regular buses from Central Bus Station stop nearby. The White House Visitor Centre is in Johnny Lane, off Bird Cage Walk, Otley, LS21 3JL. Open April-Oct inc. 1pm-4.30pm Sat & Sun, Nov & Dec 1pm-4pm Sun only. Closed Jan-Mar inc.*

☎ *Countryside Ranger on Otley (0943) 465023. Café on 0943-467566.*

Clayton Woods

Clayton Woods, Daffy Wood and Spring Wood are part of the same complex in the valley to the east of Horsforth. It remains one of the very best wildlife strongholds in North Leeds. The trees are mostly oak and birch but the presence of dead and dying elm trees has created a superb habitat for birds that loving rotting tree trunks. Green, greater-spotted and lesser-spotted woodpeckers are found, as well as nuthatches and treecreepers. The woods also support fair populations of all the commonest warblers in spring and summer.

The Old Mill Beck is good for dippers and grey wagtails The two mill ponds off Low Lane have mallard, moorhen, common snipe and attract woodcock. Wildflowers include yellow archangel, marsh violets and winter heliotrope.

☛ *Of numerous access points, the easiest is off Low Lane, opposite its junction with Springfield Close. There is a large network of paths through the woods, although in summer some are obscured by the greenery. Get Yorkshire Rider bus service to Woodside from Central Bus Station.*

Eccup Reservoir

Most visitors to this, the main holding reservoir for Leeds drinking water, miss the interesting birdlife to be found out on the man-made lake. It is perhaps the best place for a breath of fresh air in Leeds, and there is no danger of getting lost. A well-made path can be followed for approximately three-quarters of the shore, and by using a network of lanes and public footpaths on the north side of the reservoir, it is possible to have a good two-three hour walk. For bird-watchers, Eccup is recognised as an internationally important refuge for many wintering wildfowl

from Greenland and Siberia. The best time for these is between September and March. Then, the water surface has sometimes thousands of ducks: mallard, pochard, tufted, teal, wigeon and goldeneye. However, the real VIP of the bird world at Eccup is the goosander, which has its largest wintering population here. This has been as many as 200 but 50 is a more usual number. The population seems to increase when there is severe weather on the Continent. There are many Canada geese and, in autumn, 50 or more great-crested grebes. Sometimes 30,000 gulls roost here in winter, and it is worth keeping a watch for rare glaucous and Iceland gulls in the crowd.

☛ *Access is easiest from Alwoodley Lane, or from Harrogate Road. There are convenient Yorkshire Rider bus services from Central Bus Station.*

Fairburn Ings

On the eastern fringe of Leeds, Fairburn Ings is a reserve managed by the Royal Society for the Protection of Birds. But don't be put off by that: Fairburn is just as good a place to take kiddies in pushchairs to feed bread to the ducks, geese and swans, as it is for seri-

A meeting of swans: one of the lakes at Fairburn Ings Bird Reserve.

ous birdwatchers. The area is scattered with lakes, ponds and marshes produced by mining subsidence, all neatly confined between the A1 in the east and the A656 in the west. For those with binoculars and telescopes, there are three public hides, reached by walking along the causeway and footpath below the village of Fairburn. The best times are the spring and autumn migrations, when many unusual birds stop to feed or roost on their passage north or south. Look for black terns, little gulls, yellow wagtails, greenshank, smew, whooper swans. But anything can turn up, and Fairburn is a twitcher's paradise. The surrounding area attracts large numbers of newly arrived redwings and fieldfares. You can usually count on seeing most of the common wildfowl species: mallard, tufted, teal, wigeon, pochard, shoveler and gadwall. Helpful display boards make Fairburn a good place to introduce children to birdwatching. The RSPB has a visitor centre, with much information and advice. If the weather's bad, there are several lay-bys on the road between the A656 and Fairburn village, from which to birdwatch.

☛ *From centre of Leeds, take A63 Selby road past Garforth, turning south on A656 Castleford road to signposted left turn. One mile along the road, near end of lake on right, is the visitor centre with parking and toilets, open at weekends from 10am to 5pm.*
☎ *0977-673257.*

Gledhow Valley Wood

In deepest suburbia, this ribbon of wood fills Gledhow Valley, which runs between Harrogate Road and Roundhay Road. All the common species of woodland birds are present, with the important addition of the sparrowhawk, which nests here, as do tawny owls. Dabchicks, or little grebes, nest on the pond, which is amazing in view of the regular disturbance they must get. Herons are also regular visitors. The most interesting flower is the broad-leaved helleborine, a member of the orchid family. An excellent place in spring to hear the dawn chorus.

☛ *The wood is on the north-east side of Gledhow Valley Road. Yorkshire Rider bus service for Moortown, alighting at Gledhow Valley Road stop.*

Hetchell Wood

It is easy to get lost in this fine woodland on the eastern edge of Leeds, and in summer many of the paths become overgrown. That's how it should be, because Hetchell Wood is a 29-acre nature reserved leased by the Yorkshire Wildlife Trust, and while public access is unrestricted, visitors have to proceed with care. The wood has some fine beech trees, plus some oak, ash, hazel and hawthorn but the area's most notable feature is its exposed quarries of limestone which were opened by the Romans. Much insect life in the undergrowth is studied by local entomologists; in spring and summer there are willow warblers, chiffchaff and blackcap to be seen. Plant life includes dog's mercury, sanicle and toothwort. Lower down there is an alder swamp where meadow sweet and panicled sedge grow. Watch for sika deer .

☛ *Several access points. One is half a mile along Milner Lane from Thorner. Keep right at triangular intersection and see reserve entrance on left (there is a small parking area on the verges). Can also be reached via a signposted public footpath off the A58 Wetherby road at Rowley Grange.*

The Kirkstall Valley

At one time huge parts of the green wedge that carries the Leeds and Liverpool Canal and the River Aire to the heart of Leeds were earmarked for development. But the acres of supermarket car park and the rest have been mostly held at bay and in the 1990s the accent is on keeping the Kirkstall Valley as a unique wildlife corridor, with improved footpaths, nature trails and other facilities. The best areas are:

Kirkstall Nature Reserve. This first specially created £200,000 nature reserve in Leeds has been established partly on derelict land beside the River Aire and partly on the site of the former Kirkstall Power Station. It has over 15,500 trees and shrubs of 18 different species, a new wetland habitat for birds, insects and plants, a new meadow area with many species of classic British wildflowers which modern farming methods have virtually banished from the countryside. While there is no public access to an island in the Aire, there is almost a mile of new footpaths and country lanes on the south side of the reserve.

Kirkstall Wildflower Garden. This strip of land amounting to no more than half an acre between the busy Kirkstall Road and a River Aire goyt (mill stream) has been planted with various species of wildflowers and trees to create a unique pocket of countryside close to the heart of the city. Among the species to be seen are fritillaries, bird's foot trefoil, salad burnet, ox-eye daisy, orange hawkweed and wild carrot. In the wet area there is yellow flag and bullrushes. The site is managed by the Kirkstall Valley Countryside Ranger and members of the British Trust for Conservation Volunteers, who have planted cherry, ash and birch trees, plus gorse, hazel and broom. New interpretation boards will help you identify the various species.

Bramley Fall Wood. This wood forms much of the south side of the Leeds-Liverpool Canal between Kirkstall and Rodley and is considered one of the best places in Leeds for fungi in September and October. There are many good walks through the gently sloping mix of the common deciduous trees, and although not classed as "ancient" woodland it has a management-free feel, whereas most of it was actually planted. Of the fungi, the death cap, the deadliest of them all, is the most notable. It is easy to confuse with edible mushrooms, so beware—there is no known antidote. Bird life includes great and lesser-spotted woodpeckers, bullfinches, long-tailed tits, willow warblers, chiffchaffs and blackcaps, tawny owls and sparrowhawks.

Leeds-Liverpool Canal. Designated a Site of Special Scientific Interest (SSSI) for its rare freshwater plants, this famous canal has many important species of wildlife that are perhaps easier to see. Kingfishers, for example, regularly come right into the city centre, and there are at least four species of dragonfly. The larger ones, such as the brown-winged Aeshna grandis, are a superb sight in August as they patrol the stretch of water that forms their territory. Watch out too for the common blue damselflies skimming the water. For a classic urban wildlife "safari", take the towpath west from the Hilton Hotel on Neville Street. Here you can see kingfishers, grey wagtails, herons, bramblings and even blackcaps. Wildflowers to look out for are coltsfoot, toadflax, Michaelmas daisies and ragwort, lady's smock and the commoner meadowsweet. Wherever you get lady's smock there is always a good chance of finding orange tip butterflies in May. The butterfly's small oval orange eggs are laid on the flower stalks near the canal. In the water, there are sticklebacks and pike.

☛ *The Kirkstall Nature Reserve is off Redcote Lane. The Wildflower Garden is opposite Grandways Supermarket, Kirkstall Road. Bramley Fall Wood is off the Leeds & Bradford Road. There is a car park down the bumpy track. The canal has many access points between Neville Street and Calverley. The area is managed by Leeds Countryside Service as the Kirkstall Valley Country Park.*

☎ *The Ranger is on Leeds 753568.*

The Meanwood Valley

To have one green artery (the Aire valley, with river and canal) leading to the heart of the city is good enough but to have a second and one as rich in wildlife as the seven-mile Meanwood Valley, makes Leeds very fortunate indeed. The valley cuts straight through North Leeds, drained by the Adel Beck which becomes Meanwood Beck south of the outer ring-road, and forms a wedge of woodland, parkland and farmland providing a variety of habitats for 100 species of birds, numerous wildflowers, mammals, butterflies, moths, insects and assorted amphibians. Public access could not be better, especially along the Meanwood Valley Trail, which is well signposted and maintained by a full-time Ranger, employed by Leeds City Council Countryside Service. There is a Visitor Centre at Meanwood Park, where displays on local wildlife can be seen. Various events are organised here, such as guided walks, tadpole rescues, and making bird nesting boxes. Few other cities can boast woodpeckers, partridges, kingfishers, cowslips and orange tip butterflies within a mile of their shopping centres. The area that includes Meanwood Park and Woods, The Hollies, Scotland Woods and Adel Woods have been designated a Local Nature Reserve. (See also Breary Marsh).

Woodhouse Ridge. A well-established wood of oak, beech, sycamore and holly a stone's through from Woodhouse Moor, it is a conduit along which much wildlife in the city passes. Foxes, grey squirrels, magpies, jays, sparrowhawks, kestrels, stoats, weasels, rooks, jackdaws, green and great-spotted woodpeckers tits, warblers, frogs, toads—the list is long. Many paths provide good access but get muddy, so good footwear is required here and on other valley paths. There is a new frog pond on the north side of Grove Lane.

Sugarwell Hill. On the opposite side of the valley Sugarwell's rural character is maintained by the Meanwood Valley Urban Farm (see page 37). As a result, partridges are found here.

Meanwood Park and Woods and The Hollies. Nuthatches have generally increased in numbers over the last 10 years, but the Hollies had them in profusion even when they were considered rare. Many oak, beech, willow and alder trees. Mammals include foxes, roe deer, woodmice, pygmy shrews, bats and moles. There are kingfishers, dippers and grey wagtails. Among the summer warblers are willow warbler, chiffchaff, blackcap and the occasional woodwarbler. Numerous berry-bearing bushes and trees attract large numbers of redwings, fieldfares and mistle thrushes in autumn. Jays, magpies and all three British woodpeckers are present, the great-spotted being the most numerous. In May and June, in the damp area between Hustlers Row and the ring road, watch for the orange tip butterflies (like a cabbage white but with the eponymous tips) feeding on the beautiful lilac petals of the cuckoo flower, or lady's smock.

Scotland Woods, Adel Wood and Moor. One of the best woodlands in Leeds for wildlife, particularly notable for its wood warblers (they are usually identified as being greener than other common warblers) which unfailingly appear each spring and make the wood its only nesting site in the city. The woods extend from the ring-road to Stairfoot lane, hiding the seven arches (a Victorian aqueduct once connecting Leeds's first water main with Eccup) and rocky out-

A mile from the city centre—Woodhouse Ridge.

crops. The rich heather of Adel Moor is where you'll find common lizards, brown and red soldier beetles, and tree pipits (a summer visitor plumper than the meadow pipit and with a stouter bill). By the beck, look for the beautiful ragged-robin, with its long pink petals. In summer, there are common hawker dragonflies.

The Meanwood Valley Trail. The footpaths along this valley have been linked together to form a good walkway virtually from the city centre to the urban fringe, and there is more than wildlife to see. The trail, signposted and maintained by Leeds Countryside Service, is seven miles long and the recommended walking time is four and a half hours. Start at Marsden's Statue on Woodhouse Moor. Proceed down Raglan Road, right on Rampart Roads, over Woodhouse Street and up Delph Lane from where the trail along Woodhouse Ridge is met. Just north of Monk Bridge Road is Highbury Works, where sheepskin curing takes place, one of the few survivors of what was once a common Leeds industry. It was built by the brewer, Samuel Smith, in 1857. Hustlers Row was built in 1850 for local quarry workers. In Scotland Wood, see the ruin of Scotland Mill, the original mill used in 1788 by James Marshall and his engineer, Matthew Murray, for the birth of the world-famous Leeds flax industry. It was destroyed by fire in 1906.

☛ *There are numerous access points through the Meanwood Valley. The Meanwood Valley Visitor Centre is signposted from the car park at the bottom of Green Road. Open Saturday afternoons, 12-4pm, Easter to the end of August. Telephone for news of forthcoming events, or check local listings.*
☎ *Leeds 782951.*

Middleton Woods
Now designated a Local Nature Reserve, these 200 acres of ancient, broadleaved woodland (continuously wooded since at least 1600) on the south side of Leeds form the largest such area in the city. The trees are mainly oak and birch but there are some introduced species like sycamore,

beech, lime and sweet chestnut. An interesting feature of the woods is the large number of "bell" pits, an early form of coal mining, which go back to before the 14th century. You can still see their bowl shapes today among the trees. The wildlife is typical of woodland, including great-spotted and green woodpeckers, nuthatches, treecreepers and five species of tit. Nearby grassland attracts partridges and skylarks. Mammals include foxes, stoats, weasels, grey squirrels, rabbits, hares, hedgehogs, field and bank voles. In spring there is much wild garlic and a fine carpet of bluebells, and in May-June look out for the more unusual yellow archangel. Autumn fungi include the spectacular fly agaric, a white-spotted scarlet-capped ball on a stem. Others are milkcaps, shaggy ink caps and stinkhorns. A newly restored pond is being stocked with frogs and other aquatic life. There is a large network of bridleways, footpaths and tarmac cycleways, the latter also intended for wheelchairs. Nature and history trail leaflets are on sale from the café and Leeds Countryside Ranger. There are a number of organised events and guided walks.
☛ *Main entrance is on Town Street, off the Ring Road, Beeston Park, which in turn is off Dewsbury Road. Countryside Ranger is at 218 Town Street, Middleton LS10 3TN.*
☎ *Leeds 715811.*

Milman Ox-bows
These ox-bows—a flooded area left by a former meander of the River Aire—form one of the most important wildlife sites in the area. There is a good public footpath, from which you can see (in season) bird species such as green and

common sandpipers, redshanks, curlews, snipe, woodcock, green and great-spotted woodpeckers, teal, heron, jay, cuckoo, long-tailed tits, and many other small birds. Countless interesting waterside plants and pondweeds make it a worthwhile walk for botanists.
☛ *Off Apperley Road, Apperley Bridge. Path runs north between Leeds-Liverpool Canal and Elm Tree Farm.*

Washburn Valley
The valley, with many good walks and important wildlife areas, actually lies within the boundaries of Harrogate District Council, but it is included in this book because of its great significance to the people of Leeds. For here are the reservoirs that supply tapwater to almost every house in Leeds. Lindley Wood Reservoir, the closest to Leeds, was the first to open in 1875, and there is a fine walk along the wooded north shore (small car park at Lindley Bridge, near the fish farm). The lake is especially good for herons, and flocks of white-fronted geese in winter. Walking north through Norwood Bottom is one of the best rambles in the Leeds area. Watch out for sparrowhawks, great and lesser-spotted woodpeckers, and large flocks of goldfinches in late summer. There is also a good crop of autumn fungi. The next reservoir is Swinsty, which opened in 1876. It is this water that is pumped to Eccup and the kitchens of Leeds. There are fine woodland paths (good for common warblers in summer) on either side, to the bridge at Fewston Reservoir (opened in 1879). The most northerly is Thruscross, opened in 1966, below which is the old village of West End. Take OS Landranger Sheet 104, and the excellent Washburn Valley Map and Guide produced by the West Riding Ramblers Association, on sale at Leeds bookshops and Tourist Information Centre.
☛ *Take the A660 from Leeds to Otley. Lindley Wood is reached by right turn over Wharfe and following B6451. Thruscross, Fewston and Swinsty Reservoir are found by turning right off the Otley-Blubberhouses road.*

Leeds Area Footpaths

When you are out walking, if you find a public footpath obstructed, a signpost missing or a stile which needs repair, call the Public Rights of Way officer.

☎
Leeds 326444.

Architectural & Historical Features

Leeds is one of the outstanding cities of the Industrial Revolution, and there is no finer symbol of Victorian civic pride in Britain than Leeds Town Hall. Yet there are many more buildings and corners of Leeds which, in their own way, were also important in the development of the city. And while some—Cuthbert Brodrick's famous Oriental Baths in Cookridge Street to name but one—did not stand the test of time, Thornton's Arcade and many others are still part of today's Leeds townscape. More than just representing the time in which they were built, these structures often testified to the character and generosity of the greatest Leeds citizens. The enormous wealth that was produced by the mills and factories allowed their imaginations to wander. As a consequence, bizarre industrial buildings like Temple Mill and St. Paul's House rose among the smokestacks of the urban landscape. There are literally hundreds of these architectural gems worthy of investigation. The buildings and places of interest in this section are

A Journey Through the Leeds Past

Information about guided walks is available from the following:
Leeds City Tourism. Year-round programme of walks led by expert guides, to explore the streets of Leeds
☎ Leeds 478301/2/3.
Leeds Civic Trust. Organises conducted tours, concentrating on history and architecture of the city.
☎ Leeds 439594.
Murray Freedman. Specialist on guided walks round Leeds's Jewish past. Groups only.
☎ Leeds 692955.
Otley TIC. Series of walks in Otley in summer.
☎ Leeds 477705
Wetherby TIC. Occasional walks in Wetherby in summer.
☎ Leeds 477253.

not the ones that have been turned into museums like Armley Mills. Such a transformation would seem absurd at Armley Prison or the Leeds General Infirmary. Even the Corn Exchange, amid the clamour of tourists and shoppers, is still venue for the weekly Leeds corn market. Other sites on the following list, such as Beckett Street Cemetery and the feast of Georgian and Victorian features in Otley, are included because they deserve wider attention. The following should stimulate your interest to explore even further.

☞ *See also—University of Leeds p. 27, Leeds Library p. 30, Kirkstall Abbey p. 43, Middleton Railway p. 43, Temple Newsam p. 44, The Waterfront p. 45-46, Armley Mills p. 47, Fulneck Moravian Settlement p. 48, Museum of Georgian Leeds p. 49, Thwaite Mills p. 50, City Varieties p. 76.*

Adel Church

The Church of St. John the Baptist, Adel, is justly famous for the elaborate stone carvings of its porch and chancel arch. The little Norman church is, from a distance, rather plain. It was built in the middle of the 12th Century, around the same time as the remarkably less decorated Kirkstall Abbey was taking shape beside the River Aire three miles away. But when visitors walk through the graveyard to the south doorway, they find a feast of pictures in stone. It is considered the finest Norman doorway in England. There are five receding "rainbow" arches with a zigzag design. Among the images carved above them are Satan, the Cross and the Lamb of God, the sun and moon and the Son of Man. Figures on either side represent the evangelists—an eagle (St. John), a bull (St. Luke), a lion (St. Mark) a human face with an angel's wings (St. Matthew), plus the lamb for Jesus Christ. Although some have eroded with time you can still make out the main features. There are other rich carvings on the arch inside the church itself, which is the only Norman church left in Leeds. See also the memorial window (1681) and heraldic glass (1701).

☞ *The Church of St. John the Baptist is on Church Lane, Adel, Leeds LS16. Apart from during services, visitors can view the interior 9am-5pm daily.*

Armley Prison

On a hill to the south-west of the city centre stands what looks like a medieval castle, complete with battlements and towers. It is Armley Prison, one of the most deceptive buildings in England. It was actually built in 1847 and its architects, Perkins and Backhouse, were specifically asked to produce a design suggestive of the severe regime of a castle's dark dungeon. Originally, the prison housed 334 inmates but such was the crime rate in Leeds that it soon became overcrowed and an extension was built in 1857. Public executions were regular outside the main gate, the last being held on 10 September, 1864, when two murderers were hanged. Within its walls, the most famous execution was that of the notorious burglar and master of disguise, Charlie Peace, who went to the gallows there for murder on 25 February, 1879. Peace is now one of the "residents" of the Chamber of Horrors at Madame Tussaud's. More recently, Peter Sutcliffe, the Yorkshire Ripper, was held there while awaiting his Old Bailey trial in 1981. The prison has remained overcrowed through most of the 20th century, with as many as 1300 inmates, although a new extension should alleviate the crush. It holds men on remand from the courts of Yorkshire and Nottinghamshire and prisoners serving short sentences.

☞ *Armley Prison is on Gloucester Terrace, off Canal Road, Armley.*

The Bear Pit

Many passers-by look at this stone structure in Headingley and assume that it was a folly in the grounds of one of the suburb's grand 19th century houses. It certainly looks like some kind of ornamental fortress with its crenellated turrets and Norman arches. But it is a surviving relic of the Leeds Zoological and Botanical Gardens, which were opened in 1838. Unfortunately, the

Gardens were a commercial disaster, not least because of the muddle its shareholders got into over the question of Sunday opening. After the suggestion was denounced from the pulpits of several Leeds churches and chapels, some of the Gardens' wealthy backers threatened to pull their money out. Others made a similar threat, arguing that Sunday opening was *necessary* because the Sabbath was the only day the working classes could visit. In the end a compromise was reached. Sunday opening would be permitted, so long as the hours did not clash with church services. And so long as the tickets were purchased the day before, thus ensuring that there was no Sunday trading. But in 1848 the Leeds Zoological and Botanical Gardens went bust and the land was sold. The Bear Pit, which was restored in the 1960s by Leeds Civic Trust, contains an open circular pen where the beasts were exhibited. Visitors climbed spiral staircases inside the two turrets and looked down into the pit.

☛ *On the east side of Cardigan Road, Headingley, between Victoria Road and Spring Road.*

Beckett Street Cemetery

This splendid corner of the city has hardly changed since Victorian times. It opened on 14 August, 1845, as Leeds (Burmantofts) Cemetery for the burial of a nine-month-old boy, and since then more than 180,000 bodies have been interred in 28,000 graves. Now known as Beckett Street Cemetery, its huge collection of interesting funerary art makes it one of the most fascinating municipal cemeteries in the North of England and is now conserved by the council. Visitors entering by the gates opposite St. James's Hospital (Stanley Road end) will see one of two lodges. Two were required because the cemetery buried Church of England and Dissenters well apart. The path straight ahead leads to the grave of the cemetery's most famous "resident"—Sir John Barran. Look for the large grey granite memorial at the entrance to Barran Row, on the left. He founded the world's off-the-peg clothing industry in Leeds, was a Leeds MP and also the man responsible for the city's purchase of Roundhay Park. Another of the cemetery's most fascinating features is a large collection of "guinea graves". These are found by walking east up the slope of Dissenters Walk turning right on Guinea Grave Row, where numerous ordinary Leeds citizens bought themselves graves for one guinea (£1.05 in present money) to avoid the disgrace of being buried in unmarked pauper's graves. Off Anglican Walk on the south side of the cemetery you will find gravestones and memorials to men who fought in the Crimea (including the Charge of the Light Brigade), the Indian Mutiny, Waterloo, and who perished in Japanese POW camps. As you walk, you will find your attention constantly hijacked by interesting stone carvings and memorials, many of them telling sad stories of the death of ordinary people through 150 years of Leeds history.

☛ *Beckett Street Cemetery is directly opposite St. James's Hospital, Leeds. It is accessible by foot from Roundhay Road and York Road. An excellent leaflet with a map of all the most interesting gravestones can be purchased at the Leeds Tourist Information Centre.*

The fading light of a winter's afternoon projects eerie shadows in Beckett Street Cemetery.

Bramhope Puritan Chapel

A small building that is overlooked by most travellers on the busy Leeds-Otley road at Bramhope, the Puritan Chapel is unique in England. It was the only such chapel to have been erected specifically for Puritan worship during the period when Oliver Cromwell was Lord Protector. Built in 1649 by the local Dyneley family, it is a classic example of the Puritan plain style of architecture. There are no paintings, no stained glass, few decorations. When visitors walk through the door they are immediately disoriented. The "double decker" wooden pulpit stands in body of the chapel, among the fascinating wooden box pews, and some distance from the stone altar. The stone font is hexagonal, and is dated 1673. Interestingly, iron railings were fixed outside the north widows to stop curious cattle from causing unwelcome distractions during services. After a tree fell on the small bell tower in the early 1960s, the chapel was restored by the then-Wharfedale Rural District Council. Today, there are three services annually—two for Christmas carols and, in summer, one for newly elected members of Bramhope and Carlton Parish Council.

☛ *The Puritan Chapel is on the main Leeds-Otley road, on the far side of Bramhope, at the entrance to the Forte Crest Hotel. It is open for public viewing from Easter to the end of October, Sat & Sun only, 10am-4pm.*

Brangwyn Mosaics

Harehills seems an unlikely place to find an important work of art, especially in a late-Victorian church. But St. Aidan's Church on Roundhay Road houses the Brangwyn Mosaics by the great British mural artist, Frank Brangwyn (1867-1956). His other commissions included the Uffizi Gallery in Florence and New York's Rockefeller Centre. Controversially, his commemorative mural of the Great War for the House of Lords was rejected. A mural for St. Aidan's was suggested by the Leeds engineering industrialist, R. H. Kitson, who had already commissioned the Welsh-born Brangwyn to paint a frieze at his Sicilian villa. After consultation with the then-vicar, the Rev. Arthur Swayne, it was decided his work should fill the apse, the massive empty space between the high altar and the dome (some 1,000 square feet) and picture four episodes in the life of St. Aidan—the landing of St. Aidan, St. Aidan feeding the poor, St. Aidan preaching, and St. Aidan's death. A panel would also adorn each of the cancel's walls. Brangwyn began work in 1910 but stopped when he realised that the heavily polluted Leeds air might soon obliterate his mural with grime. Instead, he proposed a more durable mosaic, done with the help of a glasspainter, Sylvester Sparrow, and secured with cement. It was finally unveiled to the Harehills public on 13 October, 1916.

☛ *St. Aidan's Church is on Roundhay Road, Harehills, Leeds. The mosaic can be viewed Wed-Sat, 10am-12 noon. Or, of course, at church services.*

Civic Theatre

Highly acclaimed for his design of the new Leeds Town Hall and the Corn Exchange, Cuthbert Brodrick was asked to design yet another civic building for the growing city in 1865. It was to be a Mechanics' Institute, a cultural and educational centre for the burgeoning middle classes of Leeds. It took three years to complete and of all his buildings in the city, this contained the strongest classical French influence. Everywhere there is rich stone cornicing topped by huge urns. The finest feature is its massive entrance arch, at the

After his enormous success with Leeds Town Hall, the Hull-born architect Cuthbert Brodrick won a second competition for a major building in the city with his design for the **Corn Exchange** *(pictured above). Built to replace the original exchange in Briggate at a cost of £32,000, work on the new structure commenced in 1861 and it was opened for business on 28 July, 1863. Forever a man of surprises, Brodrick's vision was, in almost every way, the opposite of his Town Hall. This new building would steer clear of the great squares and rectangles of his famous civic commission and be dominated by the curve. The circular building—actually modelled on a Roman Colosseum—was dominated by a massive elliptical dome. If the outside was highly original, the interior was stunning in its complexity. The ribbed dome has off-centre glazing that provides an astonishing amount of light for the two-tier hall. At the height of its prosperity, there were 172 stands from which merchants traded sacks of corn. Today, there is a smaller market (Tuesdays) and the Corn Exchange is one of the most interesting speciality shopping centres, cafés and entertainment centres in Britain.*

☛ *The Corn Exchange is at the junction of Vicar Lane, Boar Lane and Call Lane, Leeds. Shops open Mon-Sat 9.30am-6pm; Sun 10am-4.30pm.*
☎ *Leeds 340363.*

top of a cascade of stone steps. The Mechanics' Institute has long since been renamed the Civic Theatre, home of amateur theatre and opera in the city. The actor Peter O'Toole made his debut on its stage in 1949. Another Brodrick commission, the Oriental Baths, was built across the street in 1866 with domes and minarets Sadly, it was demolished long ago. But next door Brodrick designed some shops which today survive as the Filling Station bar and bistro.

☞ *The Civic Theatre is in Cookridge Street, above Great George Street.*

The General Infirmary
Leeds has had first-class hospital provision for more than two centuries. On 20 October, 1767, the first patients were admitted to the new General Infirmary, a rented house in Kirkgate, and by Michaelmas the following year 89 in-patients had been treated. In 1771 a permanent building was found in what is still known as Infirmary Street, off City Square. But by the mid-19th century it was realised that even this 150-bed voluntary hospital (now demolished) was too small for Leeds's rapidly expanding population. The result was the splendid General Infirmary you can see in Great George Street. Built in 1862-68, its architect was the famous Gothic revivalist, Sir George Gilbert Scott, who was the most famous church architect of his day. The design certainly had the feel of a church, and the south façade also reminded many of the great hotel at London's St. Pancras Station, on which he was working at the same time. What makes this building especially historic is Scott's adoption of an idea by Florence Nightingale that patients would benefit from "pavilions" to maximize natural light and ventilation. A glass Winter Garden was thus built into the centre of the new building, and Scott's Infirmary was said to be one of the best hospitals in Europe. The Brotherton Wing, facing the Civic Hall, was added in 1942, originally for private patients.

☞ *Leeds General Infirmary is in Great George Street, behind the new Courthouse complex.*

The Great Synagogue
An important chapter in the history of the Leeds area was the arrival of 20,000 Jewish immigrants, who escaped the pogroms in Russia and Eastern Europe during the 1880s. Many disembarked at Grimsby and Hull, were told of a small Jewish community in Leeds, and decided to come here instead of continuing to Liverpool for the boat to America. Stepping off the train, they were directed to the squalid, insanitary houses in an area known as the Leylands, just north of Vicar Lane, between North Street and Regent Street. While their skills and hard work soon turned the Leeds clothing trade into a world leader, they quickly established a number of synagogues in and around the city centre, the first Great Synagogue being in Belgrave Street. It was built in 1860, later extended but demolished in 1985 (a Leeds Civic Trust blue plaque now marks the site). Early this century, congregations merged and the Jewish population moved up Chapeltown Road. The result was a new Great Synagogue, a red-brick building dominated by a huge green patina dome, which became one of the most distinctive synagogues in England when it opened in 1932. It is Moorish-Byzantine in style, but with a Classical Greek feel to the entrance. A mock minaret at the rear has unfortunately lost its canopy and what looks like a central heating flue is now exposed. Apparently the architect, J. Stanley Wright,

The Great Synagogue, Chapeltown Road.

had travelled widely in the Middle East while in the Army, and was influenced by what he saw. Although it now houses the Northern School of Contemporary Dance (see p. 82), visitors can still see the impressive decorations, including stone carvings, around the entrance, and great stone urns on either side of the door. By the 1980s, most of the Jewish population had moved north yet again, this time for the outer suburbs of Moortown and Alwoodley, and yet another Great Synagogue was opened on Shadwell Lane in 1986. At the front is an interesting sculpture by Naomi Black called "Shalom"—dedicated to the victims of the holocaust.

☞ *The Great Synagogue of 1932 is at 98 Chapeltown Road, Leeds LS7.*

Holy Trinity Church
Many city centre shoppers do not give this splendid church a second glance but Holy Trinity is among the most important buildings in Leeds. One of the earliest churches in the city, it was built in 1722-26 at a time when Leeds was becoming the prominent town in area, with its own newspaper (Leeds Mercury) and a new indoor cloth market. It is difficult to believe that Boar Lane was then the most fashionable residential street. Prosperous merchants had their houses there, and this was to be their church. The exterior is almost unique—a hybrid of Palladianism and Baroque that did not remain

in fashion for long. The tower replaced the original spire, which was partly demolished by a severe storm in the 1830s, and is one of the most prominent features of the Leeds skyline. Inside, Holy Trinity is more or less as it was first constructed 270 years ago, modelled on a Roman basilica. There is much rich stucco and wood carving, although the fine decorations at the end of the pews were added in late-Victorian times.

☛ *On the north side of Boar Lane, at Trinity Street. Open for public viewing 10am-4pm Mon-Fri.*
☎ *Leeds 454268.*

Lambert's Yard

In the early 17th century, most of the growing town of Leeds's commercial life was centred around what is today known as Lower Briggate. Then it was called Cloth Market because it was here that lengths of cloth were sold in open stalls, the very origin of the city's growth. The merchants built themselves "little mansions" in this area of the type with overhanging gables for which The Shambles in York is famous. The only one that survives—indeed the only three-decker, timber-framed house left anywhere in Leeds—is in Lambert's Yard off the east side of Lower Briggate. It is clearly seen on the right as you enter the yard. Although its appearance has been greatly altered through the years the original triple-decker shape still remains.

☛ *Lambert's Yard is through the gated entrance on the east side of Lower Briggate. The gate is padlocked outside business hours.*

*The centre of local government power is **Leeds Civic Hall** (pictured above) on the north-west side of the city centre. Designed by E. Vincent Harris in the shape of a triangle—but fronted by a wide Roman Corinthian portico—it cost £360,000. However, since its construction was during the early 1930s depression it provided work for local unemployed men with substantial funding from the Unemployment Grants Committee. The most distinctive features of the Portland Stone-faced building are the 170ft.-high twin towers. On each one perches a gilded bronze owl (7ft. 6in. tall and weighing half a ton) taken from the Leeds armorial bearings. Officially opened by King George V, accompanied by Queen Mary, on 23 August, 1933, the Civic Hall houses a rectangular, walnut panelled council chamber, a sumptuous 100ft long Banqueting Hall, containing panels that list the names of great people who have been associated with the city, as well as the Lord Mayor's Room and numerous council departments. The building overlooks the Nelson Mandela Gardens, so-named in 1983 as a tribute to the great South African freedom fighter.*
☛ *Leeds Civic Hall looks south between Calverley Street and Portland Crescent. There are regular guided tours of the building. For up-to-date information, check with the Leeds Tourist Information Centre.*
☎ *Leeds 478301/2/3.*

Leeds Parish Church

It was the land between this church and today's Leeds Bridge that the infant hamlet of Loidis grew at the end of the Dark Ages. The first church on this site was built of timber around AD 655, but was destroyed by fire on an unknown date. A church of stone followed, with a simple Saxon nave and small chancel. It was extended after the Norman invasion but another fire during the reign of Edward III required yet another reconstruction, this time with a nave, choir, transepts and large central tower. An organ was introduced in 1714, and John Wesley visited in 1743, 1781 and 1799. In the 1830s, a new vicar, Dr. Walter Farquhar Hook, was as High Anglican Tory as they came and feared for the Godliness of his congregation when he saw the state of their medieval parish church. He decided that the best thing that could happen was to demolish the old structure. He commissioned a new design from the architect, R. D. Chantrell and by 1841 there was a brand new—if rather outwardly rather plain—Leeds Parish Church in the 18th century Romantic style. While several memorials and monuments were kept from the old building, new fittings included Gothic galleries, a particularly high pulpit and elevated altar. Since the day it was consecrated, the only main alteration has been to the sanctuary (by the great ecclesiastical architect, G. E. Street in the 1870s) and today the interior of St. Peter's is a magnificent relic of Victorian Leeds. The city's oldest historical monument stands in the chancel. It is a partly remodelled Saxon memorial cross, which was found when the old parish church was demolished in 1838. Other fragments and a useful guide to its carvings can be seen in Leeds City Museum (see page 48). For details of choral music see page 79.

☛ *St. Peter's is in Kirkgate, Leeds LS1. Apart from services and music recitals the interior is open for inspection Mon-Fri 10am-3pm. Tea, coffee and snacks are also available at the adjoining City of Leeds Room during those hours.*
☎ *Leeds 454012.*

Leeds Town Hall

The instantly recognisable symbol of municipal life in England, Leeds Town Hall (see photograph on page 37) presides over the city in the way that York is dominated by its great Minster. It was begun in August, 1853, after a young Hull architect, Cuthbert Brodrick, won a competition for its design. His plan was for a huge square, multi-columned building on a great plinth. Like so many of Brodrick's later commissions in Leeds, it revealed a French Classical style but the famous clock tower, which was actually an afterthought, is more Baroque. The main building material, of course, was millstone grit. The great stone lions were said to have been copied from pictures of lions at London Zoo. When this great monument to northern civic pride was officially opened by Queen Victoria on 7 September, 1858, the tower was still under construction. All the city's mills were closed for the day. The project cost £122,000—over £80,000 more than the original estimate, and civic spending noticeably decreased in Leeds for many years. The great Victoria Hall, often described as being like the inside of a wedding cake, is full of rich plasterwork and worthy Victorian mottoes. The building housed the Leeds council offices until 1884, when they were moved next door to new Palladian-style municipal buildings (now the library and museum) and then to the civic hall in 1933. The city's main Law Courts and bridewell remained in the Town Hall for decades, but with the new Courthouse complex built next door, Leeds Town Hall faces a new future primarily as a major concert hall and conference/exhibition venue.

☛ *Leeds Town Hall is unmistakable, overlooking what is actually Victoria Square. Today, most people think of it as being on The Headrow. There are regular guided tours of the building, which includes a chance to visit the famous clock tower. For the latest programme, check with Leeds Tourist Information Centre.*
☎ *Leeds 478301/2/3.*

Park Square

Every Georgian town in England had its square of elegant houses and Leeds was no exception. The richest merchants and professional men lived in terraces of houses arranged round a central garden. The only one in Leeds was Park Square, begun in 1788, and much of it still survives, though it is no longer a residential area. It is likely that those who lived there objected to the soot that began belching out of Benjamin Gott's Bean Ing woollen mill, up-wind on a site now occupied by the *Yorkshire Post,* when steam engines began driving his machinery in the 1820s. As a result, by the mid-19th century the square had become more of a commercial centre and in 1878, Sir John Barran, the father of off-the-peg clothing, built an astonishing factory and warehouse along the south side of the square. St. Paul's House (pictured above) was named after a nearby church and is considered one of the finest industrial buildings in the North. Designed by Thomas Ambler, its style was Moorish-Venetian. One of its minarets disguised a chimney. Behind the terracotta façade worked 2,000 people in its heyday, but early this century it fell into disuse and was almost demolished. Today it has a new life as offices, its exterior having been carefully repaired.

☛ *Park Square is off the south side of The Headrow, opposite Leeds Town Hall.*

Looking south across Park Square to St. Paul's House.

Otley

Of all the satellite towns in the Leeds metropolitan area, Otley is the most interesting. Its core is primarily that of the Georgian market town. Victorian additions were mostly around the fringes and, because stone from the Chevin was still the main material, these new buildings did little to alter the general appearance of Otley. Today, visitors will find a charming town with many fascinating corners to explore. *See Otley Museum p. 49.*

All Saints Parish Church. There was a church on this site off Kirkgate in Saxon times, but the present structure—restored in the 19th century—is Norman. Inside, there is a fine Georgian pulpit and several fragments of Anglo-Saxon crosses. The most famous event here was the baptism of Thomas Chippendale on 5 June, 1718.

Bramhope Tunnel Memorial. In order to build the Leeds-Harrogate-Thirsk railway line in the 1860s it was necessary to cut a two-mile long tunnel under Bramhope. But during its construction, 30 men were killed in accidents. An impressive memorial, a replica of the tunnel's north portal (see below), is behind iron railings beside the Parish Church.

Jubilee Clock. Public subscription paid for this splendid clock tower in 1888 to celebrate Queen Victorian's Golden Jubilee. Attached to its walls are tablets commemorating men from Otley who fell in the Boer War, and the gratitude of Belgian refugees billeted in Otley during the Great War.

Thomas Chippendale. The man described as "the Shakespeare of English cabinetmakers" was born in Otley in 1718. His father was a joiner, and they lived in a small cottage in Boroughgate. It was demolished many years ago but a plaque marks the spot on the wall of Building Society Chambers. When his mother became ill, the young Thomas (aged 10) went to live with an uncle at what is now 3 Bondgate, occupied by the Cobblestones Team Rooms. He served his apprenticeship with his father, and it was while making furniture at Harewood that his talent was discovered. Chippendale was encouraged to take his genius to London to make furniture for the nobility and the rest, as they say, is history. A statue of Chippendale now stands outside the Old Grammar School in Manor Square.

☛ *10 miles north of Leeds on the A660. There is a Tourist Information Centre at 8 Boroughgate.*
☎ *Leeds 477705*

St. Anne's Cathedral

The Roman Catholic population of Leeds greatly increased as waves of Irish immigrants arrived to escape the Potato Famine back home. St. Anne's Church, built in 1838 at the bottom of Cookridge Street, became an RC cathedral in 1878, when the Diocese of Leeds was formed, but the building protruded into the Headrow, frustrating a plan to create a wide boulevard from Eastgate to Westgate. The council issued a compulsory purchase order in 1899 and, as the old St. Anne's was demolished (part of its site was where the Leeds Permanent Building Society offices are today) a new building was constructed just a short distance to the north, at the junction of Cookridge Street and Great George Street. The new St. Anne's, consecrated in 1904, was built in the Gothic style by Henry Eastwood and is unusually broad. Much of the detailed design work was done by Sydney K. Greenslade. The most interesting relics from the previous buildings are the pulpit, and the reredos (screens) from the High Altar.

☛ *In Cookridge Street, just north of The Headrow. Apart from services, it is open 8am-5pm Mon-Fri and 10am-5pm Sat & Sun.*
☎ *Leeds 454545.*

St. James's Hospital

Prosperous though Leeds was becoming in the mid-19th century, there was also considerable poverty in the densely populated industrial slums. There was a town workhouse at the junction of Vicar Lane and Lady Lane from 1726, which eventually housed 250 paupers. In 1846, a "Moral and Industrial Training School" was established in Beckett Street, Burmantofts, to educate the pauper children away from the influence of the workhouse. In 1861, it was decided to build a brand new Union Workhouse and chapel next to the school, accommodating 810 poor. An infirmary was built in 1874 but by 1879 there were more sick and elderly than able-bodied and the infirmary was separated to become the first Poor Law hospital outside London. As the need for a workhouse decreased, The Leeds Union Infirmary, as it was called, took over the other buildings but by 1927, when it was taken over by Leeds Corporation and renamed St. James's Hospital, it still carried the stigma of a workhouse and many older people were reluctant to be taken there. Today, the Industrial School of 1846 faces Beckett Street, on the south side of the complex. The Leeds Union Workhouse of 1861, on the north side, is now the Ashley Wing. And the Union Infirmary of 1874 is the Gledhow Wing. In 1948, when

The Bramhope Tunnel memorial at Otley's All Saints Parish Church.

taken into the NHS, St. James's was the largest general hospital in the UK. Today, it is a self-governing Trust and teaching hospital, one of the largest in Europe. And, of course, it is famous throughout Britain for the *Jimmies* YTV series. See also page 21.

☛ *St. James's Hospital is on Beckett Street, Burmantofts.*

St. John's Church

Tucked away behind Lewis's and the St. John's Centre, off the Headrow, is the church containing the most remarkable interior of any in Leeds. It is also the oldest remaining in the city centre. Work on St. John's, Briggate, started in 1631. It was paid for by John Harrison, the town's first alderman, who had inherited a fortune from his cloth merchant father. (He also built the first Charity School, next door, and in the 1620s he founded the Leeds Free Grammar School, behind the Grand Theatre and facing what is now Vicar Lane). By the time it was consecrated in 1634, St. John's was absolutely full of rich wood carvings in its pews, screens and pulpit. Rare among churches, it was also built with a double nave. St. John's was almost demolished in 1865 but good sense prevailed. As a result, today you can still see those great 17th century carvings. Although now classed as a "redundant church" it is well maintained and occasional services are held there.

☛ *St. John's Church stands on the corner of New Briggate and Mark Lane, Leeds LS2. The interior is open to the public Mon, Tues, Thur & Fri, 11am-3pm. Other times by appointment.*
☎ *Leeds 457154.*

Stank Hall Barn

One of the finest surviving tithe barns in Northern England is at Beeston, on the south side of Leeds. Built in the late 15th or early 16th century, it was founded by the Beeston family, who were Lords of the Manor at Stank Hall and, later, New Hall. As a tax, tenants had to bring a "tithe"—one-tenth of their agricultural produce—to this barn. Today, it is being restored by English Heritage

and Leeds City Council, and may be open to the public or for educational purposes in the future. At the moment, you can inspect it from a public right of way at close quarters. On the outside, it has stone walls and a stone slate roof, and wattle and daub walls and distinctive timber beams inside. The original building was altered at its southern end in the 17th century.

☛ *On left under bridge carrying main Leeds-London railway line, just as Dewsbury Road (A653) joins the ring road at Beeston.*

Thornton's Arcade

As Briggate became the main shopping street of Leeds in the 1870s, there was much competition among traders for the limited amount of shop space. Charles Thornton, who a decade earlier had bought a Georgian coaching inn called the White Swan and rebuilt it as "Thornton's New Music Hall and Fashionable Lounge" (now known as The City Varieties) provided the answer to the shortage. He would build a covered arcade which met Briggate at right angles. He commissioned George Smith, who had been architect of the new music hall, to design his development over the old Talbot Inn and yard. This followed one of the 60 medieval burgage plots which abutted Briggate, and which are still the basis of today's Briggate. In 1877-78 his Thornton's Arcade took shape, a Gothic structure as was the then-fashion

In 1838-40 John Marshall the "flax king" constructed **Temple Mills** *in Holbeck The flax-spinning mills, with the office building (detailed above) added in 1843, is regarded as the most remarkable industrial building in Leeds. The façade was actually modelled on the 2000-year-old Egyptian temple at Edfu, and was designed by the architect Joseph Bonomi, an expert on ancient Egyptian architecture The stonework was lavishly adorned with Egyptian motifs, including two winged solar discs and six columns embellished with open papyrus flowers. The Mill appeared in Benjamin Disraeli's novel Sybil and for many years—local legend has it— part of its roof had an insulating layer of turf on which sheep grazed. To provide natural light to the workers at their spinning machines, 66 glass domes were provided, held up by cast-iron columns which continued with the Egyptian theme with yet more papyrus capitals. One can only imagine what the mill looked like in its original form, with a chimney modelled on Cleopatra's Needle. Unfortunately, it became unsafe in 1852 and was replaced with a less interesting design. Leeds's great flax industry was relatively short-lived, because of competition from abroad and the switch to other fibres, and Temple Mill ceased flax spinning in 1886. Today, the building is occupied by Kay & Co., the mail order firm.*
☛ *Temple Mill is in Marshall Street, Holbeck. The best time to see—and photograph—it is on Saturday afternoon and Sundays when there are few, if any, cars parked outside.*

for any serious building. Horseshoe arches held up a glass roof over the narrow arcade and its most famous feature was the clock at the west end, a remarkable working model of the main characters in Sir Walter Scott's Ivanhoe: Robin Hood, Friar Tuck, Richard Coeur De Lion and Gurth the Swineherd. The figures, the work of Leeds sculptor John Appleyard, suddenly spring to life each time the clock strikes hours and quarters. The success of Thornton's Arcade encouraged similar developments on Briggate. Queen's Arcade, further down the street, was built in 1888-89, Grand Arcade, north of the Grand Theatre, followed in 1896-98, Victoria Arcade (where the Schofields Centre now stands, fronting on the Headrow and forming a L-shape to Lands Lane) also in 1898, County Arcade and Cross Arcade (now part of the restored and renamed Victoria Quarter) in 1898-1900.

☛ *Thornton's Arcade is off Briggate, near its junction with The Headrow, and connects with Lands Lane.*

Time Ball Buildings

The most famous shop frontage of Leeds is John Dyson & Sons, the jewellers in Lower Briggate. Although the building is thought to be Georgian, the extraordinary facade was added in the 1890s to reflect the elaborately decorated nature of many of the goods inside, including a wide range of timepieces. These adornments included two massive clocks, one of which was topped by a gilded Old Father Time. For several generations of Leeds folk, this was one of the most famous meeting points in the city centre. "I'll see you under Dyson's clock", was a popular arrangement for a night on the town. Today the façade survives as part of the new development on the south side of Boar Lane.

☛ *Time Ball Buildings are on the west side of Lower Briggate, near its junction with Boar Lane.*

Tower Works

In the mid-19th century, wealthy Yorkshire industrialists who had been on the Grand Tour returned with ideas to adorn their new mills

and factories. If the Marshalls could build a mill looking like an Egyptian Temple (see Temple Mill), Sir John Barran could make his new factory look like a Moorish palace (see Park Square) and Sir Titus Salt could have the chimney of his amazing new Salts Mill at Saltaire copied from the campanile of the Church of Santa Maria Gloriosa, Venice, then Thomas Walter Harding could demand something special for his new factory in Holbeck. He commissioned William Bakewell to design him a chimney that was based on Giotto's 14th century campanile of Florence Cathedral. Built in 1899 for his Tower Works, which made pins for the textile industry, it was named the Giotto Tower. As a Grade II listed structure, it is still in good condition. Visitors to the site will find most of the Tower Works gone, but there is good access through the car park to the east. The Giotto Tower overshadows the two other chimneys on the site. One is known as "the Leeds chimney" (also Grade II) and contained an impressively early metal dust extractor to minimise pollution. It was built in 1864 to Thomas Shaw's copy of the 12th century Lamberti Tower, Verona. The third chimney is a plain square tower.

☛ *Tower Works stand in Globe Road, Hunsley.*

Wetherby

The origin of Wetherby's growth in the 18th and early 19th centuries was its location on the Great North Road, being equidistant between London and Edinburgh and thus an ideal staging post on the 400-mile journey. Consequently, the town's splendid inns form the places of most historical interest, which is as good an excuse as you'll ever get to combine drinking with serious study. The two best surviving examples are the Swan and Talbot Inn and the Angel Inn. Between them, they formed what must have been a huge equivalent of today's motorway service stations from the start of the trade in the 1780s. As well as stabling for over 200 horses they had facilities like blacksmiths

and wheelwrights to look after the coaches. For half a century, Wetherby prospered but with the coming of the railways long-distance coaches declined and Wetherby grew as a market town. Among the other buildings of note are a Methodist Chapel (1829) in Bank Street, the foundations of Wetherby Castle (early 12th century) in Castlegate, and the impressive Wetherby Town Hall (1845) in Market Place.

☛ *Wetherby is 13 miles north east of Leeds along the A58. There is a Tourist Information Centre in the Council Offices, Westgate.*
☎ *Leeds 477253.*

White Cloth Hall

There were few more important buildings in Georgian Leeds than the White Cloth Hall. Built in 1775-76, it was a huge quadrangular market hall in which Leeds cloth merchants bought white (undyed and unfinished) woollen cloth from clothiers who came from all over the West Riding. The hall cost £4,000 to build and accommodated 1,213 stalls for the markets, which were held every Tuesday and Saturday. Most of the building was demolished by the North Eastern Railway Company in 1865 for the line that still runs east from Leeds, and the merchants were moved to new premises provided by the railway company on a site now occupied by the Metropole Hotel in King Street. But by then the trade was in decline. Today, you can still see the impressive arcaded façade of the White Cloth Hall's entrance, including the central cupola. It is now a pizza parlour. Next door, the merchants also built an Assembly Room in 1777, with a superbly decorated ballroom and card room, which became the fashionable social centre of Leeds in the late-Georgian period. Although greatly altered, it can be seen today as the Waterloo Antiques centre, and the original plasterwork can be inspected by visiting the top floor, which was added to the ballroom to create two levels. (See *Museum of Georgian Leeds* on page 49).

☛ *The White Cloth Hall and the Assembly Room are in Crown Street, behind the Corn Exchange.*

PART THREE:
Leeds Night Life

Top regional repertory theatre, contemporary dance and opera companies, the world's greatest jazz and rock stars, the most highly acclaimed touring plays and musicals from London's West End, one of the best orchestral concert seasons in England, the unique IMAX cinema experience, and some of Britain's oldest folk/roots clubs. These are just some of the facilities within reach of Leeds residents and visitors.

The range of entertainments seems to be increasing every year. Especially with home-grown entertainment like Leeds Alternative Cabaret or the city's pop-charters Utah Saints.

With the biggest concentration of theatres and live pub entertainment venues outside London, there's something happening in the Leeds area seven nights a week.

Sarah Payne in the title role of Sugar, from the stage version of "Some Like it Hot" at West Yorkshire Playhouse.

Leeds Night Life

Mozart to Melly, Shakespeare to Stoppard, The Rolling Stones to Stone Roses, Royal Ballet to Rambert Dance.

Newcomers to Leeds are usually stunned by the extent of the area's night life. And they are impressed by how accessible it is. Most venues are concentrated within the city centre, with few parking problems, nor traffic hold-ups after the show. Then there's the good quality *free* jazz, folk and blues in the area's pubs, the low ticket prices at the Leeds box offices, and the quality and convenience of the suburban cinemas. And because Bradford is so close, is is usually easy to go there for a play or a gig, adding a curry to the night out for good measure. The following pages list all the important venues in the region.

Cinemas

There is a huge and ever-growing choice of cinema screens in the Leeds area, from some of the best-preserved small cinemas in the area, traditional mutli-screen city centre complexes, film theatres, an out-of-town multiplex and the biggest screen in Britain. Despite a growing number of video outlets—there must be nearly 1,000 in Leeds alone if one includes filling stations—cinema audiences show no signs of contracting. And

with Leeds host to a highly regarded International Film Festival every year, there is much to keep cinemagoers happy in the city. A couple of those Leeds cinemas listed here have long been rumoured as closing or changing hands (the Hyde Park and the Cottage Road), and we wish them well. Meanwhile, there is still a campaign to open a National Film Theatre—North in the city. Watch the local media for details.

Cannon

A local landmark at the top of Vicar Lane, this large three-screen complex opened as The Ritz on 19 November, 1934 and became the ABC in 1959. Today, the Cannon One seats 670; Cannon Two seats 483; and Cannon Three seats 227. All are non-smoking. There is a bar for customers only and the usual pop corn and snack counter. Expect only the latest releases at Cannon, usually from the big distributors like UIP. Street parking after seven at night can sometimes be a problem

☛ *The Cannon is in Vicar Lane, Leeds LS2.*

☎ *Leeds 452665. Recorded latest programme details available 24 hours on Leeds 451013.*

Odeon

This is now the biggest regular indoor entertainment complex within Leeds city centre, with a capacity of almost 2000. The Odeon has seen many changes since it opened as the Paramount on 22 February, 1932 with a Maurice Chevalier film and, "live on stage", 24 Mangan Tiller Girls and Myrio and Desha, "sensational dancers from Paris." Plus: "Mammoth Organ!" The stage of what is now the main screen was occupied by The Beatles twice in 1963 and once on 22 October, 1964. The Rolling Stones also played here twice. Now "live" entertainment is rare, and the Odeon is a modern five-screen complex. Odeon 1 seats 980 with smoking and non-smoking sections. But it is non-smoking only in all of the others. Odeon 2 has 460 seats, Odeon 3 has 198, Odeon 4 has 172 and Odeon 5 has a nice intimate atmosphere with 126 seats. There is a full range of snacks, and a bar for ticket holders. The Odeon gets all the Rank releases and many others from the big distributors. Parking can be a problem after seven, and beware of wheel clampers in nearby private car parks. There is late parking at the Merrion Centre. No advance booking for shows.

☛ *The Odeon is at 10 The Headrow, at the junction with Briggate.*

☎ *Leeds 436230. Recorded programmes on 430031.*

Cottage Road

Like the Hyde Park, the Cottage Road has survived (at the time of writing) against the trend of small cinema closures. It opened as The Headingley Picture House on Monday, 29 July, 1912, after being converted from a motor garage. Before that, the Victorian building was thought to have been a dairy. Today its programmes are mixture of big blockbusters and first runs of the less commercially attractive films. There is seating for 468, a non-smoking area and "pullman" seats which provide more leg-room.

☛ *3-5 Cottage Road, Headingley, Leeds LS6.*

☎ *Leeds 751606 (recorded programme when unattended).*

What's On?

Besides flyposters and leaflets, at music/record shops, galleries & libraries there are three main sources of Night Life events information for the Leeds-Bradford area.

Northern Star. Formerly known as Leeds Other Paper, NS is quite simply indispensable if you're out & about in Leeds at night. The fullest What's On listings, reviews and much more. Especially good coverage of rock & pop, disco nights/raves, roots & jazz, gay & lesbian scene and alternative cabaret but covers theatre/orchestral/dance too. Published on Thursdays.

Artscene. Free magazine and listings guide published by Yorkshire & Humberside Arts, the regional arts association. Available monthly at libraries, public buildings and information centres. Big on dance, theatre, orchestral concerts and recitals but covers everything from rock to children's shows.

What's On in Leeds. Regularly updated free listings brochure produced by Leeds City Council. Covers events mainly at established venues—music, theatre, ballet, dance, opera, etc. Find it at libraries, galleries & information centres.

Hyde Park

One of the best-loved cinemas in the north, the Hyde Park lurches from one financial crisis to another. It is the one cinema in Leeds that could close at any time although it is difficult to believe it would not remain as some sort of film theatre. Thankfully, at the time of writing it is still in business, surviving largely through a combination of loyal support from its own fan club, "The Friends of Hyde Park Picture House" and the dogged persistence of its owners. Opened on 7 November, 1914, it started life as a classic suburban cinema serving a tightly knit community. But whereas most similar cinemas have disappeared, the Hyde Park has survived because it is bang in the middle of student bed-sit land, and during term time students account for a large part of its custom. The choice of films reflects this: numerous cult films like "The Blues Brothers", art house and golden oldies mixed with the more fashionable of the latest releases. The Hyde Park is often one of the few places in Leeds where a late-night film can be seen (Fri & Sat nights 11pm start during term time only). The cinema itself featured in "Wetherby" and "The First of the Summer Wine." There are 350 seats, non-alcoholic refreshments, pop corn, ice-creams, etc. Use it or lose it.

☛ *73 Brudenell Road, Headingley, Leeds LS6.*
☎ *Leeds 752045.*

The Lounge Picture House

This is one of only half a dozen small purpose-built cinemas in the country that is still open in its original form. And the atmosphere of bygone picture shows can almost be touched, because the Lounge's interior has been lovingly maintained since the day it opened on 2 October, 1916. The foyer is an essay in wood, metal and glass and the hall itself has much elaborate cornice work and other rich decoration. As a result, it draws its audiences from well beyond the Leeds area. Going to see a film here, for many middle-aged and older people, is a trip back into childhood. Owned by the same independent company that has the Cottage Road Cinema, The Lounge now gets the big films on their first run. There are often matinee screenings in school holidays (when the top films for the under-16s are programmed) and on Saturday afternoons. There is also a late show on Friday evenings. There is seating for 691 (531 downstairs, 160 in the balcony) with a non-smoking rule for all left-hand seats. A notable feature of The Lounge is its excellent stereo sound. Also, there is a useful seats booking facility for Saturday evening shows, but you must book at the office from 2pm that day. Late night shows on Friday (11pm start) in term-time are usually cult films or recent blockbusters.

☛ *The Lounge is in North Lane, Headingley, Leeds LS6.*
☎ *Leeds 751061. Recorded programme when unattended.*

Evening light at Headingley's Lounge Cinema.

Showcase

This multiplex cinema on the southern fringe of Leeds opened in 1990 but has done little to reduce the popularity of the long-established city centre cinemas. Showcase's 10 screens seem to draw customers from a wide area of West and South Yorkshire, being strategically placed near the M62 and M62. But get there early, for the film you want to see may have sold out and you will find yourself going in to watch your second, third or fourth choice. The complex offers a huge programme of the top releases and more obscure titles. Good parking, bar and refreshment facilities. There is no smoking allowed in the cinemas.

☛ *The Showcase complex is on Gelderd Road, Birstall. From Leeds, take A62 off M621.*
☎ *Recorded programme: 0924-420071. Other information: 0924-420622.*

The Apollo

This cosy Shipley four-screen complex shows latest releases, permitting the population of a wide area of Airedale (including Guiseley, Yeadon, Rawdon & Menston) to have a night at the pictures without going into Leeds or Bradford. Screen 1 has 89 seats; Screen 2 has 72 seats; Screen 3 has 121 seats; Screen 4 has 94 seats. All are non-smoking and there is good wheelchair access. Matinee performances on Saturdays and Sundays.

☛ *The Apollo is in Bradford Road, Shipley.*
☎ *0274-583429.*

Leeds International Film Festival

From its beginnings in 1987 as a small, one-off programme of films put together by a group of local cinema buffs the festival has become one of the best in the UK, with audiences growing by 25 per cent every year. Although primarily film-based, it includes many side events like talks, seminars,

workshops and exhibitions. The programme includes celebrity guests and UK premieres. The core of the festival is its screenings, more than 60 different features in the course of more than two weeks in mid-October. Each year there are several themes to the programme, such as censorship, the role of music in movies, or the cinema of a particular country. The programme is available at galleries, libraries and information centres in September

☎ *The Festival Office is on Leeds 478389. The Box Office is on Leeds 476962. Credit card bookings are taken on Leeds 455505.*

Pictureville

A spin-off from Bradford's successful IMAX screen, this luxury cinema provides a programme of old classics, foreign films, some first releases and cult films. Its speciality, however, is Cinerama, a short-lived precursor of Cinemascope, that uses three projectors to put an image onto a wide, curved screen. Pictureville has 306 seats (all non-smoking), and a bar and snacks area. There are two evening performances daily, matinees in school holidays.

☛ *In Pictureville, next to the National Museum of Photography, Film & Television, Bradford.*
☎ *0274-732277. Seats bookable in advance.*

Bradford Film Theatre

A two-screen art house cinema that is well used by Leeds residents. The shows are artistically acclaimed films, first and second-run mainstream productions, old classics, cult films, re-releases and the best of current foreign cinema (sub-titled). It runs seven nights a week, 40 weeks a year but there is no film on the Sunday before a week of theatre at Bradford Playhouse, with which it shares accommodation. The large screen has 286 seats, the 2nd has 50 seats. Programmes are listed in *Northern Star* and combined with IMAX programmes available at libraries and information centres.

☛ *Bradford Playhouse & Film Theatre is in Chapel Street (off Leeds Road), Bradford BD1.*
☎ *0274-720329.*

Leeds area residents are fortunate to have Britain's biggest cinema screen within half an hour, by bus or car, from the city. Called IMAX it is at the heart of the National Museum of Photography, Film & Television in Bradford (see also page 158). The screen is 64 feet 8 inches wide and 52 feet 4 inches high—the height of a five-storey building. Combined with its six separate sound channels—four behind the screen and two in the auditorium—the effect is one of being totally engulfed by the film. The action and sounds surround one's entire field of vision and range of hearing. IMAX was invented in Canada and although there are now chains of the large screen throughout the United States, Japan, Russia and Europe, there is still no prospect of another being built in the UK. The screen is used to its best effect with a number of films specially made for IMAX. They have been shot on film using the largest frame yet invented for the cinema—5.23 square inches, four times bigger than the 70 mm frame used on conventional cinema screens. The 340-seat cinema is an average of 60 per cent full at each performance. There are five, sometimes six shows each day (but it is closed on Mondays, including May Day, but open other Bank Hols.) The first performance is usually 12 noon although an 11am show is put on for schools mid-week. At weekends, there is a 5pm show and evening performances, starting at 7.30pm, on Thursday and Friday.
☛ *IMAX is in Pictureville, off Prince's Way, Bradford BD5 0TR. Bookings are accepted by telephone 10am-5pm seven days a week. Also book in person at the NMPFT 11am-7.30pm Tues-Sun. Access & Visa accepted. Booking essential for disabled in wheelchairs because of limited space.*
☎ *Box office: 0274-732277.*

Theatres

If one views Leeds and Bradford as a single metropolis—as do many residents of the two cities—then the sheer quantity and quality of theatre on offer here is second only to London's West End. The area's theatregoers want for nothing—they get the big West End musicals, the best RSC productions, top repertory theatre at West Yorkshire Playhouse and the best British companies on tour. Add traditional Music Hall at the City Varieties, vibrant "fringe" theatre at several Studio theatre and some of the most pioneering acts in alternative cabaret in the concert rooms of pubs and every taste is catered for. And, of course, a city like Leeds is also virtually self-sufficient in theatre if one includes the large number of amateur productions available every week of the year. The following pages are a guide to main venues.

West Yorkshire Playhouse

The finest new arts facility to be built in Leeds this century is the West Yorkshire Playhouse, a stunning £13.5 million repertory theatre, gallery and bar/restaurant complex on the eastern edge of the city centre. Opened by the actress Diana Rigg on 8 March, 1990, it replaced the Leeds Playhouse on the University campus which had been built as a temporary theatre and lasted 20 years. The new Playhouse has two auditoria—The Quarry Theatre (750 seats, open thrust stage) and The Courtyard Theatre, a rectangular space similar to The Cottesloe at the National, with adjustable seating for 350. The bar and restaurant has space for regular cabaret/live music, and there is also a coffee shop, a gallery, rehearsal and recording studios, function rooms, workshops, and a costume hire service. With productions 52 weeks a year, 17 were mounted in the first 12 months. The plays are primarily classic British and European drama and new writing, the latter including world premiers of works by Trevor Griffiths, Kay Mellor and Dario Fo. Besides its own Playhouse companies (featuring names like Rosemary Leach, Reece Dinsdale and Marius Goring), there are visiting theatre companies including the RSC. During the day there are numerous events for all age ranges, such as music workshops, playreadings, circus performers and puppeteers. Pick up the current free brochure for details. In the theatres, usual performance times are as follows. Quarry—Mon & Sat 8pm, Tues-Fri 7.30pm, Sat matinees 4pm, Wed matinees 2pm. Courtyard—Mon & Sat 7.45pm, Tues-Fri 7.45pm, Sat matinees 4pm, Wed matinees 2pm. The Playhouse is especially well equipped for the disabled, or people with seeing and hearing problems. There is an induction loop system for the benefit of hearing impaired people and each repertory production has one performance interpreted in British sign language. Seat numbers and signs have been put into braille. and there is an audio description facility for the visually impaired.

☞ *The West Yorkshire Playhouse is in Quarry Hill Mount (on east side of Leeds Markets, off St. Peter's Street), Leeds LS9 8AW. Programmes are available at libraries and information centres throughout the Leeds area. Write or call to be placed on free mailing list. Box office is open 9am-8pm Mon-Sat. Booking also by post. Pay by Artscard/Access/Visa/Amex. There are numerous discounts available. See programme or ring for details.*

☎ *Box office: Leeds 442111; Minicom textphone for deaf people: Leeds 445346; General information: Leeds 442141.*

❏ *See what goes on behind the scenes at the West Yorkshire Playhouse. Free tours are arranged for parties on Thursday afternoons. Or for a small fee, join the regular Saturday lunchtime tour at 1pm. Call Leeds 442141 for further details.*

The West Yorkshire Playhouse in Quarry Hill Mount.

Grand Theatre

By far the biggest Leeds theatre, with a 1,550 capacity (88 seats less if the orchestra pit is extended for larger productions). The Grand has been packing them in since 1878 and while the interior is a classic Victorian proscenium with Stalls, Dress Circle, Upper Circle, Balcony, Upper Balcony and boxes for 4, 5 or 8 persons, there is also the latest sound and lighting equipment. By virtue of its size and facilities it is *the* venue east of the Pennines for the big touring musicals hot from the West End or London bound. These usually remain for between one and three weeks. In summer, dramatic productions are more normal, of the Agatha Christie or Francis Durbridge school. Throughout the year there are celebrity concerts by top variety performers.

☛ *The Grand Theatre & Opera House is in New Briggate, Leeds LS1 6NZ. Box Office open 10am-7.30pm Monday to Saturday. Bookings taken by post. Enclose s.a.e. to the above address, making cheques payable to Grand Theatre, Leeds.*

☎ *Information about latest/future programme: Leeds 443509. Bookings by telephone (Access/Visa/Diners Club/Amex): Leeds 459351 or 440971. New service allows you to purchase/reserve tickets by fax: Leeds 465906.*

Civic Theatre

Somewhere between the theatre styles of the West Yorkshire Playhouse and the Grand is this mixed-programme venue, once the former Leeds Mechanics Institute designed by Cuthbert Brodrick, the architect responsible for the Town Hall, in the French style. (See page 64). Extensively and expensively refurbished in the 1980s, the Civic is where one can expect to see anything from contemporary dance, touring plays, recitals and ethnic music to concerts featuring well-known TV entertainers. These professional acts now co-exist with what was for many years the Civic's mainstay—local amateur companies. The best of the Leeds area Thespian life still perform here: drama and music productions all the year round. The Civic has a house capacity of 521, and an excellent bar and buffet (also open lunchtimes) which accepts advance orders for drinks to avoid waits during the interval.

☛ *In Cookridge Street, Leeds LS2 8BH. Box office open for bookings 10am-8pm Mon-Sat. Opens 6.45pm for Sunday performances. Access & Visa payments accepted. Also postal bookings, cheques payable to Leeds City Council, plus s.a.e. Write or telephone to be put on free mailing list.*

☎ *Box office: Leeds 476962/ 455505. General enquiries: Leeds 456343.*

The City Varieties

England's oldest music theatre is the famous City Varieties, home of TV's The Good Old Days between 1953 and 1983. Entertainment has been provided on this site from the 18th century, first in a pub called the White Swan and then the City Palace of Varieties, opened in 1865. In the early days artistes like Lily Langtry, Houdini, Bud Flanagan and Marie Lloyd performed here. And several years in advance of achieving fame in the early days of Hollywood, Charlie Chaplin appeared on the City Varieties stage. Now it is one of a few music halls surviving in Britain, and most certainly the best preserved. A change of ownership in the 1980s has breathed new life into its programmes. While there is still a twice-yearly Music Hall season (Friday and Saturday nights each April and October), there is a wide range of traditional and contemporary entertainment—comedy "farce", rock 'n' roll musicals, Light Opera, clairvoyance, hypnosis, brass bands, alternative cabaret, stand-up comics like Bernard Manning or old pop stars on their "Silver Jubilee" tours. There's also an annual drama pantomime season. Bars are open half an hour before performances and in the interval. The Circle Bar remains open after the show (within licensing hours). There is a City Varieties Friends club, a sort of fan club for the theatre. Volunteers are also invited to help staff the theatre, often allowing them to see performances free of charge.

☛ *The City Varieties is on The Headrow, Leeds LS1 6LW .*

☎ *Box Office bookings (Mon-Sat 10am-7.30pm performance days and 10am-6pm non-performance days): Leeds 430808. Programme and other enquiries: Leeds 425045.*

The Studio Theatre

Although part of the faculty of Cultural and Education Studies at the Leeds Polytechnic campus, The Studio Theatre leads a separate existence except when presenting the Poly's Student Union Drama Society productions. Most of the time, it is the only permanent, regular venue in Leeds for "fringe" theatre, offering two full seasons a year of productions by nationally acclaimed smaller professional touring companies. Its aims are to be fresh, provocative and entertaining and generally achieves them by presenting im-

Old-fashioned Leeds entertainment—Music Hall at the famous City Varieties.

aginative theatre from around Britain and abroad. A purpose-built black-box type of theatre, the house capacity is 89 but usually feels good even with an audience of 50. The stage is big enough for the meatier productions. Look out for The Studio's free glossy programme at information centres, libraries and galleries or call/write and ask to be placed on the free mailing list for news of forthcoming productions. All of the advertised performances are open to the public. All seats are one price (subject to change) and very good value. A bar is open before each show and during the interval.

☛ *Part of Leeds Polytechnic City Campus, Leeds LS1 3HE. Faces Woodhouse Lane, on left just before BBC.*

☎ *Leeds 833134.*

Leeds University Theatres

There are four theatres within the campus, only two of which are open to the general public.

The Raven Theatre, run by the University Union, stages 10-15 productions a year in a 200-seater "black box", situated in a basement of the main Union building. Mostly student drama, with occasional touring company featured.

The Riley Smith Hall, also in the Union building, has a regular programme of big musicals, cabaret and light opera, performed by three of the university's theatre/operatic groups.

Open to students and academic staff only are the **Studio Theatre** (in the Emmanuel Institute) and the **Workshop Theatre** (in the Arts Block). Each seats 60. They are part of the School of English. About a dozen under and postgraduate productions a year.

☛ *Leeds University is in Woodhouse Lane, Leeds LS2.*

☎ *Information line giving details of current and forthcoming productions at the Raven and Riley Smith—Leeds 314253. Studio & Workshop Theatre information—Leeds 334720.*

Alternative Cabaret

From small beginnings in the 1980s alternative cabaret has entered the mainstream of British comedy. Acts like Vic Reeves and Jerry Sadowitz got their own TV shows, as did Leeds favourite Henry Normal. Performances ignore traditional boundaries between such things as theatre, poetry, stand-up comedy, juggling, mime, impressionism and music. They are predictably unpredictable, irreverent, often politico-satirical and never boring. An important change from the days of the *Jokers Wild* school of comedy is that they are non-sexist and non-racist. New events in West Yorkshire are being advertised all the time and it's worth keeping a regular eye on the "performing arts" pages of the *Northern Star* What's On guide. *NS*, incidentally, have done much to encourage alternative cabaret in the region by sponsoring a competition.

Leeds Alternative Cabaret. Richard Mason is one of the AC pioneers and his shows have included names like Henry Normal, Spitting Image's Steve Coogan (we'll miss his spluttering Roy Hattersley) and Hattie Hayridge from Red Dwarf to name but three. His shows get packed out early when there's a big name on so be there in good time.

☛ *Leeds Alternative Cabaret's regular night is the 1st Sunday of the month at the Duchess of York, Vicar Lane, Leeds. Start at 7.30pm. Starting 1993, also every second month at the City Varieties. For programme, see Northern Star or send s.a.e. to LAC at 12b Archery Street, Leeds LS2 9AS.*

☎ *Leeds 460128.*

The Bradford Alhambra

The Alhambra's domes are just as familiar to theatregoers from Leeds as they are to the population of Bradford. Probably the best-preserved Edwardian theatre outside London, some of the greatest actors and entertainers have appeared on its stage, from Stan Laurel, Gracie Fields and Ernie Wise to Laurence Olivier and Rudolf Nureyev. Many of today's top stars are also regular visitors, as the Alhambra puts on pre and post West End musicals and plays and one of the country's top comedy pantomime seasons. It also receives regular visits from the Royal Shakespeare Company. In the same building is the Alhambra Studio, which accommodates 250 people in a moveable space. It is a Cottesloe-type venue for contemporary theatre, workshops and other events and has a regular programme. It has a particularly successful season of Alternative Cabaret featuring top names.

☛ *In Morley Street, off Princes Way, Bradford. Reached by either a 30-min drive from many parts of Leeds or via train/bus. For programme, write to Bradford Ticket Centre, Bradford BD1 1JS.*

☎ *Programme information: 0274-757575. Credit card bookings (Access & Visa) Mon-Sat 9am-8pm: 0274-752000. Book in person in Leeds at Artlink, Interchange Travel Club, Cavendish Travel, Bond Street Shopping Centre, or the Civic Theatre; in Otley at Waye & Son; in Ilkley at the Information Centre.*

New Leeds entertainment—Alternative Cabaret at the Duchess of York.

Theatre in the Mill

A small Black Box studio theatre on the University of Bradford campus. Its programme reflects the tastes of younger audiences, and usually consists of productions by small-scale touring companies. In tandem with the terms, there are three ten-week seasons a year. Seating is normally for 100, although 140 can be accommodated at some productions. There is a bar selling bottled beers, wines and spirits.

☛ *In Richmond Road, Bradford BD7 1DP. The entrance is off Shearbridge Road. Write for the forthcoming season's programme. Performances always start at 7.30pm.*
☎ *For bookings or information: 0274-733466 ext. 8416.*

Bingley Arts Centre

An impressive theatre for such a small town as Bingley, it seats 375. It is basically a "hiring" theatre, which means that most of the productions are put on by travelling theatre companies, big promoters seeking a medium-sized venue in the safe knowledge that

a large number of regular theatre-goers live out in the Leeds-Bradford-Ilkley triangle. Next door is the well-respected Bingley Little Theatre, which puts on 10 of its own productions a year. There is a bar & café.

☛ *At Main Street, Bingley, BD16 2LZ (next to the Bradford & Bingley Building Society HQ). Box Office is open 10am-5pm Mon-Sat.*
☎ *Bookings: 0274-567982 or 0274-752000. Programme information: 0274-566369.*

Ilkley Playhouse

Home of the Ilkley Players, an amateur company that has been going for over 60 years. A programme of eight plays is staged annually in their theatre close to the River Wharfe, each one running for 10 performances (often more if it's a musical). The Theatre, which has been fully modernised, has a raked first-floor auditorium, with seating for 130, and a 40ft. deep proscenium stage that is large for such a small venue. It allows the Players full scope with larger productions. There is a bar on the ground floor (interval drinks may be ordered in advance). Leaflets giving the full programme are available from public buildings and libraries in Wharfedale or from tourist information centres.

☛ *Ilkley Playhouse, Weston Road, Ilkley, LS29 8DW. Box office open for personal/telephone bookings from Monday before each production to end of run. Open 11am-2.30pm and 6.30pm-8pm.*
☎ *0943-609539.*

Harrogate Theatre

A good regional repertory theatre run by an independent charitable trust, the Harrogate Theatre puts on its own productions from September through to May. These are a series of eight straight plays, plus a family pantomime running for a month through the Christmas season. From May to late-August local groups take over, plus one-nighters by touring professionals. Built in 1900, the theatre seats 500 and has a bar. A small Studio Theatre, seating 50, is used for occasional performances by small professional companies. Write or phone for free programme.

☛ *Oxford Street, Harrogate, HG1 1QF.*
☎ *Box office: 0423-502116 (Access/Visa/Amex bookings). Other enquiries: 0423-502710.*

Other Theatres

Although there are enough theatres in the Leeds-Bradford area to satisfy all tastes, don't ignore the other theatres in the region.

Dewsbury. A good small local authority run theatre is Dewsbury Arts Centre (capacity 176) in Upper Road, Batley Carr, Dewsbury. Home of Dewsbury Arts Group, which puts on six major productions a year. Also occasional performances by small touring companies.
☎ *0924-461706.*

Huddersfield. Small touring companies enjoy playing the Venn Street Arts Centre (capacity 200), at Venn Street, Huddersfield.
☎ *0484-422903.*

Richmond. One of only two Georgian theatres left in Britain is the Georgian Theatre Royal at Richmond, the "capital of Swaledale". Bristol has the other. Well worth a visit, perhaps at the end of a day in the Dales. In Victoria Road, Richmond, North Yorkshire, DL10 4DW. (Write or phone for mailing list).
☎ *0748-823021.*

Scarborough. Famous for Alan Ayckbourn premiers is Scarborough's excellent Stephen Joseph Theatre in the Round. If you've planned at day at the Yorkshire coast, it might be worthwhile rounding it off with a performance here. Write or call for programme. In Valley Bridge Parade, Scarborough YO11 2PL.
☎ *0743-378863.*

Sheffield. A city with several theatres, the best being the modern Crucible, a two-theatre complex with an artistic policy similar to Leeds's West Yorkshire Playhouse. At 55 Norfolk Street, S1 1DA. There's also the beautifully restored Lyceum Theatre, for more traditional touring theatre with top names. Close to the Crucible in Norfolk Street.
☎ *For both venues: 0742-769922.*

Wakefield. The splendid Theatre Royal & Opera House gets many good variety shows and medium-sized touring productions. Appropriately, in Drury Lane, Wakefield. ☎ 0924-366556.

York. The refurbished Theatre Royal is easy to reach by train and a performance can be taken in at the end of a day trip to the walled city. Medium-sized touring plays, musicals and fine repertory theatre. Call or write for programme. In St. Leonard's Place, York YO1 2HD.
☎ 0904-623568.

Music & Opera

Leeds is renowned as one of the foremost regional cities in Europe for its musical life. While its concert seasons receive many distinguished visitors from Britain and abroad, the essence of Leeds's cultural success is the important part played by the city's own community. For Leeds is home to numerous highly regarded names in the music world, from the internationally famous triennial Leeds Piano Competition and its founder, the local piano teacher Fanny Waterman, to one of the finest regional opera companies in Opera North. And few cities can boast such a wealth of home-grown talent like the Leeds Festival Chorus, the Leeds Philharmonic Chorus and the English Northern Philharmonia. Throughout the Leeds area, for 52 weeks a year, there is always a concert or recital

to be found. Many are in historic settings, like the Long Gallery of Temple Newsam, one of the greatest stately houses in Northern England, or the Victorian splendour of Leeds Town Hall and Leeds Parish Church. Others allow a rare opportunity for townsfolk to visit Leeds Grammar School and the Clothworkers' Hall of Leeds University. With festivals, and the special events that they spawn, becoming a regular summer occurrence in the area, the outlook seems bright for the Leeds concert-goer of the 1990s. The following venues and events represent the regular musical life of Leeds but, of course, there are many one-off concerts and seasons advertised in local listings magazines.

Harewood Summer Classics
This highly acclaimed series of open air orchestral concerts in summer is very popular with Leeds audiences. Making the most of being outdoors, performances are often accompanied by fireworks, torch and candlelight. They are truly memorable when the weather's fine. The stage is set in the Capability Brown-designed grounds of Harewood House, home of Lord Harewood, the Queen's cousin.
☛ *Harewood House is on the A61 Leeds-Harrogate road at the junction with A659. For booking and concert information, write or*

phone Performing Arts Management Ltd., 103 South West Avenue, Bollington, Macclesfield, Cheshire, SK10 5DX.
☎ *0625-573477.*

Lunchtime Chamber Music
A well-established programme of recitals takes place in the lecture theatre of Leeds City Art Gallery every other Wednesday from September to May. Lasting around 50 minutes, they range from piano or harp soloists to quintets. Admission is free, but there is a collection. A programme for the forthcoming season is available at libraries and information centres each summer.
☛ *Leeds City Art Gallery faces The Headrow, Leeds.*
☎ *To check date of next recital, call Leeds 478303.*

Lunchtime Organ Music
The great Victoria Hall of Leeds Town Hall is dominated by one of the largest organs in Europe, installed between August 1857 and April 1859. The massive cast iron casing was designed by the building's architect, Cuthbert Brodrick, and was played for the first time at its official opening by Queen Victoria. Today, having been virtually rebuilt in 1972, the organ is played at an (almost) weekly Tuesday lunchtime recital, starting at 1.05pm, often by the Leeds City Organist Simon Lindley or by a guest performer. Works can include Bach, Handel, Mozart, or Vaughan Williams, Elgar or Ireland's O'Connor Morris. As many as 500 people attend each of these recitals. The season runs from September to June, admission is free but there is a collection. A programme for the forthcoming season is available at libraries and information centres each summer.
☛ *Leeds Town Hall is on The Headrow, Leeds.*

Leeds Parish Church
The beautifully restored interior of the Parish Church of St. Peters (consecrated in 1841) makes a fine setting for choral music. Besides its daily evensong, the church has a regular programme of recitals by its own Choir and by St. Peter's Singers & Chamber Orchestra.

Leeds Civic Arts Guild

Would you like to get involved in a theatrical, musical or operatic production yourself? The Leeds Civic Arts Guild is an association of amateur companies using Leeds Civic Theatre. They include:

Cosmopolitan Players
Dance Roundabout
Headingley Amateur OperaticSociety
Leeds Amateur Operatic Society
Leeds Art Theatre
Leeds Arts Centre

Leeds Children's Theatre
Leeds Gilbert and Sullivan Society
Leeds Insurance Dramatic and Operatic Society
Leeds Theatre Dance Company
Leeds Thespians
Leeds Youth Opera Group
Pioneer Players
Proscenium Players
Screaming Blue Murder Theatre Co.
Tinderbox Theatre Company
West Riding Opera
Youth Theatre North

☛ **For details of performances or involvement in productions write to the Honorary Secretary of the group that interests you, c/o Stansfield Chambers, Great George Street, Leeds LS1 3DW.**

The former, a chamber choir of 36 mixed voices, is widely regarded as one of the best in Yorkshire, and they are renowned for music of the baroque period, especially by J. S. Bach. In this they are supported by the Chamber Orchestra.
☛ *Leeds Parish Church is in Kirkgate, on the south-eastern fringe of Leeds city centre. Concerts are advertised in local events listings and by leaflets at libraries, etc.*

Leeds International Concert Season

Leeds City Council regularly wins awards for the best music provision by a local authority. Backbone of its annual programme, and of the city's cultural life for decades, has been this season of 20 or more symphony concerts in the cavernous Victoria Hall of Leeds Town Hall, once described by the Illustrated London News as "one of the noblest public rooms in the country". Held on Saturday evenings from September to June, the programme is tailored to suit the largely conservative tastes of Leeds audiences. So expect to see much Beethoven, Brahms, Chopin, Handel, Mendelssohn, Mozart, Schumann and Tchaikovsky. But there is usually a more adventurous end to this diet, with works by Mahler, Stravinsky and Shostakovich; sometimes English music by Elgar and Vaughan Williams; and American composers like George Gershwin,

Bernstein or Copland. A free programme listing all concerts in the season is available throughout Leeds every summer. You can obtain discounts between 10%-20% for booking all or several concerts at once. There are also reductions for pensioners, students, families and the unwaged. A closed loop system for the hard of hearing has been installed in Leeds Town Hall.
☛ *All concerts are in Victoria Hall, Leeds Town Hall, The Headrow, Leeds LS1. Concerts begin Saturday nights, September to June, at 7.30pm. A free pre-concert talk about the evening's programme begins at 6.45pm. For booking information, call the City Centre Box Office, Leeds Civic Theatre, 10am-8pm Mon-Sat.*
✆ *Leeds 476962 or Leeds 455505.*

Temple Newsam International Chamber Music

Some of the leading players in the world of Chamber Music appear at this annual, justly popular season in the Long Gallery of historic Temple Newsam. The series of eight concerts is one Tuesday evening per month, from October to May, and consist of all styles and tastes, from brass ensembles to harpsichord, classical guitar and the more traditional string ensemble. All concerts start at 7.30pm and finish at approximately 9.30pm. Refreshments are available during the interval. Discounts of 20% are available for bookings

of all eight concerts; a 15% discount is available for bookings of four concerts.
☛ *Temple Newsam is on the east side of Leeds, signposted off the A63 Leeds-Selby road. For booking information, contact the City Centre Box Office 10am-8pm Mon-Sat.*
✆ *Leeds 476962 or Leeds 455505.*

City of Leeds College of Music

The city's centre of excellence for the study of music promotes many good concerts. They include regular Wednesday evening performances, and the accent is on surprise with such features as Indian classical and 16th and 17th century guitar music, or big band sounds, jazz or symphony concerts. The CLCM has, since the 1960s, put on a festival every March with venues including Leeds Town Hall and the Leeds Institute Gallery at the Civic Theatre. The broad programme provides a showcase for the college's students, of which there are 350 in full-time study and over 2,500 in part-time education. They provide some of the liveliest music available in the city.
☛ *The college's concerts are advertised in leaflets, widely available in the Leeds area, and in the various What's On listings. Information about concerts is available from the main College Office, 43a Woodhouse Lane, Leeds LS2 8JT.*
✆ *Leeds 432491. Tickets box office: Leeds 462453 or 476962.*

Leeds University Concerts

One of the most important developments in the musical life of Leeds in the last 20 years was the conversion of the former Cavendish Presbyterian Church to the Clothworkers' Centenary Concert Hall at the University of Leeds. Whilst retaining most of the church's original features, an acoustically pleasing auditorium has been developed with its own grand piano, harpsichord and chamber organ. The hall is the setting for a number of regular concerts throughout the year. These may be performed by the Sinfonia of Leeds or another of the area's leading orchestras, or by orchestras and ensembles from else

A symphony concert at Leeds Town Hall.

where. Being a medium-sized venue the programmers can afford to take risks, making for some-times unusual concerts.

☛ *The Clothworkers' Concert Hall is on the campus of the University of Leeds, off Woodhouse Lane, Leeds LS2 9JT.*
☎ *Leeds 334082.*

Opera North

The cultural reputation of Leeds was greatly enhanced by the establishment of this professional opera company in 1978. And it has gone from strength to strength, with audiences steadily increasing both at its Grand Theatre base and on tour. Although founded as the northern branch of English National Opera (but on the model of the Welsh and Scottish companies) it achieved its full independence in 1981 and is recognised as one of the UK's five full-time opera companies. Up to 10 different productions are presented at the Grand Theatre each year, playing to audiences in excess of 90 per cent of house capacity. The scope of Opera North's productions ranges from Verdi's melodramatic Rigoletto to the side-splitting humour of L'Etoile and The Love For Three Oranges. But the company really excels with opera on the grand scale like Boris Godunov. The principal singers are guests drawn from the international pool of opera singers in order to ensure the best casts possible. These have included such

big names as Dennis O'Neill, Josephine Barstow, John Treleaven, Janice Cairns, Sergei Leiferkus and John Tomlinson. When the operas close in Leeds, they go on tour to major provincial centres like Nottingham, Manchester, Sheffield, Birmingham and York. There have also been overseas tours to Dortmund and Wiesbaden in Germany and to Rotterdam. Essential to Opera North's success has been its orchestra, the English Northern Philharmonia, which enjoys an independent existence. Altogether, the company employs 160 people, which comprises the 54-member orchestra, a standing chorus of 36, music staff of 14, technical staff of 36 and around 20 administration. Subscription brochures for each new season are available from libraries, public buildings and information centres around Leeds, or by post from Leeds Grand Theatre.

☛ *Opera North is at The Grand Theatre, 46 New Briggate, Leeds LS1 6NZ. Write or call to join free mailing list. Booking office is open from 10am-7.30pm Mon-Sat. Payment by post (with s.a.e.) or by phone (Artscard/Access/Visa/Amex/Diners). Seating is: stalls, dress circle, upper circle, centre balcony, upper and side balcony, dress circle and upper circle boxes.*
☎ *Opera North Hotline: Leeds 445326. Grand Theatre box office: Leeds 459351/440971.*

The Leeds Conductors' Competition

This exciting biennial event, first started in 1984, has become one of the most popular music competitions in the North of England. It was devised by a former council music officer, Michael Johnson, who saw that while there were contests for brass, pianists, singers, string players and woodwind there was a glaring lack of competitiveness among conductors. The idea was an immediate hit, and over 70 conductors aged under 35 applied for the first Leeds Conductors' Competition. Around 20 are finally put to the test each time, and the reputations of previous winners—Sian Edwards, Grant Llewellyn and Martyn Brabbins—speak volumes for the standard of entries the competitions attracts. Contests have attracted a dozen different orchestras each time for the concerts at Leeds Town Hall and the Institute Gallery of the Civic Theatre, including the Hallé, Royal Philharmoic, London Philharmonic and English Sinfonia.

☛ *The Competition is run by Leeds City Council. Events are listed in Artscene and What's On. For further information, contact The Music Officer, Leeds Leisure Services Department, 19 Wellington Street, Leeds LS1 4DG.*

Leeds International Pianoforte Competition

This triennial event is the foundation of Leeds's cultural fame world-wide, and it has brought some of the top young pianists to the city in the last quarter of a century. Perhaps only Moscow's competition is more prestigious. Past winners and famous participants have included Murray Perahia, Radu Lupu, Rafael Droxco, Dmitri Alexeev, Vladimir Ovchinikov, Andras Schiff, Mitsuko Uchida, Bernard D'Ascoli and Ju Hee Suh. So many entries are received that a preliminary selection (by past awards) has to take place to fit the competition into its usual two weeks in September. In the past the event has been split between first stages at Leeds University, finals (which are televised) at Leeds Town Hall. The founder and chair-

Geoffrey Dolton and three masqueraders in Opera North's "Masquerade".

man, Fanny Waterman, is herself a highly respected member of juries at international musical events.

☛ *The Competition's address is: Woodgarth, Oakwood Grove, Leeds LS8.*

☎ *Leeds 655771.*

Bradford Orchestral & Choral Season

Bradford still has the fine Orchestral and Choral seasons founded by European immigrants in the mid-19th century. It was through their enthusiasm that the famous Hallé Orchestra made Bradford its second home. As in Leeds, the programming used to be traditional, but today 20th century works are included. Orchestral and Choral Seasons are now combined in the famous 1,800 seater St. George's Hall. The season runs from September until May and contains around 15 concerts: 12 orchestral and three choral (The Hallé still accounts for half the Orchestral season). The Choral season is by the Bradford Festival Choral Society. Performances, on Friday and Saturdays, begin at 7.30pm and last about two hours. There is a pre-concert talk at 6.45pm.

☛ *St. George's Hall is in Hall Ings, Bradford BD1 (next to Bradford Interchange). For a free copy of the season's programme, write to Bradford Theatres Box Office, 64-66 Morley Street, Bradford BD7 1AQ. For bookings, contact Bradford Ticket Centre below.*

☎ *Bradford (0274) 752000 & 567982.*

Bradford Chamber Season

Bradford Cathedral, with its impressive medieval nave, is a first-class venue for these concerts with internationally respected artists such as the London Mozart Players, John Lill, New Budapest String Quartet and the Albion Ensemble. The season runs from October to April, on the first Friday of the month, starting at 7.30pm. There are about 350 seats, bookable in the centre nave, north and south aisles.

☛ *Bradford Cathedral, Church Bank, Bradford city centre. For free programme, write to Bradford Theatres Box Office, 64-66 Morley Street, Bradford BD7 1AQ.*

Ilkley Concert Club

At least seven chamber concerts are held annually at the King's Hall, Ilkley, with outstanding artists of the calibre of Lindsay String Quartet. The season runs from October to May and is usually a sell-out.

☛ *For further information, contact the Booking Secretary, Ilkley Concert Club, 22 Sunset Drive, Ilkley, LS29 8LS.*

☎ *Ilkley (0943) 609744.*

Best of Brass

Some of the best Brass Bands in Europe are from Yorkshire, and this annual season of concerts features famous names like the Grimethorpe Colliery, Brighouse & Rastrick, John Foster Black Dyke Mills and the Yorkshire Imperial. The concerts are once a month, October to March, at Morley (Saturdays), Yeadon (Wednesdays) and Garforth (Thurdays). All are 7.30pm start.

☛ *Venues are—Morley Town Hall, Queen Street, Morley; Yeadon Town Hall, High Street, Yeadon; Garforth Comprehensive School, Lidgett Lane, Garforth. Tickets bookable at City Centre Box Office, Civic Theatre, Cookridge Street.*

☎ *Leeds 476962 or Leeds 455505.*

Ballet & Dance

Despite being 200 miles from London, the Leeds area misses nothing when it comes to ballet and contemporary dance. All the famous names pay frequent visits, while the region's top home-grown companies have programmes of regular performances locally. Smaller events also turn up in unusual places like church and school halls and it is worthwhile checking the "Dance and Mime" section of the free monthly listings magazine *Artscene*. In particular, Leeds is renowned for its dancers from the multi-racial inner city. Harehills Middle School provides the seeds that produce some of the best youth dancers in Britain.

The Grand Theatre

Still the major ballet venue in Leeds with annual visits from the Birmingham Royal Ballet and London Contemporary Dance. Occasional visitors include the Ballet Rambert, London Festival Ballet, the Northern Ballet Theatre and one-off high profile appearances by major international companies like the Harlem Dance Theatre. The Grand has around 1,500 seats—stalls, dress circle, upper circle, balcony, upper balcony and boxes for 4, 5 or 8.

☛ *The Grand is in New Briggate, Leeds LS1 6NZ. Box Office open 10am-7.30pm Mon-Sat. Bookings also taken by post. Enclose s.a.e. to the address above making cheque payable to Grand Theatre, Leeds.*

☎ *Information about latest/future ballet programme: Leeds 443509. Bookings by telephone (Access/Visa/Diners/Amex) on Leeds 459351 or 440971. Or book by fax machine: Leeds 465906.*

The Bradford Alhambra

Mobile Leeds residents are often attracted by the programme at this fine Edwardian theatre. The Alhambra receives twice-yearly visits, in the spring and autumn, from two top companies—Northern Ballet and English National Ballet—plus performances by the Scottish Ballet, the Birmingham Royal Ballet and contemporary works by such names as the Rambert Dance Company.

☛ *In Morley Street, off Princes Way, Bradford. Reached by either a 30-min drive from many parts of Leeds or via train/bus. For programme, write to Bradford Ticket Centre, Bradford BD1 1JS.*

☎ *Programme information: 0274-757575. Credit card bookings (Access/Visa) Mon-Sat 9am-8pm: 0274-752000.*

The Dome Theatre

Home of the Northern School of Contemporary Dance, this former Great Synagogue is a lively centre for all aspects of dance. Opened in 1985 with funds from Leeds Education Authority, its main brief was to provide vocational dance training for young people who previously had to leave Leeds to find their professional training. But the school has steadily expanded to draw talented young dancers from throughout the country. At the heart of the school's work is its three year course in contemporary dance. But there is also training in other aspects of dance including classical ballet, choreography, allied arts, music, lighting and costume design. Full-time course work is just one aspect of the school's life. The school does much work in the community, and tens of thousands have benefited from its regular evening and weekend part-time classes for children and adults. The Dome has seating for around 200 and the school promotes performances for the public there most Saturday nights, usually beginning at 7.30pm. Ring or write for free programme of forthcoming events.

☛ *Northern School of Contemporary Dance, 98 Chapeltown Road, Leeds LS7 4BH.*
☎ *Leeds 625359.*

Phoenix Dance Company

A string of major awards confirm Yorkshire's only professional dance company as a growing force on the world's contemporary dance stage. From unambitious origins in November, 1981, the Phoenix has grown into a highly respected touring repertory company that proudly promotes its Leeds background wherever it plays. As a reviewer for the *Washington Post* said, "Why it should seem surprising that a troupe as sensationally fine and exciting as Phoenix Dance Company should hail from Leeds, England, I'm not so sure." The Phoenix started life as an all-male company of three dancers, quickly expanded to five and brought in female dancers at the close of the 1980s. Still the only predominantly black touring contemporary dance company in Europe, its policy is to constantly seek new audiences for dance, especially in a multi-cultural society. It tours nationally and internationally for around six months a year. Each programme consists of five or six varied works, from short solo pieces to full company works sometimes with live musicians. Although it has its own internal choreographers, the performance programme also contains work choreographed by major guests from home and abroad. Locally,

venues used by the Phoenix include the West Yorkshire Playhouse, The Dome (home of the Northern School of Contemporary Dance) and the Wakefield Theatre Royal. These annual seasons are advertised in Artscene and other listings. For the remaining six months the company pursues an "Access Programme" which enables the Leeds community to become involved with the Phoenix at its studios in rehearsals, workshops, professional classes, etc. If you would like information about this programme write to the the address below.

☛ *Phoenix Dance Company's base and studio (within the Yorkshire Dance Centre) is at 3 St. Peter's Buildings, St. Peter's Square, Leeds LS9 8AH.*
☎ *Leeds 423486.*

The Phoenix Dance Company in "Sacred Space".

Yorkshire Dance Centre

Want to explore or expand your children's or your own dancing talents? One of the finest resources in Leeds is the Yorkshire Dance Centre. In a refurbished former clothing factory beside West Yorkshire Playhouse, it provides dance experience covering artistic, social educational, health and recreation interests. The centre is open seven days a week for pupils aged three and upwards. Styles taught include classical ballet, jazz dance, tap and mime, through contemporary dance and keep fit, movement for pregnancy and birth as well as many international dances.

☛ *Yorkshire Dance Centre, 3 St. Peter's Buildings, St. Peter's Square, Leeds LS9 8AH. Write or call for free brochure.*
☎ *Leeds 426066.*

Jazz

Live jazz is on offer in the Leeds area every week, and almost every night if you include the regular and one-off pub and café bar gigs. Styles range from New Orleans & Trad by greatly respected Leeds pub players like the Ed O'Donnell Band, through frequent visits to the city by British mainstream jazz luminaries like Humphrey Lyttleton and George Melly, *avant-garde* improvisation at The Termite Club and top contemporary jazz names from the United States, Latin America and Europe promoted by Leeds Jazz. This section deals with the well-established venues/promotions, but new gigs—especially free jazz in pubs—may be added from time to time.

Leeds Jazz

One of Britain's most successful jazz promoters is Leeds Jazz, a small group of fans who got tired of having to drive to other northern cities for their entertainment. Since 1984, they have brought to the city luminaries like Memphis Slim, Steve Lacy, Art Blakey and John Scofield. But since they do it for the love of jazz rather than profit, they are prepared to lose money on more esoteric acts like Renee Rosnes or the jazz drummer Jack Degohnette. The annual programmes are a juggling act between big names like Leeds-born guitarist Alan Holdsworth (ex-Colosseum, Soft Machine & Lifetime), which make a profit, and those that are known only to the *cognoscenti* and, often, wipe out the profit. Many of the acts they promote play only Leeds and London in their European tours, so Leeds Jazz draws fans from a wide area of the north and the midlands. Venues depend on the drawing power of the act. Biggest is the Irish Centre (up to 800, drinks served in hall). Next is the University's Riley Smith Hall (up to 600 but no drinks in hall). Smallest is the West Indian Centre (200, drinks in hall). They promote around 15-20 concerts a year from October to May, working out at two per month.

☛ *The main Leeds Jazz venue is the Irish Centre, York Road, Leeds LS9* ☎ *Leeds 480613. Other venues are Leeds University Riley Smith Hall, Woodhouse Lane, Leeds LS2* ☎ *439071; West Indian Centre, off Chapeltown Road, Leeds LS7* ☎ *Leeds 629496. For list of forthcoming promotions, send s.a.e. to Leeds Jazz, 5 Coniston Avenue, Leeds LS6 2BD. City centre ticket outlet is Jumbo Records, St. John's Centre.*
☎ *Leeds Jazz enquiries: Leeds 742486.*

The Gallery

The only true late-night jazz club venue in Leeds for many years has been at The Gallery, under different names, and at the time of writing promoted as Dig. It happens every Wednesday night, 10pm-2am, and features good life modern jazz from the best local bands and top names from London. The promoters describe it as "Hard Bop-Latin-Organ-Grooves-Acid Jazz-Soul-Fusion-Grooves." In an adjoining room, there is Jazz/Latin disco the same evening called Arcadia, and customers are free to drift between the two. Very popular with older students and academic staff during term time.
☛ *Lower Merrion Street, Leeds LS2.*
☎ *Leeds 575165.*

Termite Club

Starting off way back in 1983 as the sole provider of avant-garde jazz improvisation in Leeds, The Termite has gradually tried to extend its brief. As a result, there have been recent forays into Industrial Thrash Metal territory and groups who have arrived at improvisation via house and rock rather than jazz. But jazz is still the central force demanded by The Termite's small but consistently loyal audiences. Top British names in jazz improvisation like Derek Bailey and Fred Frith are joined by stars from Europe and the United States. Audiences are mostly in the 30-50 range, over 100 for the bigger names. With grants from Leeds City Council and Yorkshire Arts, the Termite seems set to continue serving improvised jazz etc. in Leeds for the

foreseeable future. The programme runs all year and is usually monthly, on a Friday night (8.30pm start) at one of the venues below.
☛ *The Termite Club uses three different venues, according to availability. They are: Haddon Hall, Bankfield Road, LS4.* ☎ *751115; The Adelphi, Leeds Bridge, LS10* ☎ *456377; The Three Legs, The Headrow, LS1* ☎ *456316. For information about forthcoming gigs, watch Northern Star or contact the promoter Paul Buckton.*
☎ *Leeds 742006.*

Jazz at West Yorkshire Playhouse

The top traditional jazz venue in Leeds has become the West Yorkshire Playhouse, with an annual season of Sunday night concerts in its 750-seat Quarry Theatre. The biggest names on the British jazz scene over the last 30 years appear here—George Melly, Humphrey Lyttleton, Acker Bilk, Ronnie Scott and Kenny Ball. But there is also room for highly acclaimed newer acts like the Pasadena Roof Orchestra and the Pizza Express All-Stars. Before the shows, there is usually free jazz in the Playhouse's Huntsman Bar. Concerts are one Sunday per month, October to March, and start at 8pm.
☛ *West Yorkshire Playhouse is in Quarry Hill Mount, Leeds LS9. Jazz season programme is available free throughout city (libraries, etc.) from August.*
☎ *Tickets available from the Playhouse (Leeds 442111) and from City Centre Box Office at the Civic Theatre, Cookridge Street (Leeds 476962 or 455505).*

CLCM Jazz

As the sound of saxes, double bass and drums often testify to bus stop queues opposite the Merrion Centre in Woodhouse Lane, the City of Leeds College of Music is a lively centre for jazz. The college is home to several good jazz combos and a Big Band, and promotes regular concerts at its own auditorium, the Institute Gallery, which is part of Leeds Civic Theatre. Concerts are throughout the year in term time (October to

June), usually on Wednesday evenings at 7.30pm. (This programme incidentally, is mixed with classical concerts as described on page 80). But centrepiece of the college's jazz promotions is its annual jazz festival, held each February. Every evening from Monday to Saturday, there is a top act like George Melly and the National Youth Jazz Orchestra. During the festival there is also free lunchtime and late-evening jazz in the theatre bar.

☛ *For free details of events, write to the Concerts & Promotions Officer, CLCM, 43a Woodhouse Lane, Leeds LS2 8JT. Tickets for concerts are available from the City Centre Box Office, Civic Theatre, Cookridge Street, Leeds LS2 8BH.*

☎ *Leeds 452069 (CLCM); Leeds 476962 (Box Office).*

Alhambra Studio

An annual season of jazz runs at the Bradford Alhambra's "little brother" from September to early April. As befits a small studio theatre, there is an intimate jazz club atmosphere for such names as Jim Mullen, Martin Giltrap, Ronnie Scott, Barbara Thompson, Bobby Wellins and Clark Tracy. An audience of 250 is seated at round tables, and there is a bar. Write or call for programme.

☛ *The Alhambra Studio has its own entrance in Morley Street, Bradford BD1.*

☎ *Bookings: 0274-752000. Programme information: 0274-757575.*

Pub Jazz

A number of jazz residences at Leeds pubs and café bars have been drawing good audiences for several years. There is usually no admission charge, but there may be a collection for the band. The best window on new dates is the What's On section of *Northern Star* and the Jazz and New Music listings of *Artscene*.
Adelphi Hotel, *Leeds Bridge, Leeds LS10.* ☎ *456377.* Trad. jazz every Saturday with the Ed O'Donnell Band. 8.30pm start.
The Central, *88 Wellington Street, Leeds LS1.* ☎ *453927.* Long-running jazz night is Sun-

days, 8.30pm. Often jazz funk.
Eagle Tavern, *North Street, Leeds LS7.* ☎ *457146.* For many years the Trad. Ed. O'Donnell Band has played here on Sunday lunchtimes, 12.30pm start.
George Hotel, *Great George Street, Leeds LS1.* ☎ *453232.* For years, there's been a jazz jam session every Thursday night, featuring various members of the group Something Else. 8.30pm start.
Royal Oak, *60 North Street, Wetherby.* ☎ *Wetherby 583010.* Trad jazz every Tuesday, 8.45pm start, with the White Eagles Jazz Band.

Folk

The main folk music diet in the area is served up in pubs. While some still stay true to finger-in-the-ear traditional folk, most have adopted a contemporary approach. If you are interested in folk music it is worth getting West Yorkshire's own Folk Magazine, *Tyke's News.*

☛ *Tyke's News is available from 408 Skipton Road, Utley Keighley, BD20 6HP.*

☎ *Ring for details. 0535-606939.*

The Grove

Folk and The Grove are synonymous in Leeds. Friday nights are club night (8.30pm start) in the concert room, usually with a traditional session simultaneously in the tap room. Guests range from popular Yorkshire artists to the occasional national name. There's a jam session in the tap room on Tuesday nights, a guest playing folk or blues on Wednesday nights, and the last Thursday of each month is Bluegrass Night.

☛ *Back Row, Hunslet, Leeds LS11.*

☎ *Leeds 439254.*

Leeds University Folk Club

Every Sunday night during term time, the club is open to non-students. A mix of singers' nights and guests, with the latter usually being among the best names on the northern circuit (Bob Greenwood's Rhythm Rascals, Maggie Boyle and Steve Tilston to name a few). Tries to cater for traditional and

contemporary tastes. Based for many years at The Packhorse pub in Woodhouse Lane, possibly moving in 1993. Ring for details or students can see posters around the campus.

☛ *Club enquiries: 23 Harold View, Leeds LS6.*

☎ *Leeds 789995.*

Micklethwaite's Folk Club

A newish club that has slowly developed a strong following. Held on the 2nd and 4th Thursdays of the month (not August) at 8.30pm there are many guest nights, featuring well-known names from the national folk festival scene, plus the best of good Yorkshire talent. Club policy is to achieve a balance of traditional and contemporary. Every third night is singers night.

☛ *At Horsforth Club, near The Fleece, New Road Side, Horsforth.*

☎ *For club information, Leeds 591808.*

Bag o' Shoddy Folk Club

One of the best-respected folk venues in West Yorkshire, the Bag prefers its guests to be the big names on the national folk scene like Martin Carthy and Vin Garbutt. Shows a preference for traditional folk. The club is held every Saturday night from September to June (8.45pm start), with alternate singer/musician nights.

☛ *The Old Wine & Spirits Vaults, Huddersfield Road (A62), Birstall.*

☎ *Leeds 535387.*

Otley Folk Club

Longest running and most popular club in Wharfedale. Held every Wednesday night, alternating boisterous singers' nights and good quality guest nights.

☛ *Whittakers Arms, Kirkgate, Otley, LS21.*

☎ *0943-462773.*

The Topic

Billed as "probably" the world's oldest folk club, Bradford's Topic was established in 1956 and has seen folk revivals come and go almost as often as Elton John has announced his retirement. All the top names have appeared here, including Peggy Seeger, Ewan MacColl, Martin Carthy, The Spinners, The Watersons, Archie

Fisher. It caters for more modern tastes too with the likes of Harvey Andrews and Leon Rosselson. Well attended by Leeds folk fans for decades, The Topic now has moved to a new home in the Peel Hotel, but it still puts on only the top British folk names. The club is held every Friday evening from 8.30pm. Cheap tapes/record stall.
☛ *The Peel Hotel, Richmond Road, Bradford.*
☎ *Club information on 0535-633578.*

Irish Folk Sessions

The best things in the folk world are often free—a roaring fire, a pulsating bodhran and the heady swirl of fiddles, accordians and tin whistles. The essential pints of foaming stout have to be paid for, of course. The pubs below continue a tradition in Leeds that goes back almost 150 years.
The Globe, *116 Meanwood Road, Leeds LS7.* ☎ *624173.* Very popular Irish sessions on Friday, Saturday and Sunday nights beginning around 9pm. Very informal.
New Roscoe, *Bristol Street, Leeds LS7.* ☎ *460778.* One of the best pubs in the north for regular Irish folk music. Most nights between Wednesday and Saturday (8.30pm start). Session every Sunday lunchtime. Good Tetley ales. Get there early.
White Stag, *North Street, Leeds LS7.* ☎ *451069.* Regular sessions on Monday, Tuesday and Thursday nights (8.30pm start) and occasionally Sunday lunchtime.

Brendan Crocker—"the Blues King of the Aire Delta".

Rock & Pop

The Leeds home-grown music scene was once summed up as "Five hundred bands and ten good ones". Now the area's musicians make their mark on the mainstream. The legacy of The Sisters of Mercy and The Mission means that, to the uninitiated, Leeds is still known as "Gotham City", but other facets of the city's independent talent are coming through, as bands formerly on Indie labels are getting signed up by major record companies. If the resultant music has lost it rougher edge, it is simply because regular wages allow fewer cut corners to produce the sound they want. The Wedding Present are one such, with a marketing campaign that saw them releasing one limited edition seven-inch single per month (one side an original song, the other a favourite cover version), each of which entered the Top 20. Following in the "Weddoes" footsteps are Cud (pictured on page 88), whose energetic live performances and funky pop prompted A&M to make them an offer, and Bridewell, formed by ex-members of the soul/dance band Bridewell Taxis, whose debut single was produced by Roxy Music's Phil Manzanera. The Violet Hour and 29 Palms are two more local outfits that have made it on the major circuit, the latter having supported Marillion. While Leeds has yet to throw up any heavy rock bands of

consequence to match, for example, Sheffield's Def Leppard, some have plenty of potential—Fuzzy Logic, Honeyfungus, D-Rock and Mother Pluto to name four. So whatever you're looking for, whether to madly stage dive to surging punk rock, skank the night away to reggae rhythms, dance yourself dizzy, watch the mega-acts through binoculars at Roundhay Park or just appreciate good songwriting by some of the great survivors of rock who often play at The Irish Centre, Leeds has something for you. Of course, nothing remains the same for long in rock. Especially on the fringes, where many Leeds acts appear to be resident. The best source of news about the latest scene, and concert info, is the "Rock & Pop" section of the weekly *Northern Star*, while details of up-and-coming gigs can also be found in the Pop Post section of the *Evening Post* Saturday edition or, if you can get it, the pop section of *Leeds Weekly News.*

The Indie Scene

The city's Indie scene, always volatile to changing trends, has been healthy for several years and any appraisal can only ever be a mere snapshot in time. But let's try. Leeds is the home of Ablaze! fanzine and its offshoot record label Stuffed Cat, and also the home of the Hemiola label, which delights in bringing strange and wonderful American bands, like Thinking Fellers Union Local 282 and Unrest, to your attention. The upsurge in new American music that occurred in the early 90s has its aficionados, particularly Jellyfish Kiss and Tin Turtle Music, led by eccentric poet "The Butterfly". Edsel Auctioneers' breathless country-tinged thrash, Spectral Alice's psychedelic grunge, and Tsetse Fly's hard-edged pop are responses to the US explosion, while Cool Trader write pop songs in classic style. Big Wednesday take their cues from Joy Division, Swerve redefine the art of Indie-dance, Pale Saints continue to provide beautiful noises in English accents, and Greenhouse play music for those with an environmental conscience.

Acid/Dance Scene

The rise of Hip-Hop, Rap and House music has had a strong effect on the city, which is now one of the centres of the UK's 'acid' scene. Utah Saints' inspired sampling of Annie Lennox and Gwen Guthrie's voices sent their first single 'What Can You Do For Me' into the Top 10, LFO regularly feature in both dance and mainstream charts, and Nightmares on Wax, Ital Rockers and BTI are all acts whose latest white label releases are eagerly awaited in clubs throughout the land; Zero Zero fuse rap with scorching guitar rock samples, in a similar manner to Pop Will Eat Itself, while Mad Love are a duo that generate strong soul sounds. Both should make waves in the 90s.

Black Music

In Leeds, it is concentrated around the Chapeltown area, where acts like Royal Blood, Stone Roots, and Sister B are based. On the August Bank Holiday Sunday, before the annual Carnival, there's usually a free concert in Potternewton Park, which features local acts as well as established stars like Aswad, Cutty Ranks and Daddy Freddy, watch for the posters. Another way of tuning in to the reggae/hip-hop scene is to listen to one of the Community radio stations, like Peoples FM (105.6 FM), or Supreme (102 FM), which give you advance warning of big concerts.

Blues

The blues has always been strong here, and is still thriving in a number of small pub venues. Good local blues/rock bands include Blueprint, Square Foot Brothers, F.O.S. Brothers, The Above Average Weight Band, The John Dixon Band and The Julie Strother Band, most of whom have regular gigs at several Leeds pubs, including The Eagle, The Duck & Drake and The Central. There is a strong following for Brendan Crocker, (pictured left) the Blues King of the Aire Delta, and Steve Phillips (both members of the Notting Hillbillies with Dire Straits' Mark Knopfler), who very occasionally play in the Central or The Grove.

Anarcho-Punk

The Thatcher Years left an interesting footnote to the Leeds scene. A number of so-called anarchist punk bands purvey a strong political message, among them Chumbawamba, a musicians collective whose chaotic cabaret attracts plenty of like-minded followers. The Mekons, original agit-prop popsters of the punk years, are still in business and have embraced both country and dance music. Their various guises include The Church of Country & Western Music and The Regal Yams.

Rock Venues

In Leeds and Bradford, and a half-hour drive down the M1 to Sheffield Arena, local audiences get most of the world's top acts. And many of tomorrow's megastars. From smoky pubs to Roundhay Park Bowl, these are the venues—

Astoria

Spacious without being cavernous, The Astoria has two venues, the Ballroom, which hosts the odd major concert and disco. Meanwhile the cosy downstairs room hosts small gigs by local bands and occasional folk acts. Buses from outside Lewis's in New Briggate will get you there.
☛ *339 Roundhay Road, LS8.*
☎ *490914*

Colosseum

This venue, Leeds's first cinema, has seen many bands in its long history, most recently The Mission, Cud, Wedding Present, 808 State, Boogie Down productions and The Jesus & Mary Chain. Coveted by London's Town & Country Club, who see it as one of the medium-sized quality venues in northern England, featuring top British and American acts. It's difficult to believe it will not remain a good live rock venue in some form.
☛ *Cookridge Street, Leeds LS1.*

Duchess of York

The only venue in the city offering live music seven nights a week, and established as *the* place where smaller Indie bands (especially those from the USA), stop off on UK tours. There's something different every night, such as heavy rock on Wednesdays, "Indie-pop" on Thursdays, and folk/acoustic music/cabaret on Sundays. The Duchess likes to give good up-and-coming local bands a try with regular Awareness Nights. All this mayhem goes on around what is essentially a pub with pint-supping regulars.
☛ *Vicar Lane, Leeds LS1.*
☎ *Leeds 453929.*

The Irish Centre

The Irish Centre hosts concerts by some of the better known Irish acts like Brendan Shine (check their ad in the *Evening Post* on Saturdays), and is also the venue used by Duchess promoter John Keenan when booking medium-sized bands like Mega City Four, or survivors from the 60s and 70s like Wishbone Ash, John Martyn, Christy Moore, Roy Harper, Robert Fripp, Joe Ely and Richard Thompson.
☛ *York Road, Leeds LS9.*
☎ *Leeds 480613.*

Leeds University

Firmly established as one of Leeds' most important venues, the University Refectory's played host to most of the big names of rock and pop down the years. Both The Who and John Martyn have recorded live albums here. Tom Petty and the Heartbreakers even once played it as a support! When packed, it can be quite a crush and the nearest beer's a five-minute walk away. In the Union building there's the Riley Smith Hall, which is similarly unlicensed, where some of the medium-sized bands on the circuit stop off when on tour.
☛ *Woodhouse Lane, Leeds LS2.*
☎ *Leeds 439071.*

Leeds "Polytechnic"

Smaller than the University, but with no less an eye to quality. The Poly has always had the knack of attracting the mega-stars of the future. Acts as diverse as Pink Floyd, Dire Straits, Clash, The Sex Pistols and Nirvana have played here in their teeth-cutting days and look where they ended up! Can be a

bit of a crush at the front but the size of the place means that everyone gets a view.
☛ *Calverley Street, Leeds LS1.*
☎ *Leeds 430171.*

Phoenix Club
Situated off Chapeltown Road, The Phoenix is where to go for good reggae music. Most of the major names from Jamaica stop off here when touring.
☛ *58 Francis Street, Leeds LS7.*
☎ *623619.*

Bradford Queens Hall
One of the busiest venues in the region, The Queens gets most of the top medium-named acts on tour, from The Fall to Joan Armatrading. Part of Bradford College Students Union, the "ballroom" has a capacity of around 900, which makes for an excellent atmosphere. Ticket prices are usually good value.
☛ *Queens Hall is in Morley Street (up the road from the Alhambra), Bradford.*
☎ *0274-392712.*

St. George's Hall
Neighbouring Bradford has one of the top venues east of the Pennines. The St. George's Hall, a grand Victorian building that holds 2,000, is regularly used by Leeds audiences. All medium-sized names on tour top off here—from Prefab Sprout to Motorhead, Julia Fordham to Fairport Convention. Events finish conveniently at 11pm, enabling trains and buses back to Leeds to be caught from the nearby Interchange terminus.
☛ *Hall Ings, Bradford BD1.*
☎ *Bradford (0274) 752376.*

Roundhay Park Bowl
Away from Wembley Stadium and Knebworth, Roundhay Park is the biggest outdoor venue in the UK. The Bowl is a superb grassy amphitheatre and was "christened" in 1982 with the Rolling Stones playing to a 90,000 sell-out audience. Since then, other megastars like Bruce Springsteen, Genesis, Madonna, Simple Minds and Michael Jackson have packed them in. Viewing from the front is usually OK, but further back the performers can look like fleas strutting around a postage stamp, and binoculars are a distinct advantage. Traffic can be chaotic.
☛ *Roundhay Park is on Princess Avenue, Leeds LS8.*

Sheffield Arena
Apart from Roundhay Park, this is Yorkshire's only gig for Platinum-selling artists, from oldies like Paul Simon and Dire Straits to modern biggies like Wet Wet Wet. They draw audiences from Leeds and the rest of the north. It's an easy 30-minute drive down the M1.
☛ *In Broughton La., Sheffield S9.*
☎ *0742-565500 (Information), 0742-483456 (tickets).*

The Warehouse
A long-established small venue, with past rosters including Prefab Sprout, Marc Almond and The Mission. It caters for a wide diversity of tastes. There is a good stage set-up and, when packed out for the bigger names, the atmosphere is second to none. Positioned just off the bottom of The Headrow.
☛ *19 Somers Street, Leeds LS1.*
☎ *Leeds 468287.*

West Indian Centre
Entertainment hub of Leeds's sizable Afro-Caribbean community, and the venue for frequent black and Third World music events which go beyond rock, usually promoted by Soundjata. African, Reggae, South American salsa, etc. Watch *Northern Star* for programme.
☛ *Laycock Place, Leeds LS7.*
☎ *Leeds 629496.*

Cud—Major record label signings from Leeds.

Pub Rock

Many pups have rock/pop/blues/skiffle nights. The list is constantly changing but below are some of the best-established.

The Central, *Wellington Street, Leeds LS1* ☎ 453927. Live music at least two nights a week. Aspiring local bands playing their first gigs, but also some luminaries on the local scene.

Duck & Drake, *Kirkgate, Leeds LS2* ☎ 456806. Great Real Ale bar with mature rock/blues end of live music on Sun, Tues & Thur nights from 8.30pm.

The Eagle Tavern, *North Street, Leeds LS7* ☎ 457146. Has live music Thur, Fri, Sat & Sun nights, 8.30pm start.

Haddon Hall, *Bankfield Road, Leeds LS4* ☎ 751115. Haddon Hall has its own music room for local bands playing their first gigs, to the delight of friends and family, or occasionally a bigger local name. Usually Fri & Sat, 8.30pm.

Royal Park, *Queens Road, Leeds LS6* ☎ 757494. The upstairs music room plays host to both local acts and indie pop/rock bands on debut UK tours, and bands can be found playing at least on Thurs & Fri nights from 8.30pm.

Nightclubs

A few years ago Leeds was not exactly renowned as a nightclubbers' town. All it had was your typical "suit and tie at the weekend" type of place and the odd Goth club left over from the mid 80s. Then came the club revolution, House music and—whether we like it or not—a burst of renewed interest in clubs. People wanted to dance—not just see bands—and Leeds entered into the spirit of things as much as anywhere else. Local promoters and clubs started taking advantage of the change. Suddenly, nights like Kaos and Joy were up there with events in allegedly trendier places like London and Manchester. People even started travelling to Leeds for nightclubs, not just out of it. The city has become—as a result—home to a lively club scene where you can hear a variety of music and relax in all kinds of different atmospheres. In addition to the clubs here, there is a develop-ing scene with one-off events. For example, the Corn Exchange—Leeds's very beautiful and fashionable shopping centre—is being hired at weekends by promoters. Also, both Leeds Polytechnic and Leeds University are used by the major club promoters. Ark at the Poly as well as thrash, 80s and indie nights make this a popular and busy venue and the Uni is beginning to move in the same direction. And watch out for clubs buried away in the satellite towns of Leeds. Unfortunately, they don't always last but a notable example at the time of writing was After Dark at Morley, the home of Orbit, one of Yorkshire's finest rave nights. Unlike a lot of events in the city centre Orbit has a very authentic feel and you don't suspect they've just called it a "rave" and turned the sound up a bit. Clubbers travel from all over the country to wait outside this venue at 7pm. With a new lease of life and the influx of ideas in Leeds, things have never looked—or sounded—so good.

The Warehouse

Most clubs are in the city centre. And Leeds's best known club for some time is The Warehouse. It was big in Goth days and then it was one of the first clubs to start playing House music. It still holds very popular mid-week house events (like Kaos and its sister club Soak) and Fridays and Saturdays are House too. The crowd at weekends has a reputation for being on the younger side but that keeps it lively if nothing else. Rigid security and queues are also a feature. The Warehouse holds mid-week monthly rock and 80s nights and overall its popular because it looks and feels right. At the time of writing it's not an old glitzy club trying to be something else but just what it says—a former warehouse. It's the kind of place you'd never wear a suit to.

☛ *19 Somers Street, Leeds LS1.*
☎ *Leeds 468287.*

The Gallery

Nowadays the Gallery is probably at least as well known as the Warehouse. It houses three clubs in all: Rickys, the Gallery and Arcadia.

Rickys is an underground haunt that is, of course, ridiculously popular. Once a favourite Kaos venue house seems to have dropped off and instead there are rock, 60s psychedelic and student nights galore. The house music has moved upstairs and the Gallery is host to some very popular nights. Bliss (Friday) seems to be the most successful and is run by local band, the Utah Saints. During the week you can hear 70s funk and even jazz. Arcadia is the very smart upstairs part and nights there cater for the smarter, maybe more grown-up clubber generally speaking. Whilst you might feel happy in the Gallery in t-shirt and jeans you'll find designer clothing more appropriate in Arcadia.

☛ *In Merrion Street, Leeds LS1.*
☎ *Leeds 450923.*

Mister Craigs

Just round the corner from the Gallery is Mister Craigs. A former cinema, Craigs is big (it can get in 800) and flashy with mirrors, high stools, lights up the stairs and everything. A real traditional "smart" place and the weekend you still need to be "smartly dressed" to get in, which means no jeans, t-shirts or trainers. You can dress up and have a laugh here, in the old style. During the week, however, Craigs lets its hair down a bit with student and house nights bringing them in. Many Leeds clubbers feel a certain fondness for the sheer unabashed glitz of Craigs, even if the music or clientele is not always to their taste. Flashy menu.

☛ *54 New Briggate, Leeds LS1.*
☎ *Leeds 422224.*

Digbys

Tucked away in the commercial quarter of the city centre is this more traditional club. Expensively fitted out with comfy seating and homely decor, it is small, neat and intimate and attracts an older crowd. It's a famous haunt of the married, the dangerously close-to-being unmarried, the divorced and the still free and single (if not quite as young as they think they are). During the week it caters for students but most often it's glad rags only to get in here.

☛ 20 York Place, Leeds LS1.
☎ Leeds 443590.

Ritzys

Another club in the same vein as Digbys. Upstairs in the Merrion Centre this venue is not black and silver (like Craigs) but more muted colours like pink. It's suit and tie at the weekends and fairly traditional but during the week there are student and over 25s nights on offer with music to match.
☛ The Merrion Centre, Merrion Street, Leeds LS1.
☎ Leeds 431448.

Le Phonographique

Better known simply as The Phono. A basement venue that must be the longest established club in the city. The Phono had its real heyday in the Goth era and it still provides nights out for the people who like to wear a lot of black (of which there is still a remarkably large number in Leeds). At the time of writing it was playing virtually no house music, preferring alternative, indie, sub-pop and the like. You could say it's kept true to its roots and for certain people it is simply the *only*

On the Razzle in Leeds

1. Whilst door prices are not too bad drinks do tend to be higher than pub prices in the clubs. If you're on a budget look out for midweek drinks promotions or simply drink more in the pub first. Buy tickets in advance if possible.
2. Almost without exception clubs shut at 2am. If you want all-nighters you're advised to look further afield to Bradford, Huddersfield and other places.
3. To a certain extent house clubs have eased out hip-hop and soul. Look in Bradford and listen to pirate radio for details of one-off events in the region.
4. Best sources of information about what's on in the clubs are the Northern Star or leaflets at Jumbo Records in the St. John's Centre and Crash Records on The Headrow and in the Merrion Centre.

place to go.
☛ The Phono is in a Merrion Centre basement, off Merrion Street, Leeds LS1.
☎ Leeds 433688.

The Music Factory

Renamed from Rockshots, which used to be Leeds's main gay club. Now there have been major changes at this Lower Briggate venue, with some extremely popular and nationally renowned events—Back to Basics in particular. This is on Saturdays and at the time of writing is Leeds's most successful non-hardcore night. The music is a mix of house, funk and softer sounds. Clubbers are encouraged to dress up, at least a bit. On other nights you can hear hardcore, indie, 80s, 70s, pop and all sorts whilst the ever-popular Chocolate Factory is still upstairs on Fridays. There you'll get everything from Hawkwind to Carter.
☛ 174 Briggate, Leeds LS1.
☎ Leeds 449474.

Riffs

Just outside the city centre near the Sheepscar Junction, Riffs mainly stages nostalgia discos, like "The Time Tunnel" and "The Lizard Club" for 60's buffs, "Glory" for New Romantics, or "Stereo Shoestring" (Thursdays) for noise/hardcore addicts. Sometimes Rolling Stones or Smiths special. Riffs is cheap and something like Rickys.
☛ North Street, Leeds LS2.

The Phoenix

The legendary Phoenix in Chapeltown has bags of what used to be called Street Cred. Formerly Cosmos, before that Roots and even a famous punk venue the F Club, it is now an easy going place that attracts some students and a certain older patron who doesn't want the fuss of the city centre. Despite being located in the heart of the West Indian community, it's not necessarily a reggae, funk or soul venue but a pleasing mix of musical styles and periods. You don't have to dress up, it isn't particularly fashionable.
☛ 58 Francis Street, Chapeltown, Leeds LS7.
☎ Leeds 623619.

Gay & Lesbian Scene

Leeds has well-established centres of social life for its gay & lesbian community. There's also some crossover with the Bradford scene. For local events, see the weekly *Out in The North* listings in *Northern Star*.

Clubs

At the time of writing, there are two main late-night drinking/social centres in the region.
Primo's II, *Westminster Building, 41-43 New York Street, Leeds LS2*. This basement venue is currently the main late-night haunt in Leeds. Two DJs playing a wide variety of music for gays and lesbians of all ages. Open Mon-Sat 9pm-2am.
Mr. B's, *5 Barry Street, Bradford BD1*. Large gay/lesbian club on two floors. Open Mon-Sat 9pm-2am and Sundays 9pm to 1am.

Pubs

The following have been publicised by listings and helplines for a number of years:
Bananas, *Call Lane, Leeds LS1 (below Music Factory)*. A particular favourite with the young.
Bavaria Tavern, *corner of Heaton Road and Church Street, Bradford BD1*. Prominent in Bradford young gay/lesbian scene, with disco on Saturday nights and lesbian social on Tuesday evenings.
Bridge Inn, *1/5 Bridge End, Leeds LS1 (corner of Call lane)*. Popular, not too noisy. Quiz night on Wednesday.
The New Penny, *Call Lane, Leeds LS1*. Across from Bananas. Another favourite haunt of young gays/lesbians, but some older people find it somewhat hectic. Famous for its Karaoke Night (Tuesdays).
Old Red Lion, *Thwaite Gate, Leeds LS10*. More relaxed and, consequently, attracts somewhat older gays/lesbians. Leeds Gay Switchboard holds a social evening here each Monday at 9pm. Pub quiz every Tuesday night.
The Sun, *124 Sunbridge Road, Bradford BD1*. There are discos on Wednesdays and Sundays. Good bar food.

PART FOUR:
Pubs & Restaurants

There is an increasingly international flavour to Leeds. Going out to eat and drink these days often entails making choices between noisy American bars/diners, Continental-style cafés (especially outdoor ones in summer) and a whole range of eastern cuisine.

Thankfully, traditional Yorkshire food and drink is still widely available, perhaps more appreciated than before when seen against some of the glitzy modern pubs and restaurants.

The following pages try to present a cross-section of what's on offer in the Leeds area, with preference given to places that we consider offer excellent value for money or which have special character. There is something here for all age-groups, tastes and pockets.

Savita serves with a smile at Bobby's Sweet & Kebab House, Leeds (see page 110).

Leeds Pubs & Café Bars

A revolution is taking place in the once-humble Leeds bars—now it's CD jukeboxes, low-cholesterol grub and "world" beers. But traditional pubs survive.

No area of social activity in the Leeds area is undergoing so much change than going out for a drink. Apart from the 11am-11pm opening hours, the main difference is in style. Café bars are increasingly common, with more than a dozen in the city centre, and spreading out to the suburbs. These make a big thing of lager, wines and cocktails and fast-food like pizzas and hamburgers. By and large, they are frequented by the young and young-at-heart. Thankfully, the old-fashioned pub is still alive and well in West Yorkshire. Leeds has some of the best, such as the famous Whitelocks and the glorious Garden Gate. Since the last edition of *Leeds Fax*, there has been a significant increase in the number of pubs with No Smoking areas. Hopefully, the all-No Smoking pub is not too far off.

Central Bars & Pubs

In the city centre, or within walking distance, most pubs have a mixed clientele during the day and sub-30 drinkers at night. There are one or two exceptions to this—most notably the Victoria and Whitelocks—but by and large the "oldies" tend to prefer to stay in their suburban neighbourhoods for night-time liquid refreshments. As the next pages show, it's worth venturing into new territory.

Adelphi Hotel

The nearest Tetleys tap to the brewery and one of the best-kept pints in town. This ornate street corner Edwardian boozer has the widest range of customers—locals, jazzers, punks, students, GTI drivers, OAPs, middle-aged darts n' dominoes players as well as office workers in this expanding part of town. In short, the whole of Leeds life. The interior is beautifully preserved wood panelling, green tiles, engraved glass, red-leather seating. Four-rooms downstairs, and the famous upstairs concert room

(regular Jazz on Saturday night). Good food at lunchtimes: pie & peas & sandwiches on Monday and Tuesday; bigger range of meals Wednesday to Friday.
☛ *Leeds Bridge, Leeds LS10.*
☎ *Leeds 456377.*

The Bank

Possibly the best-known of the city's "wine" bars, the Bank is a very central basement that's glitzy and LOUD! It has a resident DJ who seems to talk a lot, and it's probably not the place for spending a whole evening. But it's an essential stop on the city centre crawl for the under-25s. The name, by the way, is not a cynical reflection of the loadsamoney cash registers, but a reminder of the fact that it's in the basement of what used to be the Bank of England. During the week, its customers seem to be mainly from local offices judging by the requests read out by the DJ—"Michelle at Eagle Star, Hayley at National Westminster ..." Fashion beers like Budweiser. Cheap or expensive wines. Good value cocktails.
☛ *South Parade, Leeds LS1.*

Barney's

This very popular pub in the quaint yard next door to the City of Varieties is almost a museum of music hall memorabilia, photographs, shelves of books etc. The theatre was actually an extension of the pub (formerly called the White Swan) in 1865. Despite major refurbishments, a traditional feel has been retained—though more of an early 20th Century style than anything that reflects its earlier life as a coaching inn. It's very popular with young and old. The beer is the Tetley range (bitter and mild, three lagers & Guinness). Barney was the late Barney Colehan, founder and producer of *The Good Old Days*, the long-running TV series filmed next door.
☛ *Swan Street, Leeds LS1.*
☎ *Leeds 450064.*

The Bond

Another stop on the restless crawl of city centre bars by the Leeds young, especially on Thursday, Friday and Saturday nights. Then, it's packed with singles, mostly groups of lads and lasses. Their length of stay depends on the quality of the talent. Loud music and video monitors give the atmosphere of a disco. Tetleys ales.
☛ *32/34 Albion Street, Leeds LS1.*
☎ *Leeds 432092.*

Boulevard

One of those classy joints in Leeds that blur the old differences between pub and wine bar. Owned by Tetleys, so beer is still very much in evidence, though the youngish clientele like their lager (three kinds on draft and any number of "world beers" in bottles—all at reassuringly high prices). The Boulevard stands on the "Rue de Headrow". Open plan and somewhat "art deco", the interior design lends an informal cafe-atmosphere—thus the wine bar feel. Loud music at night makes this not a place for serious conversations. More likely, serious flirting with the eyes. Food is served lunchtimes only, Monday to Friday.
☛ *The Headrow, Leeds LS1.*
☎ *434172.*

Cafe Society

Housed in the basement of Leeds Corn Exchange, the idea seems to be a cross between Rick's in *Casablanca* and Harry's Bar in New York City. So far it's a case of style lagging some way behind aspiration, probably because it's that little bit on the fringe of the more established Thursday-Friday-Saturday night crawl that centres on Albion Street and Boar Lane. But it really does merit a visit—all that black and silver decor is just too good to waste. Tetleys beers and "house" lagers, reasonably priced cocktails, and a wide variety of pizzas for eats. Gets busy when the shops close and then again later in the evening, but Café Society's days of being *the* fashionable place in Leeds cannot be too far away.
☛ *Corn Exchange, Cloth Hall Lane, Leeds LS1.*
☎ *445314.*

Central

A long-established unpretentious boozer, catering for office workers from the nearby business centre, journalists from the *Evening Post/Yorkshire Post* down the road, and thirsty travellers from the nearby Wellington Street Coach Station. At night, the Central "Station" as it was once called (the 1850s LNER station across the road closed in 1967) frequently has live music. Folk, blues & jazz seem to dominate, bringing a wide assortment of customers from the leather n' jeans brigade to finger-in-the-ear types in Fair Isle sweaters. Excellent meals at lunchtime, such as home-made pies, chilli, pie & peas. Fine Tetleys ales.

☛ *88 Wellington Street, Leeds LS1*
☎ *Leeds 453927.*

City of Mabgate

This fine old pub (c.1840) is easily missed, stuck as it is in the shadow of the New York Road flyover at the foot of Eastgate but it is worth seeking out. The beers are Whitbreads, including the excellent Castle Eden, and serves the increasingly popular Murphy's Stout. It's interior is old but not kitsch, with a vast collection of beer mats the main attempt at decoration. The customers are "mature"—business reps from the many offices in this part of Leeds and medics from St. James's hospital up the road. In the evening, it is sought out by the less scene-searching students. There is no jukebox, just tapes. The games room fills with locals who have used the pub for decades, playing darts and doms. Food at lunchtimes is very varied—home-made pies, chilli, curries, toasties, sandwiches, giant Yorkshire puds with onion gravy, chip butties.

☛ *Mabgate, Leeds LS9.*
☎ *Leeds 457789.*

The Coburg

An always busy pub, where students and staff from the Poly on one side and Leeds City Council workers from Merrion House on the other converge for their Tetleys ales and good value bar lunches. The food makes few concessions to diets, being of the steak pie & chips, pie and peas variety. A

once-famous jukebox of good vinyl now, alas, replaced by CDs. But little else has changed in this pub for many a decade.

☛ *Claypit Lane, Leeds LS2.*
☎ *Leeds 457886.*

Conservatory

A sprawling basement café bar with a split personality. During the day, it's a stylish stop for shoppers of all ages, who like its good coffee and bar snacks. But things change at the happy hour, when in come the younger office workers and by nine it's heaving with wall-to-wall singles. As the name implies, there's much verdant decor, plus an attempt at giving it the feel of a book-lined study in some corners. But the clientele seem more video age than bookish. They quaff draught Budweiser, Fosters and Ruddles County, and numerous cocktails. Most of the men prefer their beer from the bottle.

☛ *Albion Place, Leeds LS1.*

Cullens Wine Bar

In the heart of the Leeds business quarter, Cullens has an upstairs and a downstairs but both essentially cater for executives and office workers. Tetleys beer and a good range of wines, plus very tasty food at lunchtimes (ie. chicken & ham pie, Chinese beef, cheese & onion flan). Various inducements are made to keep its customers after the early evening rush has finished, including occasional live music (blues, folk, contemporary). Gets a mostly well-heeled clientele.

☛ *5 York Place, Leeds LS1.*
☎ *Leeds 450556.*

Duck & Drake

Loved by some, loathed by others. But there's no denying the appeal of the biggest range of hand-pulled cask-conditioned beers in Yorkshire and some of the best free live entertainment in Leeds several nights a week. A former

Within weeks of the last edition of Leeds Fax, an excellent bar and diner called the **Filling Station** *opened up and thus missed our recommendation. Standing at an aloof distance from the city centre's other stylish bars, it thankfully misses most of the excesses of the asphyxiating perfumes and after-shaves of the Saturday night crawlers who pack out the Albion Street-Boar Lane area bars. In an beautifully restored building designed by Cuthbert Brodrick (the architect responsible for the Town Hall and the Civic Theatre, which is across the road), the bar's happy hour runs till 8pm and offers the most delicious—and enormous—cocktails in town. All the usuals are there—comfortable screws and pina coladas—and there's nothing naff about paying a couple of quid for a tankard of fruity wondrousness. Students, crisply dressed office workers, and people with fresh giros alike head for the Filling Station. Unfortunately, the students usually get there first and nick the high stools. What was that line again about poor students?*

☛ *43-51 Cookridge Street, Leeds LS2.*
☎ *Leeds 422990.*

CAMRA Pub of the Year, it regularly has up to 20 different beers on offer. There are two bars. The bigger is full of Aran sweater wearing and grizzle-bearded Real Ale fanatics, students and bikers who share a common interest in the English hop. The second is an ordinary boozer, used by doms-playing older men and women who've come here for years to kill an hour before catching their bus from the local bus station. The beers include Marston's Pedigree & Owd Roger, Taylor's Landlord, Theakston's Old Peculiar, Boddingtons, Ruddles. Sunday lunchtime jazz, and folk/blues/etc on Sunday & Thursday evenings.
☛ *Kirkgate, Leeds LS2.*
☎ *Leeds 465806.*

Eagle
Still hugely popular with Real Ale fans, who enjoy the full range of Timothy Taylor's excellent beers (Golden Best, Landlord and the fruity winter brew, Ram Tam), plus guests. Very popular at lunch-times, when good bar meals are available (especially the traditional Yorkshire Sunday lunch), and also when live jazz/blues/folk is on the menu in the large tap-room at night. The lounge is cosy and inti-mate until about eight, then gets extremely busy. The large tap-room has the music, loud enough to enjoy at just the right volume through in the lounge. The graffiti in both the ladies and gents is leg-endary. "This wall is now avail-able in paperback". If only.
☛ *North Street, Leeds LS7.*
☎ *Leeds 457146.*

Eldon
Located directly opposite the Uni-versity Engineering Department, this pub is, not surprisingly, full of students in term time. Very friendly in the summer, and popu-lar with people stopping off for a drink on their way out to Headingley and points north. Has a tap room, lounge and games room (pool table & darts). Beers are the standard Tetleys brews, Bitter and Mild, plus Skol and Castlemaine XXXX lagers, Gaymers Old English Cider and Guinness all on draught.
☛ *Woodhouse Lane, Leeds LS2.*

Faversham
If you've been away from Leeds for a while you may find the changes at the Faversham quite a shock to the system. Located al-most within the University this pub has traditionally been the haunt of rock stars (well-known and ob-scure) and a never-ending flow of goths, hippies, rockers, students and miscellaneous poseurs doing what used to be called "making the scene". It has recently been re-vamped but the clientele seems oblivious to the smart new look. The Fav still attracts huge crowds, especially on Friday and Saturday nights, when it's full of people who've arranged to meet their friends. Searching for the afore-mentioned offers excellent chat-up lines. Bouncers, very loud music, DJs and queues for the toilet that can make a girl weep give the Fav a nightclub atmosphere, and ru-mour has it . . . For the moment though, it remains the only pub in the city that you could ever call trendy. Ever. Oh, and the beers are . . . who cares?
☛ *1 Springfield Mount, Leeds LS2.*
☎ *Leeds 458817.*

Fenton
Second home to several genera-tions of university and poly stu-dents/lecturers, the Fenton is best seen at night, when cultish 20-30 year olds predominate. Once the most radical chic of all Leeds pubs, these days you're more likely to overhear a conversation about CDs than CND. The social mix includes a large number of ex-students who find the Fenton a rather comfy time warp, sundry musicians, student crowd hangers-on, artie-farties, staff from the Beeb across the road, and the oc-casional weirdo. Also draws smart-suited types who live locally lest they become suburbanites. And the Fenton is a world away from the suburbs. Well kept Tetley ales, lunches if you're feeling rich, and somewhat sporadic live mu-sic. A Leeds institution, many would consider their lives poorer without The Fenton.
☛ *161 Woodhouse Lane, Leeds LS2.*
☎ *Leeds 453908.*

Fox & Newt
Despite being one of the best pubs in Leeds for cask conditioned ale, the Fox's customers are mainly the beer bellyless side of 30, probably thanks to its close proximity to Park Lane College and numerous university departments. Beers in-clude the own-brewed Willow and Burley Bitter, plus a variety of ales that at any one time can include Theakston's Old Peculiar and, Marston's Pedigree. Drinkers of Irish stout are well catered for—both Guinness and Murphy's on draught. And a wide range of bot-tled lagers is sold alongside sev-eral draught. The pub has an old feel to it, but it actually opened in the seventies. Food is good and plentiful, with vegetarian dishes often taking prominence on the menu. But not on Sunday lunch-time, when the traditional roast, veg and puds are served. Best time is early evening, before the crowds arrive.
☛ *Burley Street, Leeds LS3.*
☎ *Leeds 432612.*

George Hotel
Like the nearby Victoria, the George gets packed with assorted medics, legal eagles and journal-ists during the week, and becomes a stop on a crawl of Leeds pubs later at night and at weekends. De-spite almost total lack of nearby housing, it has a staunch "local" element—people who bus in or drive from other parts of Leeds to do their drinking here. Good Tetleys beers, games nights and occasional live music. Excellent value meals at lunchtime. Leeds lads hang around at night blatantly chatting up nurses from the nearby infirmary.
☛ *67-69 Great George Street, Leeds LS.*
☎ *453232.*

Guildford
Most people are gob-smacked the first time they walk into this pub. The art deco lights and brasswork and French Impressionist prints on the walls combine to give not just a splash but bucketfuls of colour and life. This has the effect of keeping out the yob element, who wouldn't be seen dead drinking in a pub like this. Therefore, it can

be almost elite in its clientele during the week, although it still suffers the hordes that squeeze into other city centre bars on Fridays and Saturday nights. An attempt at being even more popular by putting on discos may alienate those who found it a rare, genuinely stylish place for Leeds. Good lunches, Monday to Saturday. Tetleys beers. Unique.

☛ *The Headrow, Leeds LS1.*
☎ *Leeds 423468.*

Harveys Cafe Bar

Whereas certain other café bars in the city centre are in danger of becoming seedy, Harveys still draws the more sophisticated types. Solidly constructed with lots of wood panelling, a feature wrought-iron spiral staircase, tiled floor and cane furniture, it is a popular meeting place during the day. A wide range of bar meals and very good coffee attract all age groups. At night, it's mainly for young people showing off their new clothes or sun-tans. Or theatre/opera goers who have time for a drink before moving across to The Grand. Packed out from about nine Thursdays to Saturdays, it is owned by Tetleys but you won't see any pumps for bitter beer on the bar—this is very much a lager and wine place. Thirst quenchers are Kir Royale, Pimms, Bucks Fizz and Sangria by glass or jug.

☛ *26-30 Merrion Street, Leeds LS2.*
☎ *Leeds 432332.*

Highland

Lovers of real pubs cherish this classic back-street boozer, of which there are precious few left in Leeds. Sympathetically restored a few years back, nothing was done to alter the character of the long, two-roomed pub beside the RSPCA animal home. Sepia photographs of old Leeds street scenes cover the walls. An amazing, leather-upholstered wall seat curves round the main room, but standing at the Highland's bar somehow seems more appropriate. Very popular with journalists/printers from the nearby Yorkshire Post building, and other shift-workers in the area. Renowned for its well-kept Tetleys bitter

☛ *Cavendish Street, Leeds LS3*
☎ *Leeds 457092.*

Hoagy's Bar

Once called Hoagy's Piano Bar with a house pianist in the evenings who would serenade your loved one for the price of a drink. Sadly, both the piano and pianist have disappeared to be replaced by piped music and discos. Still, a good range of Youngers' beers, McEwans and excellent Becks lagers, autumn gold and Dry blackthorn ciders, plus Guinness. Newkie brown (bottled) for the brave. CD jukebox and a pool hall upstairs with nine tables attract a predominantly young male clientele.

☛ *46 Eastgate, Leeds LS2.*
☎ *Leeds 453421.*

Jacomelli's

The street-level restaurant at Jacomelli's has been an established meeting place for decades, but the large cellar bar's immense popularity with the young, largely working class of Leeds, is something of a recent phenomenon. The description "spacious"—which it is—becomes redundant at night, when there is a shoulder-to-shoulder crush. Very loud music kills the art of conversation stone dead, and it's really just a question of lads drinking their bottled beers and lasses their pernod and black as stylishly as possible. Tetley beers, but the Holstein lager and the wines on draught seem more popular.

☛ *56 Boar Lane, Leeds LS1.*
☎ *Leeds 452555.*

Joseph's Well Tavern

In an area where the pubs are verging on the grimy and packed full of young people Joseph's Well is an oasis of soothing luxury and calm. On the edge of student-land and on the edge of town (just over the footbridge from the Leeds General Infirmary in Great George Street) the Well is spacious, and very popular with office workers at lunchtimes, who devour huge platefuls of home-cooked meals like meat pies, curries, chillis and daily specials. In the evening it's largely the haunt of smarter, less demonic students. Beers are bass, stones and Worthingtons, plus guest bitters. Has a no-smoking area at lunchtime.

☛ *Hanover Walk, Leeds LS3.*
☎ *Leeds 451634.*

Len's Bar

For many years, Len's has been a favourite watering hole for white-collar workers in this part of town. The big cellar is a warren of rooms, with lots of intimate corners where those secret/dangerous office liaisons can be nurtured. Stella and Heineken lagers on draught, plus Boddingtons bitter and Murphys stout. Great value lunches, like roasts and salads. Busy early evening, gets its second wind around nine when the more mature clubbers are out.

☛ *20 York Place, Leeds LS1.*
☎ *Leeds 443590.*

New Roscoe

The original Roscoe stood at the bottom of Chapeltown Road, a small pub with much character,

The—ahem—eye-catching mural on an exterior wall at the New Roscoe.

narrow passages, low ceilings, roaring coal fires in winter and a predominantly Irish clientele. It also served a beautiful pint of Tetleys and, therefore, was much revered by Real Ale (as well as Real Pub) devotees. Since its demolition in March, 1982 its reputation has become greatly enhanced by the golden mists of time. There is even an annual wake on the very spot, against the relentless roar of traffic from all sides. The New Roscoe, less than half a mile away, opened in late 1988 and is nothing like the original. It is big (including a large pool room) and bright and plush. The beer is good and all the paraphernalia of copper pans, jugs, brass kettles and lanterns are there and The Hills of Sweet Mayo still plays on the jukebox. There is a wood & glass replica of the original inside but you can't design atmosphere. The landlord puts on Irish "sessions" and balladeers and still serves an exemplary pint of Tetleys.
☛ *Benson Street, Leeds LS7.*
☎ *Leeds 460778.*

Observatory
Well named, this is a place to see and be seen. Another of the city centre's wine bar kind of venues, but not many of the regulars seem to sit down to admire a bottle of *Chateau Cheval-Blanc* in the age-old wine bar manner. Rather, this is a big and brash bar that shifts a lot of beer and lager, cocktails and a vast selection of bottled beers. On the Thursday to Saturday night crawl by the young and trying-to-be-young, the bouncers at the door might put some folks off. It is possibly the most elegant of all Leeds bars, being in an amazing Classical building once owned by the Midland Bank. It gets packed out at happy hours. Great place if you can stand the pace.
☛ *40 Boar Lane, Leeds LS1.*
☎ *Leeds 428641.*

The Pack Horse
Virtually an off-campus Leeds University Union Bar, the Pack Horse's customers for around nine months of the year are predominately students and academic staff. It serves as the meeting place for several of the university's clubs & societies, and has a long history of folk music on Sunday nights. Modernisation in the mid-80s did not alter its beautiful interior, especially the amazing wooden bar. And, thankfully, the traditional multi-roomed lay-out was retained. It's a beer drinking pub, with good Tetleys bitter and mild on draught.
☛ *Woodhouse Lane (near junction with Clarendon Road), Leeds LS2.*
☎ *Leeds 453980.*

Parkers Bar
One of those bars that's full of sharp-suited businessmen during the day and early evening and swingers and nightclubbers later on. Parkers has been going a long time. It has one of the longest happy hours known to mankind—3pm-11pm daily (4pm start on Fridays) and now an excellent range of hand-pulled beers—Boddingtons, Castle Eden, Tetleys. And Murphys Stout. Although it's dropped the word "wine" from its name, the grape is still very much in evidence, with specials on offer. Good value, imaginative lunch counter.
☛ *12 Park Place, Leeds LS1*
☎ *Leeds 451919.*

Pig & Whistle
After doing all that shopping in Morrisons, where better than to nip for a quick drink than the Pig & Whistle on the edge of the Merrion Centre? Four hours later, you find it's quite a job getting home with all that shopping and no bus fare. That aside, the Pig is a very pleasant pub where students and townsfolk mix and drink amicably. It's friendly and there's plenty of seating. Definitely a place to unwind. Tetleys beers, plus "guest" Burtonwood. Good lunches include salads, home-made pies, scampi. Very occasional live music by students from the College of Music across the street. Other pubs may exist just so you can get wound up, hyped up and ready to go crazy at some nightclub but this is not the case at the Pig. Sit, drink, talk and . . . try not to spend your bus fare.
☛ *East Wing, Merrion Centre, Leeds LS2.*
☎ *Leeds 445354.*

The Ship
While tourists and professional people squeeze into Whitelocks, further up Briggate is another narrow yard giving access to this gem of a Leeds pub. More workaday than Whitelocks, but with bags of charm. Lead windows and wood panelled walls, the latter virtually covered by photographs, engravings and drawings of steamships, sailing ships, Royal Navy frigates and other nautical vessels. A basic beer pub (Tetleys Ales), popular with all age groups, especially at lunchtimes when food that is not designed to aid diets is served up. Included is the popular Dutch dish of chips accompanied by various dips like garlic mayonaisse and thousand islands dressing.
☛ *Ship Inn Yard, Briggate, Leeds LS1.*

Sparrow's Wharf
This kind of bar is all the rage in the former docklands of London, Hull and Liverpool. Converted to a pub from an 1830s warehouse on the north bank of the Aire Calder Navigation, it is a huge cellar with exposed brick walls and vaulted ceilings, and a polished wooden floor. Windows and a balcony overlook the Aire, and it is clear that this is the first of a number of such pubs which will eventually open in the greatly improved waterfront area of Leeds. Cask conditioned ales are a speciality, including Bass, Worthington and Taylor's Landlord, plus a well selected range of wines. Prices ensure that customers are of above-average income. Food (Mondays to Saturday 11.30am-2.30pm) is farmhouse and Continental cheeses & pates with crusty bread.
☛ *32 The Calls, Leeds LS1.*
☎ *Leeds 446801.*

Stumps
When the weather's good, the customers of this large, cavernous bar below the library/museum spill outside to sit on tables and steps. Even in winter, Stumps is one of the most popular pubs in town, especially with young single men and women. The former go there hoping to bowl a maiden over and the maidens, often, want to play. Much cricket memorabilia in glass

cases. Prints/cartoons continue the cricket theme, as well as sepia photographs from the days when Yorkshire County Cricket Club won things. Naturally, Stumps is a place that shifts vast quantities of lager—Budweiser and Fosters on draught, plus "designer" bottled beers. Also at the pumps are Ruddles and Websters ales. Lunchtime food is varied, from a good range of salads to roasts, burgers and fried fish.

☛ *Centenary Square, Leeds LS1.*
☎ *Leeds 458842.*

Town Hall Tavern

Facing Cuthbert Brodrick's baroque ediface across Westgate is this small pub, highly popular with m'learned friends, solicitors and assorted miscreants and their families/friends from the nearby Courthouse. Although there are seats, it's mainly a standing-up pub, and more suited to beer drinkers (Tetleys) than young lager quaffers, who are likely to feel more at home in The Boulevard a few doors along. Bar snacks are minimal, mainly filled rolls.

☛ *17 Westgate, Leeds LS1*
☎ *Leeds 453966.*

Victoria

The Vic has been a popular meeting place for all classes of Leeds people since the 1860s. Close proximity to the Town Hall, the Courthouse, a number of colleges and the General Infirmary makes it particularly well patronised by musicians, lawyers, doctors, journalists and academics. The Victoria Family & Commercial Hotel, to give its full name, is very definitely the thinking (and drinking) man's and woman's pub in Leeds. There are three bars—the Windsor (also called Bridget's Bar or Bridie's Bar, after the popular long-serving barmaid); the Albert, which has some fine caricatures on the walls; and the Long Bar. The latter is extremely noisy, more likely to attract large groups of "lads" or "lasses" doing the rounds and to be avoided if you want a serious conversation. Good hot and cold lunches.

☛ *Great George Street, Leeds LS1.*
☎ *451386.*

West Riding Hotel

Extremely popular with executives, lawyers, accountants and the rest of the business community in this part of town. Clean, comfortable and roomy—it is a very long, narrow bar and many of its well-dressed customers prefer to stand to do their talking/drinking/yammering into cellphones. Tetleys beers, wines on draft and an exceptionally stylish CD jukebox. One of the few city centre pubs with a relaxed atmosphere on the hectic Thursday-Saturday nights. Good hot and cold bar meals during the week.

☛ *38 Wellington Street, Leeds LS1.*
☎ *Leeds 453660.*

The White Stag

A lively pub a five-minute walk from Vicar Lane that is a long-established home of the Leeds Irish community. But it's also popular with a wide range of backgrounds, including a "street-cred" haunt of denim-wearing art types and media-folk. Many of the wall pictures relate to its Irish clientele (maps of the Emerald Isle, pcitures of Dublin pubs, etc) and there are regular "sessions" in the superb wood-panelled tap room. The CD juekbox has plenty of Phil Collins and the like but you're still more often than not going to hear the Fureys. Well-kept Tetleys beers.

☛ *North Street, Leeds LS7.*
☎ *Leeds 451069.*

Few pubs have been enthusiastically endorsed by a poet laureate, but Sir John Betjeman was clearly impressed by **Whitelocks**. *"It is the Leeds equivalent of Fleet Street's Old Cheshire Cheese", he wrote, (and the aforementioned Cheese is probably the most loved pub in London). He added, "it is far less self-conscious and does a roaring trade. It is the very heart of Leeds." Indeed. And enormously popular, with its feast of Victorian and Edwardian features, and some interesting art nouveaux glass. Originally called the Turk's Head when it received its first license in 1715 (Whitelock was the name of a family which bought it in 1880) the yard outside is still known as Turk's Head Yard. It is said to have been the first place in Leeds to have an electric light. Inside, the Youngers Ales are very popular, served across a high glass, brass and tile bar. There is another, more recent, bar further up the yard and outside seating round barrel tables. The food is served off a great marble slab to one side of the bar—traditional English fayre like meat and potato pie, mushy peas, Cornish pasties, bubble & squeak. The roast beef sandwiches with red cabbage are famous.*

☛ *Turk's Head Yard, off Briggate, Leeds LS1.*
☎ *Leeds 453950.*

Suburban/Country Bars & Pubs

Away from the city centre, there are mainly two types of bars and pubs. One is the traditional neighbourhood ale house. Another is the big pub—usually surrounded by acres of car park or gardens—that serve meals and cater mostly for adults and their children. We have selected what we consider to be among the area's best/most popular in both these categories, with special emphasis on places of character or with good bar meals and family facilities.

Albion

If men get that feeling of *déjà vu* when they're standing outside the Albion, you *have* been there before, but in a Lilliputian sort of way. So archetypally 19th Century English pub is The Albion that it was used as the model for miniature "Railway Hotels" in thousands of Hornby 00 Gauge toy train sets. The brick and tile frontage and the original Peter Walker & Sons of Warrington sign have been carefully preserved. Which is more than can be said for the neighbourhood, which has been more or less flattened to make warehouses and hypermarkets. Inside, the three-roomed bar has been tastefully renovated. A pool table exists in a back room; there is a piano for the occasional singsong, a good jukebox, open fires, mirrors, and pictures of old Leeds on the walls. Not surprisingly, the Albion's got almost as many preservation orders on it as Stonehenge and is justly promoted as a "Pub of Character" by Tetleys Brewery. Very popular with "locals"—many of them have to walk a fair distance because most of the streets it once served have been pulled down—and with lovers of real pubs. And, of course, real ale fans like it too. Definitely worth seeking out.

☛ *86 Armley Road, Leeds LS12.*
☎ *Leeds 456729.*

Although this elegant pubs is hugely popular with all classes and incomes, the **Cardigan Arms** *has been colonised by 25-50 year-old middle classes from the Headingley-Burley areas who've been dispossessed of their own locals by students. The interior is richly decorated in stained glass, wood, mirrors and brass. The long, spacious taproom still has a quaint "ladies only" door at the side. The big central bar has—alas a new CD jukebox—the Campaign for Vinyl Jukeboxes starts here. There are also three rooms of varying sizes, the big front one being much favoured by persons of a Greenpeace/CND disposition. At lunchtime, the Cardigan's giant Yorkshire puddings are much relished. You may recognise the pint-pulling landlady, Joyce Kennedy, a well-known character TV actress, appearing in things like All Creatures Great and Small and Coronation Street.*

☛ *Kirkstall Road, Leeds LS4.*
☎ *Leeds 742000.*

Bay Horse

A small, two-roomed beer drinkers' pub across the road from the cobbled Otley market square, it is extremely popular at weekends. A recent change of landlord has led to the introduction of "guest" beers, but more than any pub outside Leeds the Bay Horse is famous for serving a fine drop of Tetleys. There are two rooms, both low-ceilinged and small and although there are tables and chairs, the Bay is a popular stand-at-the-bar pub. There are darts & doms nights on Mondays and Thursdays (large plates of sandwiches and sausage rolls passed round for all) and bar snacks at lunchtimes include home-made pie & peas, beef & sausage butties.

☛ *Market Place, Otley, LS21.*
☎ *Otley (0943) 461122.*

Bingley Arms

In the *Guinness Book of Records* as England's oldest inn, it dates from AD953 and was mentioned in the *Domesday Book*. The Bingley Arms is also credited as England's oldest brewhouse but today the beer is Tetleys. A tunnel once linked it with the nearby Saxon church and you can still see the "priest holes" in the bar walls where the monks hid when raiders came. And there were frequent raids in those days—Scotland played away a lot. Good bar meals, an excellent beer garden for families and a famous Sunday roast carvery—as much as you can get on a plate for what you'd pay for a starter in some restaurants.

☛ *Bardsey Village (off A58 road to Wetherby).*
☎ *Collingham Bridge (0937) 572462.*

Black Bull

Fronting what's left of Horsforth village's ancient village green, the Black Bull is very big, allowing it to cater for all age groups. At lunchtime, when it has a very good hot meals counter, it has a mixture of businessmen, retired people and some young drinkers. There's a no-smoking area until 7pm, and an excellent beer garden with kiddies playground at the rear. In the evening, it soon fills up and becomes one of the busiest pubs in the area, drawing mostly the under-30s from a wide area of North Leeds and Aireborough. NEXT-dressed lager lovers stand around drinking out of their bottles and groups of girls return their glances from the seating, which includes sofas. The eponymous bull's head glowers menacingly over this from above the cavernous fireplace, where logs burn brightly when temperatures fall. There's chintzy country sitting-room style, with old racing prints in the "public bar" (though it's all open plan now) and floral pictures in a conservatory area.

☞ *Town Street, Horsforth.*
☎ *Leeds 586925.*

Bridge Inn

Like a list of vicars in a church, The Bridge displays a chronology of all its landlords right from the day it opened on Good Friday, 1868. It's been modernised a few times since then, but the atmosphere of a Victorian pub has survived if not the original features. Tetleys beers, and an utterly addictive "Genius" computer game. But what makes The Bridge different from most pubs is its large range of country-style pies. Each one has an intriguing name ("Crofters", "Manor", "Huntsman", "Harvesters", etc.) There's also a barbecue at weekends when the weather's fine. All in all, The Bridge is fine pub to have as a local, and good to visit if you live elsewhere in North Leeds.

☞ *Woodside, Horsforth.*
☎ *Leeds 582792.*

Chemic

A neighbourhood local in Woodhouse, the Chemic is a bit like Dr. Who's tardus—inside, it's much bigger than you think. At the front is a long lounge, popular with locals and students. The large tap room at the back has as wide a social mix as you'll find in any Leeds pub. University lecturers, media-folk, muttering Irishmen, Anarcho-veggies, New Age hippies, and radical feminist groups. Extremely busy (and smoky) after 9pm on most nights. Good drop of Tetleys bitter.

☞ *Johnston Street, Leeds LS6.*
☎ *Leeds 420226.*

Chequers

The only pub in the Leeds area that still has only a six-day licence. Around 400 years ago Lady Elizabeth Hastings of nearby Ledston Hall decreed that there should be no Sunday drinking—and it still applies today. The Chequers is a fine old building, cloaked in ivy outside and indoors a warren of low-ceilinged, oak-beamed small rooms much decorated with antique toby jugs, brasses, plates, etc. The beers are Youngers and Theakstons and the bar meals are home-made English dishes like toad-in-the-hole and steak pies. There's also an upstairs restaurant (booking advisable for Saturday nights). Twice a year it still hosts an old tradition—the rent dinners. Local farmers gather to pay their rent to the local estate. The menu has been the same for centuries— a three-rib and four-rib of beef, leg of lamb and one large chicken. Outside, there is a popular beer garden.

☞ *Claypit Lane, Ledsham (between Kippax and the A1).*
☎ *South Milford (0977) 683135.*

The Chevin Inn

A very popular, relaxing refuge for the over-40s from a wide area of North Leeds, Otley, Menston, Guiseley, Horsforth, Yeadon and Rawdon. No thumping jukebox here, or hunting in vain for a seat. On the north side of Otley Chevin, it is an 18th century farmhouse converted many years ago to a pub, and modernised inside without tearing away its character. The beer is John Smiths, which has much improved in recent years. Has a quaint room down some steps at the back. The Chevin's the sort of place many older people dress up for on a Saturday night.

☞ *Chevin End (high road out of Otley to Menston).*

Deer Park

Considering there are probably more millionaires living in northeast Leeds than anywhere else in Yorkshire, there is an extraordinary lack of decent pubs. This is about as comfortable as they get, a very large pub where people are prepared to pay a bit more for an expensive, soothing environment, and with the carpets deep enough to provide a soft landing when they faint at the cost of a round. Popular with all age groups, but most seem well-heeled and there's a lot of swapping glances as eyes search for the Deer Park's celebrity regulars. Very good meals at lunchtimes and evenings. There is a non-smoking area. The name, incidentally, is a hangover from days of yore when nearby Roundhay Park was a hunting park for the local nobility. Yep, the rich have always lived around here.

☞ *68 Street Lane, Leeds LS8.*
☎ *Leeds 667372.*

Drysalters Arms

A large, brightly lit and expensively modernised Tetley house on the ring road, within walking distance of Leeds United's Elland Road stadium. It is one of the smartest pubs in south Leeds, and a popular lunchtime halt for those businessmen who always have their jackets neatly hanging in backs of company cars. They stop off again in the evening for a glass of Perrier (honest, officer) on their way to or from places like Batley and Dewsbury. CD jukebox for all tastes, but with a surprising amount of heavy metal for such a plush place. However, a little on-board computer has calculated that this is very much a Simply Red place. Beers include Tetleys and Newquay Steam Bitter. Large range of fish/chicken/steaks/salads on bar menu (eating area is no smoking).

☞ *Elland Road, Leeds LS11*
☎ *Leeds 700229.*

Fox and Hounds

Bramhope is a sprawling amorphous place mostly lacking in village atmosphere. The exception is around the junction of Eastgate and Moor Road, where this fine pub is situated. The lounge is one of the most interesting in Leeds, dominated by two large inglenook fireplaces, one containing a remarkable stove. The whole place is packed with antiques. Up-market locals enjoy Tetleys beers, but also low-alcohol beers and ciders. Good quality bar lunches.

☞ *Moor Road, Bramhope.*
☎ *Leeds 842448.*

Gaping Goose

This was set up as an inn to serve travellers on the "new" turnpike from Leeds to Selby in the 18th century, and it still gets a lot of passing trade. Pubs of such wonderful character are hard to find on the east side of Leeds, and the Gaping Goose—still with some of its Melbourne Brewery insignia intact—has bags of appeal. As you walk through the door, there's an interesting tiled mosaic of the eponymous goose in the hall. Some remarkable coloured glass window designs decorate the snug, while the main bar is full of horse brasses and copper kettles. Tetleys, who took over the late-lamented Melbourne brewery in the 1950s, now run the place and their beers and lagers are on offer. Limited range of bar snacks.

☛ *Selby Road, Garforth, Leeds LS25.*

☎ *Leeds 862127.*

Garden Gate

It's a toss-up whether the Gate or Whitelocks has the most splendidly preserved, ornate interior of any Leeds pub. It is an oasis of Victorian architecture in a desert of new housing in this part of Hunslet and so much of its surroundings have been flattened that the Post Office had to give it a new address. The façade is a magnificent essay in cream and chocolate tiles. Inside, there are many rooms decorated with glorious glass, wood, brass, a fine mosaic floor and yet more elegant tilework. Built in the 1820s it was first used as a pub in 1833. The decoration was probably turn of the century. The beer is Tetleys and the customers are predominantly locals, although the "Pub of Character" status draws many others from all parts of town. Lunches are traditional northern stodge like Yorkshire pudding, with onion gravy or with casserole, and dishes which are just as much part of the modern English diet—chilli, curries and burgers.

☛ *37 Waterloo Road, Leeds LS10.*

☎ *Leeds 700379.*

Hare & Hounds

An excellent family pub. There is a large beer garden with parasol tables on a former bowling green, safe for children to play in the tree house or use the roundabout, swings and climbing frame while their parents relax with a drink. Inside, the bar is big and gets busy at weekends. Pool tables, darts and dominoes and fruit machines are there for the games-minded. Beers are Tetleys (plus three lagers, Guinness and wines) and the bar meals are all home-made—pies, casseroles, Yorkshire puds, roast beef sandwiches.

☛ *Bradford Road, Menston.*

☎ *Menston (0943-873998).*

Harewood Arms

As you'd expect, an up-market bar in the estate village attached to the Stately home of Lord Harewood, the Queen's cousin. Sam Smiths beers and lagers, a cocktail list, and above-average bar meals at lunchtimes and evenings (6pm-9.30pm) such as roast sirloin salads, casseroles, fish and chicken plus blackboard specials. No apparent dress restrictions but leave the leather jacket and ripped jeans at home—you'll be well out of place. More of a Laura Ashley/Austin Reed sort of place. The furnishings are chintzy and comfortable; the fireplaces look like they've been borrowed from the Robert Adam-designed interior of Harewood House. Prices are not as fancy as you might think.

☛ *On A61 Harrogate Road at Harewood.*

☎ *Leeds 886566.*

Hyde Park

Has one of the most promising façades of any Leeds pub, but unfortunately the interior's not much different to any other refurbished Tetleys house. Open plan to squeeze in vast numbers of the mainly student clientele in term-time. In particular, it's used by the less fashion-conscious students, and those who are too lazy to walk much further than round the corner from their rented flat/shared house/bedsit. Karaoke nights are very popular and lively and the pool is well subscribed, too. There is a video jukebox and staff are friendly. Relatively quiet at lunchtimes, but evenings are manic! You have been warned. Late on,

the cigarette smoke may be a problem for non-smokers.

☛ *Hyde Park Corner, Headingley Lane, Leeds LS6.*

☎ *Leeds 759352.*

The Ings

The stunning stained-glass entrance to this pub on the fringe of Guiseley reveals an almost over-the-top Victorian kitsch interior. Sitting down on one of the well-stuffed sofas or at a scrubbed pine antique table, one begins to fill in the detail—the game fish "trophies" in glass cases, the period engravings and prints on the wall. And yet there is a strangely modern feel to the place. It may be something to do with the Rolling Stones playing on the CD jukebox, or maybe the strong smell of baking pizzas (served all night). Still, the Tetleys beer is as good as it's always been, and there's a nice selection of wines and lagers.

☛ *45 Ings Lane, Guiseley.*

☎ *Guiseley (0943) 873315.*

The Junction

Since the last edition of *Leeds Fax*, the Junction seems to have gone in and out of fashion with the under-25s as other pubs in Otley have courted this huge, and otherwise uncatered-for market in Wharfedale. At the time of writing, it's extremely popular again, especially at weekends and for the famous/hilarious Wednesday night quiz. Being a free house, beers include Tetleys, Taylors and Theakstons. The oak-beamed interior is adorned with brasses and horse leathers, and sepia photos of old Otley cover the walls. In winter, the real fire warms the old bones of its loyal over-35s customers. Fine jukebox full of golden oldie vinyl now, alas, replaced by CD selection. Big-portion bar meals at lunchtimes.

☛ *Bondgate, Otley.*

☎ *Otley (0943) 463233.*

The Mansion Hotel

Beer gardens don't come much better than this—tables and chairs overlooking a fine swathe of Roundhay Park. The Greek Revival-style Mansion was built for the Nicholsons, the rich former owners of Roundhay park, in 1826

with an enormous Ionic portico. When it was bought by the Leeds ready-made clothing king John Barran in the 1870s it was originally planned to be an art gallery. It was "temporarily" used as a hotel and . . . well, you know what temporary things have a habit of becoming. Inside, there are numerous bars, popular with all age groups. Beers and lagers include Websters, Ruddles, Bass, Fosters, Holstein, Beamish and Guinness. Speciality wines also available. Good meals are served in the Darcy Bar—things like lamb chops, baked trout, stuffed tomatoes, asparagus omelette.
☛ *Mansion Lane (off Prince's Avenue) Roundhay Park, Leeds LS8.*
☎ *Leeds 661341.*

Mustard Pot
For the moment the MP seems to have become the most popular pub with the young in Chapel Allerton, after years of domination by The Regent on the other side of the busy Harrogate Road. It is a large place, serving Mansfield Beers (and draught Red Stripe), and in summer one of its main attractions is the large south-facing garden. This sun-trap has a large number of timber picnic tables, and a kiddies play area. Inside is a plush, sitting-room atmosphere where all ages and social groups mix freely at lunchtime and early evening. It is after nine that the 18-25s seem to predominate.
☛ *Clough House, Stainbeck Lane, Leeds LS7.*
☎ *Leeds 696284.*

New Inn Eccup
Eccup is a village with a population of around a couple of dozen people but the local pub gets packed. For this is a popular watering hole for many people in North Leeds, especially those living in the seemingly endless suburbs of Adel and Alwoodley who don't have a traditional pub like this nearby. The New Inn started off serving tea & coffee only to the workers who built the nearby Eccup Reservoir in the 1840s. Today, it serves fine Tetleys ales, good bar meals and its regulars are fond of darts, doms and quizzes (quiz night Wednesdays). Its fam-

ily room and beer garden make it an ideal place if you have children.
☛ *Eccup Lane, Eccup.*
☎ *Leeds 886335.*

New Inn Wortley
To generations of Leeds people waiting for a tram in Duncan Street or City Square, the New Inn was a famous destination on the line running along Tong Road to Wortley. It was at this pub that the trams terminated and one wonders how often the excuse "Sorry, luv, I missed me tram" was used by men getting late home from work after nipping in for a swift half. Today, the New Inn has a room devoted to the tram route's history, with many old photographs on the wall. The pub is as good as you'll find with many Victorian fittings and a kind of bar skittles—unique in Leeds—called "Devil Amongst the Tailors". Good Tetleys beers and a juekbox of vinyl 45s! Play it while you can.
☛ *366 Tong Road, Wortley, Leeds LS12.*
☎ *Leeds 637084.*

Newlands
Unlike most pubs in the big flat/ besitland the Newlands is somewhere to go for a quiet drink. It's not full of students, karaoke or rugby teams. Instead it's actually frequented by that endangered species in transient-dominated Leeds 6, the local population. All ages, ethnic backgrounds and classes mix in a relaxed atmosphere, with good Tetleys beers on tap. Refur-

bished, but stylishly so—no attempt at roping in the trendies here. Busy after nine most nights.
☛ *Hyde Park Road, Leeds LS6.*
☎ *456908.*

The Oddfellows
Another one for lovers of real pubs, "the Rag" as it is known by Yeadon drinkers is three 18th century weavers' cottages knocked into one. Low-roofed and stone-faced, it has retained its character down the years despite several modernisations. And well-kept Tetleys ales have made it a veteran of *The Good Beer Guide*. The strange name comes from a 19th century Northern society described as the "working man's freemasons", the founders of which were popularly believed to be "odd fellows".
☛ *The Green, Yeadon, LS19.*
☎ *Leeds 503819.*

Old Bridge Inn
There is probably no bigger or better beer garden in the Leeds area than this riverside haven. It has to be said that the River Aire, as it slides eastwards through this part of the Kirkstall Valley, is not exactly the Dordogne. But trees screen the busy traffic and electricity pylons, and in summer it is an amazingly popular sun-trap. When the weather's fine, a big barbecue is lit. Inside, there's a large bar meals menu. The bars (there's one upstairs and in the stone-flagged cellar) sell a good range of drinks: Boddingtons, Stones,

A rare waterside beer garden in Leeds—the Old Bridge Inn at Kirkstall.

Tetleys, Theakstons bitters; four draught lagers, two ciders, and Guinness. The pub is popular with the young; the beer garden a great hit with young families.

☞ *Bridge Road, Kirstall, Leeds LS5.*

☎ *Leeds 749508.*

Original Oak

This popular pub overlooks what used to be the centre of Headingley village but nowadays the shopping centre is to north and the Oak, along with the Skyrack over the road, form the social centre. Despite being long out of favour with Real Ale buffs because of the lack of handpumps, the Oak has got to be one of the busiest pubs in Leeds between 9pm and 11pm seven nights a week when the students are around. However, it's not all students. The youngish Leeds population who sincerely believe that student pubs must be where the action is make up a sizeable chunk of the custom. And so does the 12-months-a-year Headingley population, from pipe-sucking old timers to balding hippies. In summer, there's a good beer garden around a classic billiard-table bowling green, a real sun-trap at lunchtime. The bar lunches (12-2pm Monday to Friday) are definitely among the best in the city. Great home-made meat pies and rib-stickers like stew and dumplings a speciality, but also receives complements for its vegetarian dishes. Traditional puddings like treacle sponge and custard and jam rolly polly. The multi-roomed pub gets very crowded after Test matches at the nearby cricket ground, and it's worth going for the atmosphere alone, especially when the Aussies are in town.

☞ *2 Otley Road, Leeds LS6.*

☎ *Leeds 751322.*

Pack Horse

On Gelderd Road, just up the hill from the ring road, this particular Pack Horse—it's a common name for pubs in Yorkshire—is extremely popular for the quality of its bar meals. Young business types pile into cars from the city centre and escape here for an hour. Part of its appeal is that it's not

particularly expensive, yet the quality is high. As well as pies/fish/chips/chicken there are some pretty fancy specials. The portions are generous and, last but not least, the gravy is delicious. Recently, meals have been put on in the early evening too. Beers are standard Bass—Stones, Carling lager, two ciders and Guinness.

☞ *Gelderd Road, Leeds LS12.*

☎ *Leeds 638217.*

The Queens Hotel

In one of the dreariest parts of Leeds, the handsome Victorian façade of the Queens shines like a diamond. Inside, lots of dark wood and tiles, beautifully etched windows and shiny brass captivate the attention. Why, you almost forget you should be watching our for those famous faces from the nearby Yorkshire Television studios who do their Tetleys beer drinking here. Other regulars include locals from this part of Burley, and a fair smattering of students in term time.

☞ *Burley Road, Leeds LS3.*

☎ *Leeds 459024.*

Red Lion

The big car park is evidence that this pub is popular with more than just the villagers of Shadwell. With large areas of North Leeds lacking pubs of real character, many suburbanites like to drive out to the Red Lion. Locally, it is the hub of village life at Shadwell. Tetleys beers, with the addition of Burton Ale, are on sale, along with four draught lagers, Guinness. Acknowledging that many of its customers are driving, there is a good range of low-alcohol beers and ciders. During the week there are bar meals, mostly roasts and home-made pies. The big lounge fills up very quickly at night, mainly with under-30s, and the large back room is where older villagers drink.

☞ *Main Street, Shadwell.*

☎ *Leeds 737463.*

Regent

Once the busiest and trendiest pub in north-east Leeds, the Regent at Chapel Allerton is still very popular with the smarter under-30s set despite competition from the

nearby Mustard Pot. At lunchtime and in the early part of the evening it has a staunchly local custom, but after eight the Armani Army and pouting young women invade the big two-level lounge from other parts of Leeds to see and be seen. Many a romance has started with a bit of light-hearted banter across the shoulder-to-shoulder forest of bodies. Good bar lunches Monday to Saturdays. Well kept Tetley bitter prevents the Regent from becoming a lager lounge.

☞ *Regent Street, Leeds LS7.*

☎ *Leeds 683354.*

Rising Sun

Overshadowed but not eclipsed by a huge railway viaduct built to carry the Leeds-Thirsk railway, the Sun has survived when the traditional back-to-back Leeds houses it once watered have disappeared. A popular haunt of Rugby League fans—the Loiners' ground is just up Cardigan Road—this Victorian pub serves a fine drop of Tetleys (it is promoted as one of the brewery's "Pubs of Character"). You can hardly fail to notice the superb engraved windows.The Rising Sun may not be as trendy as the nearby Cardigan Arms, but there is a lot of atmosphere and you can find elbow room (even a seat) on Friday and Saturday nights. Lunchtimes bring in a mix of office and factory workers for bar meals (roasts, pies, curry, chilli, pasta, sandwiches) and the evening brings in many aspiring Leeds people who live in Burley.

☞ *Kirkstall Road, Leeds LS3.*

☎ *Leeds 751046.*

Royal Park

For as long as Leeds 6 is the student heartland (ie until the end of time) the Royal Park will be one of the busiest pubs in town. It was once claimed that Tetleys shifted more beer here than anywhere else in Yorkshire. For years, it was almost a headquarters for hippies, punks, Goths, assorted leather-jackets and whatever was the latest cult. So revered was it that members of The Clash popped in for an impromtu set here way back in the 80s. However, a refurbishment has cleared many old timers out, but still the place gets packed.

In term-time, you're positively geriatric at 25. Video jukebox, pool and some addictive computer games keep many a mind occupied. Local bands play regularly in the upstairs room. Hand-pulled Tetleys, the usual range of three lagers (weak, medium and strong). It can take a long time to get served and drinkers often buy a couple of rounds at once. The Royal Park is an acquired taste to some, a way of life to others.
☛ *Queens Road, Leeds LS6.*
☎ *Leeds 757494.*

Royalty Inn

Perched on the top of Otley Chevin, with stunning long-distance views west to Bradford and north across Wharfedale, this former 18th century farmhouse is very popular. A large family room and outdoor beer garden with playground (tree house, climbing frames, swings and bouncing castle) make it an especially good for children. It is a Tetleys house, serving good English food that can include toad-in-the-hole, jumbo Yorkshires and lamb chops. The Royalty puts on a bonfire and fireworks display every November 5th.
☛ *Yorkgate, Otley Chevin, reached by lane off A658.*
☎ *Otley (0943) 461156.*

The Skyrack

The best times to go to the Skyrack are during the day and during the summer. At all other times it is packed full of students and assorted Headingley youth. A few years back it had a predominately Heavy Metal air to it but slowly things have changed and there's now probably more house music being played on the CD jukebox than anything else. The denim crew are still there but looking more weary and outnumbered by the day and seem to have been relegated to the large pool area at the back. On summer evenings, drinkers from here and the Original Oak across the busy Otley Road spill out over the pavements and surround area, making it one of the liveliest parts of town. Being a Whitbread pub, the beers include Castle Eden, Trophy, Moosehead and Murphys.
☛ *Otley Road, Leeds LS6.*
☎ *Leeds 752123.*

The Stables Bar

This was part of the stables block to the Mansion that was the manor house to a large part of north-east Leeds until the 1870s. Today, it is a popular bar with the young, especially on fine summer evenings when its front yard tables and chairs get the sun's full blast. Inside, draught beers include the lovely but expensive Becks, McEwans lager, Theakstons Old Peculiar and Bitter, and Younger's Scotch Bitter. Pizzas and other meals. Quiz night is Tuesday; Golden Oldies disco on Wednesdays; and live bands on Thursday.
☛ *Prince's Avenue (opposite Tropical World), Roundhay, Leeds LS8.*
☎ *Leeds 668435.*

White House

Converted from a beautiful stone Victorian detached house on the edge of Roundhay Park, the White House is popular with all age groups in an area rather devoid of decent pubs. Most people tend to drive here, and there's a large car park. Beers include Greenalls and Tetleys, and lagers are Labatt's, Castlemaine and Stella. Food has become such an integral part of the White House that it could just as easily be described as a restaurant. Geared to family tastes, with special prices (and portions) for children and senior citizens. The menu is mostly English in style, with steaks, fish, chicken, casseroles, scampis and home-made meat pies. Also salads and vegetarian pasta dishes.
☛ *55 Wetherby Road, Leeds LS8.*
☎ *Leeds 655834.*

All hands—a game of dominoes in progress at a Leeds public house.

Eating Out Around Leeds

From Thai to Polish, Caribbean to Gujarati, Vietnamese to Burgers, Punjabi to Greek, French to Fish & Chips, Italian to Bacon Butties, Pizzas to Tacos.

In the 1990s, Leeds has assembled a remarkable range of different cuisines. Only a couple of decades ago, the best meals in town were usually served at a handful of posh hotels but today—with incomes higher than ever and people eating out more and more—the choice is vast. Since the first edition of *Leeds Fax*, there have been some exciting new restaurants opening up, not least in the expanding Chinese community of Leeds, and the introduction of Thai cuisine. In order to keep the information as up-to-date as possible, we decided not to include opening times or say which credit cards are accepted, since these often change. Instead, we offer the following advice—

Opening Times. Trying to keep up with the opening times of some restaurants is a hopeless task. While many have kept the same hours for years, some are constantly altering them. But the rule of thumb is that the majority are open Tuesday to Saturday evenings. Many, especially those in the city centre, serve lunches Monday to Saturday too. It's on the Sunday lunchtime and evening and Monday nights that some close. If you are going to try a restaurant for the first time, especially if it involves a special journey, it is advisable to telephone first to check that it is open.

Credit Cards. Another moving target is the range of credit cards accepted by different restaurants. Again, some change according to what deal they're getting with the credit card company. All the establishments listed in the following pages, unless otherwise stated, accept Access & Visa. Many also take American Express and Diners Club cards.

Tipping. Many restaurants at the higher end of the market apply a 10% service charge to the bill. Where we know this is the case, we have stated it. Ocassionally, a waiter might still leave the "tips"

section free on the credit card slip, expecting a further hand-out.

Booking. Most restaurants take bookings, but the busiest do not. Instead, they have bars at which you can have an aperitif, sometimes giving your order there so that the first course is already served when you sit down.

Bistros

The biggest growth area in Leeds restaurants is the catch-all bistro, one that offers something for every taste and pocket. Their menus often change at least by the season, and the combination of ingredients can be truly inspirational. Some call themselves American diners, others have a Continental bias, but most defy categorization. Except, of course, as bistros.

Boston Exchange

Always good value, the Boston Exchange squeezes an astonishing range of cuisines onto its menu—truly the United Nations of nosh. Dishes include American, Mexican, Creole, Japanese via New York, Italian via Boston and Louisiana via Leeds. Burgers, tacos, enchiladas, steaks and scampi represent the basic side of the menu. Elsewhere, is the more unusual stuff. The desert list makes you put on a few ounces just reading it—sundaes, fudges, cheesecakes and Death by Chocolate! There is a large cocktail bar, with good value drinks, while you're waiting to be seated, and occasional live entertainment. Set in a large car park with easy access to town for businessmen at lunchtime and close enough to the better suburbs for the evening trade, the Exchange gets very busy. An ideal place for groups in which the older members have rather conservative tastes and others are more adventurous/vegetarian. All tastes are catered for here.

☛ *St. Anns Lane, Leeds LS4.*
☎ *Leeds 755404.*

Brasserie Forty Four

This is yet another sign of the shape of things to come in Leeds, a superb brasserie occupying warehousing and flour mills beside the Aire Calder Navigation. The smart dining room overlooks the water, and in the short time it has been open has become among the top half dozen restaurants in Leeds. First-time diners usually have to do a double-take at the pianist in the bar—it's a dummy. Part of the much-acclaimed 42 The Calls hotel next door, its menu has an extremely varied international feel, representing many of the world's classic meals and ingredients, each given an extra special touch. The most basic example is the Yorkshire pudding with port-enriched gravy. Starters include tempura-cooked seafood, and melon with smoked duck. The main courses can be reasonably priced, like the chopped steak burger with a cheese fondue sauce, or expensive like the New York prime rib of beef steak, serve simply with its roasting juices. Some dishes are more original, like the lamb and apricot pie. The sweets often depend on the season, and can include summer pudding, rhubarb crumble and—a real surprise in such a place—bread and butter pudding. There is a pretty impressive wine list.

☛ *44 The Calls, Leeds LS2.*
☎ *Leeds 343232.*

Ferret Hall Bistro

There has been a bistro in this Headingley location, under different names, for the last couple of decades. This one seems to have found a winning formula—good food and reasonable prices, a constantly changing menu, and quick service. Although small, it squeezes a surprising number of tables into a dining room decorated with Punch-style cartoons. The dishes are often imaginative. Besides the usual garlic mushrooms and home-made pate there things like mixed bean taco and "soup of the century" (cream of madeira and mushroom). Main courses depend on how much you want to pay and range from char-grilled steaks at the top end, through chicken and asparagus pie, stir-fry lamb, and salmon mornay en croute. Vegetarians are well catered for with things like vegetarian taco, and a French style pancake. Burgers and pasta dishes complete the regular menu, supplemented with blackboard specials in season. Optional 10% service charge added to the bill.

☛ *2 The Parade, North Lane, Headingley, Leeds LS6*

☎ *Leeds 758613.*

Glenn's

Unfortunately, there are not many good bistros in South Leeds but this is one of the exceptions. Glenn's theme is Caribbean—the owner, Glenn Evans, was born in the Cayman Islands—but by no stretch of the imagination could it be called a Caribbean restaurant, with Yorkshire Pudding and roast beef with the trimmings on the Sunday lunch menu. Other dishes include clam chowder, curried eggs, shark steaks, peppered steaks. Occasional live entertainment, including a Caribbean Steel Band. Booking advisable.

☛ *283 Dewsbury Road, Leeds LS11.*

☎ *Leeds 705187.*

Ike's

A well-established, very busy restaurant that is extremely popular with the young. Although advertised as an American restaurant, it has one of the widest menus in town, an international collection of dishes ranging from burgers, Italian pizzas and pastas, Mexican, French, Greek and other dishes. Carnivores will love the plate-filling T-bone steaks, while vegetarians have some of the best veggie meals currently on offer in Leeds. They include rice and hazelnut burger, vegetarian stroganoff, aubergine and mushroom lasagne, vegetarian chilli, butterbean and vegetable moussaka and wholemeal and wallnut casserole. There's a kiddies menu, and a large American-ish sweets board. The big cocktail bar has plenty of seating, if you have to wait for a table. Very busy on Thursday, Friday and Saturday nights.

☛ *Cross Belgrave Street, Leeds LS2.*

☎ *Leeds 433391.*

Korks

Out in the uncivilized wastes of Wharfedale, Korks is an oasis of good food. Officially, it's a wine bar and you can come in and sit drinking from the extensive list. But its food has steadily become the focal point, a constantly changing and surprising menu of ingredients that you would never have believed would be seen in a bed of rice or lettuce together. It's a safe bet that the steak, chicken, lamb, freshwater and sea fish, duck, rabbit and pasta is not like how mamma used to make it. There's also a range of homemade burgers, and an extremely fattening sweet menu (boozy icecreams, creme brulee, hot chocolate fudge, etc.)

☛ *40 Bondgate, Otley.*

☎ *Otley (0943) 462020.*

Outside Inn

Another pizza-pasta-burger place, but above-average quality. The decor, if you don't already know, creates the illusion of eating outdoors whilst indoors. Facades of Victorian shops and courtyards surround the dining area, where you tuck into the medium-priced food or go for the top-end meals like steaks, veal and seafood. Sinful sweets like knickerbocker glory and hot chocolate fudge.

☛ *6 Town Street, Horsforth.*

☎ *Leeds 581410.*

Strawberry Fields

With the BBC across the road and the University and Poly on either side, Strawberry Fields has had to be conscious of modern eating habits to survive. It manages very well on its menu, a mixture of wholefoods, international specialities and—above all—its excellent range of vegetarian dishes. These include vegetarian lasagne, pancakes stuffed with nuts and mushrooms, three bean stroganoff, red bean moussaka There's burgers and steaks too, and often good "share-a-pizza" deals for two. Sweets are things like fudge brownies, cheesecake, Mississippi mud pie. Excellent value litre carafes of house wines.

☛ *159 Woodhouse Lane, Leeds LS2*

☎ *Leeds 431515.*

A revolution in eating tastes has happened in Leeds in the last 25 years. Foreign cuisines now predominate, and pubs are often the last bastions of traditional English "fayre". Some restaurants also doggedly fly the flag—

The Adam Restaurant

The great manor house that once had the whole of Roundhay Park as its front garden became a hotel in the 1870s and for almost as long its restaurant has been a noted eating place in Leeds. Most of its customers come for the table d'hôte (fixed price) menus, whether the executive lunches during the week or the immensely popular Friday and Saturday nights when the meal includes dancing until 1am. Food varies from classic fish, chicken and red meat English food with some Continental food too, especially on the a la carte menu. Sunday is family day, with two sittings for traditional roast lunches—12.15pm and 2.30pm.

☛ *Mansion Lane (off Prince's Avenue), Roundhay Park, Leeds LS8.*

☎ *Leeds 661341.*

Bingley Arms

The oldest licensed premises in England has a long established upstairs dining room. The a la carte menu contains mostly good English food, as befits an old English inn, with some interesting seafood dishes like poached salmon flakes in a crepe topped with asparagus and coated with Champagne sauce. Main courses include the very popular roast rack of Yorkshire lamb, peppered fillet steak, roast ducking and one of the rare places these days that serves up Surf & Turf. That is, fillet steak with lobster and prawn sauce. Sheer decadence! There are some good vegetarian alternatives like potato goulash, nut and vegetable pancake and cauliflower chasseur. Fattening deserts and a fine range of Yorkshire Dales, English and French country cheeses.

☛ *Bardsey Village, off the A58 Wetherby Road.*

☎ *Collingham Bridge (0937) 572462.*

Brigg-Shots

Named after a traditional refreshment enjoyed by the woollen cloth merchants whose market in this part of Briggate in the Middle Ages was the very foundation of modern-day Leeds. Brigg-Shots is hidden away in a recently renovated court and is the sort of small, stylish bistro that one normally finds in country towns. The menu various according to season but in summer can be interesting combinations like the following starters—smoke salmon asparagus and hazelnut salad in a hazelnut dressing, grilled dates wrapped in bacon with a mild mustard sauce, or asparagus mouse with quails eggs and cheesy wafers. Main courses are similarly unusual. If it's on the menu, try the lamb fillet topped with mustard and garlic and served with a sauce of redcurrant and sour cream. Good range of sweets, including delicious lemon syllabub.

☛ *Queens Court, off Lower Briggate, Leeds LS1.*
☎ *Leeds 425629.*

Whitelocks First City Luncheon Bar

For many living on the fringes of Leeds, this is the only place to eat when in town. The restaurant section of this nationally famous pub (see page 97) remains more or less just as it was designed over 70 years ago. There's wood panelling, stained glass windows, brass fittings, a coal fire, good solid tables and leather-upholstered seating. And the food is in harmony with all of this—beautifully cooked classic English dishes like roast beef, giant Yorkshire puddings and onion gravy (for starters), a beef and ale pie and lamb chops, all served with three vegetables. For afters, the jam rolly pool or the treacle sponge are great if you have room; there's also apple pie with cream or ice cream. And, of course, no English restaurant would be complete without a whole stilton, scooped out with a spoon. Although Whitelocks keep a good wine list, the majority of diners prefer to order beers to brought through from the bar.

☛ *Turk's Head Yard, Briggate, Leeds LS1.*
☎ *Leeds 453950.*

Fish & Chips

Leeds and the West Riding form the fish and chips capital of the world. If the region has made any contribution to the national cuisine, it is the jumbo haddock fried in dripping, never vegetable oil. What affect this has had on the local health nobody knows, but there are still plenty of spritely octogenarians walking around who have been eating their "land and sea" since they were kids. Today, Leeds has still got the best fish and chip restaurants.

Brett's

Charlie Brett runs the famous café and takeaway first established by his father in 1919, and it has become a Headingley institution. Its fan club extends to numerous past and present players in the England cricket team, who have been known to sneak off here for their haddock and chips after a Test Match at the nearby cricket ground. The late great cricket commentator, John Arlott, even had his retirement party here. Apart from the sheer character of the place—a tiny fish & chip shop fronted by a carefully manicured garden that could put some country houses to shame—what makes people love Brett's is the quality and the prices (high and low respectively). Fine fresh cod, haddock and plaice are always on the menu in a variety of sizes, as well as more recent additions of scampi, chicken, sausages and burgers. Side orders include mushy peas and baked beans. Tea and bread and butter are the traditional partners, for there is no license. Save room for the afters, particularly the famous steamed treacle pudding. You get to the café by walking behind the counter of the shop. No credit cards. Always closed Sundays.

☛ *4 North Lane, Headingley, Leeds LS6.*
☎ *Leeds 755288.*

The Americans and Japanese have three stops in Yorkshire when they'e on holiday. One is York Minster, the other is the Brontë Parsonage at Haworth, and the third is **Harry Ramsden's** *at Guiseley. Well, soon they may not bother. The company has now opened branches (or is it chips off the old block?) in New York, Hong Kong and Heathrow Airport. Perhaps the next one will be in Moscow, where they know all about standing in queues. For apart from the quality of the food and the crystal chandelier dining room, that is what most people remember about going to Harry Ramsden's. A few years back, 27 coach-loads of hungry people once rolled up at the same time! The food is, as you might expect, predominately fish and chips in a variety of portions and with peas, beans, etc. and the essential pot of tea and bread and butter. In these health conscious days, Harry Ramsden's still use getting on for half a million pounds of haddock a year.*

☛ *White Cross, Guiseley.*
☎ *Guiseley (0943) 874641.*

Bryan's

Bryan's was once judged "Fish and Chip Shop of the Year" by the *Good Food Guide* and anyone who knows the place will tell you the standard has been maintained for years. A large, brightly lit restaurant at the top end of Headingley, Bryan's offers brisk and very cheerful service. Cholesterol watchers throw caution to the wind and feast on fried fresh (never frozen) cod, sole, plaice and halibut and *real* chips. But the famous Bryan's meal is the haddock. The jumbo and chips arrive on a gleaming oval charger and takes up most of the table. Accompaniments include mushy peas, baked beans, pickled onions, coleslaw and pickled cucumber. Most people wash all this down with scalding hot tea. The takeaway shop next door is always busy.

☛ *Weetwood Lane, Leeds LS16.*
☎ *Leeds 785679.*

Cravens

One lady set the editor of *Leeds Fax* a test. "I'll soon find out how comprehensive your book is," she said with a twinkle. "Does it have Cravens at Pudsey, my favourite fish restaurant?" Whereupon the editor turned to page 48 and showed her the appropriate entry. "Oh dear," she sighed, looking slightly pale. "I suppose the prices will go up." As far as we know, they haven't. Craven's is still a fine fish and chip restaurant, much overlooked in the Leeds area. Surrounded by marine decor (things like divers' helmets, ships' wheels) you tuck into large helpings of fresh haddock, halibut, place or scampi. There's a takeaway too.

☛ *32 Lowtown, Pudsey.*
☎ *Leeds 551396.*

Nash's Tudor Restaurant

The 18th century building once housed the Kemplay's Academy for Young Gentlemen, three of its former pupils going on to become signatorys to the American Independent Bill. How many chippies have got that sort of history? Nash's upstairs restaurant serves classic Grimsby-fresh fish and chips like haddock, plaice and halibut. Other features include rainbow trout, Dover sole, salmon and scampi. And if you're really into seafood, start off with the "prawns on draught". That is a half-pint of whole prawns. The restaurant also does steaks and lamb chops. Popular with generations of stars appearing at the nearby Grand Theatre and City Varieties.

☛ *17 Merrion Street, Leeds LS2.*
☎ *Leeds 457194.*

French

Despite its reputation, French food has never been widely available in Leeds. The following restaurants have been going for some time, and have built up good reputations.

L'Escargot

In a good Yorkshire stone house set back from one of Headingley's main thoroughfares, once discovered L'Escargot becomes a favourite restaurant. The staff are French and if you enjoy speaking the language they'll engage you in conversation. The food comes from a regularly changing menu and there is always a wide choice. There's an excellent selection of steaks from the char-grill, while fresh fish often depends on what's on the market. Comprehensive wine list. L'Escargot is not exactly cheap, but by the standards of its food and other French restaurants its prices are reasonable.

☛ *13 Shaw Lane, Leeds LS6.*
☎ *Leeds 788400.*

La Grillade

A cellar restaurant with a good atmosphere, La Grillade has been going a long time and is justly popular. The set menu, at a very reasonable price, is usually good enough for most people, until they look at the blackboard for specials like Moules Marinières, and whatever else is straight from the market. The menu, by the way, is in French and although words like *poulet, canard, veau* and *pommes* are understandable to those who don't speak French, some explanation might be required. Excellent wine list.

☛ *In the basement of the Wellesley Hotel, Wellington Street, Leeds LS1.*
☎ *Leeds 459707.*

Sous Le Nez En Ville

There's been a high-quality restaurant here for many years, popular with the business community by day and for its romantic candlelit atmosphere at night. Although most of the dishes are named in English, there is a distinctly French character to the food. Among the starters, few can resist the French black pudding. The blackboard specials are dominated by fish. Also a wine bar, there is a wide variety of bar snacks at lunchtime.

☛ *The Basement, Quebec House, 9 Quebec Street, Leeds LS1.*
☎ *Leeds 440108.*

Le Mange-Tout

On a summer's evening, the tables and chairs outside this restaurant and the strings of lights are an inviting site to travellers on the Otley road. Inside, the decor is a traditional French bistro, with green chequered tablecloths and posters of classic French cafés. The menu is not as wide as some in Leeds, but that's a sign that everything is extremely fresh. Good fish dishes like turbot and halibut steaks, Dover sole and monkfish. Very reasonably price. Makes a thing of Bastille Day (July 14).

☛ *473 Otley Road, Leeds LS16.*
☎ *Leeds 610201.*

Greek

With Greece rivalling Spain as the number one European holiday destination for the British, it's surprising that there aren't many Greek restaurants in the area. The two below are just the place to go to re-acquaint your tastebuds with retsina and ouzo. Oh, and the food's good as well.

Olive Tree

A smart restaurant rather than a taverna, set back from a busy ring road roundabouts. Good kebabs and specials like kleftiko, the classic pot-roasted lamb dish. Other more standard food like stefado and moussaka are included. There are various good-price set meals, such as at off-peak times and business lunches.

☛ *Oaklands, Rodley Lane, (off the ring road) Rodley.*
☎ *Leeds 569283.*

Scorpio

If smashing plates is good therapy, this place should be available on the NHS. The Green smithereen culture is alive and well at the Scorpio. Diners dance to loud bazouki music on Fridays and Saturday nights. Most of the time, however, the Scorpio is a basic taverna. Greek-Cypriot in style, with dips like taramasalata, humous and tsatsiki, plus kefthethes and dolmathes. There's the unusual bourtheto, a Corfu fish dish baked with onion, tomatoes and paprika. And there's the kebabs. Advance booking for plate-smashing essential.

☛ *11 Merrion Way (at the rear of the Merrion Centre), Leeds LS1.*
☎ *Leeds 451389.*

Italian

After Asian, Italian food is the most popular in Leeds. And three of the city's busiest restaurants— Bibi's, Flying Pizza and Le Celle—are Italian. Some can be really expensive, others allow eating on a budget. All serve pizzas, pasta dishes and a wide range of speciality meat and vegetarian dishes. And the Italian wines, if you've never got beyond Chianti and Valpolicella, are wonderful.

Bibi's

The best-know name in Italian food in Leeds, Bibi's moved upmarket a few years back and managed to become the busiest restaurant in town. The quality of the food is very high, and prices range from medium to expensive. You can't book so at peak times there's the inevitable wait at the bar. The huge menu encompasses a wide choice of antipasti, then pastas, pizzas, steaks, veal, guinea fowl, turkey, chicken, duck and fresh fish like prawns, swordfish, squid and sole. The sweets are gorgeous with lots of cream, chocolate sauce and fudge liberally splashed around. Good value carafes of house wine. A 10% service charge is added to the bill.

☛ *Minerva House, 16 Greek Street, Leeds LS1.*
☎ *Leeds 430905.*

Flying Pizza

Where conspicuous consumption in Leeds is most conspicuous. Very popular with the wealthy who live in this part of town (and many who don't) it is, however not so highly priced that it's the exclusive habitat of Gold Cards. The food is classic Italian cuisine, a huge range, and is very good. Like the main menu, the antipasti has cheap and expensive ends. The latter includes Bresaola (cured fillet of beef with pickles and olive oil) which is absolutely delicious. Good steaks and veal dishes. Blackboard specials. Extremely busy, and there is often a wait for a table at night. A good outdoor seating area for fine weather.

☛ *60 Street Lane, Leeds LS8.*
☎ *Leeds 666501.*

Alfresco eating at the Flying Pizza, Roundhay.

Italian Job

A small, almost intimate café-type place near Leeds Bridge, with reasonable prices. It does burgers as well as pizzas and pastas, and specials like steaks, veal and poultry. Among the starters is a very good tonno fagioli (tuna, beans and onions in oil dress). Popular at lunchtimes and early evening.

☛ *9 Bridge End, Leeds LS1.*
☎ Leeds 420185.

Le Celle

Established in the former Ireland Wood police station, Le Celle contains one or two hints of its former use, but mostly it's a medium-priced ristorante. The large bar seating/standing area is evidence that there can be quite a wait for your table at peak times, but the wait's usually worth it. A huge menu contains few surprises in the pizza and pasta dishes but it's in the more expensive main courses like veal, chicken, steaks and fish that Le Celle pulls out the stops. Incredibly popular at both lunchtimes and evenings.

☛ *151 Otley Old Road, Leeds LS16*
☎ *Leeds 611297.*

Pizza Express

One of the key buildings in Leeds history was the White Cloth Hall, opened in 1776. Most of it was knocked down to build the railway line that runs to York, but the gatehouse with its distinctive cupola survived. Like the Corn Exchange it faces, it has found a new role in the regeneration of this part of town. Pizza Express are at the fast-food end of the pizza market, but the standard is good. Over a dozen pizzas, plus lasagne, cannelloni, and various dishes with doughballs. Limited range of Italian wines, but like the food they are budget-priced.

☛ *Crown Street, Leeds LS2.*
☎ *Leeds 465207.*

Salvo's

After Harry Ramsden's, Salvo's probably has the most famous queue in Leeds. Perhaps not as long as the celebrated fish and chip emporium, but its diners are no less determined to get their tables. Salvos is small and has a good at-

mosphere, which is too rare in Leeds restaurants. The menu is limited but imaginative, and there's always good blackboard specials. For such high quality, the prices are quite low—thus the queues.
☛ 115 Otley road, Leeds LS6.
☎ Leeds 755017.

Polish

After browsing through the Eating Out section of the last edition of Leeds Fax, a number of readers felt moved to point out that there was one glaring omission. So here it is.

The Polish Catholic Centre
On the first floor of this large hub of Leeds's closely knit Polish community is a restaurant that is open to the general public. The dining room is long and extremely ordinary—diners come here for the food. The dishes are Polish and other East European cuisines. The menu changes from time to time but can include goulash, rissoles and pierogi (a kind of large, oval ravioli stuffed with mincemeat. The price includes potatoes (chips are served for a small extra charge) and any two vegetables from a range that includes beetroot, sauerkraut, cabbage and pickled cucumber. Sweets include apple cakes and pancakes. Prices pay scant attention to inflation, and service is cheery. The Christmas dinners in December are especially good value.
☛ Woodfield, Newton Hill Road (off Chapeltown Road), Leeds LS7.
☎ Leeds 628019.

Vegetarian

Vegetarian alternatives are available in most Leeds restaurants. Places like Ike's, Strawberry Fields and Maxi's have particularly good choices of vegetable dishes, but here are three which specialise in meat-free cookery.

Bhavani Junction
A new addition, like its sister restaurant The Shabab next door, the Bhavani Junction offers good quality Indian cuisine in stylish surroundings. A favourite is the thali, which brings several dishes together. These can include various daals, or vegetables like aubergine, leaf spinach, okra or mushrooms.
☛ 2 Eastgate, Leeds LS2.
☎ Leeds 423299.

Curlew Café
This Otley café has an international flavour to its menus, which can include Mexican, American, Italian, Greek, North African and East European. During the day, there are cakes and snacks with teas and coffees and good home made lunches dishes like soup, salad, nutroasts, omelettes, humous, curries, baked potatoes. Vegan food available.
☛ 11-13 Cross Gate, Otley.
☎ Otley (0943) 464351.

Hansa's
Hansa's Gujarati restaurant has a large menu, studied over a drink before moving into the three-level dining rooms. There are Thali complete meals, and specialities like massalla dhosa, a spicy mixture of vegetables rolled in a pancake. The vegetable curries include paneer (cottage cheese) and peas, spinach and potato, cauliflower, Indian runner beans and aubergine. Finish off with an Indian desert like kulfi or the gulab jamu, fried golden milk powder balls dipped in syrup and served hot.
☛ 72-74 North Street, Leeds LS2.
☎ Leeds 444408.

American

With American 50s culture swamping leisure fashions in Britain, the food is also everywhere. Much of it—burgers, chilli and fried chicken—has been assimilated by the menus of many different restaurants. Even chop suey is a Chinese-American invention. And, of course, there is McDonalds and Burger King. Not surprisingly, therefore, there are a few specialist American cafés. Here's two of them.

Jake's Diner
Upstairs at Belushi's, a shrine to the dead cult hero star of The Blues Brothers, is this weird place. Pictures of John Belushi stare down at diners tucking into mainly pizzas and fast-food pasta. It's fast, basic and very low priced. Being at Hyde Park Corner, heart of student/bedsit land, its customers are mainly young. Licensed, and serves wine, Rolling Rock beer, Red Rock cider and Skol.
☛ Hyde Park Corner, Woodhouse Lane, Leeds LS6.
☎ Leeds 746075.

The Manhattan Diner
In the basement of the Corn Exchange, the Manhattan has the biggest range of burgers in town, all with names like Hollywood (turkeyburger & mayonnaise), Brooklyn (beefburger with bacon & cheese), and Miami Vice Burger (chilli relish, onion ring & cheese). American breakfasts served all day, and there's spare ribs, fried chicken, real hot dogs, vegetarian and Mexican meals.
☛ The Corn Exchange, Crown Street, Leeds.
☎ Leeds 432252.

Caribbean

With a large West Indian population in Leeds, there are surprisingly few opportunities to sample the distinctive Caribbean food. An exception is Dr. B's.

Dr. B's
The low prices charged for the excellent food here arise from the fact that Dr. B's is used to train staff for the catering industry. Green decor and plants create a tropical environment, and the food includes such things as the Jamaican national dish of Ackee (a yellow, soft, sweet fruit looking like scrambled egg when cooked) and salt fish. Others are sprats and dumplings, fried chicken, West Indian curried goat and rice, rice & peas, fried plantins. Popular at lunchtimes.
☛ 191/193 Chapeltown Road, Leeds LS7.
☎ Leeds 626362.

Asian

Great new restaurants are opening up all the time, and places like Wetherby, Otley and Horsforth have all got good quality Asian cooking on their doorsteps. In

Leeds itself, competition is fierce. The following are our recommendations for all tastes and budgets.

Ayesha

Popular with students, because of its location and its low prices, the Ayesha has a large range of dishes. Not all are of the "all brown unless it's with spinach" variety and instead there are some good creamy, spicy, vegetarian and speciality meat dishes. The staff—or to be more exact, the one man who seems to be there all the time—is friendly and patient, even when some of the student diners get rather excited.

☛ *Victoria Road, Leeds LS6.*
☎ *Leeds 758826.*

Corner Café

With a recent facelift, the Corner Café—not a greasy spoon but a good budget-priced curry house—at last looks like it's in the catering business (before, it could have been someone's private house).

But the food hasn't changed. It's still good value, especially its vegetarian meals which draw diners from all over Leeds. Inside, there are two rooms and the curries come in soup plates. Most people order chapaties rather than rice. No credit cards.

☛ *83 Buslingthorpe Lane (near the bottom of Scott Hall Road), Leeds LS7.*
☎ *Leeds 623958.*

Darbar

An extraordinary place! No restaurant in Leeds has such an interior. Wood panelling, a carved wooden door that is a work of art, stained glass roof-lighting, deep pile carpets, linen tablecloths, and expensive furniture make the Darbar a real treat. Considering its location deep in the heart of the city centre, the atmosphere is calm. After all that, the food has a lot to live up to and fortunately it is wonderful. There's a limited range of tandoori and other Indian dishes,

but each one we tried was a knock-out. And the pillao rice seemed to put everyone else's in the shade. Of course, it's expensive but well worth it. Recommended by the Curry Club, the Darbar has raised the standards of up-market Asian restaurants in Leeds.

☛ 16/17 Kirkgate, Leeds LS1.
☎ Leeds 460381.

Mandalay

Close to the Grand Theatre and two of the biggest cinemas, a visit to the Mandalay is often combined with the night's entertainment. Still one of the highest quality in Leeds, and one of the most expensive. The tandoori dishes are what it does best, but there's also a wide selection of vegetarian meals. The vegetable kofta, in particular, will get even carnivores coming back for more. Any of the 12 vegetable dishes can be ordered as a main course for an additional 50% charge. Many of the dishes are delicately flavoured with ingredients like cream, yoghurt, fresh ground herbs, nuts, tomatoes and lemon slices.

☛ *8 Harrison Street (off New Briggate), Leeds LS1.*
☎ *Leeds 446340.*

The Moghul

Horsforth residents have a choice of several good Indian restaurants and the Moghul is perhaps the most upmarket. Quite small by Leeds standards, it always seems busy as customers tuck into a good range of tandoori and vegetable dishes. Booking advisable.

☛ *8/9 The Green, Town Street, Horsforth.*
☎ *Leeds 590530.*

Mumtaz Mahal

Situated between the Junction Inn and Korks Wine Bar & Brasserie, this corner of Otley seems to be hogging some of the best eating and drinking places in Wharefdale. The Mumtaz is very good for a "country" curry house, and the locals know it. Excellent tandoori dishes, including a fine tandoori chicken tikka massalla, are the centre of a huge menu—dansaks and dopiazas, bhunas and kormas, biryani and vindaloo. The downside of being next to the

The very friendly Thukral family have for many years run the much-admired **Bobby's Sweet & Kebab House** *on Roundhay Road, a frequent stop for many on their way home to the suburbs of Roundhay and Oakwood. Although it has the appearance of a shop and most of its customers buy takeaways, there are some limited facilities for eating here, if you don't mind cardboard plates and plastic cutlery. But the food is authentic Indian cuisine, and it regularly receives plaudits from local newspaper reviewers. The small, bright shop is dominated by shelves of mouth-watering sweets. There are also trays of good starters like great vegetable samosas, potato & onion pie (weekends only), various kebabs, pakora and chicken tikka. Many eat a starter while waiting for their takeaway. The large variety of main courses include an excellent chicken massalla and several interesting vegetarian dishes (try the vegetable kofta). All come with chapaties or rice. No credit cards.*
☛ *156 Roundhay Road, Leeds LS8.*
☎ *Leeds 490205.*

Junction is that it can get somewhat noisy after eleven at night, so go early.
☛ *44 Bondgate, Otley.*
☎ *Otley (0943) 464301.*

Nafees

For tens of thousands of students at the nearby University, Nafees was the place they had their first real curry. Sloppy curry houses (that is, mop it up with your chapati rather than use a knife and fork) are rare outside Leeds-Bradford, Manchester and some areas of London and the Midlands. Nafees has grown in size, but its food is still as good. A classic Nafees meal is the onion bhaji followed by chicken bhuna and three chapatis. More recently, they've introduced tandoori specialities. Nafees is licensed and does takeaways.
☛ *69a Raglan Road (at the southern end of Woodhouse Moor), Leeds LS2.*
☎ *Leeds 453128.*

Raja's Tandoori

High quality Indian food (Raja once worked at the more upmarket Mandalay) but at medium-budget prices. With a new extension, the difficulty of fitting all his customers in has been solved. The main attraction is the superb, authentic North India tandoor-cooked dishes. The kitchen is in the dining room, so you can see dishes being prepared. Among the specialities are the karai gosht, a rich lamb dish, and jeengha massalla, the spiciest of shrimps. Choose the strength of your curry as mild, medium or hot and if you really want to clear your sinuses, order a dish of fresh green chillis on the side. Vegetables dishes are available as side dishes or main courses.
☛ *186 Roundhay Road, Leeds LS8.*
☎ *Leeds 480411.*

Shabab

This upstairs restaurant is top quality Indian cuisine, complete with over-the-top interior decoration like high-backed cane chairs and pendant basket-woven lights. The clay tandoor is clearly always busy, for tandoori dishes are what

the Shabab does best. For those who've never been, it is worth trying the thali on that first visit. Then you get to try a little of several different dishes. All the starters are mouth-watering, and the vegetable side orders threaten to eclipse some of the main courses. The business lunch, Monday to Friday, is one of the best value meals in town.
☛ *2 Eastgate, Leeds LS2.*
☎ *Leeds 468988.*

The Sheeba

Another good curry out in the sticks, The Sheeba is the tiniest of places in an old stone cottage close against what used to be known as the Great North Road at Wetherby. Good Indian tandoori meals at medium prices, and especially wide range of vegetable dishes. The editor thought the lamb pasander was the best he'd had for years. Like all country Asian restaurants, it's not a good idea to go when the pubs have just turned out.
☛ *North Street, Wetherby.*
☎ *Wetherby (0937) 583694.*

Thai

Down the centuries Thailand, formerly known as Siam, has received many a trampling army. Several different eastern cuisines have been left behind, combining to make Thai cookery some of the most exciting there is. There are the strong flavours of Szechuan Chinese food, the tropical flavours and sweetness of Malaysia, the coconut and fire of South India and the milder spices of Arabia. It is only in the 1990s that Thai food has come to Leeds, and it seems to have become very popular.

Maitai

Named after a popular Thai cocktail, the Maitai's menu is quite limited but that is often a sign of everything being absolutely fresh off the market. Many of the meals are flavoured with herbs like coriander, basil, lemon grass and citrus leaves. Other distinctive ingredients are chillis, peanuts and coconut milk. The result is a sweet, but sometimes hot dish (you can ask for it mild, and they'll go easy on the chilli). The main meats are

beef, pork and chicken—already cut into bite-sized portions. Fish includes some you've never heard of and the more familiar squid and prawns. Good value business lunches, and friendly service.
☛ *159 Lower Briggate, Leeds LS1*
☎ *Leeds 431989.*

Thai Siam

Return visits to the Thai Siam, a large upstairs room, reveal a distinctive identity in the food. For a start the kaeng ped curry dishes can be very, very hot. In other dishes the sauces are soupy, usually with coconut milk, and the rice gently steamed with vanilla. There is much use of peanuts, lime and pandan leaves and bananas to give surprising flavours to chicken, beef, pork and prawns. To explore them, start off with one of the excellent value set menus for two or more persons. Try the chicken (gai) or beef (neua) green curries for something really different, or exquisite pad poh taek seafood. Macho men will enjoy the aptly named weeping tiger, a spicy sirloin steak. And, of course, the beef/chicken sate should not be missed.
☛ *68/72 New Briggate, Leeds LS1.*
☎ *Leeds 451608.*

Vietnamese

As you might expect, Vietnamese food owes much to both Chinese and Thai cuisine, but has its own character. For a start, water rather than oil is used in most of its cookery, and many of the dishes are almost like soup. The food is richly aromatic and definitely worth investigation.

The New Asia

The menu here is predominantly Chinese but it is the list of Vietnamese dishes that wins it a place in this book. The main accompaniments are vermicelli (fine noodles) and steamed rice, for meats like prawns (tom), chicken (ga) and beef (bo). The sauces in which they arrive are runny and delicious.
☛ *Vicar Lane (next to the Cannon Cinema, Leeds LS2.*
☎ *Leeds 343612.*

Chinese

The most exciting development on the Leeds restaurant scene in the 1990s has been the increased competition amongst the top quality Chinese restaurants in the city. With two enormous newcomers—Maxi's and the Lucky Dragon—the standards have leapt up, and prices have become ever more competitive. The basis of a significant Chinatown now exists in Leeds.

Dynasty

The Dynasty's Cantonese and Pekinese food is of an unusually high standard for a suburban site, and it is always busy. Popular with students' parents taking them out "for a proper meal" and with Headingley locals who know they don't have to worry about finding a place to park, its menu is every bit as varied as the bigger places in town. The cost of having such a conveniently situated restaurant, however, is not cheap. Service is usually slick unless there's a big run on the Dynasty's telephone order takeaway service. There are set meals for two, three and four persons and some good steak dishes

The entrance to Maxi's.

which arrive hissing and spitting on iron griddles. Seafood dishes, including some excellent fresh crab with ginger and spring onion (when available), are particularly numerous.

☛ *4 St. Anne's Parade, Headingley.*
☎ *Leeds 782130.*

Jumbo

For years, the quality end of the Chinese restaurant market in Leeds was dominated by the Jumbo and the Whan Hai. These days, the Jumbo's food is as good as ever but in the light of what we've come to expect at Maxi's and the Lucky Dragon (see below) its menu seems small. The Dim Sum is still popular with the Chinese community, and the main meals like chicken in a paper bag, fried chicken with fresh lemon and the Peking Crunch Duck in chinese mushroom sauce are still favourites at this basement restaurant. And on a cold winter's day, nothing warms you up more than a bowl of its Peking sour and chilli soup. Besides good food, what keeps the Jumbo busy is its keen prices.

☛ *120 Vicar Lane, Leeds LS2.*
☎ *Leeds 458547.*

Lucky Dragon

A vast cellar restaurant, the Lucky Dragon is a sign that the huge Chinese community in Manchester is expanding into Leeds. Cantonese food that is truly first rate, both in quality and value. For atmosphere alone, it is worth a visit when Dim Sum is being served during the day and extended families from Leeds's growing Chinese community sit round big tables. The air is full of excited chatter, and waiters and waiters cruise, ready to help. Dim Sum dishes are usually "snack" types, which added together form a substantial meal, although the chicken feet may be an acquired taste. The massive menu will no doubt repay numerous visits.

☛ *Templar Lane, Leeds LS2.*
☎ *Leeds 450520.*

Maxi's

The splendour of Maxi's has to be seen to be believed. The exterior photograph (see left) hints at the lavish decoration inside. A huge dining room, which seat up to 300, has hardly a square inch of space unembellished with Chinese birds and dragons, and at the centre is a sort of decapitated pagoda temple, containing yet more tables and chairs. Maxi's is very popular, and the Cantonese and Pekinese food is top rate. Portions are huge. Dim Sum is served during the day, and at weekends is eaten by large numbers of Chinese and their families. A sign at the door warns of the consequence of allowing their children to wander off. "They will be sold as slaves!" it says. It is difficult to imagine that a single dish has been left off the vast menu, but Maxi's still offers to cook anything not included. There is a good bar, which diners might see a lot of at weekends as they wait for their tables. Bookings at peak times essential. One of the best—and most interesting—restaurants in Leeds.

☛ *6 Bingley Street (at the start of Kirkstall Road), Leeds LS3.*
☎ *Leeds 440552*

Sang Sang

Still one of the best Cantonese restaurants in Yorkshire, a verdict only confirmed by comparisons with its new competition, the excellent Lucky Dragon. Among its best dishes are the Hong Kong Roast duck, the steamed king prawns with garlic and black bean sauce (utterly habit-forming). There is a small range of vegetable dishes some of which (notably the Two Winters bamboo shoots and mushrooms) make a good main course for vegetarians.

☞ 7 The Headrow, Leeds LS1.
☎ Leeds 468664.

Whan Hai

This big upstairs restaurant still appears in "best Chinese restaurants in England" lists. It was the first place in Leeds one could enjoy crispy aromatic Szechuan duck with pancakes, julienned spring onions and cucumber, coated with sweet sauce. And there is no rival for its Mongolian hotpot. The Whan Hai is strictly Pekinese, with more pungent flavours than many of their Cantonese equivalents. A big favourite after all these years is the Imperial mixed hors d'oeuvres, and a bowl of fried shredded seaweed with grated fish. If you can get a party together, ask for the banquet—a real Imperial occasion with nine courses.

☞ 20 New Briggate, Leeds LS1.
☎ Leeds 435019.

Cafés & Tea Rooms

After many years of fairly indifferent coffee bars in the city centre, Leeds has seen a tremendous growth in the number of good quality cafés and tea rooms. This is mainly as a result of the restoration of historic buildings like the Corn Exchange, and the renovation of other parts of town. As Leeds became the region's principal shopping centre, so the demand for light snacks and hot drinks grew. There are also some good cafés outside the city.

Cobblestones Tea Room

Few tea rooms can boast that a famous figure once sat down to eat and drink there, but the Cobblestones is one such place. For here lived Thomas Chippendale, sometimes described as the Shakespeare of Cabinetmakers, from the age of 10 until he left to become the most famous furnituremaker in the 18th century. It was the home of his uncle, and today it is set behind the eponymous cobbles in Otley's Bondgate. The one-roomed café is small—just six lace-covered tables—but service is good and the snacks and meals are excellent. A sideboard contains plates of scones and cakes, from which you can choose. Or there's home-made soups and main courses. Just the place to pop into after a walk on the Chevin but, unfortunately, it is not open on Sundays. (See page 68).

☞ At 3 Bondgate, Otley.
☎ Otley (0943) 467874.

The Cornucopia Café

This has got to be one of the most popular cafés in Leeds. Its location is certainly one of the best in the North of England. As the photograph shows, many of the tables are smack in the middle of the historic Corn Exchange, and above soars the magnificent replica of the Wright Brothers' first aeroplane. As the name implies, the menu is all-encompassing, with savoury pastries, cakes, scones, toasties, sandwiches (in soft white, granary or wholemeal bread or French stick). There's interesting snacks like toasted bagel with cream cheese, creamed mushrooms on toast and a range of meals that includes steaks, scampi and tuna croquettes. The Cornucopia has a vegetarian menu, with daily specials added to a good selection of regular meals and snacks.

☞ In the basement of the Corn Exchange, Call Lane, Leeds LS1.
☎ Leeds 450715.

The Cornucopia Café in the Corn Exchange.

Georgian Café

Up two flights of stairs in the Waterloo Antiques Centre, formerly the Assembly Rooms (see Museum of Georgian Leeds on page 49). It's an absolute gem of a place, with lace tablecloths, and a relaxed, almost Palm Court atmosphere. The food is all good quality, and ranges from cream teas with home-made scones, toasted teacakes, sandwiches, quiche, soup and a constantly changing menu of hot meals and salads. Now recommended in a national guide.

☞ *Waterloo Antiques Centre, Crown Street (behind Corn Exchange), Leeds LS2.*
☎ *Leeds 444187.*

HG's

The impressive Victoria Quarter has this splendid courtyard café, with more seating on two floors inside. It starts off at eight every morning except Sunday by serving a range of different breakfasts, including English, Swiss, German, French, American and vegetarian. The price includes tea or coffee. But most customers come for its snacks like crumpets, toasted teacakes, muffins, croissants, Welsh rarebit. The coffee is among the best in town with a wide choice, like Jamaica Blue Mountain, and served either at a large pot or "bottomless" cup (frequent refills). Like many of the establishments listed here, HG's also serves complete meals, things like "Desperate Dan's Meat Pies", and lasagne, chilli, quiche, a la carte menu on the blackboards.

☞ *The Victoria Quarter, between Briggate and Vicar Lane, Leeds LS1.*

Lakeside Restaurant

Although now called a restaurant, the Lakeside is mainly a café on the edge of Waterloo Lake, Roundhay Park. It has a fine terrace, which is a pleasant place to sit when the weather's fine. Inside, there's a long, spacious conservatory-style room with much greenery and in winter the weak sun in here can actually feel warm. It is also good in summer, especially for elevenses before the crowds arrive. It can get very busy. The menu is mostly teas, coffees and snacks, but you can get some hot meals with jacket potatoes with fillings, and burgers. Good value breakfasts from 10am.

☞ *By foot, beside Waterloo Lake, Roundhay Park. By car, access is off Park Avenue, Leeds LS8.*
☎ *Leeds 651804.*

Leeds Parish Church

Just a short walk from Vicar Lane and the market areas, the Leeds Parish Church tea room is a sanctuary of cloistered calm and ridiculously low prices. Run by volunteers, it serves a limited range of snacks, including home-made scones and cakes, and freshly made sandwiches. Teas and coffees, cup-a-soups are the drinks, and customers sit in a long room with stained glass windows on which are wonderful little Victorian homilies like "Blessed are the poor in spirit". If you've never been here before, take the time to inspect the interior of St. Peter's Parish Church (see page 66). The tea room is always open 10am-3pm on Monday to Friday and 10am-4pm on Saturdays. Closed on Sundays.

☞ *St. Peter's is on Kirkgate, Leeds LS2.*
☎ *Leeds 454012.*

The Merrion Coffee House

Above the hurly burly of shoppers streaming in and out of the Merrion Centre is this basic café, which has an "outdoor" seating area on the balcony complete with parasols. Several people claim it serves the best bacon butties in town, and they are certainly good. Despite the parasols, there's nothing flashy about the place and its menu contains numerous permutations of sausage, egg, beefburger, beans and chips. There's also a wide range of sandwiches, and snacks.

☞ *44 Merrion Centre (up the stairs at the Merrion Street end), Leeds LS2.*
☎ *Leeds 454372.*

Pablo's

Pablo's is the coffee bar at Leeds City Art Gallery, a calm haven away from the hectic Headrow. As you might expect, it's popular with culture vultures who like a little Camden Town with their courgette and mushroom pie. Good quality snacks and light meals, and excellent tea and coffee, all at non-auction room prices. Vegetarians are well catered for.

☞ *On the main floor of Leeds City Art Gallery, off The Headrow, Leeds LS1.*

Pasta Romagma

This place used to be best known as the only place in Leeds you could buy freshly made pasta. But it has steadily expanded, first with a few tables for coffees and slices of home-made pizza inside and now—thanks to the pedestrianization of Albion Place—it has spread outside in summer. There are numerous attractions, not least the diligent service of its Italian owner. Opera booms from the shop door, as she serves cups of wonderful cappuccino and espresso, freshly baked chocolate croissants and pizza slices.

☞ *26 Albion Place, Leeds LS1.*
☎ *Leeds 451569.*

Perry's

Tucked away in the small Horsefair Centre, Wetherby, Perry's is a smart, self-service café with white lace table cloths, and an outdoor seating area in summer. There's a good range of hot snacks like toasted sandwiches, and some complete meals. Most people are struck by the large range of home-baked scones, including cherry, lemon and orange, and "breakfast" scones.

☞ *9 Horsefair Centre, off North Street, Wetherby.*
☎ *Wetherby (0937) 581561.*

Victorian Tea Rooms

On the balcony at the Corn Exchange is this classic English tea shoppe. With stripped pine chairs, lace tablecloths, Victorian nursery paintings on the walls, the atmosphere is authentic. Beautiful speciality and herbal teas, and some unusual coffees. The food is the usual cakes, scones and pastries, but with small meals like quiches, omelettes and salads. No smoking room.

☞ *The Corn Exchange, Call Lane, Leeds LS1.*
☎ *Leeds 430668.*

PART FIVE:
Leeds Area Shopping

Leeds has always been at the forefront of shopping developments. The great arcades of late-Victorian times—most can be seen today—were among the first in Britain. One of the world's earliest department stores was opened by Snowdon Schofield in 1921—a modern version is also still there on The Headrow. And the Merrion Centre was one of the first shopping malls in the UK.

By the 1990s, Leeds has become the top shopping city east of the Pennines, especially for Christmas shopping. With an expensive face-lift and further pedestrianization the city centre is an increasingly pleasant place to wonder. A feature is the many good speciality shops in which to browse.

But Leeds also as interesting neighbour shopping areas, especially in satellite towns like Otley, Wetherby and Morley and it is worthwhile visting them for a few hours. You never know what you might find.

In the beautifully restored County Arcade section of the acclaimed Victoria Quarter, Leeds.

Shopping for Pleasure

Walking round the Leeds shopping precincts and arcades, markets and malls has become one of the top day's out in Yorkshire.

Shopping is Britain's most popular leisure activity these days. Browsing through markets and shops is enjoyed by millions every day. In Leeds, this fact was recognised over a century ago by the pioneering men who built the famous Leeds arcades. Make the shopping experience as pleasant as possible, they reasoned, and customers won't be able to stay away. Today's Leeds continues that philosophy by providing ever more indoor shopping centres, refurbishing its arcades and extending pedestrianization to allow tables and chairs to take the place of traffic. In particular, the pedestrianization of Briggate—historically the main shopping street in Leeds—will have an enormous impact, leaving most of the city centre completely traffic-free. With Landmark Leeds (the major lighting, seating and decorative project) now a distinctive part of the city centre, Leeds has all the comfort and facilities of the big out-of-town malls that have sprung up at Gateshead and Sheffield. But Leeds also has more than *four times* the number of shops in its central area. The theme of this section, therefore, is largely shopping for enjoyment in Leeds and its sat-

ellite towns. It lists all the most interesting new ventures, from the imaginative Booths Yard at Pudsey to the emergence of Otley as a fine country shopping town. And, of course, it is a guide to all the exciting developments in Leeds city centre.

Central Leeds

Between the arcades, the shopping centres and the great Kirkgate Market, there is more covered shopping in Leeds than anywhere else.

The Arcades

Long before the Merrion Centre become one of the first large indoor malls in Britain in 1964, Leeds was a warren of arcades and today they contain some of the most interesting "speciality" shops in Leeds. Refurbishment proposals for some are unlikely to alter their essential character. The best known one is **Thornton's Arcade** (see page 69), which opened in 1878, and has a famous clock. It has many high/medium fashion boutiques, jewellers and good quality gift shops. More of the same awaits you further down Briggate in **Queens Arcade,** built in 1888-89. Almost at the foot of Briggate is the more modern **Burton Arcade,** famous as the site of The Leeds United Collection, where footballers and supporters go for the latest kit, videos, etc. On the east side of Briggate is **Market Street Arcade**, with more leisure clothing, jewellers and craft shops. Moving back up Briggate, the arcades have been turned into The Victoria Quarter (see below). Finally, running between New Briggate and Vicar Lane, the well-named **Grand Arcade**, opened earlier this century and now containing some of the best-known shops in Leeds—that is if you are an angler, a sportsman (The Trophy Shop) or a pet/tropical fish lover.

☞ *All the arcades join Briggate, the historic main shopping street of Leeds.*

Victoria Quarter

By roofing over Queen Victoria Street with Europe's largest stained glass canopy and magnificently restoring County Arcade and the smaller Cross Arcade, developers have given Leeds one of the most stunning retail areas in the country. Paying close attention to detail and using only the best materials they have created a stylish environment that reflects the quality of its shops and goods. For example, there are three beautiful mosaic floor-panels in County Arcade (see foreground of the photograph on page 115). Mahogany and glass was used for the shop fronts, their names in gilded Art Nouveau lettering. Queen Victoria Street—built when Leeds was the clothing capital of the world— is now the top fashion centre in Yorkshire. All the big names are represented, such as Jean Paul Galtier, Cerruti, Paul Smith, Armani, Bruce Oldfield, Katharine Hamnett and many more. One sees immaculately dressed men and women shopping here that are, somehow, never encountered elsewhere. Beside the boutiques, there are shops selling jewellery, sportwear, fine art prints, computer software, maternity wear, kitchen gadgets, flowers, luggage, unusual loose teas and coffees, quality pork pies and many more. There is enough in here to keep you occupied for several hours, especially with a courtyard café (HG's—see page 114) to restore your energy.
☞ *The Victoria Quarter runs between Briggate and Vicar Lane, north of King Edward Street.*

The Shopping Centres

When the Merrion Centre opened in 1964, few could have imagined that such developments would appear in every town and city in Britain. Leeds now has four in the central area, and one out at Cross Gates. Still one of the busiest, the **Merrion Centre** is dominated by its huge Morrisons and Woolworth stores, but also contains many good speciality shops, a Georgian

Leeds Lights

The famous Leeds Christmas Lights are switched on in Mid-November and can be seen until Twelfth night. Eight miles of festive lighting in Leeds and surrounding towns, all produced by one of the city council's departments. The biggest Christmas lights display in the country— even London has fewer—it drawns coachloads of shoppers from all over the North of England.

☞ The lights are switched on between 3.30pm-4pm and 12 midnight, seven days a week.

Arcade, and a Superstore in which many new and second-hand goods are sold at extremely low prices. The next to open was the **Bond Street Centre** (1978), in which there are large Boots and British Home Stores, as well as numerous small shops. The **St. John's Centre**, opened in the late 1980s, seems to be the busiest of them all, thanks to many good outlets for clothes, kitchenware, cards, records and hi-fi, but also because it has become the main thoroughfare from The Headrow to the Merrion Centre. The most recent is the **Schofields Centre**, perhaps the most stylish of them all. It contains a new Schofields Department store—the original was set up here in 1921—and a large Marks & Spencer. Its Circus Food Court serves sandwiches, fish and chips, burgers and fried chicken, pizzas and pasta, health foods, pies and roasts, jacket potatoes, cakes and pastries, and Chinese meals.

☛ *The Merrion Centre is between Merrion Street and Merrion Way; The Bond Street Centre is between Boar Lane and Bond Street; the St. John's Centre is between Dortmund Square and Merrion Street; the Schofields Centre is off The Headrow and Lands Lane.*

Leeds Markets

Leeds owes its very existence to the development of a market in the later Middle Ages. Then, it was right on Leeds Bridge and was mainly for trade in woollen cloth. Today's markets sell just about everything. Around 800 traders and sometimes as many as 100,000 shoppers on a single day pack the newly restored Kirkgate Market, an Edwardian building famous for its ornamental dragons, and its huge open-air market. The main market is always lively and there are specialist areas for fresh poultry, game (this is the place to come for grouse on or after the Glorious Twelfth), fish, meat, fruit and vegetables, and bread like the famous Yorkshire oven cakes. The flower stalls are among the cheapest you will find. The fresh fish market sells things like yellow-tail snappers, octopus, red mullet, blue jacks, Greenland halibut, Dover sole, all kinds of shellfish and white fish, and occasionally fresh lobster. The large steel building, a "temporary" structure erected in 1976 after a fire destroyed two-thirds of the original market, houses a large number of stalls. There are specialist units selling leather goods, cosmetics, electrical equipment, motor accessories, greetings cards, bedding, lighting, Asian & Oriental foods, home brew, china/earthenware TV/Radio/hi-fi, jewellery, DIY goods, fabrics, needlework goods, cake ingredients and many more. For anyone setting up home and starting from scratch to build up the basic kitchen and household equipment, it is the obvious place to come. The outdoor market, where Michael Marks first set up his stall that was to grow into Marks & Spencer, offers goods at extraordinary low prices, and some stallholders even allow you to haggle. The Thursday fleamarket draws antique collectors from a wide area.

☛ *On the east side of the city centre, between Vicar Lane and the Central Bus Station. Kirkgate Market is open Monday to Saturday, 8am to 6pm, with half-day closing on Wednesdays at 1pm. The Open Markets run on Tuesdays, Fridays and Saturdays. There is an open flea market on Thursdays and on Mondays a clothes mart with special provision for second-hand clothing, bedding, curtains and fabric items.*

☎ *Further information about all Leeds Markets—Leeds 476948.*

A sea of fruit and vegetables at Kirkgate Market—the biggest market in the North of England.

Corn Exchange

The magnificent Corn Exchange is now a unique speciality shopping hall, a bright and spacious marriage of Victorian splendour with 1990s style. Originally opened in 1863 as the main West Riding centre for corn trading (see page 64), it is now a Grade I listed building. The architect, Cuthbert Brodrick, modelled it on a Roman colosseum. The design of the roof allowed natural light to flood the interior, so that traders could assess the quality of the corn. But by the 1980s a wider use was sought. Though corn merchants still trade from their desks on the concourse every Tuesday, their 54 units have become speciality shops on three levels, the huge dome above being dominated by a replica of the Wright Brothers' Kitty Hawk aeroplane which made the first manned flight in 1903. There are several fine cafés and restaurants, a modern café-bar in the basement, and all sorts of small stalls keep appearing to sell things you'd forgotten existed. Among the shops, many specialise in good quality American 50s and 60s clothes and accessories. Others sell Oriental crafts, records and videos, herbal remedies and animal-friendly cosmetics. A jelly bean shop sells the original American bean in an astonishing range of flavours. Another unit offers things like "karma visualisation" and other therapies. One is devoted to teddy bears, while another—the Condom Shop—has turned the once-humble rubber Johnny into a cult object. With an Antiques Fair every Sunday and a Book & Stamp fair every second month (ring the events coordinator on Leeds 439556 for date of next one) the Corn Exchange is always one of the busiest parts of town at weekends. There are also regular fashion shows and exhibitions featuring top names.

☛ *Call Lane, Leeds LS1. Open 9.30am-5.30pm seven days a week.*
☎ *For further information— 340363.*

Waterloo Market and Antiques Centre

Housed in the historic Assembly Room, the elegant hub of Georgian society in Leeds, the Waterloo Market and Antiques Centre houses a large range of traders. It is a complex of over 30 small and medium-sized units, selling a wide range of antiques and bric-a-brac. There are specialists in clocks, antique fireplaces and surrounds, Victorian/Edwardian clothing, jewellery, furniture and household goods, pottery and porcelain, Victoriana and Kitchenalia, Art Deco and Nouveau, pictures, prints, books, records, and carefully restored radios from the 40s and 50s. On the floor below the Antiques Centre is held a Flea Market every Friday, Saturday and Sunday. While the Friday market is aimed at antique collectors, buyers and dealers, the Saturday and Sunday traders target their goods at students, Bohemians and assorted bargain hunters. On the top floor is the Museum of Georgian Leeds (see page 49) and the Georgian Café (see page 114).

☛ *In Crown Street, Leeds LS2. Antiques Market open Tues-Sun 10am-5pm; Flea Market open Fri-Sun 10am-5pm.*
☎ *Leeds 444187.*

Queens Court

A small courtyard of shops formed behind an 18th century cloth merchant's house. The buildings now

The balcony and Sunday antiques fair at the historic Corn Exchange.

converted into shops, a pub and restaurant were where woollen cloths trade on the historic Leeds market outside in Briggate were finished off. Other such courtyard refurbishments off Briggate are likely.

☞ *Lower Briggate, Leeds LS1.*
☎ *Leeds 569144.*

Granary Wharf

Variously promoted as "Leeds's answer to Covent Garden" and "Camden Lock comes to Leeds", all comparisons are unfair. Granary Wharf has no equal in the UK. It is a colourful shopping arcade built in the warren of vaulted tunnels known as the Dark Arches below Leeds City Station. Outside, it opens onto the historic basin of the Leeds-Liverpool Canal, where there is a marvellous picnic area, food and drink stalls and entertainment at weekends. The shopping arcade is a well-lit collection of 20 or so shops, many of them selling good that are unobtainable elsewhere in Leeds. Among the busiest is Paradyllic, with its fantastic array of excellent value clothes and crafts. The emphasis is on hand-made goods—hand-dipped candles, hand-carved masks, hand-printed postcards, hand-woven rugs, hand-painted jewellery. Highly colourful and buzzing with young people. Nearby is another unique Leeds shop, Knock on Wood, which specialises in Third World acoustic instruments, from a jaws harp to a didjeridoo, pan-pipes to Nepalese whistles. As the name suggests, there is a large range of drums and other percussion instruments. Other shops sell Celtic items, pine furniture, cake decorations, custom printed t-shirts, bridlewear, teddy bears, pictures and old photographs of Leeds. On Sundays, there are over 60 shops and stalls open, many selling crafts, fashion and design. Some offer on-the-spot services like aromatherapy and face painting (see photograph on the right). The first Sunday in every month is Sunday Funday. You can leave children with the resident Children's Entertainer for games and prizes whilst you shop. There are regular special events like Dickensian Festivals.

☞ *The easiest access is from Neville Street, below the railway bridges. There is also car access off Water Lane.*
☎ *Further information about events—Leeds 446570.*

Leeds Car Boot Sale

This amazing bazaar of second-hand goods is set up every Sunday morning throughout the year. Anyone can bring along surplus possessions to sell from the back of their car. Simply turn up, sign the Council's terms and conditions relating to sales, and hey presto you're in business! Shoppers find some real bargains. The market is open at 6am Sundays and usually closes around 2pm.

☞ *Held at Leeds City Council's Wholesale Market, Cross Green Industrial Estate, Pontefract Lane, Leeds LS9.*
☎ *Further information—Leeds 476948.*

Retail Parks

More and more out-of-town shopping centres are springing up. They are purpose-built developments, ranging from some speciality shopping arranged round one or two big supermarkets, to full-blown retail parks. All offer the convenience of close parking, huge choices of goods and many bargain prices. Some also have a bar and restaurant. The following are the major ones in the Leeds Area, but more are in the pipeline:

Aireside Centre. Close to the city centre, the stores are grouped round the central car park. Retailers have changed several times but include MFI, Carpetland, The Jolly Giant (toys), Kingsway Suites, World of Leather.

☞ *Off Whitehall Road, Leeds LS1.*
Crown Point Retail Park. A vast new shopping centre just south of the River Aire. Outlets include Texas Homecare, Allied Carpets, Paul Ayre Carpets, Rumbalows Atlantis, Shoe City, Homestyle, Harveys (curtains, beds, carpets, suites); Poundstretcher; Curry's, Children's World; Miller Brothers electrical.

☞ *Opposite Tetleys Brewery, Hunslet Lane. Reached via Crown Point Bridge, turning right then left.*
Owlcotes Centre. On the very western fringe of Leeds, near Pudsey railway station. Dominated by a massive Marks & Spencer and an ASDA.

☞ *Off the A647 Stanningley Bypass, between Leeds and Bradford.*
Moor Allerton Centre. Sainsbury's store, Homebase DIY and garden centre, plus several other shops, a pub and library.

☞ *Off the outer ring road and Alwoodley Lane, Leeds LS17.*
Tesco Centre. A huge Tesco, Texas DIY and Garden Centre.

☞ *Off Roundhay Road, Oakwood, Leeds LS8.*
Killingbeck. On the eastern side of the city, there is a Rumbalows Atlantis, B & Q, McDonalds and an ASDA.

☞ *Just off York Road, next to Killingbeck Hospital, Leeds LS14.*

Behind a painted smile—face decoration at Leeds's excellent Granary Wharf.

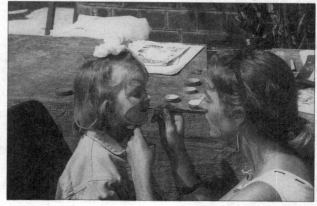

Good Food & Drink Shops

Leeds is well-off for such shops. Below are listed some selling foods/drinks that are otherwise unavailable in the area, or which offer a massive choice and good value.

Le Croque Monsieur. Excellent French-style patisserie. Also sells a variety of Continental salads, pates, cheeses and breads. Open Sunday morning.
☛ *251 Otley Road, West Park.*
✆ *Leeds 787353.*

Kendal Moore. A fine delicatessen, with terrific range of quality meat pies, home made pastas and quiches, unusual fresh breads and rolls, cheeses, cooked meats. Open on Sundays.
☛ *74 Otley Road, Headingley.*
✆ *783439.*

Gloucesters Cheese & Wholefoods. This Otley shop is the best in the area for unusual Yorkshire Dales cheeses, many made in small quantities.
☛ *5 Newmarket, Otley, LS21.*
✆ *Otley (0943) 466935.*

Maumoniat International Supermarket. A breathtaking range of spices, herbs, pulses, rices, flours, oils, and other ingredients for foreign cookery, especially Asian. Low prices.
☛ *39 Brudenell Grove, Leeds LS6.*
✆ *Leeds 782432.*

Hing Fat Supermarket. A massive range of Chinese foods and cooking utensils. One of the biggest in the north.
☛ *Templar Lane, Leeds LS2.*
✆ *Leeds 348168.*

Pasta Romagma. Freshly made pasta, Italian breads, cheeses, coffee, olive oils and other ingredients for Italian cookery.
☛ *26 Albion Place, Leeds LS1.*
✆ *Leeds 451569.*

The Ale House. Mind-boggling array of bottled and draught beers to take away. Also sells organic wines. If only all off-licences were like this.
☛ *79 Raglan Road, Leeds LS2.*
✆ *Leeds 455447.*

Great Northern Wine. Wholesale prices of hundreds of wines, bought per case. Can mix bottles. Vast range.
☛ *Dark Arches, Canal Basin, Leeds LS1.*
✆ *Leeds 461200.*

Outer Leeds

Beyond the city centre there are many good shopping areas, both in the suburbs and the satellite towns of Leeds. The following are the most interesting.

Cross Gates. The biggest out-of-town shopping centre, with a massive indoor shopping mall, the Arndale Centre. Gets customers from all over Leeds.

Garforth. The shopping area is along Main Street. There is an open market (36 stalls) each Saturday.

Headingley. Some boutiques in North Lane. Also wholefoods and much more. There's a long parade of shops at the Arndale Centre.

Horsforth. Town Street is a pleasant shopping area, with some good food shops.

Moortown. Good food shops, clothes, books, fancy goods and gifts.

Morley. Queen Street has many interesting shops. Windsor Court, next to the Town Hall, is an indoor development. Morley Market Hall, established in 1880, is large and famous for low priced goods.

Oakwood. Two pleasant parades of shops on either side of Roundhay Road, with good quality food shops, books, clothes etc.

Otley. One of the best small towns for shopping in the region. Good shops in Bondgate, Kirkgate (an excellent arcade), Boroughgate, Manor Square and the Market Place, where there are two new courtyards. Busy market days (50-90 stalls) Friday and Saturday.

Pudsey. Booths Yard and the Trinity Shopping Mall, side by side, have a number of interesting small speciality shops. There's an open market at Pudsey (45 stalls) every Tuesday, Friday and Saturday.

Wetherby. Centres round the old Market Place, North Street, Church Street and Bank Street, where there are numerous small speciality shops. A good place to browse, especially on the Thursday market (24 stalls).

Hyde Park Corner. For many years has been home to a wide variety of student boutiques, book and record shops, and trendy furniture stores. Always lively.

Yorkshire Markets

Thousands of Leeds residents prefer to visit neighbouring towns on their regular open market days, many of which have not changed for centuries. The following is a complete list of all these ancient market days in Yorkshire and North Humberside. HD means half-day.

Batley—*Mon, Wed, Fri, Sat, HD Tues;* **Barnsley**—*Wed, Sat, HD Thurs;* **Beverley**—*Wed, Fri, HD Tues;* **Bingley**—*Wed, Fri, HD Tues;* **Birstall**—*Thurs;* **Boroughbridge**—*Mon, HD Thurs;* **Bradford**—*Mon, Tues, Thurs, Fri, Sat;* **Brighouse**—*Wed, Sat;* **Castleford**—*daily;* **Cleckheaton**—*Mon, Sat, HD Wed;* **Dewsbury**—*Wed, Sat, HD Tues;* **Doncaster**—*Tues, Fri, Sat;* **Driffield**—*Thurs, Sat, HD Wed;* **Easingwold**—*Fri;* **Elland**—*Fri, HD Tues;* **Featherstone**—*Thurs, HD Wed;* **Goole**—*Mon, Wed, Fri;* **Halifax**—*Fri, Sat;* **Hemsworth**—*Tues, Fri, Sat, HD Wed;* **Hebden Bridge**—*Thurs, HD Tues;* **Heckmondwike**—*Tues, Sat;* **Holmfirth**—*Thurs, HD Tues;* **Hornsea**—*Wed, Sun;* **Huddersfield**—*Mon, Thurs, Sat, HD Wed;* **Hull**—*Tues, Fri, Sat, HD Thurs;* **Harrogate**—*daily, HD Wed;* **Hawes**—*Tues, HD Wed;* **Yeadon**—*Mon, Fri;* **Ilkley**—*Sat (small);* **Keighley**—*Wed, Fri, Sat, HD Tues;* **Knaresborough**—*Wed, HD Thurs;* **Knottingley**—*Fri, Tues, HD Wed;* **Normanton**—*Tues, Sat, HD Wed;* **Ossett**—*Tues, Sat, Fri, Sat;* **Otley**—*Tues, Fri, Sat, HD Wed;* **Morley**—*Fri, Sat;* **Morley** *(Peel Street)*—*most days;* **Pickering**—*Mon, HD Wed;* **Pontefract**—*Wed, Sat, HD Thur;* **Pudsey**—*Tues, Fri, Sat;* **Richmond**—*Sat;* **Ripon**—*Thur, Sat, HD Wed;* **Rotherham**—*Mon, Fri, Sat, HD Thurs;* **Rothwell**—*Sat, Mon, HD Thurs;* **Selby**—*Mon, Fri, Sat, HD Thurs;* **Settle**—*Tues;* **Shipley**—*Fri, HD Wed;* **Sheffield**—*Mon, Tues, Wed, Fri, Sat;* **Skipton**—*Mon, Wed, Fri, Sat, HD Tues;* **South Elmsall**—*Tues, Fri, Sat, HD Wed;* **Tadcaster**—*Thurs, HD Wed;* **Todmorden**—*Wed, Fri, Sat, HD Tues;* **Thirsk**—*Mon, Thurs, Sat, HD Wed;* **Wakefield**—*Mon, Tues, Thurs, Fri, Sat, HD Wed;* **Wetherby**—*Thurs, HD Wed;* **York**—*daily.*

PART SIX:
Sports & Fitness

One of the main advantages of living in, or visiting, a city is the abundance of good sport and leisure facilities such major population centres have to offer. From Premier League football at Elland Road to Test cricket at Headingley, from the beautifully restored Edwardian swimming baths at Bramley to the hundreds of free tennis courts throughout the area, Leeds has everything you need.

In particular, the area has some exceptional public sports and leisure centres, and what is regarded as the best Sports Development scheme in the UK. Even obscure sports like t'ai chi and octopush are available in Leeds.

The next nine pages cover the most popular activities, and provide all the details you need to get involved. Opening times, or news of forthcoming fixtures, are available with a simple telephone call.

Left: Competitors in the annual Leeds Marathon run east along Wellington Street.

Spectator Sports

Top soccer and rugby league clubs, a modernised look to Yorkshire cricket, international swimming and cycling, and great racecources.

Sports Action is seven days a week, 52 weeks a year in the Leeds area. And it's some of the best in the country. After winning the First Division Championship in 1992, Leeds United is back among the top English soccer clubs, while across the city at Headingley, Leeds RLFC has become one of the strongest teams in the Rugby League. Next door, Headingley Cricket Ground is one of the world's historic test match venues. Some of the classic meetings on the racing calendar are within easy reach of Leeds. And more sports are being served up all the time, like American Football and international cycling events. The following pages show the range of spectator sports on offer in the 1990s.

Soccer

For many people throughout Britain, Leeds means Leeds United. Despite its mixed fortunes in the last 20 years, the club has been one of the city's main ambassadors at home and abroad. But while the team is well supported in Leeds, with some of the biggest gates in the country, there is also considerable interest in Yorkshire teams in the lower divisions, notably Bradford City. And—heresy—there is

even substantial local support for Manchester United. But since this is *Leeds Fax*, we have decided to concentrate here on the local side.

Leeds United

Even in the topsy-turvy world of English League football, few clubs have Leeds United's history of astonishing achievements followed by abysmal failure. Admitted to the Second Division in 1919 after Leeds City had been expelled for "irregularities", its first 40 years were spent in obscurity. But from the day in March, 1961, that the late Don Revie took over as manager, Leeds United began a long spell as one of the greatest clubs in Europe. By 1964-65, they had finished as runners-up in both the League and the FA cup. Under Revie, they won the Football League Championship in seasons 1968-69 and 1973-74, the FA Cup in 1972, the League Cup in 1968, the FA Charity Shield in 1969 and reached the finals of all three European cup competitions, winning the Fairs Cup in 1968 and 1971. But when Revie left in 1974, the club's fortunes took a nose-dive which a long series of managers like Brian Clough, the late Jock Stein and Revie squad skipper Billy Bremner failed to halt. To make matters worse, the club's

supporters were briefly notorious for their behaviour at away matches, although crowd trouble at Elland Road was rare. By their previous high standards, therefore, United were almost at rock-bottom in 1988 (lying 21st in the Second Division) when yet another manager, Howard Wilkinson, was appointed from Sheffield Wednesday. Within 18 months they had won the Second Division Championship. The Glory Days finally returned to Elland Road at precisely 50 seconds past 5.09pm on 26 April, 1992, when their winning of the First Division Championship was confirmed. Their future in the Premier League seems bright. This growing strength on the field is matched by a modernised stadium at Elland Road, which was bought by Leeds City Council in 1985 for £2.5 million. The first fruits of this partnership are a new 17,000-seater East Stand and a new 450-seat Banqueting Suite for business customers. For the mid-1990s Elland Road is one of just a handful of grounds in the country to have an all-seater, sheltered capacity of 40,000. There is also a major commitment to attracting families. In Leeds at least, soccer has been reclaimed as an enjoyable and comfortable sport to watch at the stadium rather than from the sitting room.

☞ *Elland Road stadium is two miles south west of the centre, just off the M621. On matchdays regular buses run from Swinegate, Leeds.*

☎ *Leeds 716037 (general enquiries); 710710 (ticket sales); 0898-121680 (Ticket Call); 0898-121180 (Club Call); 0836-401831 (Route Line).*

Cricket

Although there are dozens of Leeds area cricket clubs worth watching (Pudsey St. Lawrence to name but one) cricket in Leeds really means Headingley Test matches and Yorkshire's County Championship games. The first cricket at Headingley was played on 27 May, 1890. Among its numerous records are a local one-day crowd (39,000 for England v Australia on 26 July, 1948) and the first triple century

Match day at Elland Road

in Test history (Don Bradman's famous 334 runs on 11-12 July, 1930). Today, the ground is still on the Test circuit, although since 1989 it has had to join a rota with others and is not guaranteed a test match every year. When there is no test at Headingley, there are two one-day internationals.

☞ *The Headingley ground is between St. Michael's Lane and Kirkstall Lane, Headingley, Leeds LS6. Parking near the ground at Test match time can be a problem. It would be easier to take a Yorkshire Rider bus from Infirmary Street (off City Square) or take a train to Burley Park Station, which is just a short walk from the ground.*

☎ *For credit card ticket bookings, call Leeds 787394 (Access/Visa/Diners accepted). For personal callers, the ticket office is open 9am-5pm Monday to Fri.*

Yorkshire County Cricket Club

More than any county, Yorkshire has a great cricketing tradition. Between 1893 and 1968 the White Rose team won the County Championship 29 times, almost twice the number of wins of any other county. But with the exception of the occasional cup win (Gillette Cup in 1969 and Benson and Hedges Cup in 1987, Sunday League in 1983) Yorkshire's great cricketing days appeared to be over. The county seemed destined

to be a quaint footnote to county cricket history, with its strict rule that only men born within its own boundaries could be selected to play, and the constant bickering between various factions off the field. However, the early 1990s have seen a relaxation of the Yorkshire-only policy for the team which will undoubtedly put the club on a more equal footing with other county sides. As a result, the next few seasons at Headingley will be the most interesting for two decades. The best way to enjoy cricket at the home ground is become a member of Yorkshire County Cricket Club. A list of benefits too long to print here includes free admission to the ground, pavilion and members enclosures at Headingley, Scarborough, Sheffield, Middlesbrough, Harrogate and Bradford for Yorkshire matches in the Britannic Assurance Championship, as well as the Sunday League, Benson & Hedges Cup zonal matches, Tilcon Trophy, and others. You also get a reduced admission charge at Test Matches. Championship matches draw crowds averaging 5,000; many more for Sunday matches.

☞ *Yorkshire County Cricket Club is at Headingley Cricket Ground, St. Michael's Lane, Leeds LS6 3BU. See above for directions.*

☎ *Leeds 787394. Cricketline (for all the latest news and scores updates for Yorkshire County Cricket Club matches): 0891-567-518.*

The 13-a-side code Rugby League has for decades been the region's favourite rugby. Leeds and Hunslet were among the 20 clubs which set up the breakaway Northern Rugby League on 29 August, 1895, at the George Hotel, Huddersfield. The Rugby League's headquarters are in Leeds, and the game is increasingly prominent on many of the area's school playing fields.

Leeds RLFC

For many years, the top club in the city has been Leeds RLFC, which plays at Headingley. Its record crowd was 40,175 for a match against Bradford Northern in May, 1947, but today crowds in excess of 12,000 are normal, with over 20,000 for the more important fixtures. The "Loiners" have won everything: League Champions six times, Challenge Cup winners ten times, Premiership Trophy winners twice, Championship Play-Off victors three times, Yorkshire Cup 17 times, John Player Trophy winners twice, and the BBC2 Floodlit Trophy winners once. Prospects look bright in the 1990s with a series of major signings.

☞ *St. Michael's Lane, Headingley. Regular Yorks. Rider services from the bus station or Infirmary Street.*

☎ *Leeds 786181. Club call number (for team & game information) is 0898-121530.*

The famous Headingley Cricket Ground

Bramley RLFC

Bramley joined the Northern Union a year after it was formed—in 1896—and have won just one major honour, the BBC2 Floodlit Trophy in the 1973-74 season. They have never been one of the major forces in the game, but despite this they have a very strong local following.

☛ *Bramley play at McLaren Field, Town St., LS13 3EN. Regular trains to Bramley from Leeds City or Yorkshire Rider buses from Corn Exchange and Central Bus Station.*

☎ *Leeds 564842.*

Hunslet RLFC

Like Leeds, Hunslet are a club with a famous past, being one of the founder members of the Northern Rugby Football League. They were League Champions back in 1937-38; Division Two champions twice; Challenge Cup winners twice; Yorkshire Cup winners three times; and Championship Play-Off victors twice. After 85 years at Parkside, they moved to Elland Road in 1973.

☛ *Hunslet play at Elland Road, Leeds LS11. Buses from Vicar Lane.*

☎ *Leeds 711675.*

Rugby Union

Although somewhat overshadowed by Rugby League in Yorkshire, Rugby Union can still draw big crowds for important matches, especially when it is a local derby. Of the four main Leeds area clubs, the most successful down the years has been **Headingley** (which actually plays in Kirkstall). They won the Yorkshire Cup in 1988 and play in the National League. The long-running saga of their merger with National League rivals **Roundhay** was being completed as we went to press and it seemed likely that the new combined club would play at a purpose-built ground off the Outer Ring road, Adel, from September, 1993. The other two top sides in the city are **Morley** and **Otley**. Most matches are on Saturdays.

☛ *For the moment, Headingley play at Bridge Road, Kirkstall, Roundhay play at Chandox Park, Chandos Ave., Lidgett lane, LS8.*

But watch for announcements about merger in 1993. Morley play at Scatcherd Lane, Morley; Otley play at Cross Green Ground, Pool Road.

☎ *Headingley, Leeds 755029; Roundhay, Leeds 661815; Morley, Leeds 533487; Otley, 0943-461180.*

Horse Racing

Besides Wetherby, Leeds has eight good racecourses within reach. Yorkshire has always been one of the sport's major centres, with famous stables at Malton and Middleham. Scarcely a week passes without one of the Yorkshire courses being in action. There are 150 days of racing on the flat or over the sticks, including prestigious races like the International at York and Doncaster's St. Leger, the oldest of the world's "Classics".

☛ *For a complete guide to all the courses listed below, contact "Go Racing in Yorkshire" at Freepost HG112, Wetherby, West Yorkshire, LS22 4YY.*

☎ *Wetherby (0937) 580051.*

Wetherby

National Hunt meetings at Wetherby have been going since 1891. Of the 14 fixtures a year between October & May (all of them jumping), the best-attended are usually Boxing Day & day after; Easter Mon & Tues; and Spring Bank Hol. Monday. The biggest prizes are the Charlie Hall Memorial Chase (late-Oct/early-Nov) and the Castleford Handicap (27th Dec.) worth over £26,000 each.

☛ *Wetherby Racecourse, York Road, Wetherby, LS22 5EJ*

☎ *Wetherby (0937) 582035.*

Pontefract

The flat season begins here in early April and continues with a busy programme to the end of October. Clearly seen on the south side of the M62 (exit on junction 32).

☛ *Pontefract Park Races., 33 Ropergate, Pontefract, WF8 1LE.*

☎ *0977-703224.*

York

Meetings every month from May to October inclusive, the biggest be-

ing on the Tuesday, Wednesday and Thursday before the August Bank Holiday weekend, with a crowd of over 80,000 for the three days. The meeting has the year's richest race in the International.

☛ *The Manager, York Race Committee, The Racecourse, York, YO2 1EX.*

☎ *York (0904) 620911.*

Ripon

Ripon describes itself as "Yorkshire's Garden Racecourse" and makes a big effort with floral displays during its 12 meetings a year, from April to August Bank Holiday. The big event of the course's calendar is the Great St. Wilfred Handicap, usually in mid-August.

☛ *Ripon Race Co. Ltd., 77 North St., Ripon, North Yorks HG4 1DS.*

☎ *Ripon (0765) 602156.*

Doncaster

The St. Leger Festival takes place over four days every September. Doncaster is one of the busiest courses in Yorkshire, with both flat and jumping fixtures on 10 months of the year.

☛ *Doncaster Racecourse, The Grandstand, Leger Way, Doncaster DN2 6BB.*

☎ *Doncaster (0302) 320066.*

Catterick

Famous for its Army barracks and its twin-code racecourse, which is one of the busiest in the country. There are meetings every month of the year.

☛ *For the year's programme contact: The Secretary, Catterick Racecourse, First Floor, Ebor Court, Westgate, Leeds LS1 4ND.*

☎ *Leeds 422221.*

Beverley

Flat season racing which begins in March and continues to September.

☛ *The Beverley Race Co. Ltd., 19 North Bar Within, Beverley, N. Humberside HU17 8DB.*

☎ *Hull (0482) 867488.*

Thirsk

Racing on the flat, beginning in April and continuing each month to September.

☛ *Thirsk Racecourse Ltd., Station Road, Thirsk, N. Yorks. YO7 1QL.*

☎ *Thirsk (0845) 22276.*

Redcar

Eighteen days of racing on the flat from April to October at this popular racecourse on Teesside.

☛ *Redcar Races, Redcar, Cleveland TS10 2BY.*

☎ *0642-484068.*

Other Sports

Away from the Big Four there are many other spectator sports on offer in the Leeds area. And new events are being attracted all the time. Keep an eye on the What's On listings. The point of this section is not to mention occasional events/meetings like snooker and athletics but to describe some of the more regular, up-and-coming spectator sports.

American Football

After several nomadic years the Leeds Cougars have finally found what looks like a permanent home at the ground of Farsley Celtic, and field a strong team in the Coca Cola National Division. The Cougars play a season that begins in early May and finishes in August. At their home games there is all the razzmatazz of hot dog and chilli stands, bands and cheerleaders (the same ones, incidentally, that have entertained the Elland Road crowd). Average gate is 1200. The Cougars also have a junior side, with over 60 15-18 year olds on their books.

☛ *Home games are on Sundays, May-August, 3pm kick-off. Farsley Celtic's ground is in Throstle Nest, Newlands, New Street, Farsley, Leeds LS28.*

☎ *Cougars Info on Leeds 691728.*

Baseball

In just a few years the Leeds City Royals have grown from a single team playing in the infant Yorkshire League to a club with two senior and two junior teams and a permanent baseball ground off York Road. The 1st team plays in the National Premier League, the 2nd in the Northern League. The junior sides are based the home ground, known as the Leeds Baseball Diamond, while another is at Lawnswood YMCA. The season is April to September, and home games start 2.30pm on Sundays.

☛ *Leeds Baseball Diamond is at the former Swarcliffe Cricket Ground (opposite Red Lion),York Road, Leeds LS14.*

☎ *For news of fixtures ring Ian Smyth on Leeds 612571.*

Speedway

The only speedway team left in the area is the Bradford Dukes, who ride at Odsal Stadium, Bradford. Fast action and a fanatical following of over 2,000 from all over West Yorkshire characterize their weekly meetings from late-March to early October.The Dukes have seven riders (inc. two reserves) and there are 16 heats. Meetings are on Saturdays, starting at 7.30pm and lasting around two hours.

☛ *Odsal Stadium is in Rooley Avenue, Bradford (off the main Manchester road out to the M606). Odsal Stadium venue may change. Contact: Northern Speedways Ltd.*

☎ *Bradford 0274-690614.*

Formula One Stockcar Racing

Between April and October, usually on Bank Holiday Mondays or the final Saturday of the month, Stockcar Racing takes place at Odsal Stadium, Bradford. Up to 4,000 spectators enjoy at least four races per meeting, 16-30 drivers in each. Meetings start at 7.30pm and run until 10pm. Bar, refreshments.

☛ *Odsal Stadium is in Rooley Avenue, Bradford (off the main Manchester road out to the M606). Odsal Stadium venue may change. Contact: Bamforth promotions.*

☎ *Huddersfield (0484) 850081.*

Cycling Events

The 1990s have seen the sudden rise to prominence of Leeds as a venue for major cycling events. With the finish of the Kelloggs Race, the World Cyclo-Cross Amateur, Junior and Professional Championships (drawing a total crowd of 50,000) and the Wincanton Classic all brought to the city, Leeds is now firmly established on the international cycling map. You will find up-to-date details of future events in local What's On listings. For times and venues, call the Leeds Tourist Information Centre.

☎ *Leeds TIC, 478303. Sports Information Desk, Leeds 478303.*

Swimming

Leeds International Pool, one of the few 50-metre pools in Britain, hosts many top swimming events each year. These can range from European Junior Swimming and Diving Championships to national championships and trials. There is a great atmosphere when the 1,000-capacity seating area is full and local competitors, who are among the top in Europe, are doing well. Events usually take place on Fridays, Saturdays and Sundays.

☛ *The International Pool is in Westgate, Leeds LS1 (a short walk west of Leeds Town Hall). For news of forthcoming events, see the regular What's On listings available in the city, or telephone the Sports Information Service.*

☎ *Leeds 443713.*

Greyhounds

Unfortunately, the greyhound stadium at Elland Road has long since gone but there are several regular race meetings within an easy drive of the city. Among the most popular are:

Askern Stadium. There are meetings on Mon, Wed and Fri evenings. Busiest night, with a crowd of 500 or more, is for the open races on Saturday nights.

☛ *Selby Road, Askern, near Doncaster.*

☎ *0302-701550.*

Castleford & Whitwood. Also racing several nights a week. This greyhound stadium is even closer to Leeds.

☛ *Altofts Lane, Whitwood. Ring for programme.*

☎ *0977-559940.*

Equestrian

The four-day Bramham Horse Trials are one of three international equestrian events held in Britain each year (the others are Badminton & Burghley). The Bramham Trials are always the weekend following the Spring Bank Holiday. Around 20,000 spectators follow 130-plus competitors. The main event during the trials is the two-day Cross Country.

☛ *Bramham Park is reached through Thorner, to the east of Leeds, or off the A1 northbound carriageway.*

☎ *Boston Spa (0937 from Leeds) 844265.*

Sports & Fitness

Great public and private sports facilties, top sports development schemes and a vast programme of fitness courses

Most recreational sports are available in the Leeds area, from archery to athletics, korfball to karate, wrestling to weightlifting. By far the biggest provider of facilities are the 23 public Sports & Leisure centres, which also encompass many fitness courses. These are detailed on pages 129 & 130. But there are also numerous private sports clubs, specialising in such things as snooker, martial arts, squash, bowling, tennis, and golf. You will find them listed in the *Yellow Pages* and *Thomson Directory*. If, however, the recreational sport you seek is not available in Leeds, you will probably find it somewhere else in the region. Check the Sports list in the Clubs & Societies section of *Leeds Fax* (beginning on page 131). And if you're still stumped for a contact, try the Leeds Sports Information Desk, which maintains an up-to-date list of all sports contacts in the Leeds and West Yorkshire area. Below are some of the most popular recreational sports that require special facilities.

☎ *The Sports Information Desk is on Leeds 443713.*

Tennis

There are literally hundreds of free tennis courts available throughout the Leeds area. Most are attached to Leeds parks, even the smaller ones, and are open from dawn to dusk seven days a week. The only pay-courts are at Roundhay, where there are 14 good hard-surface courts next to Canal Gardens. Their location is excellent, and a game checker is there from early morning to dusk. There is no regular indoor tennis at the sports centres in Leeds. The biggest purpose-built tennis centre in the region is the Graves Tennis Centre at Sheffield. It has 6 indoor plexicushion courts, 12 outdoor plexipave courts (8 floodlit).

☛ *Graves is at Bochum Parkway, Sheffield S8 8JR.*
☎ *0742-839900.*

Golf

While an acute shortage of courses in southern England causes long queues from dawn to dusk, Leeds has the luxury of 22 fine golf courses. Sixteen of them are private (listed in the *Yellow Pages*) and five are good municipal courses. These are at Middleton, Roundhay, Gotts Park and two at Temple Newsam. In addition, there is a brand new public-private 18-hole course at Oulton Park in south Leeds (another 9-hole courses was opening in 1993). Designed by Dave Thomas to competition standards, this has all the facilities of a big private club, including a Professionals shop with a resident Class A Pro, bar and catering facilities in The Barn Restaurant, plus changing rooms in a purpose-built development. No membership is required, but ring in advance for booking details. In the same complex is the Oulton Golf Driving Range, where you can practice on any of the 16 indoor bays, using your own clubs or a set hired at the range. You hire baskets of around 95 balls.

☛ *Oulton Park is off the main Leeds-Wakefield Road at Oulton, near Rothwell. Open from dawn to dusk, seven days.*
☎ *Leeds 823152.*

Ten-pin Bowling

There are two good indoor bowling complexes in Leeds. The well-established Leeds Bowl, part of the Merrion Centre, has 30 lanes and computerised scoring. Prices are per person per game. There's a bar and fast food café. Open 9.30am-Midnight seven days. On the south side of the city is LA Bowl, which has 26 lanes, computerised scoring, and American food & drink bars. Open 10am-Midnight seven days. It also offers Flat Green Bowling on a fully carpeted arena, Mon-Sat 1pm-5pm.

☛ *Leeds Bowl is in Merrion Way, at the rear of the Merrion Centre, Leeds. LA Bowl is in Sweet Street,*

Holbeck (near M1/M621 junction), LS11.
☎ *Leeds Bowl, 451781; LA Bowl, 421330.*

Skiing

There are two artificial ski slopes in the Leeds area. The Harrogate Ski Centre has two main slopes, one 100 metres leading into an intermediate 80-metre slope, plus two nursery slopes where "taster" sessions are held for beginners. Boots, skis and poles are included in the ticket price. The other facility is the Halifax Ski Centre, a 90-metre-long slope, plus beginners' slope. Equipment is provided.

☛ *Harrogate Ski Centre is at Hookstone Wood Road, Harrogate. Halifax Ski Centre is part of the Sportman Leisure Complex, Swalesmoor, Halifax.*
☎ *Harrogate (0423) 505457; Halifax (0422) 340760.*

Ice Skating

The nearest Ice Rink to Leeds is in the centre of Bradford, just a five minute walk from the train or bus station. It has a 180ft by 80 ft. skating pad which can accommodate 2,250 skaters at once but 500-800 skaters a session is more normal. Skates are for hire or for sale. You can also get involved in ice hockey—there are three teams and a junior side. Disco requests are taken for evening sessions.

☛ *Little Horton Lane (behind the Photography Museum), Bradford BD5 0EA. Open: Mon-Thur 2pm-4pm; 7.30pm-10pm; Fri 2pm-4pm; 5.30pm-6.45pm (children session, parents free); Sat 11am-1pm, 2.30pm-5pm, 7.30pm-10pm; Sun 11.30pm-1.30pm, 7.30pm-10pm.*
☎ *0274-733535.*

Indoor Cricket

The last decade has seen a tremendous growth in the popularity of year-round indoor cricket. No longer do good cricketers allow themselves to get rusty in the winter months. Below are the three main indoor facilities in the Leeds area.

Cricket Wicket. Part of the big LA Bowl sports complex just south of the city centre, Cricket Wicket is a fast and furious game for 8 players a side, played for 75 min utes a session. There are two cricket courts, and all players bat and bowl for equal periods.

☛ *Sweet Street, Leeds LS11 9DB. Near start of M1 and M621.*
☎ *Leeds 421330.*

Yorkshire Cricket School. Next to the historic Headingley Cricket Ground, the school's Indoor cricket programme flourishes with competitions running throughout the year. They include Kwik Cricket in summer, competitions for under 13s, under 16s, adult teams and inter league teams.

☛ *41 St. Michael's Lane, LS6 3BR.*
☎ *Leeds 754622*

Speedball. This purpose-built complex in Bradford draws teams from all over the region. Eight players per team play on a court 38 x 22 yds with a slow surface and a softened ball of yellow leather, so no protective gear is required.There are 16 overs per side (7-ball overs). Speedball has four courts.

☛ *At Horton Park Avenue, Bradford BD5 0NL. Open 10am-midnight, seven days.*
☎ *0274-394307.*

Synthetic Turf Soccer & Hockey

The only full-sized pitch in the area is at Fearneville Sports Centre in North Leeds. Bookings must be 28 days in advance for the floodlit pitch, which is available from 9am to 10pm seven days a week. It is marked out for soccer (both 11 and 5-a-side are played) and hockey. There is a Master Turf League at Fearneville, with 16 soccer teams split between two divisions. But you can hire the pitch for informal games.

☛ *In Oakwood Lane, LS8.*
☎ *Leeds 402233.*

Target Shooting

The well-established Airedale Rifle & Pistol Club in Leeds has two full-bore ranges and one air pistol range, each with four points.

☛ *At Leeds Firearms International, Unit 6, Tower Works, Globe Road, Holbeck.*
☎ *Leeds 460003.*

Athletics

There are two long-established Athletics clubs in Leeds. They both cover the four main running categories—road, track and field, cross-country and fell-running. The city's main athletics facility is the synthetic track at Leeds Polytechnic—Carnegie School.

☛ *Leeds City Athletic Club, Mr. T. Burton, 8 Moseley Wood Green, Leeds LS16 7HB; Skyrac Athletic Club, Mr. G. Agar, 23 Milner Bank, Otley, LS21 3NE.*
☎ *Carnegie Track Info, 832600.*

Marathons and Fun Runs

In the last decade these events have become a major part of the local sports calendar. Many compete to test their personal fitness, or to raise money for charities.

Leeds Marathon and Half-Marathon. The region's premier running event takes place annually on the last Sunday of October. Over 3,000 runners participate. ☎ *Leeds 443713 for info.*

Leeds Swimming Marathon. At the International Pool over 8 days from the 3rd week of November each year. Swim 100 lengths (5000m.) or 50 lengths. Over 1,000 participate each year. ☎ *Leeds 438696 for info.*

Pudsey 10K. This 10 kilometre run is held in early April from Pudsey Leisure Centre. About 250 take part. ☎ *Leeds 568903 for info.*

East Leeds Biathlon. On 2nd Sun of October each year. Is a 500 metre swim, followed by 10 kilometre run. About 200 take part. ☎ *Leeds 648802 for info.*

South Leeds Fun Run. A five-mile jog from South Leeds Sports Centre. Date varies. ☎ *Leeds 457549 for info.*

Sports Development Programmes

Recreational sports in the Leeds area are promoted through a large range of council-run schemes. The aim is to make people aware of the sports opportunities and facilities available in the area, to encourage them to participate in sport and physical recreation, to enjoy these activities whether as participants or spectators, and the raise standards of excellence at all levels. Directed by Sports Development Officers who are specialists in their respec-

tive sports, they encompass all the most popular activities. Each one includes short courses through the year, ranging from one day, one weekend or six consecutive weeks. Adult courses are at weekends, while junior courses are held during school holidays. If you are an individual, the first point of contact is the Sports Development Officer who is responsible for the sport of your choice.

Football

Generally regarded as the best Football Development Scheme in Britain, it promotes football at all levels, from League soccer to junior and senior leagues, colleges, schools and groups. Courses are held at a number of sports centres and around 700 youngsters a week are benefiting from the scheme. Among the courses are schoolboy/girl holiday courses for players aged 7-13 throughout the city; Football Association Coaching Centre Sessions to provide coaching for boys and girls aged 7-13 years (one-hour sessions after school between October and March); and advanced coaching for boys aged 7-9; the Football Association/Leeds Centre of Excellence for the most promising 10-13 year old boys (weekly sessions at Fearnville Sports Centre and possibly selection to the FA National School); coaching sessions for girls aged 7-13 at Scott Hall Sports Centre; plus courses for coaches and referees.

☛ *Football Development Officer, Elland Road Stadium, LS11 0ES.*
☎ *Leeds 717609.*

Cricket

There are 120 cricket clubs in the Leeds area, many of them with junior sides playing at under 11s, under 13s, under 15s and under 18s. They cover all standards, and if you want to find a club to play with (for yourself, son or daughter) the Leeds Cricket Development Scheme may be able to help. The centre of excellence for the area is the Yorkshire Cricket School, which is across the road from the famous Headingley Cricket Ground. Coaching courses are available for all ages and abilities, usually running for 10 weeks. There are also holiday courses in Christmas, Easter summer and half-term holidays. The age range starts at under 9s, through under 14s, under 18s, men and women to senior citizens. Plus specialist courses for those showing real promise, and there's always the chance of being talent-spotted by the Yorkshire County Cricket Club coaching staff!

☛ *Cricket Development Officer, Yorkshire Cricket School, 41 St. Michael's Lane, LS6 3BR.*

☎ *Leeds 754622*

Fitness

Besides the huge community fitness programme (see Sports & Leisure Centres) Leeds has a much-acclaimed Fitness Clinic at the International Pool. It includes a Sports Injuries Service, with doctors and chartered physiotherapists with specialist skills in sports medicine. They offer diagnostic surgeries, physiotherapy and gymnasium rehabilitation. There is also a Fitness Training and Counselling service. The staff will assess your health-related fitness and lifestyle and help you achieve a higher standard of fitness. This is especially valuable to men and women over 40. Finally, there is a an extensive Corporate Fitness service.

☛ *The Fitness Development Officer, Leeds Sports Development, Leeds International Pool, Westgate, Leeds LS1 4PH.*

☎ *Leeds 424000.*

Sports for People with Disabilities

This sports development scheme seeks to encourage sport and recreation opportunities for the disabled in the Leeds area. There are regular sessions to involve disabled people in a variety of specialist sports, such as wheelchair basketball, but the main theme is one of integration—involving disabled people in all areas of sport and recreation. Also, disabled persons are encouraged to become sports coaches. The scheme produces a news sheet detailing activities.

☛ *Development Officer, Sport for People with Disabilities, Leeds Sports Development, International Pool, Westgate, Leeds LS1 4PH.*

☎ *Leeds 443713.*

Gymnastics

Leeds is well supplied with gymnastics opportunities, especially at the excellent Carnegie Region Gymnastic Centre at Beckett Park, which is one of the largest such permanent facilities in the UK. Branches of the sport being coached in Leeds include men's and women's artistic, sport acrobatics, rhythmic gymnastics and jumping gym-minies (for ages 1-4). Sports Acrobatics is one of the city's top sports (Leeds had one of the first acrobatic clubs in the country) with many world-class performers starting here.

☛ *The Gymnastics Development Officer, Carnegie Regional Gymnastic Centre, Beckett Park, Leeds LS6 3QS.*

☎ *Leeds 833162.*

Outdoor Pursuits

Based at Leeds Sailing Centre, Yeadon Tarn, a freshwater lake nine miles from the centre of Leeds, the Outdoor Pursuits Centre runs activities like dinghy and keelboat sailing, windsurfing (including a fleet of junior windsurfers for the 9-14 age range), canoeing (at swimming pools, Yeadon Tarn and local rivers), orienteering, caving and climbing.

☛ *The Development Officer, Leeds Sailing Centre, Yeadon Tarn, Yeadon, LS19.*

☎ *Leeds 503616.*

Racket Sports

Badminton, squash, tennis, short tennis and table tennis courses are organised throughout the Leeds area by the Racket Sports Development Unit. The badminton scheme is claimed to be the best in the country, with over 50 weekly classes catering for players of all ages and standards. At Rothwell Sports Centre is the National High performance Centre, where players are coached to international standard. There are also 50 squash coaching courses at sport centres in Leeds each year, and over 20 teams competing in two divisions providing casual players with some competitive play. Tennis coaching for juniors and adults is extensive, especially at beginner level, and lessons take place all year round. Short tennis is a good introduction to racket sports for children aged 5-12.

Weekly classes are held at five sports halls in Leeds. And for budding table tennis players, classes are held for juniors in the city.

☛ *The Racket Sports Development Officer, Rothwell Sports Centre, Wakefield Road, Oulton, Leeds LS26.*

☎ *Leeds 829319.*

Rugby League

The 13-a-side game is part of the Leeds sporting heritage and this development scheme provides coaching courses to promote the sport at all levels. Basic skills courses take place for ages 9-19. Week long school holiday courses are offered around the city. There are also Stage Two courses at sports centres for those wishing to improve their handling, passing, tackling, positional play, etc.

☛ *The Rugby League Development Officer, International Pool, Westgate, Leeds LS1 4PH.*

☎ *Leeds 443713.*

Swimming

Leeds International Pool is the acknowledged centre of excellence for swimming in the UK and this is reflected in the scope of its vast Swimming Development programme. Encouraged by the Olympic Gold Medal of City of Leeds Swimming Club member Adrian Moorhouse and its team of world-class coaches, there is a comprehensive training scheme for all levels of physical ability or disability. There are 700 swimmers in full-time competitive training; every year around 300,000 private swimming lessons are given at the pools throughout Leeds; there is a vast programme of schemes from ante-natal training, aqua-robics, diving, water polo, synchronized swimming, octo-push, life-saving, sub-aqua and much more. Children in the 6-13 age range can start in "E-groups" at many local pools and after introductory coaching two or three times a week, can move into higher levels. Initial contact is your local pool manager; for more the specialised stuff ring the Swimming Development Unit.

☛ *The Swimming Development Officer, International Pool, Westgate, Leeds LS1 4PH.*

☎ *Leeds 421959.*

Sports & Fitness Centres

Don't let the use of the word "Sport" put you off. These centres, scattered throughout the Leeds area, offer a great deal more than gruelling work-outs. There is everything from tea dances to indoor bowls, sunbeds, to yoga. Indeed, something for everyone. Of course, the centres house a large amount of sport-related facilities. Leeds has Britain's largest community fitness programme. Health-related fitness activities for both sexes, all ages and every level of fitness take place in hundreds of exercise classes each week at Sports & Recreation Centres and swimming pools across the area. These include "Bodyline Fitness" programmes (see The International Pool below). Exercise classes include aerobics, step, circuit training, weight training, body tuning and conditioning, gentle exercise, 50-plus, ante and post natal, water workouts, remedial classes and exercise for people with disabilities. There are 17 public squash and badminton complexes (in addition to numerous private clubs: see *The Yellow Pages*), swimming pools, weight rooms, and sessions in volleyball, martial arts, roller skating, and trampoline. Back-up services include a sports injuries service, fitness testing and counselling, and courses for instructors. All leisure centres and pools are available 7 days a week, throughout the year. There is no membership scheme. For details of latest activities, telephone or call at the sports centre nearest your home, or the one that offers the facilities you seek.

Aireborough Leisure Centre

Aerobics, activity room, badminton, bar/cafe, basketball, bowls, creche, climbing, dancing, fitness, football, gymnastics, martial arts, netball, orienteering, weights, roller skating, rugby, sauna, self-defence, snooker, squash, solarium, swimming, diving table tennis, tennis, volleyball.

☛ *The Green, New Road Side, Guiseley, LS20*

☎ *Bookings, Guiseley 877131; Enquiries, 871035.*

Armley Leisure Centre

Aerobics, activity room, badminton, bar/cafe, basketball, bowls, fitness, football, gymnastics, hockey, martial arts, netball, weight lifting, roller skating, rugby, sauna, self-defence, snooker, squash, solarium, swimming, table tennis, tennis, trampoline, volleyball.

☛ *Carr Crofts, Armley, LS12 3HB.*

☎ *Leeds 795858.*

Bramley Baths

Recently restored to its superb Edwardian glory, complete with poolside changing cubicles and steam room. It is almost a museum of the period's municipal baths, with old photographs of swimmers. Modern facilities include a weights and conditioning room, aerobics area and sunbeds.

☛ *Broad Lane, Bramley, Leeds LS13*

☎ *Leeds 571795.*

Bramstan Recreation Centre

Badminton, basketball, fitness, football, gymnastics, martial arts, netball, weights, roller skating, rugby, snooker, volleyball.

☛ *Intake School, Calverley Lane, LS13.*

☎ *Leeds 566627.*

Chippendale Swimming Pool

Fitness and swimming, but with ongoing expansion of dry facilities and some outdoor facilities. These improvements will be accompanied by an eventual change of name to

The area's top indoor sports facility is the **Leeds International Pool** *(pictured above), a landmark for everyone who travels along the inner city ring road on the west side of Leeds. Centrepiece is one of the few 50 x 17 metre swimming pools in the UK, which ranges in depth from 0.9 metres to 1.8 metres. This is home to the world-class City of Leeds Swimming Club, but also a popular pool with swimmers of all abilities at sessions which include early birds, lunchtime, homeward bound and evenings. In addition, there is a small pool (17.7m x 7.3m, with a depth between 0.8m to 1.3m) and a 7m x 17m diving pool, which is five metres deep, with fixed platforms at 5m, 7.5m and 10m, plus springboards at 1m and 3m. Other facilities in this huge sports complex include three saunas, two aerotone baths, six sunbeds and five solariums. There are two "body line" fitness and conditioning rooms, The Studio and The Basement, with varied programmes for all abilities. The Studio emphasises aerobic fitness, while The Basement concentrates on muscular fitness and endurance. Other facilities include a Fitness Clinic (see page 128) with well-equipped physiotherapy and sports fitness testing suites. And, of course, there is a café serving snacks and refreshments.*

☛ *Leeds International Pool is in Westgate, Leeds LS1 4PH. Best foot access is by walking west on south side of The Headrow, past Leeds Town Hall. Motorists access is off Wellington Street. Coins required for car park, refundable at reception. Ring for charge, and opening times.*

☎ *Leeds 438696.*

Prince Henry's Sports Centre.
☛ *Prince Henry's Grammar School, Otley, LS21.*
☎ *Otley (0943) 466852.*

East Leeds Leisure Centre

Aerobics, activity room, badminton, bar/cafe, basketball, boxing, bowls, creche, cricket, fitness, football, martial arts, netball, roller skating, rugby, solarium, swimming, table tennis, volleyball.
☛ *Neville Road, LS15.*
☎ *Leeds 648802.*

Farsley Recreation Hall

Activity rooms for weights, circuit training, martial arts, etc. plus large badminton hall, five-a-side, etc. Bookings for latter taken for Sat, Sun & Wed. Other days, apply to Farsley Celtic Football Club.
☛ *Newlands, Throstle Nest, Farsley, LS28.*
☎ *Activity room and hall bookings Leeds 568903; hall bookings on Mon, Tue, Thur & Fri only Leeds 561517.*

Fearnville Sports Centre

Body Line fitness, aerobics, all weather pitch, activity room, badminton, bar/cafe, basketball, dancing, fitness, football, gymnastics, hockey, martial arts, netball, weights, roller skating, rugby, squash, swimming, table tennis, tennis, volleyball, yoga.
☛ *Oakwood Lane, LS8.*
☎ *Leeds 402233.*

Garforth Squash & Leisure Centre

Aerobics, activity room, badminton, bar/cafe, basketball, bowls, dancing, fitness, football, gymnastics, martial arts, netball, weights, rugby, sauna, snooker, squash, solarium, table tennis, volleyball.
☛ *Ninelands Lane, Garforth, LS25.*
☎ *Leeds 860225.*

Holt Park Leisure Centre

Aerobics, all weather pitch, badminton, bar/cafe, basketball, cricket, dancing, fitness, football, gymnastics, hockey, martial arts, netball, weights, roller skating, rugby, sauna, self-defence, squash, solarium, swimming, table tennis, tennis, trampoline, volleyball, yoga.
☛ *Holt Road, LS16 7QD.*
☎ *Leeds 679033.*

John Smeaton Sports Centre

Body Line fitness, aerobics, all weather pitch, activity room, badminton, bar/cafe, basketball, climbing, cricket, dancing, fitness, football, gymnastics, hockey, martial arts, netball, rollerskating, rugby, sauna, squash, solarium, swimming, table tennis, tennis, volleyball, yoga.
☛ *Smeaton Approach, LS15.*
☎ *Leeds 601853.*

Kippax Sports Centre

Aerobics, badminton, bar/cafe, basketball, fitness, football, gymnastics, martial arts, netball, weights, roller skating, rugby, sauna, solarium, swimming, table tennis, volleyball.
☛ *Station Road, Kippax, LS25.*
☎ *Leeds 868882.*

Kirkstall Leisure Centre

Aerobics, activity room, badminton, bar/cafe, dancing, fencing, fitness, football, gymnastics, martial arts, netball, weights, rugby, sauna, squash, solarium, swimming, table tennis, yoga.
☛ *Kirkstall Lane, LS5.*
☎ *Leeds 786878.*

Middleton Leisure Centre

Aerobics, all weather pitch, activity room, badminton, bar/cafe, basketball, cricket, fitness, football, martial arts, netball, weights, roller skating, rugby, self-defence, squash, solarium, swimming, table tennis, tennis, volleyball.
☛ *Middleton Ring Road, LS10.*
☎ *Leeds 770021.*

Morley Leisure Centre

Aerobics, activity room, badminton, bar/cafe, basketball, bowls, fitness, football, gymnastics, hockey, martial arts, netball, weights, roller skating, rugby, sauna, snooker, squash, solarium, swimming, diving, table tennis, volleyball.
☛ *Queensway, Morley, LS27.*
☎ *Leeds 530001.*

Otley Open Air Pool

Swimming (summer only).
☛ *Wharfemeadows, Otley, LS21.*
☎ *Otley (0943) 466426.*

Pudsey Leisure Centre

Aerobics, aqua-aerobics, activity room, badminton, bar/cafe, basketball, bowls, creche, dancing, fitness, football, gymnastics (pre-school, rhythmic & acrobatics), keep fit for disabled, martial arts, netball, weights, roller skating, rugby, squash, "slim 'n' trim", solarium, swimming, volleyball.
☛ *Market Place, Pudsey, LS28.*
☎ *Leeds 568903.*

Richmond Hill Recreation Centre

Aerobics, badminton, basketball, fitness, football, gymnastics, martial arts, netball, weights, roller skating, rugby, snooker, table tennis, volleyball.
☛ *Pontefract Lane, LS9.*
☎ *Leeds 488056.*

Rothwell Sports Centre

Aerobics, activity room, badminton, bar/cafe, basketball, bowls, creche, climbing, fitness, football, gymnastics, martial arts, netball, weights, rugby, sauna, self-defence, snooker, squash, solarium, swimming, table tennis, trampoline, volleyball, yoga.
☛ *Wakefield Road, Oulton, LS26.*
☎ *Leeds 824110.*

Scott Hall Sports Centre

Body Line fitness, Aerobics, activity room, badminton, bar/cafe, basketball, boxing, creche, fitness, football, gymnastics, martial arts, netball, weights, roller skating, rugby, self-defence, squash, swimming, table tennis, tennis, volleyball.
☎ *Scott Hall Road, LS7.*
☛ *Leeds 624721.*

South Leeds Sports Centre

Body Line fitness, aerobics, activity room, badminton, bar/cafe, basketball, boxing, dancing, fitness, football, gymnastics, martial arts, netball, weights, roller skating, rugby, self-defence, snooker, squash, solarium, swimming, table tennis, tennis, volleyball.
☛ *Beeston Road, LS11.*
☎ *Leeds 457549.*

Wetherby Swimming Pool

Body Line fitness, aerobics, activity room, bar/cafe, fitness, football, martial arts, weights, sauna, solarium, swimming, table tennis, yoga.
☛ *The Ings, Wetherby, LS22.*
☎ *Wetherby 65125.*

PART SEVEN:
Clubs & Organizations

You can have as many fancy restaurants and shops as you like, but the true mark of a great city is a rich and varied community life.

The Leeds area has groups involved in every conceivable activity, from naturists to tortoise breeders, a Star Trek fan club to the Yorkshire Dialect Society. Campaigners fight for the rights of Leeds cyclists, or the rights of tribes to survive in the Third World. Charities raise money to buy guide dogs for the Leeds blind, or food for children in East Africa. And there are support groups for everyone from parents with crying babies to owners of personal computers.

The following pages provide a cross-section of communal activity in Leeds and West Yorkshire. There are thousands of opportunities to meet new people, help worthwhile causes, and learn more about a sport or hobby.

Hands-on at the hive: members of Leeds Beekeepers' Association at their apiary. See page 133.

Community Involvement

How to join a local club, volunteer your time for charity, fight a cause, make new friends, or start your own special interest group.

The named contacts listed here fall into two categories. One, the driving force in the club or organization, who will probably always be so. And two, an annually elected office bearer, usually secretary. In the latter case, the named individual should be able to point you in the direction of the current contact if he/she is no longer involved. If not, try the appropriate Primary Source (see below).

Voluntary Action Leeds

The city's umbrella organization for community and voluntary groups, charities etc. Can advise on setting up a new club/campaign, finding membership, limited start-up funds, "off-the-peg" constitutions.
☛ *34 Lupton Street, Leeds LS10.*
☎ *Call diversions/new number notification on Leeds 448921.*

Leeds Volunteer Bureau

A "Job Centre" for volunteers. More help constantly required with community work, including children, environment, elderly, education, driving, day centres, sports. Training provided, where required.
☛ *Contact through Voluntary Action Leeds (see above).*

Primary Sources

This section is an edited version of four databases for local organizations. If the contact listed here is no longer involved with their respective club etc. the following should have been notified of the most up-to-date contact—
Leeds Societies Index. The main list of local clubs, campaigns, charities, etc in the Leeds City Council area. Can be inspected at most branch libraries, or the "master" copy is held at Leeds Reference Library.
☛ *Third Floor, Central Library, Calverley Street, Leeds LS1 3AB.*
☎ *Leeds 478282.*
Leeds Community Health Council. Has most recent contacts for many health-related charities and

support groups. Can advise on setting up a new one.
☛ *3-4 Vicar Lane House, Templar Street, Leeds LS2 7NU.*
☎ *457461.*
Yorkshire & Humberside Arts. Updates lists of many arts/entertainments groups and individuals in the region.
☛ *21 Bond Street, Dewsbury, WF13 1AX.*
☎ *0924-466522.*
Yorkshire & Humberside Council for Sport & Recreation. Has a constantly updated directory of sports/leisure clubs, leagues etc.
☛ *Coronet House, Queen Street, Leeds LS1.*
☎ *Leeds 436443.*

Activities

Adel Horticultural Society. Friends Meeting House, New Adel Lane, Leeds LS16. ☎ 674231.
Aireborough Bridge Club. Mr. C. Taylor, 9 Tranfield Close, Guiseley. ☎ 874853.
Airedale Speakers Club. S. Wyatt, 22 Moseley Wood Avenue, LS16. ☎ 672062.
Airienteers. G. Mason, 90 St. Anne's Road, Leeds LS6. ☎ 785357.
Alwoodley Chess Club. Mr. J. Dobson, 2 Buckstone Way, Leeds LS17 5HD. ☎ 689243.
Alwoodley Gardening Club. Alwoodley Community Hall, The Avenue, Leeds LS17. ☎ 678773.
Army Cadet Force. Leeds Area ACF, Churchill Barracks, Whitelock Street. ☎ 459570.
Barwick-in-Elmet Horticultural Society. Mrs. M. Scarlett, 8 Gasgoine View, Barwick, LS15 4LU. ☎ 812563.
Boston Spa Chess Club. Deepdale Community Centre, Deepdale, High Street, Boston Spa. ☎ 0937-842095.
British Butterfly Conservation Society, C. Watson, 28 Arlington Road, Leeds LS8 2RU. ☎ 403313.
British Cactus & Succulent Society. Mr. J. A. Briscoe, 10 Stocks

Bank Drive, Mirfield, WF14. ☎ 0924-497239.
British Trust for Conservation Volunteers, Hollybush Farm, Broad Lane, Kirkstall, Leeds LS5 3BP. ☎ Leeds 742335. (Involves volunteers of all ages and backgrounds in practical conservation projects; runs training courses in skills; grows mature trees and wildflowers. Has a fine wildlife garden that is open to the public).
Caravan Club. B. Hewitt, 50 Hawkhill Gardens, Cross Gates, LS15 7PU. ☎ 648558.
Cats Protection League, 7 Broadgate Avenue, Horsforth, LS18. ☎ 586218.
Chapel Allerton Allotment and Gardens Association. Mrs. E. Thirsk, 21a Farrar Lane, Leeds LS16 6AD. ☎ 612120.
First World War Aviation Historical Society, Crag Cottage, The Crag, Bramham, LS23 6QB.
Garforth Bridge Club, Mrs. J. Varley, 1 Manor Garth, Ledsham, LS25 5LZ. ☎ 0977-682134.
Geranium Society. c/o Leeds Paxton Hall, Kirkstall Lane, Leeds LS6. ☎ 648028.
Gledhow Valley Allotment Association. Mrs. H. Knibbs, 16 Oaklea Gardens, Leeds LS16 8BW. ☎ 612724.
Goss Collectors Club. Mr. D. Porter, 4 Devonshire Crescent, Leeds LS8 1EP. ☎ 664164.
Gritstone Club. D. Chapman, 5 Calder View, Ossett, WF5 8RF. ☎ 0924-278502.
Guiseley Bridge Club, J. Banks, 13 Banksfield Crescent, Yeadon, LS19 7JY. ☎ Guiseley 75604.
Historical Commercial Vehicles Society. J. Hanson, 116 Copgrove Road, Leeds LS8 2RS. ☎ 400308.
Horsforth Antiques Society. c/o Rawdon Conservative Club, Leeds Road, Rawdon. ☎ 0943-462525.
Inland Waterways Association Mr. T. James, 270 West Park Drive, Leeds LS8 2BD. ☎ Leeds 665273.
Ireland Wood & District Garden Association. Mrs. M. Kingswood, 371 Otley Old Road, Leeds LS16 6BX. ☎ 612310.
Jewish Historical Society. H. R. Sterne, 43 Roper Avenue, Leeds LS8 1LG. ☎ 663409.
Leeds & District Badger Group, 32 Bath Lane, Bramley, Leeds

LS13 3AT. ☎ 659402.

Leeds & District Gardeners Federation. Mr. G. Kellard, 415 Spen Lane, Leeds LS16 6JE. ☎ 674264.

Leeds Amateur Winemakers Club. L. Rushworth, 75 Coalhill Lane, Leeds LS13 1DD. ☎ 577684

Leeds and District Amalgamated Society of Anglers. Mr. D. Fulthorpe, The Leeds Anglers, 75 Stoney Rock Lane, Leeds LS9 7TB. ☎ Leeds 482373.

Leeds Animal Forum, c/o PO Box HH13, LS8 4TD. ☎ 489459.

Leeds Astrology Group, D. Fisher, 14 Ganton Close, Leeds LS6 2NF. ☎ 439484.

Leeds Astronomical Society. Mr. Stanley Bell, 4 Belvedere Grove, Leeds LS17.

Leeds Beekeepers Association. David Barrett, 23 Beck Meadow, Richmond Field Lane, Barwick-in-Elmet, Leeds LS15. ☎ Leeds 813484. (Established in 1898, the Beekeepers have an apiary at Temple Newsam, have classes for beginners in May and June and meetings from September to April. Some of the 100 or so members are pictured on page 131.)

Leeds Birdwatchers Club, M. Palmer, 26 Ludlow Avenue, Garforth, LS25 2LY. ☎ Leeds 863503.

Leeds Budgerigar Society, W. Brady, 4 Jakeman Court, Tingley, WF3 1UR. ☎ 0924-522171.

Leeds Canoe Club. D. Player, 21 The Drive, Roundhay, Leeds LS8 1JF. ☎ Leeds 667397.

Leeds CHA Rambling/Social Club. J. Haley, 4 West Grange Gardens, LS10 3AT. ☎ 777829.

Leeds Chess Club. B. Hare, 97 Shakespeare Towers, Leeds LS9 7UG. ☎ 658483.

Leeds Dog Training Club, M. Harvey, 37 Sunnydale Road, Ossett. ☎ 0924- 275563.

Leeds HF Rambling/Social Club. G. Cressey, 12 Templestowe Drive, LS15 7BR. ☎ 648517.

Leeds Horticultural Society. Mrs. V. Dutton, 8 Stainburn Crescent, Leeds LS17 6NF. ☎ 687065. (Promotes the annual Leeds Show at Soldier's Field, Roundhay Park, every August).

Leeds Naturalists' Club & Scientific Association. Mrs. P. Larner, 1 Ashleigh Road, Leeds LS16 5AX. ☎ 755173.

Leeds Naturist Group. Council for British Naturism, Assurance House, Hazelwood Road, Northampton NN1 1LL. (Trying to establish naturist centre in Leeds).

Leeds Paxton Horticultural Society, Kirkstall Lane, Leeds LS6. ☎ 759775.

Leeds PC User Group. Dr. Maparooqui, 11 Summerhill Gardens, Leeds LS8 2EL. ☎ 662028.

Leeds Philatelic Society. Mr. D. Firth, 28 Greenside Drive, Leeds LS12.

Leeds Scrabble Club, A. Marsh, 9 Hemingway Garth, Leeds LS10 2PG.. ☎ Leeds 755153.

Leeds War Games Club. J. Smith, 27 Armley Grange Mount, Leeds LS12 3QB. ☎ 793974.

Linton Collecting Antiques Society. Mrs. G. Mobbs, "Beechwood", Jewitt Lane, Collingham, LS22 5BB. ☎ 0937-573793.

Long Distance Walkers Association West Yorkshire Group. Mr. D. Light, 44 Haw Lane, Yeadon, Leeds LS19 7XG.

Mathematical Association. Dr. A. Orton, 16 West End Lane, Leeds LS18 5JB.

Middleton Dog Training Club, D. Sage, 15 Winrose Garth, Belle Isle, Leeds. ☎ 772918.

Morley Family History Group. A. Blair, 30 West Lea Crescent, Tingley, WF3 1DJ. ☎ 533598.

Morris Minor Owners Club. Ian Benn, 20 Moorside Crescent, Drighlington, BD11. ☎ 854226.

Narrow Gauge Railway Society. R. Redman, 14a Oliver Hill, Leeds LS18 4JF. ☎ 583722.

National Canine Defence League, Leeds Centre, Eccup Lane, Adel, LS16.

National Tortoise Club, 2 Laith Close, LS16 6LE. ☎ 677587.

National Trust Volunteers. Mr. P. Hine, 110 Bentley Lane, Leeds LS6 4HA. ☎ 785238.

Otley Dog Training Society, Mrs. B. Acaster, 64 Larkfield Avenue, Rawdon, LS19. ☎ 506404.

Paganlink. Feòrag, Box 333, 52 Call Lane, Leeds LS1 6DT. (Network for all who honour the Spirit of the Earth).

Pudsey & District Rambling Club. A. Thayer, 10 South Way, Harrogate, HG2. ☎ 0423-504456.

Pudsey Chess Club. P. Smart, 53

Westway, Farsley, LS28 5HS. ☎ 576576.

Pudsey Philatelic Society. Mr. P. Devine, 38 Wellstone Garth, Leeds LS13 4HL. ☎ 550148.

Ramblers' Association West Riding. Mr. G. W. Garrard, 7 Clapham Dene Road, Leeds LS15 7EB. ☎ Leeds 644949.

Reliant Owners Club. D. Gillan, 9 Chaucer Grove, Pudsey. ☎ 551015.

Richard III Society. A. Cockerill, 55 St. Michael's Lane, Leeds LS6. ☎ 751263.

Rose Forgrove Chess Club. D. Smith, 25 Dale Park Walk, Leeds LS16 7PS. ☎ 697133.

Rothwell District & Allotment Association. Mr. R. Peters, 15 Needless Inn Lane, Leeds LS26 8EH. ☎ 823419.

Rothwell Historical Society. J. Quinn, 8 Manor Crescent, Wood Lane, Leeds LS28 0RE.

Roundhay Allotments and Gardens Association. P. Armitage, 4 Moor Allerton Crescent, Leeds LS17 6SH. ☎ 691602.

RSPB Leeds Members Group, V. Metcalfe, 19 Copgrove Road, Leeds LS8 2SP. ☎ 488108.

Taverners Amateur Wine & Beer Making Circle. G. Ellerker, 27 Church Lane, Horsforth. ☎ 580875.

Thoresby Society. 23 Clarendon Road, Leeds LS2. (Study of Leeds history).

Thorner Historical Society. J. Swift, 80 Main Street, Thorner, LS14 3BU. ☎ 892516.

Victorian Society. "Claremont", Clarendon Road, Leeds LS2. (Conservation and appreciation of Victorian architecture in Leeds).

West Yorkshire Fuchsia Society. 6 Barthorpe Avenue, Leeds LS17 5PF. ☎ 608207.

Wetherby & District Flower Club. M. Madden, 2 Deerstone Ridge, Wetherby. ☎ 0937-583717.

Wetherby Bridge Club, Mrs. D. Benn, 6 Bolton Way, Boston Spa, LS23 6PT. ☎ 0937-844184.

Wetherby Family History Society. S. Parkinson, 59 Barleyfields Road, Wetherby. ☎ 0937-585507.

Wetherby Historical Society, Northgate House, Barleyfield Lane, Wetherby. ☎ 0937-65361.

Wetherby Machine Knitting Club. Mrs. J. Hocking, Kenilworth

Lodge, Clifford Road, Boston Spa. ☎ 0937-845557.

Wharfedale Family History Group. R. Rowley, 3 Holt Lane, Leeds LS16. ☎ 673220.

Wharfedale Fuchsia Society. J. Goy, 111 The Avenue, Leeds LS17 7PA. ☎ 675806.

Wharfedale Naturalists Society. Mrs. J. Hartley, The Mount, Henley Avenue, Rawdon, LS19 8MZ. ☎ 504190.

White Rose Amateur Radio Society, J. Hart, 146 Street Lane, Leeds LS8 2AD. ☎ 663789.

Woodhouse Local History Group. c/o Woodhouse Community Centre, Woodhouse Street, Leeds LS6. ☎ 787081.

Yorkshire & Humberside Keep Fit Association. Mrs. E. Fitzpatrick, 5 Brownberrie Lane, Horsforth, Leeds LS18 5SD. ☎ Leeds 585106.

Yorkshire Alsatian Training Club, D. Calvert, 71 Bronte Old Road, Thornton, Bradford. ☎ 0274-833835.

Yorkshire Archaeological Society, Claremont, 23 Clarendon Road, Leeds LS2. ☎ 457910.

Dutch Rabbit Club, J. Walker, 53 Carr Manor Drive, Leeds LS17. ☎ 683338.

Yorkshire Bonsai Association. P. Chapman, 30 Sunset Hill Top, Leeds LS6. ☎ 758649.

Yorkshire Conchological Society. Mr. D. Linley, 29 Carr Manor Avenue, Leeds LS17 5BJ. ☎ 697047.

Yorkshire Draughts Association, W. H. Leggett, 17 Hetton Road, LS8 2RT. ☎ 401585.

Yorkshire Geological Society. Dept. of Earth Sciences, Leeds, University, LS2 9JT. ☎ 812906.

Yorkshire Mountaineering Club. D. Campbell, 43 Outwood Lane, LS18 4JB. ☎ 588311.

Yorkshire Parachute Club. H. Potter, 32 New Street, Pudsey, LS28. ☎ 562258.

Yorkshire Ship Enthusiasts. Mr. Cressey, 12 Templestowe Drive, Leeds LS15 7BR. ☎ 645517.

Yorkshire Subterranean Society. G. Shooter, 33 Oakroyd, Rothwell, LS26 0BL. ☎ 826862.

Youth Hostels Association. Leeds District Group, T. Harvey, 17 Highfield Drive, Leeds LS25 1JY. ☎ 863646.

Arts/Entertainment

Adel Players Dramatic Society. V. Bate, 20 Sefton Terrace, Leeds LS11 6LY. ☎ 712409.

Aireborough Camera Club. C. Milnes, 22 Benton Park Crescent, Rawdon, LS19 6NA. ☎ 506632.

Aireborough Gilbert & Sullivan Society. D. Exley, 156 High Street, LS19 7AB. ☎ 502051.

Aireings. J. Barker, 24 Brudenell Road, Leeds LS6. ☎ 785893. (Produces twice-yearly poetry magazine, organises poetry readings, festivals, workshops, etc).

Alwoodley Art Group, P. Bond, 5 Mulberry Rise, Leeds LS16. ☎ 679474.

Alwoodley Players. c/o Alwoodley Community Centre, The Avenue, Leeds LS17. ☎ 691915.

Alwoodley Singers. Alwoodley Community Centre, The Avenue, Leeds LS17. ☎ 671056.

Bib & Braces Circus Arts. P. White, 20 Rokeby Gardens, Leeds LS6 3JZ. ☎ 626731.

Bramhope Art Club, C. Newman, 14 Manor Close, LS16 9HQ. ☎ 842689.

City of Leeds Pipe Band. J. Bill, 37 Parklands, Bramhope, LS16 9AH. ☎ 842894.

City Varieties' Friends. City Varieties Music Hall, Swan Street, Leeds LS1 6LW. ☎ 425045.

Cosmopolitan Players. Stansfield Chambers, Great George Street, Leeds LS1. ☎ 583999.

Elvis Presley Fan Club. P. Phillips, 418 Oakwood Lane, Leeds LS8 3LG. ☎ 403485.

English Folk Dance & Song Society (Yorkshire). Mr. C. Barstow, 9 Peregrine Court, Netherton, Huddersfield HD4 7SW. ☎ 0484-666034.

Garforth Amateur Dramatic Society. B. Russell, 1 Ludlow Avenue, LS25 2LY. ☎ 860922.

Garforth Art Club, Mr. L. Burrows, 43 Woodland Road, Leeds LS15. ☎ 642321.

Garforth Musical Society. J. Robinson, 107 Fairburn Drive, Garforth. ☎ 866044.

Glenlee Scottish Dancers. S. Toft, 153 Leysholme Crescent, Leeds LS12. ☎ 639204.

Hall Place Studios, 4 Hall Place,

Leeds LS9 8JD. ☎ 405553. (A centre for community/independent media. Film and video studios, 16-track sound studio.)

Headingley Amateur Operatic Society. E. Packer, 17 Long Meadows, Garforth, LS25 2BR. ☎ 863603.

Horsforth Choral Society. Mrs. J. Tunncliffe, 33 St. Margaret's Road, Horsforth, Leeds LS18 5BG.

Horsforth Gramophone Society. A. Rawnsley, 21 Carr Lane, Rawdon, LS19. ☎ 504427.

Horsforth Leeds City Band. A. Higham, 95 Woodall Road, Leeds LS28 5PW. ☎ 550684.

Hospital Radio. C. Mason, 29 Leicester Close, Leeds LS7 1LN. ☎ 429792.

Hullaballoo Community Circus. A. Raynor, 16 Knowle Mount, Leeds LS4 2PP. (Circus enthusiasts helping others to develop circus skills. Hold workshops).

Interplay Community Theatre. R. Cuthbertson, Armley Ridge Road, Leeds LS12 3LE. ☎ 638556.

Kuffdem Theatre Company. P. Osborne, 1 Roxholme Grove, Leeds LS7 4JJ. ☎ 625753. (Only black theatre co. in Yorkshire, promoting African-Caribbean arts. Devises shows for young people and summer playschemes).

Leeds Actors Company. D. Robinson, 1 Grosvenor Road, Leeds LS6 2DZ. ☎ 740461. (Profit-sharing company to give Leeds writers, actors and directors opportunities to create exciting theatre for the city.)

Leeds Amateur Operatic Society. Mrs. M. Coustol, 47 West End Grove, Horsforth, LS18 5JJ. ☎ 582192.

Leeds Animation Workshop. 45 Bayswater Row, Leeds LS8 5LF. ☎ 484997.

The Leeds Art Collections Fund, Temple Newsam House, Leeds LS15 0AE. ☎ 647321. (Join this club to become more closely associated with the work of the city's three municipally owned galleries: Temple Newsam, Lotherton Hall and the City Art Gallery.)

Leeds Art Theatre. Stansfield Chambers, Great George Street, Leeds LS2. ☎ 621465.

Leeds Arts Space Society, Unit

D, 76 East Street, LS9 8EE. ☎ 434252. (Provides studio space to visual artists and craftspeople).

Leeds Camera Club. Civic Arts Guild, Stansfield Chambers, Great George Street, Leeds LS1. ☎ 587815.

Leeds Decorative and Fine Arts Society, Miss H. B. Upton, 7 Weetwood Park Court, Weetwood Park Drive, LS16 5AD. ☎ 759669.

Leeds Festival Chorus. 9 Ashleigh Road, Leeds LS16 5AX. ☎ 751628.

Leeds Folk Dance Club. M. Norton, 29 Carr Manor Walk, Leeds LS17 5DN. ☎ 681306.

Leeds Gilbert & Sullivan Society. Mrs. G. Jealous, 98 Ring Road, LS16 6EL. ☎ 785786.

Leeds Guild of Singers. Mrs. E. Hawthorn, 19 Highbury Road, Leeds LS6 4EX.

Leeds Male Voice Choir. Mr. J. Lockett, 40 St. Catherine's Crescent, Leeds LS13. ☎ 560450.

Leeds Morris Men. D. Matthews, 21 Fairfield Avenue, Ossett, WF5. ☎ 0924-272336.

Leeds Music Club. J. Brown, 29 Vesper Gate Drive, Leeds LS5 3NH. ☎ 788378.

Leeds Painting/Sketching Club, Mr. M. Senior, 32 West Grange Gardens, Leeds LS10 3AT.

Leeds Philharmonic Society. J. S. Brodwell, 30 Jackman Drive, Leeds LS18 4HS. ☎ 433311.

Leeds Photographic Society. D. Simmonds, 3 Holt Park Drive, Leeds LS16 7RG. ☎ 671470.

Leeds Star Trek Fan Club. C. Looby, 152 Otley Road, Leeds LS16. ☎ 758596.

Leeds Symphony Orchestra. Miss D. Morton, 161 Stratford Street, Leeds LS11 7EQ. ☎ 718938.

Leeds Writers Circle. Mrs. P. Belford, 38 Drummond Avenue, Leeds LS16 5JZ. ☎ 758490l.

Loidis International Folk Dance Group. Mrs. N. Marks, 174 Street Lane, Leeds LS8 2AA. ☎ 663863

Morley Camera Club. L. Sanderson, 18 Marshall Crescent, Morley, LS27 0HB. ☎ 530902.

National Film Theatre North. B. Geoghegan, c/o Leeds Design Innovation Centre, 46 The Calls, Leeds LS2 7EY. ☎ 441188.

Otley Arts Club, 20 Cambridge Grove, Otley, LS21 1DH. ☎ 0943-463500.

Otley Choral Society. Mr. R. Walker, 130 Bowling Park Drive, Bradford BD4 7ET.

Phoenix Folk Dancers. M. Sawyer, 57 Raynel Drive, Leeds LS16 6BP. ☎ 672097.

Proscenium Players. Stansfield Chambers, 67 Great George Street, Leeds LS2. ☎ 0937-73780.

Pudsey Camera Club. B. Webber, 7 Priestley Gardens, Pudsey, LS28 9AG. ☎ 568397.

Rawdon Amateur Operatic Society. B. Mason, 37 Rufford Drive, Leeds LS19 7QZ. ☎ 502468.

Rothwell Competitive Music Festival. M. Wilks, 6 Whinmoor Crescent, Leeds LS14 1AG. ☎ 653575.

Rothwell Theatre Group. Mrs. S. Tennant, 42 Ramsgate, Lofthouse, Wakefield. ☎ 0924-826087.

Royal Scottish Country Dance Society. Mrs. J. Dyson, 19 Pegholme Drive, Otley, LS21 3NZ. ☎ 0943-461022.

Sherburn-in-Elmet Arts Club, Mrs. J. Brown 27 Oakwood Close, Church Fenton. ☎ 0937-557323.

Sinatra Music Society. G. Day, 86 Montague Crescent, Garforth, LS25 2EH. ☎ 867341.

Sinfonia of Leeds. Mr. T. Casey, 22 Ashdene Crescent, Pudsey, Leeds LS28 8NS.

St. Peter's Singers. Miss S. Chambers, 7 Orville Gardens, Leeds LS6 2BS.

Swinnow Scottish Dancers. Mrs. E. Dracup, 11 Wellstone Drive, Leeds LS13 4DZ. ☎ 566013.

Wallace Arnold Rothwell Band. Band Room, Butcher Lane, Rothwell, LS26. ☎ 822388.

Wetherby Camera Club. Mrs. P. Rollason, 15 Ullswater Rise, Wetherby. ☎ 0937-564655.

Wetherby Silver Band. The Band Room, Bank Street, Wetherby. ☎ 0937-586734.

Wetherby Light Music Singers. Mrs. M. Mason, 23 Heathfield Lane, Boston Spa. ☎ 0937-844987.

Wetherby Music & Theatre Group. Mrs. A. Baldwin, 8 Linden Way, Wetherby, LS22 4QU. ☎ 0937-582395.

White Rose Barbershop Singers. T. Timms, 109 Ring Road, Cross Gates, LS15. ☎ 603148.

White Rosettes Leeds Ladies

Barbershop Harmony Club. Mrs. J. Barker, 6 Moorside Crescent, Drighlington, BD11 1HS. ☎ 853164.

WYBC Community Radio. A. McLeish, Flat C, 24 Avenue Hill, Leeds LS8 4EY.

Yorkshire Dialect Society. S. Ellis, Fairfields, Weeton Lane, Weeton, Leeds LS17.

Yorkshire Women Theatre Co. J. Courtney, Chapeltown Business Centre, 231-235 Chapeltown Road, Leeds LS7 3DX. ☎ 626900. (Drama and writing workshops with women's groups, disabled women, bi-lingual women and girls groups).

Campaigns/ Interest Groups

A660 Joint Council (Leeds). Dr. R. F. Youell, 5 North Grange Mount, Leeds LS6 2BY. ☎ 786441.

Aireborough & Horsforth Environment Group. P. Middleton, "Anville", Morlands Drive, Yeadon LS19 6AA. ☎ 509390.

Amnesty International. L. Tidball, 12 Broomhill Drive, Leeds LS17 6JJ. ☎ 686461.

Association for Nonsmokers' Rights. Leeds Area Branch, Sandy Reid, 8 Moorbank Court, Shire Oak Road, Leeds LS6 2DD. ☎ 788250. (Excellent campaign for smoke-free areas and facilities, especially in pubs/eating places).

Campaign for Nuclear Disarmament. Leeds Group, H. Denham, 31 Cross Flats Parade, Leeds LS7 7JL. ☎ 706902.

Campaign for Real Ale (CAMRA). C. Chapman, 10 Waterloo Crescent, LS13. ☎ 572346.

Council for the Protection of Rural England. West Yorkshire County Branch, L. Bettison, 39 Southleigh Drive Beeston, LS11 5TR. ☎ 712616.

Friends of Beckett Street Cemetery. S. Barnard, 2 North Park Road, Leeds LS8 1JD. ☎ 643012.

Friends of Kirkstall Abbey. I. Crawshaw, 4 Victoria Park Avenue, Leeds LS5 3DQ. ☎ 756732.

Friends of the Settle Carlisle Line Association. P. Shaw, 33 Temple Rhydding Drive, Baildon, BD17 5DX.

Greenpeace (Leeds). 9 Moorfields, Leeds LS13. ☎ 577658.
Kirkstall Valley Campaign. Mrs. L. Raine, 12 Eden Crescent, Leeds LS4 2TW. ☎ 788475.
Leeds China Support Group. 19 Fearnville View, Leeds LS8 3DS. ☎ 625291.
Leeds Civic Trust. Dr. Kevin Grady, Claremont, 23 Clarendon Road, Leeds LS2 9NZ. ☎ 439594. (Historic building preservation. Marks structures with blue plaques explaining their importance).
Leeds Cyclists Action Group. T. Harberd, 14 Oatland Green, Leeds LS7 1SN. ☎ 428991.
Leeds Nicaragua Solidarity Campaign. 6 Harland Square, Leeds LS2 9EB. ☎ 433522.
Leeds Urban Wildlife Group. P. Larner, 1 Ashleigh Road, Leeds LS16 5AX. ☎ 755173.
National Trust. Miss D. Chant, 11 Mount Pisgah, Burras Lane, Otley, LS1 3DX. ☎ 0943-463273.
South Leeds Groundwork Trust, Environment and Business Centre, Wesley Street, Morley, Leeds LS27 9ED. ☎ 380601.
Survival International. Paul Marchant, 58 Ash Road, Leeds LS6 3EZ. ☎ 787131. (Survival for tribal peoples, upholding their human rights to live as they choose, to have land rights, etc.)
Yorkshire Wildlife Trust. 10 Toft Green, York YO1 1JT. ☎ 0904-659570.

Charities/ Voluntary Groups

Age Concern Leeds. 88a Woodhouse Lane, Leeds LS2 9DX. ☎ 672925.
British Red Cross Society. J. Gooding, 19 Greenwood Park, Leeds LS6 4LB. ☎ 779999.
Christian Aid. Area Office, Leeds Church Institute, 36 Lower Basinghall Street, Leeds LS1 5EB. ☎ Leeds 444764.
Guide Dogs for the Blind Association. E. Wheatley, 142 Moseley Wood Gardens, Leeds LS16 3JB. ☎ 672593.
Leeds & District Spastic Society. Mrs. J. Marsden, 13 Outwood Avenue, Horsforth. ☎ 584979.
Leeds Lions Club. Mr. L. Dickinson, 1 Hollycroft Court,

Leeds LS16 6AZ. ☎ 611635.
Leeds Round Table. A. Jones, 470-474 Roundhay Road, Leeds LS8. ☎ 400666.
Leeds Skyrack Lions Club. Mr. I. Hughes, 6 Fitzroy Drive, Leeds LS8 1RW. ☎ 402910.
Leeds Student Community Action. Leeds University Union, PO Box 157, Leeds LS1. ☎ 314260.
National Heart Research Fund. Concord House, Park Lane, Leeds LS3 1EQ. ☎ Leeds 347474.
NSPCC. 10 Woodhouse Square, Leeds LS3. ☎ 737331.
RNLI Leeds. Mrs. M. Rowe, 41 Devonshire Lane, Leeds LS8 1DY. ☎ 666463.
Rothwell Lions. P. Unwin, 15 West View, LS26 8TS. ☎ 824101.
United Nations Children's Fund. F. W. Chattaway, 27 Primley Park Lane, Leeds LS17 7JE. ☎ 686777.
Wetherby Lions. P. Lloyd, "Peeps", Harewood Road, Collingham. ☎ 0937-573027.
Woodcraft Folk, 272 York Road, Leeds LS9 9DN. ☎ 498359.
Worldwide Fund for Nature Conservation (WWF). P. Hogg, 22 Allerton Drive, East Keswick, LS17 9HE. ☎ 0937-572104.

Ex-Service & Retired

1940 Dunkirk Veterans Association. J. H. Else, 26 Sandiford Terrace, Cross Gates, Leeds LS15 8JL. ☎ Leeds 603903.
Age Concern, 188a Woodhouse Lane, Leeds LS2 9DX. ☎ Leeds 458579.
Burma Star Association. E. F. Kirby, 24 Rosewood Court, Rothwell, LS26 0XG. ☎ 827491.
Civil Service Retirement Fellowship. J. Corkill, 6 Highmoor Drive, ☎ Leeds 487271.
Commando Association. Polish Catholic Centre, Newtonhill Road, Leeds LS7. ☎ 670885.
D-Day & Normandy Veterans Association. J. Hodgson, 25 Wood Lane Court, Leeds LS6 2PF. ☎ 783803.
Leeds Royal Naval Association. P. Radford, 94 Wharfedale Rise, W. Ardsley, WF3 1AY. ☎ 524337.
Morley OAP Association. Mrs. W. Thornton, 27 Lewisham Court, Morley. ☎ 523143.

National Association of OAPs. M. Lumley, 46 All Saints Drive, Woodlesford, LS26 8NF. ☎ 824727.
RAF Association Headingley, c/o British Legion, St. Michael's Road, Leeds LS6. ☎ 672045.
RAF Association Airedale & Wharfedale, Grove Hill Social Club, Ilkley Road, Otley, LS21. ☎ 0943-462525.
RAF Association City of Leeds, M. Taylor, 40 Lincroft Crescent, Leeds LS13 2JN. ☎ 561789.
Royal Artillery Association, H. Stottard, 64 Broadgate Drive, Horsforth. ☎ 585055.
Royal British Legions. (There are too many in Leeds to list here, but they are to be found in the Leeds Area Phone Book).
Royal Signals Association. Mr. T. Smith, 22 Park Wood Crescent, LS11. ☎ 701587.
University of the Third Age. Enid Nicholson, 6 Mulberry Avenue, Leeds LS16 8LL. ☎ Leeds 677035.
West Riding Association of WRENS. Mrs. M. Briggs, 3 Green Moor Close, Lofthouse, WF3 3LF. ☎ 0924-822888.
Women's Royal Army Corps. M. Conley, 24 Alexandra Road, Leeds LS18. ☎ 584707.
Yorkshire Fleet Air Arm Association. J. Tuke, "Amastra", 10 West Grange Road, Leeds LS10 3AW. ☎ 707881.

Health & Parental Groups

Acne Self Help Group. A. Wood, 48 Stonebridge Lane, Old Farnley, Leeds LS12. ☎ Leeds 792362.
Action for Research into Multiple Sclerosis. MBO Therapy unit, Airedale Mills, Rawdon, Leeds LS19 6JY. ☎ Leeds 504528.
Alzheimer's Disease Society. M. Welford, 29 Henley View, Leeds LS13 EAQ. ☎ Leeds 553534.
Arthritis Care 35 Group. P. Le Gallex, Leeds General Infirmary, Leeds. ☎ Leeds 432799.
Association for Children with Heart Disorders. C. Dixon. ☎ Leeds 522316.
Leeds Speech Therapy Group. M. J. Peace, 35 Grove Farm Crescent, LS16 6BZ. ☎ 672559.

Asthma Society. Mrs. W. Hemsley, 22 Moorway, Guiseley, LS20 8LB. ☎ Guiseley 873615.

Autistic Society. Mrs. R. King, Fairmount, Park Road, Bingley, BD16 40W. ☎ 0274-564999.

British Diabetic Association. S. Horsey, 5 Beckhill Row, Stainbeck Lane, Leeds LS7 2RL ☎ 680119.

British Epilepsy Association. National Information Centre, Anstey House, 40 Hanover Square, Leeds LS3 1BE. ☎ 439393.

British Polio Fellowship. Mrs. Hendley. (Socials, help and advice). ☎ Leeds 402858.

Cancer Support Scheme. 72 Vicar Lane, Bradford BD1 5AG. ☎ 0274-370073.

Carers' National Association. J. Fitton, 1 St. Margaret's Close, Leeds LS18 5BE. ☎ 585579.

Chest, Heart & Stroke Association. Respiratory Diseases unit, Killingbeck Hospital, York Road, Leeds LS14 6UQ. ☎ 601167.

Child Growth Foundation. L. Robbins, 15 Welburn Avenue, Leeds LS16. ☎ 757810.

Compassionate Friends, P. Clark, 75 Weetwood Lane, Leeds 16. (Bereaved parents support group. Personal contact, meetings, visits etc. Newsletter) ☎ 759526.

Cot Death Support Group. B. Hilton, 463 Selby Road, Leeds LS15 7AX. ☎ 606310.

Crysis. H. Jenks. (Practical support for parents of crying babies). ☎ Leeds 521602.

Dementia Helpline. 6-8 Great George Street, Leeds 1. ☎ 422120.

Disabled Drivers Motor Club. W. Rowland, 15 Ash Dene Drive, Crofton, Wakefield. (Advice on adaptations for cars etc.) ☎ 0924-862640.

Foresight. V. Kearney. (Preconceptual care through nutritional advice). ☎ 0423-864358.

Foundation for the Society of Infant Deaths. L. Miller.(24 hour helpline/counselling service for bereaved parents and information about cot deaths.) ☎ Leeds 691585.

Haemophilia Society. (Provides advice and assistance to haemophiliacs.) ☎ Leeds 663023.

Headway. A. North, 9 Abbot Court, Leeds LS12 2JW. (Self help group for serious head injuries. Holds meetings). ☎ 791662.

Hyperactive Children's Group. V. Kearney, 2 Ridge Villas, Forest Moor Road, Harrogate. ☎ 0423-864358.

Ileostomy Association. L. Lancaster, 33 Fearnville View, Leeds LS8 3DJ. ☎ 658498.

Infertility Self-help Group. L. Manson, 71 Birchfields Rise, Leeds LS14 2JD. ☎ 736208.

Laryngectomy Club. Mr. Harrison, 29 Manor Farm Gardens, Leeds LS16 3RA. ☎ 711364.

Leeds & District Sports Association for the Disabled. Mrs. M. Griffiths, 26 Churchville, Micklefield, LS24 4AP. (An umbrella group to encourage sport and recreation for the disabled. Will direct callers to various clubs). ☎ 871176.

Leeds & District Twins Club. J. Threlfall, 34 Beech Lees, Farsley, LS28 5UZ. ☎ 564592.

Leeds Braille Group. Mrs. M. Mattocks, 23 Oakwell Avenue, Leeds LS8 4AQ. ☎ 668727.

Leeds Centre for Alternative Therapy and Medicine. 244 Wetherby Road, Leeds LS17 8NH. ☎ 589026.

Leeds Gingerbread. M. O'Connor, 1 Highfield Court, Leeds LS12.

Leeds Psychiatric Survivors Group. c/o Box 193, 52 Call Lane, Leeds LS1.

Let's Face It. (Support for anyone who suffers from facial injury or disfigurement). ☎ Helpline: Huddersfield (0484) 663673.

Limbless Support. Mr. Mills. (Will visit in hospital, and advise amputees.) ☎ Leeds 665976.

Manic Depression Fellowship. The Resource Centre, St. Mary's Hospital, Leeds LS12. ☎ 790121.

Meet-a-Mum Association. Mrs. G. Cook, 38 Brandhill Drive, Crofton, Wakefield. ☎ 0924-863028. (Support for mums with young children, mums experiencing post-natal depression).

Mencap. The City of Leeds Society for Mentally Handicapped Children & Adults, Mencap House, 142 Chapeltown Road, Leeds LS7. ☎ 622818.

Mind. 157 Woodhouse Lane, Leeds LS2 1YY. (Provides general advice and information on all aspects of mental health). ☎ Leeds 454824.

Motor Neurone Disease Association. D. Allen. (A small support group). ☎ Leeds 607513.

Muscular Distrophy Group. M. Unsworth, 24 Parklands, Bramhope, Leeds. ☎ 842861.

National Association for the Childless. A. Wilson, 22 Wensley Road, Leeds LS8. ☎ 682292.

National Association of Colitis and Crohn's Disease. J. Rothwell, 14 Victoria Walk, Leeds LS18 4PL. ☎ 588577.

National Back Pain Association. D. Sheppard, 10 Kirkfield Gardens, Leeds LS15 9DT.

National Childbirth Trust. S. Lakie, 10 Parkside Green, Leeds LS6 4NY. ☎ 759804.

National Eczema Society. L. Beech, 94 Springhill Avenue, Crofton, WF1. ☎ 0924-862149.

National Federation for the Blind. Mrs. J. Jackson, 19 Avondale Street, Leeds LS13 4DE. ☎ 575503.

National Osteoporosis Society. P. Goodacre, 67 Moorgate Road, Kippax, LS25 7ET. (Help and advice for sufferers). ☎ 868193.

National Schizophrenia Fellowship. A. Singleton, 28 Parkland Crescent, Leeds LS6 4PR. ☎ 693430.

Natural Family Planning Service. S. Pickles, 20 The Avenue, Leeds LS15 8JN. (Offers a confidential personal service in natural family planning including help for couples having problems conceiving a child). ☎ 600844.

Parents of Deaf Children. National Deaf Children's Society, Centenary House, North Street, Leeds LS2 8JS. ☎ 438328.

Parkinson's Disease Society. N. Smith, 39 Coxwold View, Wetherby, LS22. ☎ 0937-583397.

Retinitis Pigmentosa Society. E. Atkins, 70 New Bank Street, Morley, LS27 8NA. ☎ 539867.

Sickle Cell Society. L. Powell, Chapeltown Health Centre, Leeds LS7. ☎ 664893.

Spastics Society. Regional Office, 3 Brindley Way, Wakefield WF2 0XQ. ☎ 0924-828980.

Spina Bifida & Hydrocephalus Association. Mr. Booth, Brick House Farm, Askwith, Otley.

Stillbirth/Neonatal Deaths Society. L. Cheetham, 4 Park Spring Gardens, Pudsey, LS13 ☎ 568591.

Thalassemia Support Group. Mr. Iqbal. ☎ Leeds 406079.

Tinnitus Group. G. Standley, 4 Dene Hill, West Lane, Baildon, BD17 5BA. ☎ 0274-591601.

Twins Club. J. Threlfall, 34 Beechlees, Farsley, Leeds LS28. (Parent support group). ☎ 564592.

Urostomy Association. S. Speck, 12 Parkside View, Leeds 6. ☎ 756728.

Weightwatchers UK. Provincial House, Albion Street, Leeds LS1. ☎ 452423.

Yorkshire & Humberside Keep Fit Association. Mrs. E. Fitzpatrick, 5 Brownberrie Lane, Horsforth, LS18 5SD. ☎ 585106.

Housing/ Homelessness

Harehills Housing Aid, 188 Roundhay Road, Leeds LS8 5PL. ☎ 492484 (ansaphone) or 487794. (Housing/welfare advice. Urdu, Punjabi, Hindi, Bengali spoken).

Leeds Shaftesbury Project, Oxford Chambers, Oxford Place, Leeds LS1 3AX. ☎ 450267.

Nightstop, 53 Cardigan Lane, Leeds LS4 2LE. ☎ 757314. (Finds emergency accommodation for young people aged 16-25. No self-referrals).

Palace Youth Project, 92 Shepherds Lane, Leeds LS7. ☎ 620093. (For 16-25 year olds. Informal counselling, help with jobs, benefit claims, etc.)

Rokeby Project (formerly Leeds Leaving Care), 2 Rokeby Gardens, Leeds LS6. ☎ 744284. (Young people 16-18 leaving local authority or foster care).

Sahara, PO Box 94, Leeds LS1. ☎ 460401. (For black women who suffer violence from family).

Salvation Army Hostel, 36 Lisbon Street, Leeds LS1 4NA. (Men only, not suited for under 18s). Also for single women and women with children at 27 Broad Lane, Bramley, Leeds LS13. ☎ 570810.

Shelter—Leeds Branch. Charlton House, 36 Hunslet Road, Leeds LS10 1JN. ☎ 451460.

St. Anne's Shelter & Housing Action, 6 St. Mark's Avenue, Leeds LS2. ☎ 435151. (Referrals accepted from anywhere provided the person is homeless).

Theodor Foundation, 94 Harehills Avenue, Leeds LS8 3EX. ☎ 626726. (Hostel for homeless men 16-2).

Umoja House, 6-12 Sholebrook Avenue, Leeds LS7 3HB. ☎ 374059. (Hostel for single 16-25 women and men).

Local/ Community Groups

Aireborough Civic Society. Mr. D. Wagstaff, Lilac Cottage, Apperley Lane, LS19. ☎ 504139.

Alwoodley Community Association. Alwoodley Community Hall, The Avenue, LS17. ☎ 671331.

Beeston Helpline. 169 Old Lane, Leeds LS11 7AQ. ☎ 704075.

Boston Spa Village Society. Mrs. J. Newman, 298 High Street, Boston Spa. ☎ 0937-845675.

Burley Lodge Centre, 12 Burley Lodge Road, Leeds LS6 1QP. ☎ 443335.

Chapel Allerton Residents Association. Mrs. R. Dobson, 60 Henconner Lane, Leeds LS7 3NX. ☎ 625618.

Hall Lane Social Action Centre 65 Hall Lane, Leeds LS12 1PG. ☎ 634380.

Hawksworth Road Community Association. M. Rawnsley, 191 Vesper Road, Leeds LS18 4LS. ☎ 582228.

Horsforth Civic Society S. Barlow, 15 Victoria Crescent, Horsforth, LS18 4PT. ☎ 585748.

Hunslet Community Forum. Hunslet Parish Church, Church Street, Leeds LS10. ☎ 704659.

Kirkstall Village Community Association. F. Butler, 1 Hesketh Road, Leeds LS5. ☎ 788239.

Lower Wortley Community Association. Mrs. J. Spink, 138 Lower Wortley Road, Leeds LS12 4PQ. ☎ 639090.

Meanwood Community Centre, Stainbeck Avenue, Leeds LS7 2QJ. ☎ 786995.

Newlay Conservation Society. Ms. Wendy Butlin, Flat 5, 28 Newlay Lane, Horsforth, LS18. ☎ 580936.

Oulton Civic Society. M. Holt, 23 Farrer Lane, Oulton. ☎ 821548.

Rodley Residents Association. Mr. P. Bishop, 169 Town Street, Rodley, Leeds LS13 1HW.

Rothwell Civic Society. Mr. J. D. Barlow, 314 Wood Lane, Rothwell, LS26 0PW. ☎ 825225.

Roundhay Conservation Society. Mrs. M. Lester, 59 Lidgett Park Road, Leeds LS8 1JN. ☎ 662403.

South Headingley Community Association. The Cardigan Centre, Cardigan Road, Leeds LS6. ☎ 785893.

Tong/Calverley Countryside Project. Mr. B. Johnson, 4th Floor, Crown House, 310 North Parkway, Seacroft Town Centre, Leeds LS14 6LU. ☎ 734184.

Woodhouse Tenants Association. Mrs. Tinker, 21 Holborn Walk, LS6 2RA. ☎ 453359.

Miscellaneous Help & Advice

Catholic Marriage Advisory Council. Basement, St. Anne's Cathedral House, Great George Street, Leeds LS2. ☎ Leeds 432974.

Halton Moor Information Centre, Neville Road, Leeds LS15 0NW. ☎ 608901.

Leeds Claimants Union. Hyde Park Priory, 158 Hyde Park Road, Leeds LS6. ☎ 753160.

Leeds Gay Community. The Swarthmore Centre, 3-7 Woodhouse Square, Leeds LS3. ☎ 432210.

NCH Care Line. The Family Care Centre, Oxford Chambers, Oxford Place, Leeds LS1 3AU. (Counselling by telephone or face to face on all types of family problems, family therapy). ☎ Leeds 456456.

Relate. Leeds Marriage Guidance (See page 24). Rutland House, 38 Call Lane, Leeds LS1 6DT. ☎ 452595.

Samaritans. 93 Clarendon Road, Leeds LS2 9LY. (Friends to people who are feeling desperate, lonely or suicidal. Contact by phone or writing. Confidential). ☎ 456789.

South Leeds Legal Advice Centre, Hunslet Parish Church, Church Street, Leeds LS10 2QY. ☎ 704659. (Advice includes Social Security, writing letters, filling in forms, representation and appeal tribunals, legal advice, therapy). Open, 9.30am-9.30pm Mon-Fri).

National & Ethnic Groups

Association of British Muslims (Leeds). Omar House, 5 St. John's Terrace, Leeds. ☎ 621716.

Bangladesh Islamic Society. Mr. N. Ali, 41 Shepherds Lane, Leeds LS8. ☎ 625200.

Barrack House. Barrack Road, Leeds LS7. (Community health education centre for varied ethnic groups). ☎ 621035

Federation of Irish Societies. Bernard McGrath, 97 Old Lane, Beeston, Leeds LS11 7AQ. ☎ Leeds 714047.

Garu Nanak. H. S. Sagoo, 270 Crossflats Grove, Leeds LS11 7BS. ☎ 711630.

Iraqi Community Centre. 48 Colwyn Road, Leeds LS11 6LP. ☎ 771154.

Japanese Society. Mrs. S. Greavy, 77 Westfield Lane, South Milford, LS25 5AW. ☎ 0977-682604.

Kashmir Social and Welfare Association. 5 Gathorne Close, Leeds LS8 5EY. ☎ 626036.

Leeds Chinese Community. Mrs. S. Chan Lee, 4 Rocheford Walk, LS11.

Leeds Vietnamese Community Association. 55 Louis Street, Leeds LS7 4BP. ☎ 430985.

Leeds Welsh Society. Miss M. E. Pinnell, 6 Park Villa Court, Leeds LS8 1EB. ☎ Leeds 665399.

Muslim Women Association. 42 Roxholme Place, Leeds LS7 4JQ. ☎ 623221.

Otley & District Caledonian Society. J. Lee, Lyndhurst, Laxton Road, Leeds LS19 6QU. ☎ Leeds 504949.

The Jamaica Society. Mrs. L. A. Powell, School House, Bankside Primary School, Markham Avenue, Leeds LS8 4LE. ☎ 626347.

Religious Organizations

Baha'i Community. PO Box MT14, Leeds LS17 7UR.

Christian Aid. Leeds Church Institute, 36 Lower Basinghall Street, Leeds LS1 5EB. ☎ 444764

Leeds Council of Christians & Jews. Rev. Cannon Jeffrey King, St. John's Rectory, Fir Tree Lane, Leeds LS17 7BZ. ☎ 637484.

Leeds Jewish Representative Council. 151 Shadwell Lane, Leeds LS17 8BD. ☎ Leeds 697520. (Umbrella for the religious and lay organisations of the Leeds Jewish Community. Has a list of all Orthodox and Reform Synagogues in the Leeds area.)

Leeds Metropolitan Council of Churches. Rev. E. D. Murfett, St. Peter's House, Kirkgate, Leeds LS2 7DJ. ☎ 452036.

Theosophical Society. 12 Queen Square, Leeds LS2. ☎ 587074.

Welsh Church. Soroptimist House, 6 Woodhouse Cliff, Leeds LS6. ☎ Leeds 751565.

Worldwide Evangelisation for Christ. P. Banfield, 20 Hanover Square, Leeds LS3 1AW. ☎ 453650.

Yorkshire Congregational Union. 43 Hunslet Lane, Leeds LS10 1JW. ☎ 451267.

Social Organizations

Association of Speakers Clubs. For Leeds Area Clubs, contact G. Morris, 11 Stainburn Road, Leeds LS17 6NR.

Bardsey Men's Debating & Literary Society. Ian Smith, 74 Roman Avenue, Leeds LS8 2AN. ☎ 667485.

Inter Varsity Club. G. Hannant, 4 Holt Park Close, Leeds LS16 7QA. ☎ Leeds 671762. (Social and activity events for young professionals. Weekly meetings).

Leeds Association of Graduate Women. Mrs. G. Chettoe, Eastbrook House, Leyton Road, Rawdon, LS19. ☎ 503063.

Leeds Central 18-plus Group. K. Benfield, 9 Bantam Close, Morley, LS27. ☎ 536744. (Social activities for 18-29 year olds.)

Leeds Jewish Friendship Club. Mrs. Braham, 17 Dunstarn Drive, Leeds LS16. ☎ 671871.

Leeds Solo Club. R. Leuty, 66 Chandos Gardens, LS8 1QB. ☎ 663651.

Morley Rotary Club. J. Finnigan, Stoneleigh House, Syke Road, Tingley. ☎ 538111.

Oasis Social Club. The Green Community Centre, Horsforth

LS18 4RH. ☎ 612272.

Otley Rotaract Club. D. Barker, 9 Abbeydale Garth, Kirkstall.

Otley Rotary Club. B. Baker, 61 Riverside Park, Otley, LS21 2RW. ☎ 0943-462400.

Pudsey Rotary Club. C. Clough, 20 South Parade, Pudsey. ☎ 570523.

Rotaract Cross Gates. A. Gore, 14 Lea Park Vale, LS10. ☎ 713711.

Rotaract Headingley. J. Horrocks, 10 Wynford Terrace, Leeds LS16 6HY. ☎ 678575.

Rotaract Leeds. Mr. P. Girvan, 2 Gordon Drive, Leeds LS6.

Rotary Club of Leeds. H. Bevin, 14 Southfield Road, Burley, LS29 7PA. ☎ 0943-864546.

Rotary Club L. Wharfedale. T. Baines, 20 Chatsworth Drive, Wetherby, LS22. ☎ 0937-585712.

Rothwell Rotary Club. D. Thompson, 11 Rosewood Court, LS26. ☎ 820943.

Sports: Regional Contacts

Amateur Fencing Association. Miss M. McNamara, Hawthorn Cottage, Regent Street, Leeds LS7 4PE. ☎ Leeds 682205.

Auto Cycle Union. B. Jones, 38/39 Titus Street, Saltaire, BD18 4LU. ☎ 0274-585143.

Bowmen of Adel. Mrs. C. Clift, 19 Harrowby Road, Leeds LS16. ☎ 788852.

Aikido. B. Jones, 32 Fenton Street, Burley-in-Wharfedale. ☎ 0943-863857.

British Baseball Federation. Mr. J. S. Mortimer, 94 Bellhouse Way, Foxwood Lane, York YO2 3LN.

British Cycling Federation. Mrs. J. England, 46 The Sycamores, Horbury, WF4. ☎ 0977-277484.

British Gliding Association. Mr. T. A. Hollings, 1 Newlands Rise, Yeadon, Leeds LS19 7PH.

Hang Gliding Association. M. Dale, 69 Ainsty Road, Wetherby, LS22. ☎ 0937-585587.

British Horse Society. P. Higham, Mosswood House, Crayke, York YO6 4TQ. ☎ 0347-21396.

British Octopush Association. Mr. H. Pitchforth, 28 Lister Dale, Littletown, Liversedge, WF15 6EN. ☎ 0924-406128.

British Parachute Association. J. L. Thomas, 17 Hustler Road, Bridlington. ☎ 0262-673101.

British Sports Association for the Disabled. First Floor, Unit 9, Longlands Industrial Estate, Milner Way, Ossett WF5 9JN. ☎ 0924-280029.

British Sub Aqua Club. Mr. I. Furness, 5 Pinfold Road, Leeds LS15 0PN. ☎ 608185.

British Water Ski Federation. Mr. E. Hichliffe, 54 Durkar Low Lane, Wakefield. ☎ 0924-253453.

Charles Rice Junior Football League. Mr. G. Warner, 27 Acaster Drive, Garforth, Leeds LS25 2BH. ☎ Leeds 862624.

Cycle Touring Club Leeds Branch. E. Goodban, Sunset Bungalow, Bridge End Farm, Rodley, LS13 1LF. ☎ 576023.

Dales Hang-Gliding Club. Mrs. C. Clapham, Station House, Settle, BD24. ☎ 0729-822533.

Garforth Junior Football League. Mr. A. Exley, 17 Boothroyd Green, Dewsbury, WF13 2RQ. ☎ 0924-460124.

Lawn Tennis Association. 1 College Close, Beckett Park, Leeds LS6 3QH. ☎ Leeds 741410.

Leeds & District Badminton League. T. Grimbley, Cragghill View, Leeds LS16. ☎ 672347.

Leeds Aikido Club. R. Browne, 52 Beckett Park Crescent, Leeds LS6. ☎ 740436.

Leeds Sailing Club. Mrs. C. Setters, 20 Hawcliffe View, Silsden, BD20. ☎ 0535-654627.

Leeds United Supporters Club. E. Carlisle, 59 Appleton Court, Leeds LS9 7RS. ☎ 480239.

Martial Arts Commission. Mr. Ray Wilson, 649 Stanningley Road, Pudsey, LS2. ☎ 555268.

Motorcycle Riders Club. K. Illingworth, 32 St. Ives Mount, Leeds LS12. ☎ 792640.

National Skating Association. Mr. M. Phillips, 3 The Towers, Elland Road, Churwell, Morley, LS27 7PB. ☎ Leeds 533296.

North Eastern Counties Amateur Boxing Association. A. Ford, 62 Merrill Road, Thurnscoe, Rotherham S63. ☎ 0709-896694.

North of England Clay Pigeon Shooting Association. Mrs. K. Sayer, 26 Newlands Avenue, Norton, Stockton-on-Tees, Cleveland. ☎ 0642-554996.

Northern Counties Athletic Association. G. Beckett, 32 Ingfield Avenue, Huddersfield HD5 9HE. ☎ 0484-428690.

Otley Cycle Club. S. Bates, 47 Northgate, Baildon.

Panda Bowmen Archery Club. B. Skinner, 32 Springfield Rise, Leeds LS18. ☎ 585624.

Pennine Ballooning Association. Mrs. G. Waite, 1-5 Greengate, Malton, YO17 0EN. ☎ 0653-693600.

Royal Life Saving Society. Mr. D. J. Cosstick, 256 West Park Drive, Leeds LS8 2BD. ☎ Leeds 663584.

Royal Pigeon Racing Association. D. Higgins, 6 Billingwood Drive, Rawdon. ☎ 504810.

Royal Yachting Association. Sailing: Mr. Ian Cox, 42 Everard Avenue, Bradway, Sheffield S17 4LZ. Windsurfing: C. Nuttall, 92 Abbey Lane, Sheffield S8 0BQ. Sand and Land Yacht Clubs: D. Sergeant, 7 Oaktree Way, Strensall, York YO3 5TF.

Salmon & Trout Association. Mr. D. Walker, Weir House, Nidd Bank, Knaresborough. ☎ 0423-862588.

Seacroft Wheelers. N. Davidson, 16 St George's Crescent, Leeds LS26 0RN. ☎ 827879.

Shukokai Karate Union. Mr. Ken Gee, 25 Cambridge Drive, Otley, Leeds LS21. ☎ 0943-466782.

Small Bore-Rifle & Pistol Association. B. Biggs, 6 Elizabeth Grove, Morley, LS27. ☎ 524896

The Croquet Association. Mr. J. McCullough, 3 St. Nicholas Croft, Askham Bryan, York YO2 3RJ. ☎ 0904-630151.

Tug of War Association. Mr. T. Reape, 25 Coppice Close, Pinders Heath, Wakefield WF1 4TA.

West Riding County Football Association. Mr. R. Carter, Unit 3, Low Mills Road, Leeds LS12 4UY. ☎ 310101. (Responsible for football at all levels in West Yorkshire. Can provide information on league competitions, secretaries of clubs and other related matters).

West Riding Cricket League. Mr. C. Bragger, 12 Ridgestone Avenue, Hemsworth, Pontefract. ☎ 0977-612808.

West Yorkshire County Netball Association. S. Ryan, 21 Broughton Avenue, Leeds LS9 6ED. ☎ 403733.

Northern Counties Athletic Association. Mr. N. Townsend, 21 Pasture Lane, Bradford BD14 6JR. ☎ 0274-815151.

West Yorkshire Korfball Association. Mr. N. Townsend, 21 Pasture Lane, Bradford BD14 6JR. ☎ 0274-815151.

West Yorkshire Volleyball Association. Miss W. Light, 201 Legrams Lane, Bradford BD7 2EJ. ☎ 0274-575521.

White Star Ski Club. B. Hollingworth, 19 Abbeydale Gardens, LS5 3RG. ☎ 587029.

Women's Rugby Football Union. Ms. C. Parkin, 2 Norfolk Street, Bishopthorpe Road, York YO2 1JY. ☎ 0904-632895.

Womens' Football Association. Miss. F. Bilton, 44 Watton Grove, Hull HU6 9NL. ☎ 0482-805837.

Yorkshire & Humberside Amateur Gymnastics Association. Mrs. J. Clark, 7 Woodlands Drive, Harrogate. ☎ 0423-883131.

Yorkshire & Humberside Handball Association. Mr. I. Cook, Boothferry Leisure Centre, North Street, Goole. ☎ 0405-769005.

Yorkshire & Humberside Orienteering Association. Mr. D. Morgan, 23 Stopford Avenue, Sandal, Wakefield, WF2 6RH. ☎ 0924-258579.

Yorkshire & Humberside Roller Hockey Association. Mrs. L. Messenger, 158 Hightown Road, Liversedge WF15 8PU.

Yorkshire & Humberside Rowing Council. Mrs. B. J. Edwards, 4 Warren Avenue, Eldwick, Bingley BD16 3BZ.

Yorkshire & Humberside Ski Federation. U. Hughes, 49 Swillington Lane, Swillington, Leeds LS26 8QF. ☎ 860503.

Yorkshire & Humberside Volleyball Association. Mr. I. Waring, 39a Willow Rise, Thorpe Willoughby, Selby YO8 9PP. ☎ 0757-213275.

Yorkshire & Humberside Women's Squash Rackets Association. A. Johnson, 16 Willis Street, York YO1 5BE.

Yorkshire & North East Counties Air Rifle & Pistol Assocation. Mr. J. Watson, 30 Fir Tree Lane, Thorpe Willoughby, Selby, YO8 9PG.

Yorkshire Amateur Rugby League. F. Marshall, 1 Brigshaw Lane, Allerton Bywater. ☎ Leeds 862042.

Yorkshire Amateur Swimming Association. Mrs. N. Muir-

Cochrane, 60 Armley Grange Avenue, Leeds LS12 3QN. ☎ Leeds 637419.

Yorkshire Amateur Wrestling Association. Mr. H. Mansley, 87 Moorbottom Road, Holmfield, Halifax. ☎ 0422-244227.

Yorkshire Amateur Weightlifting Association. J. Mason, 33 Wood Mount, Overton, Wakefield, WF4 4SB. ☎ 0924-277202.

Yorkshire Archery Association. Mrs. D. Wright, 40 Stocksbank Drive, Mirfield, WF14 0HB.☎ 0924-494748.

Yorkshire Basketball Association. Mr. B. Sly, 1 Willowdene Garth, Eggborough, Goole DN14 0UA. ☎ 0977-661254.

Yorkshire Billiards and Snooker Association. Mr. E. Hodgkinson, 3 Eastbury Avenue, Horton Bank Top, Bradford BD6 3PN. ☎ 0274-679369.

Yorkshire County Amateur Athletic Association. Mr. G. Clarke, "Dunrunin'", 9 Whitehouse Avenue, Great Preston, Woodlesford, Leeds LS26 8BN. ☎ Leeds 862590.

Yorkshire County Badminton Association. Mrs. A. Maltby, 34 Barnsley Road, Scawsby, Doncaster DN5 8QJ.

Yorkshire County Bowling Association. Mr. P. Welch, 9 The Crescent, Redcar, Cleveland TS10 3AU. ☎ 0642-483941.

Yorkshire County Crown Green Bowling Association. Mr. D. Radley 10 New Street Skelmanthorpe, Huddersfield HD8 9BL. ☎ 0484-863147.

Yorkshire County Hockey Association. Mr. R. D. Haigh, 94 Merrygates Lane, Sandal, Wakefield WF2 7DW. ☎ 0924-255835.

Yorkshire County Indoor Hockey Association. B. Young, 8 White Rose Way, Thirsk, YO7 1JZ. ☎ 0845-522168.

Yorkshire County Lacrosse Association. Mr. C. Dale, 26 Clementson Road, Crookes, Sheffield S10 1GS. ☎ 0742-669326.

Yorkshire County Ten Pin Bowling Association. P. Noon, 65 Conway Place, Leeds LS8 5DE. ☎ Leeds 490091.

Yorkshire County Women's Bowling Association. Mrs. A. Haw, 24 Finsbury Avenue, York

YO2 1LW. ☎ 0904-623438.

Yorkshire Cricket Association (Leeds Area Council). R. Pritchard, 15 Hollyshaw Lane, Leeds LS15 7BA. ☎ 646326.

Yorkshire Cross Country Association. Mr. B. Heywood, 4 Oakes Avenue, Brockholes, Huddersfield HD7 7AT. ☎ 0484-665029.

Yorkshire Cyclo-Cross Association. Mr. Tony Lee, 6 Square Fold, Lepton, Huddersfield. ☎ 0484-604515.

Yorkshire Driving Club. (Equestrian). Mr. D. Jagger, 9 Binks Fold, Wyke Lane, Wyke, Bradford.

Yorkshire Federation of Sea Anglers. Mr. P. Newton, 154 Featherstone Lane, Featherstone, Pontefract.

Yorkshire Hang-Gliding and Microlight Centre. Woodhall, 16 Gateland Drive, Leeds LS17 8HU. ☎ 738128.

Yorkshire Indoor Bowling Association. Mr. A. Horobin, 10 Larch Close, Birstall, Batley, WF17 0EA. ☎ 0924-475199.

Yorkshire Ladies County Golf Association. Mrs. M. Elliott, Ingle Court, Lepton, Huddersfield HD8 0NN. ☎ 0484-602011.

Yorkshire Mixed Hockey Association. Mr. J. White, 4 The Sycamores, Horbury, Wakefield WF4 5QG. ☎ 0924-274620.

Yorkshire Rugby Football Union. Mr. K. Barber, c/o Morley RUFC, Scatcherd Lane, Morley, LS27 0JJ. ☎ 524300.

Yorkshire Squash Rackets Association. Mr. D. Ball, Glen House, East Keswick, Leeds LS17 9HG.

Yorkshire Table Tennis Association. Mr. K. Shepherd, 24 Hillfoot Avenue, Pudsey, LS28 7QN. ☎ 577591.

Yorkshire Union of Golf Clubs. Mr. A. Cowman, 50 Bingley Road, Bradford BD9 6HH.

Yorkshire Women's Amateur Athletic Association. D. Oxspring 16 Venetian Crescent, Darfield, Barnsley. ☎ 0226-753546.

Yorkshire Women's Cricket Association. A. Roberts, 16 Burley Wood Lane, Leeds LS4 2SU. ☎ 759455.

Yorkshire Women's Hockey Association. Mrs. Sheila Middleton, 17 Crabgate Drive, Skellow, Doncaster DN6 8LA. ☎ 0302-725917.

Women's Groups

Adel Townswomens Guild (Evening). Mrs. D. Hall, 30 East Causeway Vale, LS16. ☎ 674181.

Armley Townswomens Guild. Mrs. G. Barrett, 11 Halladay Grove, Leeds LS12. ☎ 635588.

Athill WI. T. Lumb, 5 Kingsley Road, Leeds LS16. ☎ 674034.

Bardsey-Rigton WI. Mrs. L. Astle, Blackmoor Lane, Bardsey, LS17 9DY. ☎ 0937-573368.

Burley Ladies Group. Mrs. E. Fletcher, 11 Woodbridge Vale, Leeds LS6. ☎ 787988.

Chapel Allerton Townswomen's Guild. Methodist Youth Centre, Town Street, Harrogate Road, LS8.

Chinese Women's Group, c/o Chinese Advice Centre, Brudenell Centre, Leeds LS6 1EZ. ☎ 788327.

Cookridge Townswomens Guild. Mrs. M. Midgley, 37 Haven Chase, Leeds LS16. ☎ 672045.

Cooperative Women's Guild. J. Savery, 32 Rosedale Walk, Leeds LS10.

East Keswick WI. Mrs. J. Clarke, 15 Golf Links Crescent, Tadcaster, LS24.

East Leeds Women's Workshops. 161 Harehills Lane, Leeds LS8 3QE. ☎ 499031.

Far Headingley Townswomen's Guild. Headingley Community Centre, North Lane, Leeds LS6.

Guiseley WI. R. Walton, 59 Coach Road, Guiseley, LS20 8AY.

Halton Townswomens Guild. Mrs. B. Crookes, 2 Field End Court, Leeds LS1. ☎ 642977.

Harewood WI. Mrs. A. Hullam, Elm Tree Cottage, Wykefield Farm, Harrogate Road, LS17 9JZ. ☎ 886482.

Headingley Afternoon Townswomen's Guild. Miss C. Grainger, 84 Westfield Road, Leeds LS3. ☎ 449305.

Headingley Evening Townswomen's Guild. E. Lawson, Ash Road, Leeds LS6 3LB. ☎ 751574.

Kirkstall WI. Mrs. J. Karshaw, 59 Stanmore Crescent, Leeds LS4 2SB. ☎ 755736.

La Leche League. B. Rhodes, Station House, Micklefield, Leeds, LS25. ☎ Leeds 868416.(Help with breast feeding).

League of Jewish Women. Mrs. C. Seaton, 154b Street Lane, Leeds LS8 2AD. ☎ 662072.

Leeds Business & Professional Women's Club. M. Smith, 3 North View, North Lane, Leeds LS8.

Leeds Caesarean Support Group. ☎ M. Penberthy, Leeds 692255; A. Hutchinson, Leeds 556126. (Offers moral support to any women who have to undergo, or have already had a caesarean birth, and who feel they need to talk to someone who has experienced this way of giving birth.)

Leeds Incest Survivors' Association. (Helpline for women who have been sexually abused or are incest survivors. They have a safe home). ☎ Leeds 310949, Tues 4-7pm, Fri 10-2pm.

Leeds Women's Luncheon Club. Mrs. Urquhart, 15 First Avenue, Bardsey, LS17 9BE. ☎ 0937-73228.

LIFE. 165 Low Briggate, Leeds LS1. (Support for pregnant women, counselling and practical help such as accommodation. Post-abortion counselling. Open Mon, 5-6pm, Tues, Wed & Fri 10-2pm.) ☎ 826947.

Mastectomy Association Self-Help. Leeds Methodist Mission, Oxford Place Centre, Room 2, Leeds. (Social meeting for ladies who have had breast care treatment. Family and friends welcome. Wed 2.30-4.30pm).

Miscarriage Association. PO Box 24, Ossett, West Yorkshire. ☎ 0924-830515. (Support, help and info. for women and their families who have suffered miscarriages, from women who have undergone the same thing. Newsletter).

National Association of Widows, 14 Great George Street, Leeds LS1 3DW. (Bereavement support, advice, information, social events.) ☎ 450553.

National Childbirth Trust. K. Jukes, 21 Bankfield Close, Yeadon. ☎ Guiseley 78651. (Offers support, information and practical skills to help parents with breastfeeding, ante-natal preparation, labour and post-natal care. Network of neighbourhood contact groups for mothers).

National Women's Register (Formerly the National Housewives Register. There are several groups in the Leeds area. The best way to obtain latest info. on groups in your locality is to contact—NWR, 9 Bank Plain, Norwich, Norfolk, NR2 4SL. ☎ 0603-765392.

Oakwood Evening Townswomen's Guild. Mrs. J. Whitehead, The Manor, Ladywood Road, Leeds LS8 2QF. ☎ 736354.

Rape Crisis Centre. PO Box 27, Leeds LS1. ☎ Leeds 440058. Helpline 12-4pm daily, 7-10pm Mon-Fri. (For any woman who has been sexually assaulted or raped and wants to talk to another woman or is seeking legal or medical information).

Rothwell Townswomen's Guild. Mrs. R. Sellwood, 16 Ashroyd, Rothwell, LS26 0BN. ☎ 822144.

Soroptimist International of Leeds Miss. M. E. Pinnell, 6 Park Villa Court, Leeds LS8 1EB. ☎ Leeds 665399. (Maintains high ethical standards in business and professions, develops international friendship and understanding, strives for human rights for all people and advances the status of women.)

Tinshill Townswomens Guild. Mrs. W. Agar, 66 Tinshill Mount, Leeds LS16 7AX. ☎ 672953.

Wetherby WI. P. Cobden, 15 Ullswater Drive, Wetherby. ☎ 0937-585187.

Women's Aid. (Provides help, advice and emergency & temporary accommodation for women and their children suffering from or in fear of physical or mental violence). ☎ Leeds 460401.

Women's Counselling & Therapy Service. Top Floor, Oxford Chambers, Oxford Place, Leeds LS1 3AX. ☎ Leeds 455725. (Individual/group psychotherapy. Groups for compulsive eaters, bulimia nervosa, sexual abuse. Creche facilities in mornings. Drop-in Service Tues. 2.30-5.30pm & Thurs 10-2pm. Special Drop-in Service for black women.)

Women's Gas Federation (Leeds). Mrs. J. Higson, 8 Abbeydale Vale, Leeds LS5 3RD. ☎ 580109.

Women's Health Matters. 34 Lupton Street, Leeds LS10. ☎ Number changing but try 448921. (Confidential counselling by women for women).

Youth/Children

Air Training Corps 168 (City of Leeds) Squadron, Middleton Grove, off Dewsbury Road, Leeds LS11. (Promotes among young people practical interest in aviation and the RAF). ☎ 641011.

Belle Isle Play Group. United Reform Church, Westfield Road, Leeds LS10. ☎ 776071.

Boys Brigade Leeds Battalion. R. Lolley, 16 Stanmore Road, Leeds LS4 2RU. ☎ 780192.

Busy Bees Playgroup, 66 Gledhow Wood Road, Leeds LS8. ☎ 402731.

Central Yorkshire Scout Council. J. N. Dix, 29 Broomhill Drive, Leeds LS17 6JW. ☎ Leeds 686205.

Church Lads/Girls Brigade. J. Kaye, 2 Gotts Park View, Leeds LS12 2QZ. ☎ 636743.

City of Leeds Sea Cadets. Leeds Lock, Clarence Road, Leeds LS10. ☎ 700972.

Duke of Edinburgh's Award Scheme Leeds Area. Scott Hall Middle School, Stainbeck Lane, Leeds LS7. ☎ 696420.

Girls Brigade Leeds Division. Mrs. J. Thompson, Gamble Garth House, Temple View, Lofthouse, WF3 3LN. ☎ 0924-827784.

Guiseley Youth Theatre. H. Cundell, 42 Grangefield Avenue, Burley-in-Wharfedale, LS29 7HA. ☎ 0943-863799.

Halton Tufty Club. Mrs. J. Peel 41 Templegate Close, Leeds LS15 0PJ. ☎ 642297.

Leeds Children's Holiday Camp Association. T. J. Clark, 95 Wensley Drive, Leeds LS7 2LU. ☎ 681537.

Leeds Children's Theatre. M. Perkins, 31 Jackson Avenue, Leeds LS8 1NP. ☎ 639124.

Leeds Childrens Circus. 58 Harehills Lane, Leeds LS8 4HF. ☎ 374303.

Leeds Girl Guides. E. Johns, Braeside, Newlay Wood Avenue, Leeds LS18 4LN. ☎ 586314.

Leeds Youth Opera Group. M. Shaw, 25 Newport View, LS6 3BX. ☎ 785236.

Museum Saturday Morning Youth Club. Leeds City Museum, Municipal Buildings, Leeds LS1. ☎ 462465.

PART EIGHT:
Leeds History

When the Pictish saint, St. Cadroe, crossed the River Aire around 940 he described "the city of Loidis". In fact, he meant a place with an important church. Loidis was just a tiny riverside settlement. The "city" grew with waves of settlers over the next ten centuries.

There were the Normans, the Cistercian monks who built Kirkstall Abbey, the Flemmish weavers, and the Yeoman farmers who made the medieval woollen cloth market so prominent.

In the 19th century came a flood of people off the land, caused by the Agrarian Revolution and enclosures. Thousands of Irish fled their potato famine; thousands more Jewish refugees escaped pogroms in Russia.

After immigrants from the Caribbean in the 1950s came many more from India, Pakistan and Bangladesh. Today's arrivals are white-collar workers from the South of England. So, the history of Leeds is a story of people.

Left: Between the wars, Leeds City Square looking east to Boar Lane.

Loidis becomes Leeds

How a swampside hamlet transformed into a modern metropolis through 2000 years of invasions and plague, inventions and play.

Leeds is known mainly as a product of the Industrial Revolution, but its history goes much further back than the 19th century. Even in medieval times, it was one of the main West Riding towns and an elegant Georgian centre with a grand social life for its wealthy citizens. And long before that, there was the hippo . . .

☛ *For specific details of many architectural and historical features mentioned in this section, see pages 62-70.*

☛ *For specific details of many architectural and historical features mentioned in this section, see pages 62-70.*

To 1066

The first thing that is known with certainty about Leeds is that around half a million years ago it was covered by a steamy swamp. The most tangible evidence for this is a huge hippopotamus from the period, found in 1852 at Armley. The second certainty is that it was not killed by a spear aimed by a prehistoric hunter. Man was still at least four thousand centuries and four Ice Ages away. It was not until around 8000 BC that the first settlers—nomadic hunters known as Mesolithic man—arrived in Northern England. Whilst it is known they had a camp in the

Vale of Pickering, it is doubtful that they penetrated the extensive marshes around Leeds. The first to do so are thought to have been Neolithic farmers, spreading from the continent in 3250-1700 BC. Relics of these New Stone Age peoples include a polished stone axe head found at Seacroft, another from Roundhay and one from Wyke. The central area of today's Leeds was clearly too wet for them, as it was for the Bronze Age (1700 to 500 BC) and Iron Age residents (500 BC to AD 43) who lived at Alwoodley, Tinshill, Wyke, Roundhay and Churwell. By the Roman invasion, the area was ruled by the Brigantes, uncivilized Celtic tribes who had established two towns north of what they called Loidis, or "district on the river". These were promptly taken over by the arriving Legions, led by Petillius Cerialis in AD 71, and named *Isurium* (today's Aldborough, near Boroughbridge) and *Olicana* (Ilkley).

The Romans

The Brigantes in West Yorkshire were by no means a pushover for the Romans, and such was the difficulty in keeping order that no

One of the Roman altars found at Adel. It is now in Leeds City Museum.

town of any great size was constructed here. However, there was at least one point of strategic importance that the Romans were forced to defend. It was a crossing of the River Aire, just downstream from today's Leeds Bridge. Paving stones for the ford were discovered by workmen in the 19th century. It was a vital link on the trade road from York to Chester, and in order to keep it open the Romans established what was probably the first settlement in today's Central Leeds—a small fort called *Campodunum*, or "the fort by the river bend". Traces of its earthworks could still be seen at Quarry Hill up to 100 years ago, before they disappeared under housing. However, the principal Roman settlement within today's Leeds was at Adel, a small Roman town called *Burgodunum* which at one stage seems to have been used for the manufacturing of querns, stone hand mills for grinding corn. Several Roman altars were found during rebuilding work at Adel Parish Church (see illustration).

The Dark Ages

When the Romans withdrew from Britain in AD 410, there was an immediate breakdown in law and order. Without the famous signal stations to warn of invasions, amid the chaos came waves of raiders from Ireland, Scotland and across the North Sea, particularly Germanic tribes like Angles and Saxons. Virtually nothing is known about the period between the Romans' departure and the establishment of the small kingdom of Elmet in the Leeds area (principally the land between the River Aire and River Wharfe) by the Angle King, Edwin of Northumbria, in 616-632. But he almost certainly had one of his palaces in the area. It was in AD 625 that Edwin was converted to Christianity. His chief rival, Penda, King of Mercia (the Midlands) was a heathen and set about abolishing Christianity. In AD 655, Penda's campaign came to a bloody end at Winwaed, now known as Whinmoor, to the north-east of central Leeds. He was killed by Oswi, Edwin's successor, in a victory that is hailed as being decisive in establishing Christianity in England. We know from the first printed survey of England, the Venerable Bede's *Ecclesiastical History of the English People*, completed in 731/732, that today's Leeds was little more than a river crossing in the Dark Ages and that the name Loidis was used to describe a *regio* or district rather than a town. That is what the next wave of invaders—Danish and Norwegian Vikings—found when they marched from the Yorkshire coast around AD 850. Their most important visible relic, still on show today, is the famous cross at Leeds Parish Church. But their language lives on in numerous local place names ending in "by" and "thorpe". And, of course, it was the Danes who divided Yorkshire up into the administrative "thriddings", later known as the Ridings. By the mid-10th century, the area of land around the River Aire crossing and the Parish Church had become a frontier town between Norse-Irish raiders from the west and the Danes from the east. The Pictish saint, St. Cadroe, passed through around 940 and spoke of "the city of Loidis", though the term city was used to describe a place of religious importance rather than one of great size.

The Middle Ages

From the Anglo-Saxon frontier town of Loidis, the settlement at a crossing of the River Aire became known as Leeds (initially spelt "Ledes" then "Leedes") under the Norman barons. Through the medieval period, Leeds was a growing, though still small, settlement beside the Parish Church, surrounded by marshes and dense woods, and a growing network of hamlets like Holbeck and Hunslet, Armley and Bramley, Halton and Gipton, Headingley and Allerton. Over most of these five centuries loomed the powerful Cistercian Abbots at the great monastery of Kirkstall.

The Norman Conquest

Three years after the Battle of Hastings, in the winter of 1069-70 King William marched north to put down a major uprising. The settlement of Loidis itself seems to have escaped the legendary "harrying of the north"—the slaughter of much of the population between the Humber, the Tyne and the Pennines. The rebellion suppressed, William granted a vast area of land in the West Riding to the Norman adventurer, Ilbert de Lacy, who was charged with keeping the peace and overseeing the great Domesday survey of the new kingdom's wealth, livestock and people. By the time of this survey in 1086, Leeds had clearly survived as a settlement of some importance. It was thus described: "Twenty-sevene villanes and four sokemen and four bordars have now there 14 ploughs (a total of 35 families). There is a priest and a church and a mill of four shillings and ten acres of meadow."

The de Lacys

For 250 years, Ilbert de Lacy and his descendants ruled over some 500 square miles of Yorkshire from Pontefract Castle. Within a few years, Ilbert had sub-tenanted Leeds to another Norman baron, Ralph Paynel, or Paganel. But it was Ilbert's grandson, Henry, who was responsible for perhaps the single most important event in the growth of Leeds during medieval times. Henry de Lacy had become benefactor to the Cistercian monks at Fountains Abbey, and he had promised them land for the building of a "daughter" abbey to Fountains. But the site, at Barnoldswick, near Skipton, was on high ground and not the riverside location the monks preferred. Henry's second choice was in a wooded valley beside the River Aire.

Kirkstall Abbey

Abbot Alexander, one of the austere Cistercian order's leaders, arrived at Kirkstall in 1152 to oversee the building of his new abbey. Most of the construction work, using millstone grit, had been completed by 1175 and, like Fountains, the abbey was dominated by a huge cruciform church with the usual monastic dwellings like cloisters, chapter house and hospital adjoining. The monks brought with them their sheep rearing, their farming, their mining and their iron-smelting skills, and one can only imagine the great hive of industry that Kirkstall must have been in the late 12th century. But most vital of all, the Cistercians were great spinners and weavers, and it was these crafts which introduced to the lower Aire Valley, turning the infant town of Leeds two miles downstream into the embryonic cloth and clothing capital of the world.

The Birth of Today's Leeds

Coinciding with the monks' development of the area and their increasing wool production was the establishment of a tiny market on

Leeds Population Growth

The figures below demonstrate how Leeds remained a fairly small town until the end of the 17th Century. The 19th Century—the figures are given in detail—showed the greatest growth, with the total population multiplying eight-fold between 1801 and 1901.

1086. The Domesday Book recorded 35 families (200 people).
1207. Approximately 300.
1377. Approximately 1,000, including 400 in the central area.
1600. At least 3,000 inhabitants, with 2,500 in out-townships.
1700. Approximately 11,000.
1775. 30,409, according to the first major census.
1801. Census—53,276.
1821. Census—83,943.
1831. Cenus—123,548. More than double the century's start.
1841. Census—152,054.
1851. Census—172,270.
1861. Census—207,165.
1871. Census—259,212.
1881. Census—309,119.
1891. Census—367,505.
1901. 428,968, or eight times the figure of one century earlier.
1911. Cenus—445,540.
1971. Approximately 538,000.
1992. Approximately 706,000.

the north side of today's Leeds Bridge. It was around this successful market, and not the older settlement next to the Parish Church, that the infant city grew through late-medieval times. In 1207, Leeds had been granted a borough charter by Maurice Paynel, who had succeeded his father Ralph as Lord of the Manor. Paynel was an early entrepreneur, and he saw Leeds as a lucrative New Town. The charter allowed the construction of a new street known at one stage as Wool Market, now called Briggate. It permitted the market—initially no more than 12 stalls—to spread north on rising ground to Swinegate and Boar Lane, Kirkgate and Vicar Lane. The 30 burgage plots which were established on either side of Briggate at this time still form the basis of the street and arcade layout in today's Briggate. There was almost certainly a bridge across the Aire at this point, although the earliest reference to one was not until 1384. But more than the physical change to Leeds that Paynel's charter brought, it effectively took the citizens out of feudal service. While he was still the feudal lord, now the inhabitants could pay rent rather than be held in serfdom, and this was a crucial impetus in stimulating the growth of Leeds. Despite terrible outbreaks of the plague, Leeds was becoming an important—though still small—town, helped in no small measure by the industry of the monks at Kirkstall. To match its status, in 1322 it had acquired the right to hold a June fair, and an October fair from 1341. Besides the woollen trade, with its weavers, dyers and fullers, Leeds also had a forge and at least one coal mine.

Tudor Times
After Maurice Paynel's death, the de Lacy's had regained control of Leeds and, through marriage, it became a highly valued Royal manor. For as the textile industry grew in the 15th and 16th centuries in many parts of the West Riding, so Leeds's prominence and wealth increased. Its market continually expanded because of its location on the main east-west route of Northern England. Trad-

ers came from far and wide, and its cloth was taken out to the North Sea by the Aire, which was only navigable by small craft, and exported to Holland. In 1539, when Henry VIII seized the monasteries' enormous wealth and Kirkstall Abbey was abandoned, it made little difference to the now-thriving Leeds woollen industry and market next door. Along with Halifax and Wakefield, Leeds had also become an important centre for dressing, cutting and dyeing cloth produced by cottage hand weavers in rural Yorkshire and beyond. So wealthy had some of the merchants and merchant-manufacturers become, that a private school, forerunner of today's Leeds Grammar School, was established near Leeds Bridge in 1552. It was the first sign that culturally and socially as well as economically, the town was growing in prominence. By the end of the 16th century, Leeds had up to 4,000 inhabitants living mainly in the Briggate area. Significantly, the out-townships were growing too, especially those at Armley, Beeston, Bramley, Chapel Allerton, Headingley and Hunslet.

The 17th Century

The town now extended east from Leeds Bridge by The Calls and Kirkgate to the Parish Church and Marsh Lane, west along Swinegate and Boar Lane to Mill Hill, and north on Lands Lane, Briggate and Vicar Lane to The Headrow and Lady Lane. The two main sources of water were the River Aire and the Sheepscar Beck.

Leeds becomes a "Free Borough".
Centuries of feudal rule ended in Leeds on 13 July, 1626, when Charles I granted a charter of incorporation which made Leeds a "free" Borough. This allowed the first local government of the town, establishing a Leeds Corporation of one alderman, nine principal burgesses and twenty "assistants", or councillors. However, there were no elections—all appointments were made by the King—and the earliest office bearers were to remain in charge for life. When

one died, the vacancy would be filled by co-option. Among the officeholders' many functions were the institution of Guilds to maintain crafts standards, supervise a market to be held each Tuesday, and to appoint constables to ensure law and order. A step forward though the charter was, it was deeply flawed. A small group of merchants—most of them from rich Yeoman farmer backgrounds who had moved into Leeds to take advantage of its growing wealth—used the charter to dominate local trade, causing much resentment among clothworkers from long-established Leeds families. That they were able to exclude cloth from outside Leeds also caused bitterness in other parts of Yorkshire. Today, there is an interesting relic from that 1626 charter. The Leeds coat of arms and Civic Hall feature the owls taken from the heraldic shield of the first alderman, Sir John Savile.

The Plague
An increasing number of townsfolk were packed into a very small area of central Leeds, and any additional housing requirements were simply built in back yards and gardens. It is hardly surprising that these squalid conditions and lack of sanitation lead to a terrible outbreak of the Plague. The worst year was 1645, when over 1,325 people died between 12 March and 25 December. The families most affected were those living in Lower Briggate, The Calls and Vicar Lane. Victims who had not yet died were confined in wooden cabins built on Quarry Hill. Once there, the "unclean" persons required a certificate to re-enter the town.

The Civil War
The Royalists, under the Earl of Newcastle, easily occupied the town on 23 October, 1642. But they made an unsuccessful attempt to take the staunchly Parliamentarian Bradford. Within a couple of months, Lord Fairfax's Parliamentarian forces were sent from Bradford to confront the Royalists, crossing the Aire at Apperley Bridge and setting up a camp on Woodhouse Moor before moving

in for a bloody street fight in January, 1643. However, the Royalists regained the town that summer, but when they were defeated by Cromwell at Marston Moor in 1644, Yorkshire passed into the hands of the Parliamentarians. By the time of restoration of Charles II in 1660, the councils had developed a republican bias and it required a new municipal charter to get rid of it. Obtained in November, 1661, the charter allowed the town to be ruled by a Mayor, 12 Aldermen and 24 councillors.

Religious & Social Life

The Parish Church in Kirkgate was too small for its growing population and in 1634 a new church, St. John's, was built by John Harrison, one of the wealthiest members of the new Leeds Corporation. There were also many Nonconformists among the merchant classes but persecution—including their exclusion from the Corporation—made it impossible for them to worship in the open until Charles II's "Declaration of Indulgence" in 1672. They were quick to establish churches, the first being the Presbyterian Mill Hill Chapel in Park Row. The Quakers used a house in Kirkgate. Meanwhile, we know from the diaries of the Leeds

collector and historian, Ralph Thoresby, that the merchant classes had a sophisticated social life of hunting parties, race-going, lavish banquets and dances. And for a whole month in the winter of 1684 the Aire was frozen solid, allowing the common people to hold a fair on its surface, with ox-roasting, a carnival and sports.

The 18th Century

Demand for woollen cloth was greatly accelerating. To take advantage of it, there were two major developments in Leeds which made the town pre-eminent in the woollen cloth trade and the most important commercial centre of the West Riding. They were the Aire-Calder Navigation and the great Cloth Halls—covered markets. By the end of the century Leeds had virtually doubled in population and become an elegant Georgian town. But it was already sprouting the smoke-stacks that would accelerate its growth beyond all dreams.

Daniel Defoe's Leeds "Snapshot"

The novelist Daniel Defoe, better known for writing *Robinson Crusoe*, gives us a clear description of Leeds in his *Tour Through*

the Whole Island of Great Britain (1724). "Leeds," he wrote, "is a large, wealthy and populous Town, it stands on the North Bank of the River Aire, or rather on both sides of the river, for there is a large Suburb or Part of the Town on the South Side of the River, and the whole is joined by a stately and prodigiously strong Stone Bridge, so large and so wide, that formerly the Cloth Market was kept . . . on the very Bridge itself. The Encrease of the Manufacturers and of the Trade, soon made the Market too great to be confined to the Bridge, and it is now kept in the High-street, beginning from the Bridge. The Cloth Market . . . is indeed a Prodigy of its Kind, and is not to be equalled in the World."

The Aire and Calder Navigation

Only very small craft could carry Leeds cloth along the Aire to the Humber, where it was transferred to ships bound for markets in Holland and North Germany. If the West Riding's woollen industry was to expand still further, it required an improved waterway to the growing port of Hull. In 1699, William II had signed an Act authorising the making of the Aire and Calder rivers navigable to the

A recently-discovered view of Leeds looking north from Beeston Hill, painted in the mid-1790s. In the centre is St. John's Church.

tidal Ouse. In partnership with their Wakefield counterparts, the Leeds merchants paid for the canalising and deepening of parts of the rivers. The first large vessels reached Leeds Bridge in 1700 and Wakefield the following year.

The Turnpikes

If the late-20th century is the Motorway Age, the years from 1740-60 were the Age of the Turnpike. Better road surfaces, and new wagons and stage coaches made travel easier and quicker. Also, the public hanging of the notorious highwayman, Dick Turpin, at York in 1739 had deterred other robbers, and long-distance travel became noticeably safer. As Leeds's trade grew, better communications between other towns in the region became vital. The Turnpike Trusts who built the roads did so to make money—users were charged a toll until the middle of the next century. Turnpikes connecting Leeds with Elland and Halifax (and from the latter to Rochdale and Manchester) began in 1740, and another route to Halifax via Bradford was built in 1742. In the same year, a road was cut east from Leeds to Selby, then a developing port on the tidal River Ouse. Today's A64, the Leeds-Tadcaster-York turnpike, was started in 1751. The key year for turnpikes from Leeds appears to have been 1758. Then, a road linked the town to Wakefield, Barnsley and Sheffield; another ran north-west to Skipton via Otley; and one was developed north through Harrogate and Ripon. The York and Selby routes also connected to the nation's main artery, the Great North Road, which is today's A1.

The Cloth Halls

For centuries, the cloth market on which Leeds's wealth was founded took place in Briggate every Tuesday and Saturday. But when Wakefield opened a covered market hall in 1710, Leeds clothiers had no choice but to respond with their own building. The first White Cloth Hall opened in Kirkgate on 29 May, 1711. Sheltered from the elements, cloth manufacturers from all over the West Riding sold rapidly increasing quantities of white, or undyed, cloth to the great Leeds merchants. Such was the trade's growth that a bigger hall was built across the Aire in Meadow Lane in 1756, replaced by yet a third White Cloth Hall in The Calls in September, 1776. Meanwhile, a Coloured Cloth Hall, a much larger building, had been opened in 1756 on a site now occupied by the Post Office in today's City Square. Still the demands of Leeds merchants were insatiable, and they attended cloth markets in Wakefield, Halifax, Huddersfield and Bradford. Eventually, most cloth produced in Yorkshire passed through Leeds, much of it exported via the Aire and Calder Navigation.

Life in Georgian Leeds

Leeds is mainly famous as a great Victorian city, but it was actually an elegant Georgian town of some 17,000 inhabitants. To cater for its growing middle-classes, a newspaper, the *Leeds Mercury*, appeared in 1718, with another, the *Leeds Intelligencer*, published in 1754. An Improvement Commission introduced street lighting in 1755. A general infirmary appeared in 1767, and the Leeds Library in 1768. Centre of Georgian society's social life was the Assembly Room of the third White Cloth Hall. For the lower orders, there were many ale houses off Briggate and Vicar Lane.

Mechanization & the New Entrepreneurs

Steam power revolutionised Leeds industry in the 1790s, helped by abundant cheap coal from Middleton Colliery, hauled in horse-drawn wagons (later, by rack-and-pinion) to the south side of Leeds Bridge along an impressive viaduct. The first steam-driven spinning machine was installed by Richard Paley at a new cotton mill on the east side of Leeds. In 1792 a young merchant called Benjamin Gott—keen to satisfy the increased market in army clothes brought about by Napoleon's wars—built a huge steam-powered factory on the west side of town with an unheard-of workforce of 1,200. Meanwhile, another young man by the name of John Marshall used a £9,000 inheritance from his father to open a flax-spinning water mill at Adel then, in 1791, started a mechanized flax factory—Europe's largest—in Water Lane, Holbeck. Between them, Gott and Marshall were to turn Leeds from a town known mainly for its busy cloth market into one of the leading manufacturing cities of the Industrial Revolution.

The 19th Century

Leeds was the archetypal boom town of the Industrial Revolution. From a distance of nearly 200 years, it is easy to get sentimental about the coming-of-age of a great city, but in reality Leeds was an exceptionally ugly and dirty place in the first half of the 19th century. The skyline bristled with smoking chimneys, and the central area was a warren of squalid, unsanitary housing. The vast majority of the inhabitants sacrificed their health and their sweat to produce the wealth that was the foundation of Leeds's prosperity and civic pride in the final decade of the century. By then, the grimy town had become a modernised city with much fine architecture, many public services and good quality housing areas. It is that late-Victorian transformation which forms the basis of today's Leeds fame and fortune.

Industrial Growth

At first, a lack of capital caused by the uncertainties of the Napoleonic Wars inhibited the building of many new factories. But in the 1820s, the development of Leeds entered a period of astonishing development. Dozens of woollen and flax mills sprang up throughout the Leeds area, tripling cloth production in the town between 1820-30. This expansion can be attributed to more efficient steam engines and textile machinery. It was matched by a rapid growth in the Leeds population, which was necessary to sustain the increased output of both manufactured goods and cheap coal from the mines which had spread throughout south and east Leeds. At the start of the

19th the century, there were around 53,276 people living in the Leeds borough, but by 1830 this has shot up to 123,548. This was accelerated by the enclosures driving people off the land. The result was bad overcrowding, which produced the great Leeds cholera epidemic of 1832, claiming 712 lives. In 1842, another outbreak in Leeds killed more than 2,000. When Charles Dickens visited the town in 1847 he described it as "the beastliest place, one of the nastiest I know".

The Leeds and Liverpool Canal

Although first started in 1770, the 130-mile trans-Pennine canal was not completed until 1816. Strategically, its importance was relatively short-lived—the railway was a couple of decades away—but the canal was still of immense value. Liverpool's emergence as the principal port for the increasingly lucrative trade with the Americas made a major cargo route across the Pennines from Leeds essential. In its heyday, it carried millions of tons of Leeds cloth to the Atlantic-bound ships and allowed Leeds merchants to handle one-third of all woollen cloth exports from England. Among the more interesting loads to be transported west along the canal were many thousands of wool blankets that were sold to Red Indians, and lengths of cloth that would end up on the backs of soldiers fighting on both sides of the American Civil War.

The Railways

The first steam locomotive in Leeds was developed in 1812 by Matthew Murray to pull coal wagons from the Middleton Colliery to a coal-staith in Hunslet, thus keeping pace with growing needs of the new steam-powered mills and factories. But it was not until 1834 that the first passenger and freight railway was built from Leeds, reaching Selby and its docks on the Ouse. Other lines quickly followed: the Leeds-Manchester in 1836-41, the Leeds-Derby in 1837-40 (which allowed the first direct passenger train to London on 1 July, 1840), the Leeds-Bradford in 1846, and the Leeds-Thirsk in 1845-49. For decades, Leeds was known as the northern base of the powerful Midland Railway. To cater for this expanding network, Leeds had three stations, Wellington Station (1848), Central Station (1854) and the New Station (1869) which is the only one remaining and now known as Leeds City Station, complete with its famous Dark Arches.

Law and Order

As the population grew (especially when thousands arrived from Ireland, causing much resentment), it become difficult to keep the peace. While the worst Luddite attacks on machinery were elsewhere in the West Riding, there was concern that riots might break out in the town. Cavalry barracks were built at Buslingthorpe because it was feared that Leeds was "on the verge of insurrection and rebel-

lion". In 1836 the Leeds Police Force was founded. By then, riots about atrocious living and working conditions were frequent. In 1842, crowds of workers went on the rampage in Leeds and Bradford, causing havoc by unplugging mill dams and smashing machines. In 1844, soldiers fixed bayonets and attacked a mob in Leeds town centre. Meanwhile, thieving and body-snatching was rife, and to cope with those arrested in the ever-growing crime wave a huge new gaol was built at Armley.

The Age of Reform

Locally and nationally, there were steps to improve working conditions and to enhance the town's status. Richard Oastler, himself born in slums which occupied Quarry Hill in Georgian times, mounted a campaign to end the slavery of children in factories and mills. In a series of letters to the *Leeds Mercury* in 1830, Oastler described the appalling conditions in which children as young as seven were forced to work. His letters led to Shaftesbury's Factories Act of 1833, which ended the employment of children under nine, restricted working hours of under-13s to 48 hours a week and set up a government inspectorate. Meanwhile, the First Reform Act of 1832 gave Leeds the right to be represented in the House of Commons. Two Whig MPs were elected: John Marshall junior, son of the great Leeds flax mills founder, and Thomas Babington Macaulay, the famous historian.

Leeds City Centre from Holbeck Junction as pictured by the "Illustrated London News" on 30 May, 1868.

W. E. Gladstone elected Leeds MP

The most fascinating, and forgotten, incident in the city's political history was the election of William Ewart Gladstone, the greatest British Prime Minister of the 19th century, as Liberal MP for Leeds in 1880. He had given up the Liberal Party leadership after his government was defeated by Disraeli's Conservatives in 1874 and indicated he intended to retire at the next election—he was almost 70. But such was his popularity with Leeds Liberals that they asked him to represent the constituency. Gladstone declined, but had he accepted then Leeds's name would have been associated with one of the most significant political events of the late-19th century. For Gladstone decided to stay in politics after all, and fought the 1880 General Election in the Scottish constituency of Midlothian. His famous "Midlothian Campaign" speeches condemning the policies of Disraeli are regarded as the first successful attempt by a statesman to woo the electorate with speeches reported in newspapers. Undeterred, the Leeds Liberals still entered him as a candidate in the city and when the votes were counted in April, 1880, Gladstone had been elected an MP with a majority of 11,291. In Midlothian, Gladstone had a majority of just 211 and he chose to represent that seat. Later that year, his son Herbert Gladstone was returned unopposed as a Leeds Liberal MP in a by-election to fill the seat not accepted by his father. To thank the Liberal electors of Leeds, W. E. Gladstone—now in his second term as Prime Minister—paid a three-day official visit in October, 1881. The biggest banquet ever given in the city was held in a magnificent hall specially erected over the yard of the Coloured Cloth Hall behind the Post Office in today's City Square. Over 1,000 diners sat down to a menu that included Clear Game Soup, Mayonnaise of Lobster, Venison Cutlets á la d'Orsay, Tartlettes á la Parisienne, and a music programme performed by the Band of the Grenadier Guards. In a bizarre footnote to a strange story, hundreds of tickets were sold to people who were content merely to be spectators at the lavish banquet.

Civic Improvements

Although painfully slow, there were a number of key events which gave Leeds the facilities it needed to make the transformation from town into city. The first was in 1818, when the Leeds Gas Light Company started supplying coal gas for street lighting, thus making Leeds a safer place at night, and to the households of the growing middle classes. In 1835, the Municipal Reform Act brought to an end the Leeds Corporation of 1626, and allowed the first elected council. There were 12 wards and in the first election Liberals won 42 of the 48 seats. This gave a say in the running of the city to local industrialists of a more civic-minded and philanthropic disposition than the unelected merchants who had used the Corporation to further their own ends. One of the new council's first projects was to introduce a safe water supply, piping it from Eccup in 1842 and— as housing areas and population grew—from new reservoirs at Fewston, Lindley Wood and Swinsty in the Washburn Valley, north of Otley. A municipal cemetery was opened at Burmantofts

The enormous banquet held for the visit of the reluctant Leeds MP and greastest Victorian Prime Minister, William Ewart Gladstone.

in 1845, and following the Electric Lighting Act of 1882 the council began experimenting with electric street lights and, by 1893, opened the Leeds Electric Lighting Works. That same year, Leeds won the rank of city.

The Tramways
No self-respecting Victorian city could have done without its tram system. In 1869 and 1870 they had begun operating in Liverpool and London, so the council quickly sought the Leeds Tramways Order (1871) which allowed the construction of five tramway routes in Leeds. At first, the trams were horse-drawn and, from 1883, steam-driven. The first overhead line electric tram in England started running between Sheepscar and Roundhay on 29 September, 1891, and electrification was soon extended throughout the city.

Expanding Leeds
Victorian Leeds, with a population that rose from 152,054 in 1841 to 428,968 at the turn of the century, clearly expanded physically. It spread along the principal roads to the turnpikes— Otley Road, York Road, Kirkstall Road, Hunslet Road, Armley Road, Dewsbury Road, Roundhay Road and Whitehall Road. While there was still a substantial overcrowding in central Leeds, especially to the north and east of Vicar Lane, townships of Armley, Beeston, Bramley, Chapel Allerton, Farnley, Headingley-cum-Burley, Holbeck, Hunslet, Potternewton, Wortley, Coldcotes and Osmondthorpe. This spread away from Leeds was accelerated when the tramways allowed commuting. It became easy for workers to travel from the townships into the bigger factories and offices of central Leeds.

The Changing Skyline
A period of fine architecture, from which rose today's Victorian core, was inaugurated in 1858 with Leeds Town Hall. The Corn Exchange followed in 1863 and the Mechanics Institute (now Civic Theatre) in 1865. There was a covered market in Kirkgate, and much new building in Briggate and Vicar Lane, including the shop-

Michael Marks (above left), was born at Bialystok, Russian Poland, in 1863. When murderous pogroms against Jews followed the assassination of Tsar Alexander II, Marks was one of millions of Jews who fled to Britain and America. Arriving in Leeds in 1882, he peddled small goods in the street. In 1884, he set up a stall on the open Leeds market and soon moved into the covered market, devising the famous slogan, "Don't ask the price, it's a penny". More stalls and shops followed in Lancashire and by 1890, he needed a partner. He turned to Tom Spencer (above right), chief cashier at his main wholesaler, Dewhirsts of Leeds. Thus was born **Marks & Spencer**, *the business which—more than any other—is associated with Leeds. By 1900 Marks & Spencer had 36 branches, targeting low-priced goods at the working classes who, for the first time in history, had a decent income. Tragically, Spencer died within a year of his retirement in 1903 (he was aged 53) and Marks died from overwork four years later at the early age of 44. The business was continued by their families, turning Marks & Spencer into Britain's biggest retailers with over 600 stores.*

ping arcades. In Commercial Street and Park Row appeared impressive office buildings like those for the Leeds and Yorkshire Assurance Company, the Prudential and the Bank of England. The council soon outgrew the Town Hall and built the Municipal Buildings, now the Central Library and City Museum, between 1876 and 1884.

The New Industries
The world's top producer of woollen cloth was also "Flax Capital of Britain". There were 37 flax mills in 1855, many of its 9,500 workers Irish immigrants from the terrible 1845-48 Potato Famine. Carpet, cotton and silk mills appeared, and a new engineering industry. The founder was Matthew Murray, who had built a steam engine for the Middleton Colliery Railway in 1812. Murray started building locomotives, the origin of Leeds's Hunslet Engine Company. Leeds also became a top sheepskin

and leather producer. But it was the development of the "band knife" by John Barran, who had set up a small clothing factory off Boar Lane, that pointed the way. It cut multiple layers of cloth, and with Isaac Singer's new sewing machine, Barran invented the off-the-peg clothing industry. A large number of the Jewish immigrants who arrived in the 1880s were tailors. By 1900, many had started their own businesses, making Leeds the ready-made clothing capital of Europe.

Growing Wealth
From around the mid-19th century, there was an increase in activity by banks and building societies in Leeds. Although several went to the wall in the 1840s, by the time of the Great Exhibition of 1851, there was a renewed confidence in Leeds, which led to the opening of a Stock Exchange. The growing prosperity of the working and

lower middle classes, and the demand for better housing, was mirrored in the development in 1848 of the "Leeds Permanent" with offices in Lands Lane. In 1859, the Yorkshire Penny Bank opened for business in East Parade, later moving to splendid new offices in Infirmary Street. Both are still the biggest providers of financial services in Leeds.

Poverty

Great poverty co-existed with the enormous wealth in Leeds. Despite the Improvement Act of 1842, which cleared slums and introduced fresh water, the death rate—particularly for infants—remained high in Leeds until the 1880s. Begging had been forbidden since 1662, so the old and the sick, if they were lucky, found places in the town workhouse that had been established on the corner of Vicar Lane and Lady Lane in 1726. By the 1830s it was overcrowded with 250 paupers. A massive new workhouse was opened in 1861 (now part of St. James's Hospital), accommodating 810 poor. In the 1870s, demand for housing was so great that even many people with jobs were forced to apply for admission to the workhouse.

Education

In 1846 a large Poor Law school was built at Burmantofts for workhouse children. There were 177 private schools, mostly in private houses. Many young gentlemen from the middle classes went to Leeds Grammar School, which moved into a new building beside Woodhouse Moor in 1857. And a Girl's High School was set up in 1876. When Forster's great 1870 Education Act established schools throughout Leeds, factory and church schools were already numerous. In 1831 a School of Medicine was founded, later joining the Yorkshire College of Science of 1874—forerunner of the University of Leeds.

The 20th Century

If there was a key time in Leeds's development, it was between the end of Queen Victoria's reign and the Great War. The Depression of 1873-96 had arrested Leeds's growth, and it was only after it that Leeds rose above the industrial smoke to become an important national centre for learning, sports and the arts. And for the first time in five centuries, woollen cloth was not the stable of the Leeds economy. Even the great flax industry had waned. Early in the 20th century, Leeds became pre-eminent in ready-made clothing production. Many important features of today's Leeds—from famous manufacturers, to Leeds University, to the development of Headingley Cricket Ground—appeared in those astonishing years around the turn of the century.

Early Social Life

Shorter working hours and Bank Holidays had been established in late Victorian times, and in the 1900s leisure time was becoming an important feature of Leeds life for both the working and the middle classes. Many facilities had already appeared, such as the development of Roundhay Park as "the lungs of Leeds". Very much on the edge of the city in those days, its popularity increased with the masses when it became accessible by the country's first electric cable tram service, operating from Sheepscar in 1891. But the main growth in use came in the 20th century, with the building of a boathouse on Waterloo Lake in 1902, an open air swimming pool in 1907, the Coronation House (a huge conservatory, now Tropical

Looking north from the junction of Call Lane and Lower Briggate around the turn of the century.

World), and a sports arena. Vast crowds attended many events here, like 130,000 at a military tattoo in 1926; and on 2 July, 1949, an estimated 120,000 attended Children's Day. There were numerous Music Halls (the City Varieties, the sole survivor, had opened in 1865). On 17 April, 1905, the first cinema in Leeds opened at the Coliseum Variety Theatre in Cookridge Street. The first talking films did not arrive until 1927, at the Electrocord Studios, Holbeck. For the middle classes, there was a growth in scientific, philosophical and debating societies. The major social event was the Leeds Festival, which had started in 1858. It was held every three years. The City Art Gallery, opened in 1888, built up the finest collection of British modern art outside London.

Growing Industries

By 1900, the role call of famous Leeds industrialists—names like Benjamin Gott, John Marshall, Matthew Murray—had been joined by a whole new generation of innovative factory owners. Great locomotive works were established by some of Murray's apprentices, including the Hunslet Engine Company and Hudswell Clarke. James Fowler and James Kitson, later Baron Airedale, ran the biggest mechanical engineering works in Yorkshire. Thomas Greenwood and John Batley had established their great Albion Works on Armley Road, making everything from trams to machine tools. Supported by the local industry, the Blackburn Aeroplane Company started production in Hunslet in 1909, moving to Roundhay four years later. Then there was Alf Cooke's pioneering Crown Point colour printing works (he had even secured the unique Royal Warrant of "Chromo-Lithographer to Her Majesty Queen Victoria"). John Waddington, a printer of theatre posters, became the world's biggest playing card and games manufacturer. And, of course, there were the great off-the-peg clothing factories. Besides that run by the master himself, Sir John Barran, there was Montague Burton, which employed 20,000

workers in the world's largest clothing plant at Hudson Road. Other famous names were Joseph Hepworth, John Collier, and the Leeds leather factors-turned-shoemakers Stead and Simpson. As the age of the motor car gave birth to the motor bus, two Leeds men— Wallace Cunningham and Arnold Crowe—set up the famous Wallace Arnold coach company.

First World War

As long ago as the Crimean War, Greenwood and Batley had been making machines for munitions manufacturing in Leeds. Now they were to be used at a factory in Barnbow, Cross Gates. Barnbow worked flat-out, making a total of 36 million cartridges and 25 million shells. But on 5 December, 1916, 35 women nightshift workers were killed in an accidental explosion at the factory. By July, 1915, a total of 36,000 boys and men had joined the new 15th battalion of the West Yorkshire Regiment (known as "the Leeds Pals"), the 17th West Yorkshire Regiment ("the Bantams"), 7th and 8th West Yorkshire Regiments ("the Leeds Rifles") and others. In just ten minutes on 1 July, 1916, two whole companies of the Leeds Pals were wiped out in the Somme mud.

The General Strike

As in other cities, a state of emergency was declared on 1 May, 1926, following the TUC's call for a strike by transport workers, builders and workers in engineering industries in support of miners, who were threatened by continuing wage cuts. The Baldwin government ordered the recruitment of Special Constables and volunteers to run essential services, and these were in place when the strike began on 4 May. When some tram drivers continued working, their tramcars were attacked and damaged for which 12 men and women were later jailed. By 7 May, an estimated 3,725 people had returned to work, and 50 trams were operating. The Strike was called off after nine days, because the government had been too well prepared. Certainly, it had barely touched the life of Leeds.

The Slump

Despite the diversity of its industries, Leeds did not escape the 1929-34 World Slump. Unemployment had peaked at the end of the First World War, but halved by 1927. Between 1929 and 1931 the figure doubled from around 16,000 to 32,000. Among relief schemes to give unemployed men work was the building of Leeds Civic Hall, opened in 1933. Long after the slump was declared at an end, unemployment was high in Leeds, a situation that was improved only by the war effort of 1939.

Ten Famous Leeds Residents

John Smeaton. Born in Leeds in 1724. Engineer for the Eddystone Lighthouse and Calder Navigation.

Joseph Priestley. Born at Birstall, 1733. Minister of Mill Hill Chapel in 1767-73. Famous for his discovery of oxygen in 1774.

Richard Oastler. Born at Quarry Hill in 1789. Leading campaigners against child slavery in mills and factories.

Phil May. Great cartoonist, born in Leeds in 1864. His satires of London life in late-Victorian times are much imitated today.

Arthur Ransome. In 1884, the children's writer ("Swallows & Amazons") was born in Headingley.

J. R. R. Tolkien. The writer of "Lord of the Rings" worked in the English Department of Leeds University in 1921-25.

Sir Jimmy Savile. Born on Halloween, 1926. TV show host and disc jockey. Knighted in 1990 for tireless charity work.

Keith Waterhouse. Born in Hunslet, 1929. One of the most successful and prolific British writers and journalists of the post-war. Famous for his second novel, "Billy Liar".

Peter O'Toole. Born in Ireland in 1932, his family moved to Hunslet. After acting debut at Leeds Civic Theatre, became famous as "Lawrence of Arabia".

Alan Bennett. Born in 1934 at Wortley. After fame in "Beyond the Fringe" became a top dramatist and TV actor.

Second World War

Leeds was not considered a strategically important target by Goering's *Luftwaffe* in World War II. While Sheffield's steelworks and Hull's docks suffered appalling raids, Leeds had few visits and considerably less devastation. The first attack on the city, on 1 September, 1940, caused mostly structural damage. The worst raid began minutes before the clock of Leeds Town Hall struck midnight on 14 March, 1941. More than 4,600 houses, the elegant museum in Park Row, and the Town Hall itself were damaged. Records suggest that 65 Leeds residents were killed that night, and 260 injured.

The Modern City

Lack of bomb damage meant the city was slow to join the post-war building boom. Despite the huge 1930s slum-clearance which produced the notorious Quarry Hill Flats, in 1948 sixty per cent of the city's 154,000 houses were said to require demolition. Huge new estates rose in the suburbs—many of them 17-storey tower blocks. Meanwhile, a small aerodrome at Yeadon was developed in the 1950s to become Leeds-Bradford Airport. The city was joined to the M1 motorway in the late-1950s, the M62 and M621 in the 1970s. Traffic relief for the city centre, which had become a bottleneck, came when the first phase of the Inner Ring Road opened in 1967. As the century progressed, the city became an important seat of learn-

ing. The University of Leeds, which received its Charter in 1904, grew into one of the top five in the UK. The Beckett Park Training College, the first such college to be produced by the 1903 Education Act, opened in 1913, and the Carnegie Physical Training College was added in 1935. With a number of other colleges, they were part of Leeds Polytechnic, which became the city's second University in the 1990s. Nine other colleges were established, including the Art School at which the sculptor Henry Moore studied.

Shopping

Since the 1870s, many arcades and fine stores have been a feature of central Leeds. From Snowdon Schofield's 1901 shop off The Headrow came one of Britain's first department stores. A shopping mall, the Merrion Centre, opened in 1964, followed by the Bond Street, St. John's and Schofields Centres. The first major pedestrianisation scheme, involving Commercial Street and Lands Lane, was open for Christmas 1970. In 1990s, the concept was being extended to include Briggate.

The Media

The city was now the most important media centre east of the Pennines. The *Yorkshire Post*, which had grown out of the *Leeds Intelligencer* in 1866, absorbed the *Leeds Mercury* in 1939 and became a highly respected name in British journalism. Its sister *York-*

shire Evening Post, started in 1890, similarly gobbled its competition, the *Yorkshire Evening News,* in 1963. Both moved into new offices in Wellington Street in 1970, spawning one of the country's biggest freesheets, the *Leeds Weekly News* in 1980. Radio arrived in Leeds in 1932: a radio-by-wire service. BBC Television, which had begun broadcasts to Yorkshire in 1951, opened Leeds studios in 1968. ITV programmes were transmitted by ABC in Leeds from 1956 and in 1968 Yorkshire Television built studios on Kirkstall Road. The BBC also opened Radio Leeds in 1968, and a commercial radio station, Radio Aire, appeared in 1981.

Leeds Consumes its Neighbours

A huge expansion of Leeds resulted on 1 April, 1974, when local government reorganization created Leeds Metropolitan District Council from Leeds City and nearby boroughs of Morley and Pudsey, Urban District Councils of Aireborough, Garforth, Horsforth, Otley and Rothwell, and parts of the Rural District Councils of Wetherby and Wharfedale. At 217 square miles, Leeds became the second biggest (after Doncaster) metropolitan district in England, and the second largest (after Birmingham) in population.

A City of Europe

With over 700,000 residents, Leeds had become the focal point of Yorkshire and Humberside by the 1990s. It was famous for sporting excellence (Test Match cricket at Headingley, Premier League soccer by Leeds United, Olympic Gold for its swimmers); an important arts and entertainment centre (the International Pianoforte Competition, the West Yorkshire Playhouse, home of Opera North, major rock concerts at Roundhay Park); and among the UK's principal financial, law and administrative centres. As the end of the century approached, Leeds—a mere riverside hamlet called Loidis at the last millennium—had grown so much in stature that it could project itself as one of the top non-capital cities in Europe.

Traffic relief for the city centre—building the Leeds Inner Ring Road.

PART NINE:
Beyond Leeds

No other English city has so many tourist "honeypots" within reach. If the sun makes a belated appearance at lunchtime, you can still have afternoon tea in Wensleydale or Robin Hood's Bay, the Cathedral city of Lincoln or Beatle City in Liverpool.

Within a couple of hours' drive there are four National Parks, two coastlines and literally dozens of towns and villages stuffed with historic buildings and speciality shops.

If Industrial Heritage was the growth industry of the eighties, the 1990s have seen a return to the countryside. Colour coordinated walkers and mountain-bikers swarm through the Dales, Moors and South Pennines on an increasing number of conducted tours and other special events.

The following pages describe all the most popular destinations from the city—and many little-known ones too. Leeds is at the very centre of the leisure world.

Left: Overlooking the mile-long rocky finger of Filey Brigg on the Yorkshire Coast (see page 181).

WHITBY

SCARBOROUGH

FILEY

FLAMBOROUGH HEAD

BRIDLINGTON

HORNSEA

WITHERNSEA

SPURN HEAD

GRIMSBY

CLEETHORPES

LOUTH

NORTH YORK MOORS NATIONAL PARK

YORKSHIRE WOLDS

A64

A163

BEVERLEY

KINGSTON UPON HULL

A63

SCUNTHORPE

GAINSBOROUGH

LINCOLN

DARLINGTON

A1

NORTHALLERTON

PICKERING

A170

COXWOLD

MALTON

EASINGWOLD

GREAT DRIFFIELD

STAMFORD BRIDGE

M180

DONCASTER

THIRSK

BOROUGHBRIDGE

KNARESBOROUGH

YORK

TADCASTER

SELBY

A1

M62

A1

M1

RICHMOND

LEYBURN

A684

MASHAM

RIPON

HARROGATE

WETHERBY

A58

A1

LEEDS

WAKEFIELD

BARNSLEY

M1

M18

ROTHERHAM

SHEFFIELD

CHESTERFIELD

ASKRIGG

HAWES

SEDBERGH

YORKSHIRE DALES NATIONAL PARK

BOLTON ABBEY

GRASSINGTON

SKIPTON

ILKLEY

OTLEY

A65

M621

BRADFORD

HALIFAX

HUDDERSFIELD

M62

A628

GLOSSOP

STOCKPORT

PEAK DISTRICT NATIONAL PARK

A623

BUXTON

KENDAL

LAKE DISTRICT NATIONAL PARK

ULVERSTON

LANCASTER

A65

SETTLE

KEIGHLEY

HAWORTH

M65

BURNLEY

BLACKBURN

A677

ROCHDALE

BURY

BOLTON

OLDHAM

MANCHESTER

SALFORD

M61

MORECAMBE

FLEETWOOD

BLACKPOOL

M55

PRESTON

SOUTHPORT

WIGAN

M58

ST. HELENS

LIVERPOOL

M57

M62

BIRKENHEAD

WARRINGTON

M6

NORWICH

CHESTER

ELLESMERE PORT

M56

The Bradford Area

Leeds's smaller next-door neighbour is a treasuretrove of museums, Victorian heritage attractions and curry houses.

The Bradford Metropolitan Area adjoins most of the western side of Leeds. The city grew to prominence in the second half of the 19th century by its great worsted mills, and today textiles are still at the centre of Bradford life, although tourism and conferences are now providing much work, as are jobs in the area's three big building societies. With a total population of 470,000, Bradford is the fifth largest metropolitan district in England and Wales, but visitors will not find a big city atmosphere, for the inhabitants are spread through a huge network of mill towns and hilltop villages. An important development since the 1960s has been the arrival of a large Asian community, now totalling nearly 70,000. They have brought great character to the area.

Bradford

In 1980, Bradford appointed a tourist officer and began attracting thousands of visitors to its heritage and post-industrial attractions. While the city lacks the feel of a sophisticated regional centre like Leeds, there is much to see and do, and because of its close proximity to Leeds, it is difficult to ignore. It makes a change for shopping, especially in the excellent Rawson Market. For the only complete guide, see *The Bradford Book*, the companion volume to *Leeds Fax*, on sale at Leeds-Bradford bookshops.

Essential Information

☛ By car, Bradford is nine miles (a 30 min. drive) from Leeds City Centre, well signposted via A647. Ample parking around markets, the NMPF&T, and opposite City Hall. Trains runs at least every hour from Leeds City Station. Also regular buses from Central Bus Station.

Bradford Tourist Information Centre is at the Photography Museum (see over) in Pictureville, Bradford BD5 0TR. Write or phone for specific information.
☎ 0274-753678.

Bolling Hall

Bolling Hall is partly medieval tower, and partly a typical 17th Century West Yorkshire manor house with kitchens and bedchambers kept just as they were 300 years ago. Situated in a delightful park, it is a warren of oak-panelled passageways and rooms. There are suits of armour, stags heads and weapons on the walls and its own resident ghost—the "Factory King" Richard Oastler. Some furniture by Otley's Thomas Chippendale, and fine Adam-style plasterwork in the drawing room and dining room. Spooky.
☛ *Bowling Hall Road, Bradford BD4 7LP. Signposted between Wakefield Rd (A650) and Bowling Hall Rd on south-east side of Bradford centre. Regular buses from Bradford Interchange. Open daily 10-6pm Ap-Sept; 10-5pm Oct-Mar. Closed Mon (ex. Bank Hols), Good Fri, Xmas & Boxing Day. Admission free. Limited wheelchair access.*
☎ 0274-723057.

Colour Museum

Bradford is the home of the Society of Dyers and Colourists, which tests the use of different colour processes in textiles and other materials, and this is their amazing museum. Very modern in its approach, it encourages you to make rainbows, or see how colours are perceived by dogs, fishes, birds and bees. See how colour blindness works, and how the colour of everyday objects changes our perception of them. The history of dyes from the ancient Egyptians to the modern fashion industry is covered, and interactive displays allows you to operate a dye-making factory, or use a computer to test any material for its colour.
☛ *82 Grattan Road, Bradford BD1 2JB. About 100 yds east of the Westgate-John Street junction, near the markets area, where there is good parking. Open Ap-Sep, Tue-Fri 10-12.30am & 2pm-5pm, Sat 10-4pm; Oct-Mar, Tue-Fri 2pm-5pm, Sat 10-4pm. Open for pre-booked parties Tue-Fri morning. Closed Sun, Mon & Public hols. Small admission charge.*
☎ 0274-390955.

Industrial Museum

An interesting display tracing Bradford's growth as the worsted spinning capital of the world in the 19th Century, and much more. Wool was what the city was built on, and the history of the uses that were made of this valuable commodity right from medieval times is explained. Among a large transport section is the last Bradford tram and several cars that came off the city's Jowett production lines. Don't leave without seeing the mill owner's house next door, preserved exactly as it was in Victorian times, and a complete street of Victorian back-to-back houses, furnished in authentic style. And the Horses at Work collection includes shire horses like Captain, Thomas and Ben. See their stables and the "Horsepower" gallery.
☛ *Moorside Road, Bradford BD2 3HP. On the Leeds side of Bradford, signposted between Harrogate and Fagley Roads. Open daily 10am-5pm. Closed Mon except Bank Hols; closed Good Fri, Xmas Day and Boxing Day. Admission Free. Disabled facilities.*
☎ 0274-631756.

British Wool Centre

A small exhibition at a working mill, which traces the process of British wool production from rearing of sheep, through to manufacture of yarns and the weaving of fabrics. See the treadle looms on which the world famous Harris Tweeds are woven, and an old carding machine. It's especially good for children, because of the 20 or so "live" exhibits of different breeds of sheep. Included is the spectacular Jacob, with its multicoloured fleece and four, sometimes six horns.

☛ *Run by British Wool International, Oak Mills, Station Road, Clayton, on the west side of Bradford. Open Mon- Sat 10am-5pm & all Bank Hols ex. Xmas & New Year. Party pre-booking for museum essential.*

☎ *0274-880612.*

West Yorkshire Transport Museum

Over 60 preserved motorbuses, trolleybuses, electric trams and service vehicles are housed in the 1930s Bradford Corporation bus depot at Ludlam Street. In Summer, 1994, it was moving onto a large purpose-built site at Low Moor, on the south side of Bradford, with room for open-air tramways, reconstructed Victorian streets, etc. Most of the collection—which is constantly expanding—comes from West Yorkshire. See the Leeds balcony tramcar, the

historic No 844 trolleybus, the last to operate in Bradford in 1972, and others from Halifax and Huddersfield. The oldest motorbus is a 1924 Bristol 4-tonner.

☛ *Ludlam Street Depot, Mill Lane, Bradford BD5 0HG. It is just off the main Manchester Road, 10 mins. walk from the city centre. Open, Sundays 11am-5pm. Special events through the year— telephone for list. Groups at other times by arrangement. Small admission charge.*

☎ *0274-736006.*

Undercliffe Cemetery

That this cemetery has won a national tourism award speaks volumes for its host of attractions. Most people come to see its astonishing array of memorials to the great wool barons of Victorian Bradford. There are around 125,000 people buried here, although it's possible to forget that fact as you wander round looking

at the flamboyant headstones, one of the best collections of funerary art in Britain. There are two sections: the eastern side is unconsecrated and was for Methodists and Baptists, while the western (larger) half was strictly for C of E burials. The central boulevard is the dramatic heart of the cemetery. Here you can see some of the grandest sculptures. The great mill-owning Illingworths have a mausoleum like an Egyptian temple, complete with two sphinxes. Nearby the Holden family favoured a Greco-Roman temple with carved angels. Most imposing of all is the Gothic steeple erected for Swithen Anderton—a scaled-down replica of the Scott Monument in Princes Street, Edinburgh.There is an Interpretative centre open in the New Lodge.

☛ *The cemetery lies between Undercliffe Lane and Otley Road (the A658). Frequent bus services from Interchange.*

☎ *For group bookings, ring 0274- 631445.*

Bradford Festival

Held each September, it has become an outstanding feature of the cultural and entertainment life in Northern England. Over a two-week period, one can see everything from jugglers, street theatre, classical and pop music, arts and crafts, alternative cabaret, comedy and funfairs to ballet, big-name theatre productions, special orchestral concerts, etc. But for many, the highlight is the grand finalé Asian Mela, a traditional fair or bazaar with music, dance, food & craft stalls, fireworks and other events to which Asians come from all over Britain. It is usually on the last Sunday of the festival, and revolves around Lister Park, Manningham.

☛ *A free programme is available every August throughout Bradford. Contact Bradford Tourist Information Centre (see page 157).*

Little Germany

Between 1854 and 1874 many German merchants arrived in Bradford. They formed a tight knit community on a 20 acre site at the foot of Leeds Road. Over 30 "palace" warehouses were built be-

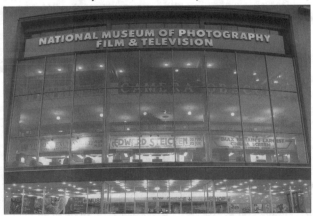

The National Museum of Photography, Film & Television *is unquestionably the jewel in Bradford's tourism crown. Not merely a collection of pictures on walls and cameras behind glass, but a truly interactive museum, where visitors are challenged to get involved with the exhibits. For example, you can become a TV news reader, ride on a magic carpet using the "Chromakey" (this is how Superman flew over Niagara Falls), or become a cameraman shooting a TV drama. Photography is covered right from the earliest cameras, to the latest optics for peering inside jet engines and human lungs. There's bags of cinema history and the famous IMAX screen (see Cinemas). This museum is one of the top attractions in the north, and a large number of those who go to its constantly changing exhibitions come from Leeds.*

☛ *Prince's View, Bradford BD5 0TR. Open Tue-Sun 10.30-6pm. Special exhibitions remain open until 7.30pm. Closed Mon except Bank Hols. Admission to Museum is free.*

☎ *0274-727488.*

tween 1854 and 1874. Among them is Treadwell's Art Mill, four floors of exhibits which have been variously described as "clinically insane", "disturbing" and "unique". The generic style is "Superhumanism", human sculptures and paintings in grotesque shapes and postures, and it is the world's largest such collection.

☛ *Little Germany is between Leeds Road and Church Bank. Treadwell's Art Mill is open daily 10-6pm except Xmas Day. Admission charges. Vegetarian café.*
☎ *0274-306065.*

Asian Restaurants

Many Leeds residents only ever go to Bradford for a curry. And there is certainly no shortage of choice. Everyone seems to have their "secret" favourites. Okay, so we'll let you into our secret. The most comprehensive survey of Bradford Asian eating is in "The Good Curry Guide", a section of *Leeds Fax's* sister publication *The Bradford Book* (on sale throughout Leeds & Bradford).

Here are some of our favourites:
Mumtaz Paan House. Vast range of starters in this authentic open-plan Indian café, and enormous helpings of freshly cooked main courses, complete with whole chillies, and mopped with naan breads. You'll need a bowl of sweet lassi, the most delicious we've ever tasted.
☛ *386-392 Great Horton Road. Open 11.30am-12 midnight 7 days.*
☎ *0274-571861.*

Sweet Centre/Kebab House. This is not exactly the most exclusive street in town, but the meals here are among the best. Excellent value, especially the balti chicken or lamb, with all fresh ingredients.
☛ *110-112 Lumb Lane, Bradford. Open Mon, 12.15-midnight, Tue-Thur 12.15-2am, Fri-Sat 12.15am-3am, Sun 12.15-2am.*
☎ *0274-731735.*

Bharat. Recommended by the Good Food Guide. An up-market, more expensive restaurant, offering classic Gujarati cuisine, highly flavoured yet delicate Specialities include king prawns and trout. The vegetable side dishes are so good they can eclipse the main meals.
☛ *496 Great Horton Road, Bradford 7. Open, Tue-Sun 12-2pm,*

6pm-midnight. Closed Mon.
☎ *0274-521200.*

Kashmir. Just up the road from the Alhambra, this basic café-style eating house always seems to be busy. The reason is good, low-priced food served quickly. The chicken or meat dishes mixed with spinach or dal are especially good.
☛ *27 Morley Street, Bradford 1. Open 11am-3am, seven days.*

Shahensha. On the west side of the city, near a busy junction, and extremely popular with Bradfordians. It is medium priced Peshwari style restaurant. Best dishes are barbecued chicken and lamb.
☛ *234 Whetley Lane, Bradford 8. Open Mon-Thur 6pm-midnight, Fri & Sat 6pm-1am, Sun 6pm-midnight.*
☎ *0274-548274.*

Haworth

Even without the Brontës, Haworth would be packed every weekend. Its cobbled main street (below) winding up the hill from the valley floor, loved by makers of Hovis commercials, is lined with shops, pubs and cafés of the sort that have colonised every other well-preserved village in Yorkshire. But the Parsonage provides that extra dimension: over 250,000 visitors annually walk through its door. Only Shakespeare's birthplace at Stratford is busier. On any day of the

The steep Main Street of Haworth

year you are likely to find at least one party of foreign tourists. There are even signposts in Japanese. But mostly, Haworth's bread-and-butter trade is the people of West Yorkshire who return frequently for its unique, brooding charm.

☛ *Easiest by Aire Valley A650 route (even with roadworks). But the best way is to take a train from Leeds to Keighley and change onto the Keighley & Worth Valley Railway (see page 161). Haworth Information Centre is at 2-4 West Lane (at top of hill).*
☎ *0535-642329.*

Brontë Parsonage

This old stone house on the edge of the Pennine Moors retains a bleak atmosphere, a legacy of the tragic stories—real as well as fictitious—that unfolded here last century. Here it was that Patrick Brontë brought his family in 1820. Within five years, his wife and two eldest children had died, leaving him to bring up three enormously gifted daughters, Charlotte, Emily and Anne, and son Branwell. In the Parsonage, you can still see the footstool on which Emily sat outside on fine days writing her romantic masterpiece, *Wuthering Heights,* as well as the sofa on which she died at the age of 28. See Charlotte's tiny shoes, wedding bonnet and writing desk, and the children's wall writings.

Off Main Street. Open daily, 11-5.30pm Apr-Sept; 11-4.30pm Oct-Mar. Admission charge.
☎ *0535-42323.*

Moor Walks

The Haworth Moors were loved by all the Brontës, but they are today mainly associated with Emily's *Wuthering Heights*. The most walks are those they described themselves to what are now known as Brontë Falls, Bridge & Chair (two miles). A mile farther on is the ruined farmhouse of Top Withens, "probably" inspiration for *WH*. A plaque by the Brontë Society says "the buildings, even when complete, bore no resemblance to the house she described". But the setting certainly does.
Leave Haworth by West Lane and follow signposted track. Allow at least two hours for return walk to Top Withens. Path muddy after rain.

Bygone Days

This memorabilia museum, in a former cinema, centres on Cooper Gate Square, a courtyard of period shops on two levels containing many antiques and artifacts that have given authentic touches to TV programmes like "Last of the Summer Wine". There are balconies and ginnels to walk through, and cream teas to be taken in a Victorian café.
At Belle Isle Road (in the valley). Open, 11-5pm Wed, Thur, weeneds and Bank Hols. Admission charge.
☎ *0535-646424.*

Museum of Childhood

A collection of mainly Victorian and Edwardian to present day toys, dolls, games and other childrens' pastimes. See the working model trains and Meccano models. The shop sells Dinky, Hornby, Trix, Triang models for dads and plenty of other things for children. No matter what your age, there is bound to be something here you remember from childhood.
117 Main Street, Haworth BD22 8DU. Open 10.30-5.30pm daily Easter-Oct, plus weekends and school holidays all year. Admission charge.
☎ *0535-643825.*

Ilkley

The town that gave Yorkshire its "national" anthem "On Ilkla Moor baht 'at'" is a genteel spa, up-market shopping centre and dormitory for Leeds and Bradford white-collar workers. Just under 12,000 people live here, but that number seems to double in the summer with tourists and conference delegates. For the people of Leeds, Ilkley is loved as a launching pad for scenic walks along the River Wharfe and over the surrounding hills.
Easy 30-min drive along A65 from Leeds or reached by frequent rail service from Leeds City or Yorkshire bus service from Central Bus Station. Tourist Information Centre in the Library, Station Road, LS29 8HA.
☎ *0943-602319.*

White Wells Museum

This is the last surviving evidence of Ilkley's spa trade. Mineral springs were trapped here in spa baths in 1756, giving birth to Ilkley, and bringing wealthy Victorians to stone plunge pools and to drink the waters as remedies for gout and melancholia. Besides this heritage, you can see wildlife and history displays about Ilkley Moor. The tea room serves vegetarian/organic foods, and the teas are made with spring water.
Not surprisingly, White Wells is at the top of Wells Road, and signposted. Open Sat & Sun, 10-6pm, Tues, Wed & Fri 11-5.30pm. No wheelchair access. No telephone at time of writing.

The Manor House

There is much evidence of Bronze Age settlements in the area and, of course, the Romans built a fort here in the winter of AD 79-80 against the northern Brigante tribes. It was known as *Olicana* and a garrison remained here for three centuries, containing 500 soldiers at its peak. The history of this, and much more, can be found

*Few cities have such a superb walks and picnics area on their doorstep than **Ilkley Moor**. A number of signposted walks radiate up the hill from the town, Cow and Calf Rocks (pictured above) being the best known. Another is to the Swastika Stone (carved with ancient markings, probably associated with fire worship) and Hebers Ghyll (6m. return) via Grove Road. There is the footpath right over to Airedale, leaving Westwood Drive. Or walk to Dick Hudson's pub from White Wells. Birds to look out for are curlews, ring ouzels and the occasional short-eared owl.*
Everything immediately south of Ilkley is classed as Ilkley Moor, but the entire hill is actually known as Rombalds Moor, extending from above Keighley, to Menston in the east. Walkers should carry the OS Landranger Map No. 104.

in Ilkley's splendid Manor House, an Elizabethan building which actually stands on the site of the original *Olicana* fort. Exhibitions change regularly.

☛ *Castle Yard, Ilkley, LS29 9DT (behind Ilkley Parish Church, through archway on Church Street). Open daily, 10-6pm Apr-Sept; 10-5pm Oct-Mar ex. Bank Hols. Closed Good Fri, Xmas Day & Boxing Day. Admission free. Wheelchair access on ground floor.*

☎ *0943-600066.*

Keighley

The second largest centre of population in the Bradford district, with 44,000 residents, Keighley is an unpretentious mix of industry and startling Pennine hill country. This Victorian mill town usually gets ignored by tourists, who never see more than its station as they change trains for Haworth, but it is certainly worth a browse, especially for shopping.

☛ *A straight run along the Aire Valley, A650, which should be even quicker with Bingley and Shipley are at long last by-passed. Or there's a regular train from Leeds City. There is a Bradford Council Information Centre at Keighley Town Hall, Bow St.*

☎ *0535-758014.*

Keighley and Worth Valley Railway

One of the best private railways in Britain, the K&WVR regularly appears in TV and films, from "The Railway Children" to "Yanks", "Sherlock Holmes" and "Poirot". It was opened in 1867 by the Midland as a branch line to Pennine mills, between Keighley and Oxenhope, but closed in 1961. Of course, steam enthusiasts wouldn't allow the line to die and reopened it seven years later. Special steam excursions include "Wine and Dine" on Saturday nights in season, and Santa Sundays nearer Christmas. Among the static attractions are splendid gaslit Victorian stations at Damens, Ingrow, Oakworth and Haworth. Ingrow is especially interesting. The station was transported from Lancashire and rebuilt here.

☛ *Runs from Keighley BR Station, platforms 3 & 4. Postal address: K & WVR, Haworth Station, Haworth, BD22 8NJ.*

☎ *Times 0535-643629. General info 0535-645214.*

Vintage Railway Carriage Museum

A spin-off from the above has been this new centre at Ingrow Station. There is an expanding collection of locomotives and carriages, beautifully restored with their original Victorian fittings. See the plush splendour of first class, and the hard wooden benches of third-class. There is also a London carriage with blackout curtains, air raid and gas mask instructions on the wall.

☛ *At Ingrow West Station yard, Ingrow, one mile south of Keighley on the A629 Halifax road. Open daily May-Aug, 11.30-5pm and weekends throughout the year (winter 12-5pm).*

☎ *0535-680425.*

Cliffe Castle

This lavish Victorian pile, which looks more like a Norman fort, was built by the rich worsted manufacturer, Henry Butterfield, and houses one of Yorkshire's biggest collections of natural history and geology. The "Molecules to Minerals" display is a dazzling show of rock crystals, fluorescent stones, etc. There are fossils, birds, reptiles, butterflies, ferns, flowering plants, bats and other mammals. Also fascinating archaeological finds, like ice age bones, Stone Age arrowheads and axe heads. And an antiques collection.

☛ *In Spring Gardens Lane, half a mile from the town centre, off A629 Skipton road. open daily 10am-5pm Oct-Mar, 10-6pm Apr-Sept.*

☎ *0535-618230.*

East Riddlesden Hall

The only National Trust property in the area, this lovely old 17th century manor house contains much of interest. Many rooms have wood panelling, beautiful plasterwork and mullioned windows. Everything on display is from the 1600s, such as the pewterware, Yorkshire oak furni-

ture, and kitchen utensils. Of course, the Hall has a ghost—the Grey Lady. Outside, the 12-acre grounds beside the River Aire contain a well preserved tithe barn with old farm arts and machinery. There is a walled garden and pond.

☛ *A mile north-east of Keighley, signposted off the A650. Open, 12-5pm weekends only and Easter week in April. Also Sat 7 Wed May-Oct inclusive. Admission charge.*

☎ *0535-607075.*

The Yorkshire Car Collection

This new museum contains such exhibits as Mick Jagger's Ford Galaxie Convertible, Roger Whittaker's Gullwing Mercedes, Robert Plant's Chrysler Imperial and the Beverley Sisters' Cadillac. There's a 1922 Silver Ghost Rolls Royce, a 1929 Aston Martin which once raced at Le Mans. Perhaps the most unusual car is the penny mini, a Mini covered in old pennies, inspired by the Beatles song "Penny Lane". Many of the vehicles are used for TV productions.

☛ *In Grange Street, round the corner from Keighley Station. Open Mon-Fri 10-5pm for parties of 10 adults by prior arrangement. Admission charge.*

☎ *0535-661177 ext. 301/275.*

Saltaire

No other Victorian industrialist left a finer memorial than Sir Titus Salt's model village of Saltaire, near Shipley. Covering over 25 acres, there were 22 streets with 850 houses, 45 almshouses, a school, hospital, an Institute, Congregational and Methodist Churches, Sunday school, park, baths, wash-houses railway station and the great centrepiece of Salts Mill itself, as long as St. Paul's Cathedral. Today, most of it survives in such pristine condition that the atmosphere of the 19th Century can almost be touched. Once discovered, Saltaire becomes a frequent destination for a short excursion. Wander round the streets, walk beside the Leeds-Liverpool canal or take a waterbus up to Bingley. There are rowing boats for hire on the Aire in summer.

☛ *Along Aire Valley from Leeds, less than 30 mins. in good traffic via A657. Signposted right beyond main Shipley lights. Yorkshire service from Central Bus Station and trains from Leeds City.*

1853 Gallery

This is one of Yorkshire's biggest international attractions, an entire floor of the former spinning shed at Salt's mill devoted to the works of Bradford-born David Hockney. The huge collection covers most of his styles, from his early days as a student at Bradford College of Art, through his swimming pool period, to his more recent work involving Xerox machines, fax machines and polaroid cameras. The wealthy can even buy an original Hockney at the gallery. For the rest of us, there's a wide range of posters on sale.

☛ *Salt's Mill, Victoria Rd., Saltaire, Shipley BD18 3LB. Open daily, 10-5pm.*
☎ *0274-531163.*

Reed Organ and Harmonium Museum

Housed in the Saltaire Institute, this museum is unique in Europe hosting over 50 English, American and French instruments. The founders, when available, will guide you through their collection, demonstrating individual organs and harmoniums if time allows. Or organists are permitted to test the instruments themselves. Many of the exhibits contain ornate carvings and inscriptions. Others have fascinating stories behind them.

☛ *In Victoria Hall, Victoria Road, Saltaire. Open daily, 11-4pm ex. weekends. Small admission charge.*
☎ *0274-585601.*

Shipley

Another mill town with a population of over 30,000 now joined to Bradford and Saltaire by urban sprawl, Shipley is good for shopping, with open bric-a-brac market on Monday and a full market on Friday and Saturday. But there are a few interesting visitor facilities in or near the town, in the Aire Valley itself or up on the tops towards Baildon Moor.

☛ *Access from Leeds as Saltaire above. There is a Bradford Council Information Centre next to the library in Wellcroft.*
☎ *0274-757016.*

Sooty's World

The little golden bear with black ears has a special place in the childhood memory of millions. This is a marvellous collection of the late Harry Corbett's glove puppet TV sets from the 1950s to the present day. See Sooty Trawlerman, Photographer, Dr. Sooty and Sooty Fisheries. There is a puppets set where parents can entertain their children.

☛ *At Windhill Manor, Leeds Road, Shipley. Open weekends Mar-Dec, Sat 1-5.30pm, Sun, 11-6pm, Bank Hols 11-6pm, school hols daily 1.30-6pm. Admission charge.*
☎ *0274-531122.*

Shipley Glen

Immortalized in song—"Meet Me Gwen in Shipley Glen"—this was a popular place for millworkers and their families in late-Victorian times. Today, the wooded scarp is quieter and probably nicer for it. For a start, there is a famous cable-hauled tramway, opened in 1895, on a steep incline through Walker Wood. The quarter-mile run on narrow-gauge cars takes just two minutes. There is a funfair, and some excellent walks.

☛ *Access is on Coach Road, off Otley Road, Shipley. The tramway runs Easter to October, Sat 1-5pm, Sun & Bank Hols 10-6pm. Also open Wed 10-4pm in June/July.*
☎ *0274-589010.*

Bracken Hall Countryside Centre

Up the hill from Shipley is this permanent exhibition on natural history of the area. The centre has a naturalist to answer questions, organises guided tours and countryside walks in summer. Features include a wildlife garden, pond and wildlife meadow.

☛ *In Glen Road, Baildon, BD17 5EA. Open, Ap-Oct 11-5pm Wed-Sun, plus Bank Hols; Nov-Mar 11-5pm Wed & Sun. Admission Free.*
☎ *0274-584140.*

*Shipley is the starting point for an excellent Waterbus service, with five stops up the **Leeds-Liverpool Canal** to the famous five-rise locks (pictured above) at Bingley. A traditional narrowboat, MB Apollo, plies the 200-year-old canal on return journeys that take three hours. Along the way there are locks, canalside cottages, and a boatman's pub.*
☛ *Operates from Wharf St., Shipley, Victor Rd., Saltaire, Hirst Wood Lock, Swing Bridge, Dowley Gap, Fisherman's Inn, Railway station car park, Bingley. Ring in advance for sailing times.*
☎ *0274-595914.*

The Harrogate Area

Colourful gardens and elegant baths, antique shops and restaurants, market towns and lonely moors, ancient ruins and modern theme parks

The administrative centre of an area of 500 square miles and 140,000 population to the east of the Yorkshire Dales and the north of Leeds, Harrogate contains many classic tourist attractions. Not the least of which is the town itself, founded on a mineral spring that was first discovered in 1571. The town grew to prominence only in late Victorian times as a fashionable spa resort and, more recently, retirement centre and international conference town. It is still remarkably well preserved, from the baths where Dustin Hoffman was filmed during the making of "Agatha", to The Stray, 200 acres of greensward protected by ancient law for walking, sports etc. They explode with crocus and daffodils every spring. Because Harrogate is at the centre of one of the most expensive housing areas in the North of England, the town is an up-market shopping centre, an antique collector's heaven, and a gourmet's delight. And, of course, Harrogate is the permanent site of the Great Yorkshire Show every July.

☛ *Ten miles or so north of Leeds, along A61. Regular buses from Central Bus Station, and trains from Leeds City, Burley Park and Horsforth stations. Tourist Information Centre is at Royal Baths Assembly Rooms, Crescent Rd.*
☎ *0423-525666.*

Harlow Carr

These Botanical Gardens, set in 68 landscaped acres on the outskirts, are the finest in the region. The Northern Horticultural Society has its headquarters here, growing plants suitable for the Yorkshire climate. The displays are interesting throughout the year, and are clearly interpreted for visitors. See spring and autumn bulbs, vegetable and fruit plots, the rock gardens, heathers, Alpine displays, roses, rhododendrons and a model village. If the rain starts, there is a Museum of Gardening, and the Garden Room Restaurant.

☛ *Harlow Carr is on Crag Lane, off the B6162 Otley Road. Open daily, 9-sunset or 7.30pm summer; 9-5pm rest of year. Entry charge.*
☎ *0423-565418.*

Royal Baths

The Royal Baths Assembly Rooms form one of the most original corners of Victorian Harrogate. Dating from 1897, the tiled Turkish baths are still open to the public, as is the Russian steam room. Modern facilities include sauna, plunge pool and sunbeds.

☛ *The Assembly Rooms are in Crescent Road. Gents sessions are Mon pm, Tues am, Wed pm, Fri pm, Sat am & pm; Ladies sessions are Tues pm, Thur pm, Fri am, Sun am & pm. Ring for bookings & times.*
☎ *0423-562498.*

Royal Pump House

This museum explains how Harrogate grew to prominence. The pump room was built in 1842 over the Old Sulphur well and became the centre of the town's spa trade for the Victorian well-to-do. Even in the 1920s, they were handing out 1,500 tots every morning. The sulphur springs still bubble to the surface and can be sampled, but they are not for the faint-hearted.

☛ *In Royal Parade. Open Tue-Sat 10-5pm, Sun 2pm-5pm. Closed Mon, Xmas, Boxing & New Year's Day. Admission charge.*
☎ *0423-503340.*

Ripley Castle

Home of the Ingilby family since the 1320s, Ripley Castle is one of the best-preserved stately homes in England. It is not as grand as Castle Howard or Chatsworth, but it more than makes up for it with original medieval wood panelling, stonework and furniture. See the Knight's Chamber, the remarkable library, and the secret priest's hiding place. There are some Georgian rooms, added in the 1780s, with chandeliers and portraits. Outside, there are Capability Brown lakes, a deer park, and gardens which now contain the National Hyacinth Collection. Ripley Village was built in the 1820s and is a blaze of floral colour in spring and summer. Foodies will love the Hopkins Porter Wine and Cheese Shops, a fine delicatessen.

☛ *Ripley is two miles north of Harrogate on A61 Ripon road. Castle open: Good Fri, Easter & Bank Hols, 11-4.30pm; Ap-Oct Sat & Sun 11.30-4.30pm; May Tues, Wed, thur, Sat & Sun 2-4.30pm; June-Sept Tues, Wed, Thurs Sat & Sun 11.30-4.30am. Admission charge.*
☎ *0423-770152.*

The tea house in Harrogate's Valley Gardens

Knaresborough

Knaresborough, like Hebden Bridge in Calderdale, has a vast number of attractions out of proportion to its size. The picturesque Market Place is the hub, including England's oldest chemist shop. There are numerous interesting shops in the warren of back alleys and ginnels, and fine walks along the curving River Nidd. There is an open market on Wednesday. Early closing day is Thursday.

☞ *Half an hour's drive, via A61 Harrogate road, picking up Knaresborough sign on new eastern bypass. The Tourist Information Centre (open summer season only) is in the Market Place.*
☎ *0423-866886.*

Castle & Court House.

High on a bluff above the Nidd stands the remains of a castle built between 1310 and 1340, the best view point for viewing the town. Admission to the castle includes a tour of the dungeon and keep, and the Courthouse Museum, a well preserved Tudor courtroom, and display of Knaresborough history, including some armour worn at the Battle of Marston Moor.

☞ *Well signposted off the Market Place. Open, daily from Easter to end of September. Entry charge.*
☎ *0423-503340.*

Mother Shiptons Cave

This cave on the west side of the Nidd is where England's great prophetess lived 500 years ago. She is said to have foretold the invasion and defeat of the Spanish Armada and the Great Fire of London. Nearby is the Petrifying Well, where porous objects turn to stone extremely fast in the cascades.

☞ *High Bridge, Knaresborough. Signposted from Market Place. Open daily from Easter to Halloween, also Boxing Day to New Year's Day and February half-term, plus Sundays. Admission charge.*
☎ *0423-864600.*

Aldborough

To the north-east of Knaresborough lies a picture postcard village that was the site of one of biggest settlements during the Roman occupation, a complete walled city called *Isurium Brigantum*. The relics can be seen at the Roman Museum, owned by English Heritage. On display is a beautifully preserved tessellated pavement, numerous coins, pottery and other items found during excavations.

☞ *Aldborough is six miles from Knaresborough on the A6055 Boroughbridge road. Museum open daily, Easter-Sep, 106pm. Admission charge.*
☎ *0423-322768.*

Knaresborough Pool

Since opening in 1990, this excellent pool has become part of an excellent family day out for Leeds families, though it's not the sort of place for doing endless lengths. It is 25m. long, and has a leisure area that includes a flume and spa.

☞ *In King James Road. Ring for details of special sessions, lessons and changeable opening times.*
☎ *0423-860011.*

Boating

This is one of the best locations in Yorkshire for leisurely boating on a fine summer's day. The Nidd is not the fasted flowing of rivers, and it slides gently through a wooded gorge past Knaresborough. The river is seen at its best from any of the rowing boats, punts and canoes for hire from Blenkhorns Boathouse. There is also a café.

☞ *At Waterside, Knaresborough. Boathouse open daily from 10am, Easter to end of October.*
☎ *0423-862105.*

Ripon

Despite its traffic problems, Ripon is a pleasant market town (officially, it's a Cathedral "city") that repays a couple of hours of wandering on a day out to the Dales. If you want to look round the shops, the busy market is on Thursdays , and avoid Wednesdays, early closing day. A tradition going back 1100 years is the Ripon Hornblower—a gentleman wearing a three-cornered hat appears every evening at 9pm to sound his horn at the Obelisk in the market place. Called "setting the watch" it originates from the times when the people of Ripon required assurance that all was well.

☞ *North through Harrogate on A61. A frequent bus service runs from Central Bus Station. Tourist Information Centre in Minster Road (summer only).*
☎ *0765-604625.*

Ripon Cathedral

Whatever you do, don't miss a visit to this splendid building. Among its many features is St. Wilfred's Saxon crypt, the oldest in England. Dating from 672, it was built to the dimensions believed to be those of the tomb in which Jesus was laid and from which He rose again. It was here that the monks travelled on Boxing Day, 1132, to begin the construction of Fountains Abbey. The Cathedral Treasury has an exhibition of ecclesiastical silver, there is a Tudor library, medieval screen, art nouveau pulpit and 15th century choir stalls with canopies, ends and misericords that are reckoned to be some of the finest wood-carving in the country.

☞ *Minister Road, signposted from Market Place. Open daily. No admission charge but a donation is invited.*
☎ *0765-604108.*

Police & Prison Museum

An unusual museum, it is housed in what was actually built as a House of Correction in 1686, then subsequently used to accommodate prisoners as Ripon Gaol. In 1887 it became Ripon Police Station, and the museum was opened in the cell block, with displays and exhibits to illustrate how law and order has been maintained in Ripon since the 10th century.

☞ *St. Mary's Gate, Ripon. Open daily, April-October inclusive. Admission charge.*
☎ *0765-690799.*

Fountains Abbey

One of Yorkshire's gems is this great Cistercian ruin near Ripon. From its birth in 1139, it grew big and wealthy as its power and influence spread across the north. The abbey was almost 400ft. long

and with 170ft. tower. There are numerous strolls through the National Trust-owned grounds. Studley Royal Country Park, next door, is 650 acres of ornamental gardens, park and woodland.
☛ *North on A61 for Ripon, then follow signpost for Abbey. Open daily 52 weeks a year. In August & September the Abbey is floodlit. Admission charge.*
☎ *0765-620333.*

Lightwater Valley

This started life as a farming theme park and became a gigantic funfare. Top attraction is classic white-knuckle ride called "The Ultimate", which is claimed to be the world's biggest rollercoaster ride. It runs for 7,475 feet, includes a drop of 162 feet, and takes nearly six minutes. There are also more leisurely boat and steam train rides, bowls and croquet lawns. Skill testing activities include BMX bikes, grand-prix go-karting and an adventure playground.
☛ *Via Harrogate and Ripon on A61, take A6108 signposted Masham. Park is 3m. further on. Special bus service from Central Bus Station in summer. Open, Easter-October, but not daily so ring for details in advance.*
☎ *0767-635368.*

Newby Hall

A famous Adam house, now carefully restored, and contents include the Gobelins Tapestry Room, a gallery of classical statuary and some of Chippendale's finest furniture. Outside, there are 25 acres of award-winning gardens, a Woodland Discovery Walk, miniature steam railway, adventure garden for children, shop, plant stall.
☛ *Signposted off the Ripon-Boroughbridge road, the B6265. Open End Mar to end Sept, Tues-Sun inclusive. Gardens, 11-5pm, Hall & railway 12 noon-4.30pm.*
☎*0423-322583.*

Nidderdale

Many visitors to Nidderdale are at a loss to understand why the area was not included in the Yorkshire Dales National Park. The answer lies in the water—it is the chief gathering ground for the City of Bradford and was left out of the Park at the last minute when it was designated in 1954, because the water engineers feared drastic controls on their reservoir schemes. But you will find most of Nidderdale every bit as beautiful as the National Park, especially the area to the north of Pateley Bridge.
☛ *Two easiest approaches are: 1, though Otley on unclassified Blubberhouses road to Greenhow, or 2, via Pool-in-Wharfedale, turning left over bridge for B6451 at Farnley. Tourist Information Centre (summer only) at Southlands Car Park, Pateley Bridge.*
☎ *0423-711147.*

Pateley Bridge

The "capital" of Nidderdale, a delightful stone-built town spreading up the hillside and attracting thousands of visitors in summer and at weekends all year. Chief attraction is the setting itself, a wonderful place to stroll, shop, play putting and lick ice-creams. The Nidderdale Museum, in an original Victorian workhouse, illustrates the background and life of Dalesfolk.
☛ *The museum is at the Council Offices, opposite the church. Open, Easter-Sept, daily. Oct-Easter, Sundays. Times, 2pm-5pm. Ring to check times. Admission charge.*
☎ *0423-711225.*

How Stean Gorge

This spectacular limestone gorge has been made a safe natural playground thanks to the building of reservoir feeder channels further up the Dale, which draws water off to nearby Gouthwaite. However, the water rises quickly after a thunderstorm and is an impressive sight. Promoted as "the Switzerland of England," How Stean is busy in summer.
☛ *In Upper Nidderdale, signposted from Pateley Bridge. Open all year, sunrise-sunset. Admission charges.*
☎ *0423-75666.*

Brimham Rocks

These grotesque formations of millstone grit are strewn over 50 acres of heather moor above the Nidd, and are one of the most popular beauty spots in North Yorkshire. The National Trust owns the property and does its best to preserve the area from the trampling hordes who arrive with picnics and children. The rocks themselves were hewn by thousands of years of frosts, ice and winds, and some of the rocks have been given strange names that fit their weird shapes, such as Dancing Bear, Druid's Skull, Baboon and Chimney Rock. The greatest marvel of all is Idol Rock, weighing an estimated 200 tons yet resting on a pivot only 12 inches thick.
☛ *Signposted off the B6165 road, three miles east of Pateley Bridge.*

Stump Cross Caverns

Limestone show caves with millstone grit on either side, an extending around four miles underground and about one-third of a mile is open to the public. There are stalagmites and stalactites, crystal rock formations and large rimstone pools, like small Grand Canyons.
☛ *Off the B6265 Pateley Bridge to Grassington road. Open daily, Easter-Oct, 10-5.30pm; Suns Nov-Dec 11-4pm. Admission charge.*
☎ *0756-652780.*

Masham

Famous mainly for its huge market place, loved by TV producers for filming period Yorkshire dramas, and for its brewery.
☛ *North from Leeds on A61, through Harrogate and Ripon, then continuing on A6108. Allow an hour for the drive at weekends.*

Theakston's Brewery

T & R Theakston have been brewing traditional Yorkshire ale since 1827, and now have a national reputation, especially for its strong dark Old Peculier. There is an interesting visitor centre, telling the story of brewing at Masham, and you can watch the coopers at work through a window. Tours of the brewery are available, involving two flights of steep stairs. Numbers are limited. Reserve places.
☛ *Signposted from Market Place. Open, Easter-end Oct, Wed-Sun 10.30-4pm; Nov/Dec, Wed/Sat/Sun 10.30-1pm, 2-4pm.*
☎ *0765-689057.*

Calderdale and Kirklees

Valleys full of Industrial Revolution heritage, Pennine hills and canal paths for bracing walks.

These two areas to the south and south-west of Leeds have between them the biggest concentration of Industrial Revolution heritage attractions in Britain. But while the towns and valleys transform into a giant theme park of Britain's former glory, the moors and countless wooded cloughs provide some of the best walking country to be found outside the National Parks.

Calderdale

There are few parts of Britain where industry and bleak countryside co-exist in such harmony. The mills, chimneys and villages clinging to the steep hillsides seem— after 200 years or so—to be rocky outcrops. As a result, there is little that offends the eye as tourists wander through the area known as The South Pennines. The heart of this area is the valley of Calderdale itself, 20 miles long and spreading from Brighouse in the east to Todmorden in the west. It takes in the fascinating town of Halifax, the Rochdale Canal and airy moors, and the totally surprising tourist centre of Hebden Bridge.

Blackstone Edge

In summer, from a distance, it looks like a hoar frost but closer inspection reveals cotton grass on this most exposed part of the Yorkshire Pennines. When Daniel Defoe trekked across these wild moors in August, 1705, he got lost in a blizzard. See the finest stretch of paved Roman Road in Britain which linked Manchester *(Mancunium)* with Ilkley *(Olicana)*. You reach it via a stretch of the Pennine Way, passing the Aiggin Stone, a medieval landmark. Blackstone Edge is a jumble of rocks offering superb long-distance views when clear.
☞ *Through Halifax & Sowerby Bridge on A58. Access from the A58 near The White House. Good boots essential, also OS Map 109.*

Cragg Vale

This peaceful corner of Calderdale was the centre of a clever counterfeit coining operation in the 18th century. Here it was that David Hartley and friends began clipping the edges of gold and silver coins and melted down the metals to forge new coins. They mostly lived in this tiny valley, through which the singing Elphin Brook flows. Some of the counterfeit coins and the tools they used are displayed in the Hinchliffe Arms and at the museum in Heptonstall.
☞ *Cragg Vale is off the B6138. Turn left at traffic lights on A646 at Mytholmroyd.*

Halifax

What was once the cloth capital of England, became the carpet capital, the toffee capital and—today—the mortgage capital. The approach to Halifax does not inspire the tourist with confidence, but once you've seen some of the Victorian shopping streets and the breathtaking Piece Hall (see below) doubts evaporate. Piece Hall also houses an Art Gallery, specialising in photography, prints and textiles. There is a Pre-Industrial Museum, telling the story of domestic cloth manufacture in Calderdale. And next door is one of the best museums in Yorkshire, the Calderdale Industrial Museum. Hear what it was like to work in the mill, smell toffee boiling at Macintoshes, see spinning jennies, beam engines, and much more.
☞ *The quickest route by car is to take the M621 and M62 to exit 26, then A58 into Halifax. Regular West Riding buses from Central Bus Station and trains from Leeds City. Tourist Information Centre at Piece Hall will give opening times and list of special events.*
☎ *0422-368725.*

Hardcastle Crags

Known locally a "Little Switzerland", Hardcastle Crags is a National Trust property. It is a popular walking and picnic area, being an uncommonly picturesque wooded clough dominated by a series of millstone grit rocks that give the valley its name. It starts just beyond Midgehole and stretches for three miles up Hebden Dale to the moors at Blake Dean. There is a good nature trail which links with several

*First opened in 1779 Halifax's truly awesome **Piece Hall** was where lengths of hand-woven cloth called "pieces" were brought to market by cottage weavers before mills and the industrial revolution. Now restored to its original glory, the huge quadrangle's colonnaded galleries contain 315 rooms that have become art and craft shops, antiques, bookshops, etc. There is regular entertainment out in the huge central courtyard, such as brass bands and jugglers, dance and theatre groups, and open air markets on Fridays and Saturdays, with a fleamarket on Thursdays. Yorkshire's only surviving cloth hall is now joined to an art gallery and two museums. See Halifax, above, for more information.*

other interesting walks in the area. A leaflet is available at the Information Centre in Hebden Bridge (see below).

☛ *Signposted off A6033 Hebden Bridge-Keighley Road.*

Hebden Bridge

There is a constantly changing programme of things to see and do in this tourist resort of post-industrial Britain so your first stop should be at the Information Centre. Wander round the streets, and find interesting shops with hardly a High Street chainstore in sight. The area gives a good example of how the Industrial Revolution developed. On the hilltop is the village of Heptonstall, where weavers worked in the cottage industry. Then, when water power began to drive looms, mills were built down in the valley, thus the growth of Hebden Bridge. In the late 1960s, when the mills were in decline, the town was "adopted" by a substantial hippy element because property was so cheap. There is much arts & crafts activity, and still a whiff of incense in the air. Highlights of the town include cruises on the Rochdale Canal, tours of Walkleys Clog Factory, and just outside town on the Keighley road, Automobilia, a museum of vintage cars and motorcycles. There is even a house of horror at Hebden Crypt in Valley Road. Best day to visit Hebden Bridge is Thursday, when there is a lively open market.

☛ *Nine miles west of Halifax on A646 (Burnley sign). Regular train services from Leeds on Rochdale line. The Tourist Information Centre is at 1 Bridge Gate, HX7 8EX.*
☎ *0422-843831.*

Heptonstall

This historic hill top village gives a unique glimpse of life in the Pennines nearly 200 years ago. Little has changed in the main street, which remains delightfully free of tourists compared with Haworth. It has its own literary connection: the American poet, Sylvia Plath, lies buried in the churchyard. Another famous resident is David Hartley, "King" of the notorious Cragg Vale Coiners (see 166). The story of the weavers' cottage in-

dustry is told in the Heptonstall Grammar School Museum. Also see the second oldest Octagonal Chapel in the world. The Methodist Chapel (1764) was planned by John Wesley and he preached in it while it was under construction.

☛ *Well signposted off main Todmorden road west of Hebden Bridge. Steep climb to top. The Museum is in the main street, and open summer weekends 1pm-5pm. Small admission charge.*
☎ *0422-354823.*

Shibden Hall

An attractive 15th century half-timbered mansion on the east side of Halifax, Shibden Hall is famous for its magnificent furniture, most of it exactly where it was at the time of Cromwell. Outside in the large parkland that surrounds the hall is a folk museum, arranged as an early 19th century village. It includes a collection of horse-drawn vehicles and a miniature railway.

☛ *On the A58 approach to Halifax. Open, Mar-Nov Mon-Sat 10-6pm, Sun 12-5pm; Feb, Sun only 2-5pm. Closed Dec & Jan. Small admission charge.*
☎ *0422-352246.*

Todmorden Amateur Astronomy Centre

The only planetarium in Yorkshire lies in a basin surrounded by hilltops near Todmorden, the perfect location to eliminate skyglow from neighbouring small towns. It accepts bookings for tours of the site, which include a camera obscura and planetarium show. Parties must be up to 25 persons. The planetarium has a dome with a white ceiling onto which is projected the night sky. A commentary is provided by the resident astronomer, Linda Simonian. "Star Parties", an American idea, are held three times a year.

☛ *At Clough Bank, Todmorden, on the A681 Todmorden-Bacup road. From Leeds area, reached on A646 beyond Halifax and Hebden Bridge.*
☎ *0706-816964.*

Wainhouse Tower

This is Halifax's equivalent of The Telecom Tower, an octagonal 270ft-high stone chimney con-

structed in 1871 for use with a dye-works but never actually brought into service. It is, without doubt, the most impressive architectural folly in the whole of Yorkshire, and it is now occasionally open to the public. The central staircase has 403 steps, and it goes without saying that the view from the elaborate balconies is stunning.

☛ *You can't miss it, off King Cross, Halifax, on the route west for Hebden Bridge. Open for group visits, maximum 50. Admission charge.*
☎ *0422-359454.*

Kirklees

The administrative area centred on Huddersfield extends from the southern boundary of Leeds, through Dewsbury and Batley to the bleak Pennine moors at Holme Moss. In between there are many heritage attractions from the Industrial Revolution, interesting markets, several important manor houses and—of course—TV's "Summer Wine" country. Besides these static features, there are numerous walks and activities.

☛ *Depending on your destination, there are several access points off the M62 between junctions 27 (Leeds end) and 22. See Huddersfield & Holmfirth for Tourist Information Centres. For guided walks and activities, call Kirklees Countryside Service.*
☎ *0484-431433.*

Bagshaw Museum

An eccentric Victorian millowner's mansion. Displays include local and natural history, oriental ceramics, ancient Egypt, divine creatures and mythical beats. An adjacent Butterfly Conservation Centre illustrates the life cycle of British butterflies and moths.

☛ *At Wilton Park, Batley. Signposted off A652 in Batley. Open Mon-Sat 10-5pm, Sun 1-5pm. Admission free.*
☎ *0924-472514.*

Dewsbury

Most visitors to Dewsbury come for what is reckoned to be the best open market in Yorkshire. There are more than 400 stalls, with cloth and yarn specialities. Traditional street snacks like tripe and black pudding abound, and there's also a well-preserved Victorian covered market. The centre of town has some fine architecture, such as the Town Hall (1888) and the Co-op Building (1878). See Dewsbury's history, especially the story of re-processed woollen cloth ("shoddy") for which it is famous, at the museum.

☛ *Seven miles south of Leeds, via Dewsbury Road (A653). Frequent trains from Leeds City and buses from Central Bus Station. Market Days Wed & Sat, bric-a-brac Fri. Museum at Crows Nest Park, Heckmondwike Rd., open Mon-Sat 10-5pm.*

☎ *Dewsbury Information Office, Dewsbury 465151.*

Huddersfield

A town of just under 100,000 population, it is not the prettiest in Yorkshire but there are some interesting corners for those willing to explore. Take the shopping centre: there are few surviving pieces of Victoriana as splendid as Byram Arcade. Also see the restored Brook Street Market for bric-a-

brac on Tuesdays and Saturdays. Around the town, see Castle Hill, off Lumb Lane in Almondbury, a striking landmark, an iron age fort now crowned by the Jubilee Tower, built in 1898 (open in summer and Bank Hols). Or see the Tolson Memorial Museum in Ravensknowle Park, including farming, transport and woollen industry galleries. Huddersfield Art Gallery is worth a visit for its 20th century British paintings, including works by Francis Bacon, Edward Burra, and members of the Camden Town Group.

☛ *Easily found off M62 junction 24. Tolson Museum is open daily throughout year, but times vary. Art Gallery above the Library in Princess Alexandra Walk, open daily ex. Sunday. Ask for leaflets from Huddersfield Tourist Info Centre, 3/5 Albion St.*

☎ *0484-430808. Tolson Museum: 530591. Gallery: 513808.*

Oakwell Hall

A gem of Tudor workmanship, this moated manor house dates from 1583. It was once occupied by the notorious Henry Batt, a sharp-deal-

ing financier who stole the bell of Birstall Church. Like the Red House, it appeared in Charlotte Brontë's *Shirley*. It is now the magnificent centrepiece of an 87-acre Country Park, with a visitor centre that includes a countryside interpretative section, barn, shop and tearoom.

☛ *In Nutter Lane, Birstall. Signposted off A652 at Birstall. Open daily throughout the year. Phone for opening times. Admission charge.*

☎ *0924-474926.*

Red House Museum

In 1660 William Taylor built the Red House and his descendants lived there until 1920. They were farmers, woolen cloth makers and bankers, playing an important part in West Yorkshire's domination of the world's woollen textiles industry. Refurbished just as it was in the 1830s, it is now open to the public. See it just as it was when Charlotte Brontë used to visit her schoolfriend, Mary Taylor. The house appears as "Briarmains" in Charlotte's novel, *Shirley*. There are craft workshops and children's activities. Admission charge.

☛ *In Oxford Road, Gomersal. Take M621, then A62 before M62, following Cleckheaton sign. Or take West Riding Brighouse/Elland service from Central Bus St. Open daily throughout year, but telephone for variable times.*

☎ *0274-872165.*

Tunnel End Canal

The Huddersfield Narrow Canal includes the longest tunnel on the highest section of canal in Great Britain. The tunnel, known as "One of the Seven Wonders of the Waterways" disappears under the Pennines at Tunnel End, Marsden. Nearby, there has been established a canal and countryside centre. Although the canal is now closed to through navigation, a short section has been restored. There are towpath walks, with picnic areas.

☛ *In Reddisher Road, Marsden. Take M62 to junction 23, then follow signs for A62 Slaithwaite and Marsden. Open Tue-Sun. Closed Mon throughout year, and Fri through winter.*

☎ *0484-846062.*

*One wonders what **Holmfirth** will be like once the popular TV series "Last of The Summer Wine" has long gone. For the moment, it's like a seaside resort at weekends and most days in school holidays. There is no denying its scenic appeal, tucked at the bottom of a steep valley. Besides the shops, craft galleries, and numerous cafés and wine bars there is a good museum full of saucy "wish you were here" postcards. And a gallery shows memorabilia from the TV series, which began in 1972. You can even buy a map to see where Nora Battye lives.*

☛ *Westbound on M62 to junction 24, then through Huddersfield on A6024. Postcard Museum, in Huddersfield Road, open Mon-Sat 1-5pm, Sun 1-5pm. Admission free. Holmfirth Tourist Information Centre is open daily at 49/51 Huddersfield Rd.*

☎ *0484-684992.*

The Wakefield Area

Good shopping, fascinating parklands, an important castle and one of the North's top museums

Three hundred years ago, Daniel Defoe passed through Wakefield and found "a large, handsome, rich clothing town, full of people and full of trade." Not much has changed, with the exception of Wakefield's growling traffic. Today, the town is the centre of a large area covering what used to be known as the Yorkshire coalfield before the industry contracted. It includes Castleford, Pontefract, Ossett and numerous mining villages that are worth exploring.

Castleford

This town on the south-east fringe of Leeds, part of the Wakefield district, was an important Roman fort called *Lagentium*. Today, it is an unexciting place jammed between the Aire and Calder Navigation and the M62, a centre of timber yards and open-cast mining activities. Castleford Pottery enjoyed a modest fame 200 years ago, and Henry Moore was born here. Now all this history is all neatly tied up at the Castleford Museum Room. There is a busy market place (open stalls Mon/Thur/Fri/Sat) and a traditional covered market.

☛ *By road, take A639 (Pontefract) sign. Regular West Riding service from Central Bus Station, and Metro trains from Leeds City. Museum is at Castleford Library, Carton St. Open, 10.30-5pm Mon-Sat; 2.30-5pm Sun.*
☎ *0977-559552.*

Nostell Priory

One of the world's finest collections of Thomas Chippendale furniture (including his famous Dolls House) is on show at this fine 18th century Palladian Mansion built by the Winn family from their coal mining fortune. Other features are paintings by Holbein and large grounds with charming lakeside walks and a rose garden. Adventure playground for the kids, and craft demonstrations.

☛ *Five miles south east of Wakefield on the A638 Doncaster road (Doncaster or Brierley/Grimethorpe bus). Open daily, Easter-October, 12-5pm or 11-5pm on Sun.*
☎ *0924-863892.*

Pontefract

It's difficult to believe that Pontefract was once the centre of government for Yorkshire. Here it was that Ilbert de Lacy, one of William the Conqueror's chief supporters, built his castle in the late 1080s. For over a century, the de Lacys ruled with an iron fist. Later, it housed Richard II, who died here, and James I of Scotland. Finally, it was wrecked by Cromwell's men in 1649. Now a scheduled monument, it is open to the public, with a visitor centre in Castle Chain. While in Pontefract, visit the superb museum in an Art Nouveau building, where Civil War history and the famous liquorice industry are well displayed. Outside there's an open market every Wednesday.

☛ *Via M1 and M62 to exit 32. Or regular West Riding bus; metro trains from Leeds City. Castle open, Ap-Oct 8.30-dusk (10.30 weekends); Nov-Mar 5pm close. Museum in Salter Row, open daily.*
☎ *0977-797289.*

Wakefield

Packed with shoppers every day, especially at the excellent Ridings Centre, one of the first conservatory style of arcades complete with food village and playgroup. The town also has two covered markets, a good range of pubs for real-ale buffs, and an outstanding museum. On the first floor is a collection of international importance, chronicling the life and work of Charles Waterton, the pioneering Victorian naturalist, traveller and explorer, who lived locally. Wakefield Art Gallery houses works by sculptors Hepworth and Moore. Architecturally alone,

Wakefield is worth a visit. See the splendid County Hall, built in 1898, the 170-year-old Court House, and the elegant St. John's Square (behind gallery).

☛ *By car, south on M1 to junction 41. Regular West Riding service from Central Bus Station, and trains from Leeds City. For leaflets on the town's attractions call at the Tourist Information Centre, Town Hall, Wood St., WF1 2HQ.*
☎ *0924-295000/295001.*

Yorkshire Mining Museum

The way things are going, this excellent museum is all that will be left of Yorkshire's once great coal industry. Find out what life is like 450ft underground, at both a modern coal face and see how it used to be dug with bare hands at a pre-mechanisation seam. Caphouse was never really modernised, and many of its best Victorian features remain, such as the pit pony, and the antiquated pit baths. The slagheaps are now picnic areas, the pithead an exhibition centre and video theatre.

☛ *In New Road, Overton. Take the M1 to 39 (Denby Dale road) and follow the A636, turning right on the A637 Huddersfield sign. Opening times vary—ring for details.*
☎ *0924-848806.*

Yorkshire Sculpture Park

One of the many nationally important facilities on the Leeds doorstep, this collection is set in the beautiful park of Bretton Hall. Weird and wonderful shapes abound, many new exhibits arriving for each new season. Of course, Henry Moore and Barbara Hepworth work is featured, along with young sculptors. There are often on-site demonstrations, and indoor facilities include a gallery, workshop, café and shop. A recent addition is the Access Sculpture Trail, bringing art and nature together with special emphasis on access for the disabled. A find day out.

☛ *South on M1 to exit 38. Take Huddersfield sing and left into West Bretton village. Parking ample. Open daily, 10-6pm (summer) and 10-4pm (winter).*
☎ *0924-830302.*

The Yorkshire Dales

A distinctive landscape of green valleys, pretty villages and gentle hills honeycombed with caves

Designated a National Park in 1954, the Yorkshire Dales cover 680 square miles of the Pennines. Most of it is within an hour's drive of Leeds, or accessible along the famous Settle-Carlisle railway line. The dominant landscape is that of flat, grassy valley bottoms drained by stony rivers, with steep bracken-covered or wooded hillsides rising to over 600 feet in height. Limestone forms the most distinctive rock, best seen around Malham, Austwick and Ingleton or in the miles of drystone walls and ancient barns throughout the park. The best way to get to know the diverse areas of the Yorkshire Dales is by joining the extensive programme of guided walks. For the programme, contact any of the Dales National Park Information Centres listed below.

Airedale & Wharfedale

Being so close to the Leeds-Bradford conurbation, these two dales are by far the busiest. They also have the highest concentration of special attractions, many of them

ESSENTIAL INFORMATION

National Park Centres
Aysgarth Falls, Wensleydale
☎ 0969-663424.
Clapham, Village Centre.
☎ 05242-51419.
Grassington, Hebden Road.
☎ 0756-752774.
Hawes, The Station Yard.
☎ 0969-667450.
Malham Village Centre
☎ 07293-363.
Sedbergh Main Street
☎ 05396-201125.
Dales Weather Forecast
☎ 0891-500748.
Map
OS Sheet 98 (Wensleydale & Wharfedale) essential for walking.

undercover if the rain starts. Everything listed here is within an hour's drive of Leeds, so that they are ideal for a quick afternoon outing. Airedale, as far as the Yorkshire Dales National Park goes, is really Malhamdale, but we have included Skipton because many often stop at the town as part of a longer day out. Wharfedale continues right up as far as Buckden and Hubberholme, where organised attractions are few, but signposted walks are many.

Bolton Abbey

The countryside straddling this long curve in the River Wharfe is hard to beat. Centrepiece is Bolton Priory, founded by Augustinian monks in 1151. At its broadest, the river runs smoothly through rocky shallows and many enjoy picnic spreads on the flat, grassy banks. Ancient stepping stones and several bridges ford the Wharfe. The Cavendish Pavilion provides everything from ice cream to complete meals. From the car park, there are numerous walks upstream, through the Strid woods (good birdwatching, fungi and wildflower identification in season) or follow the beautiful walk for the Valley of Desolation or over the moor to Simons Seat.

☛ *Via Ilkley and A65 turning right at start of Addingham bypass on B6160, crossing A59 at Devonshire Arms to Cavendish Pavilion. Limited bus services from Ilkley in season. Check with Estate Office in autumn, as some walks are closed.*
☎ *075-671-227.*

Embsay Steam Railway

This is one of the shortest private lines in Britain, running just two-and-a-half miles back and forth between Embsay and Holywell. Embsay Station was opened by the Midland Railway in 1888, a typical country station which has been beautifully restored. Holywell is a rural halt, where milk churns and

other agricultural produce were once collected for market.
☛ *Signposted off the Skipton bypass and situated approximately 2 miles from Skipton town centre. Trains run every Sunday throughout the year, Tues & Sat in July, daily in Aug (ex. Mon & Fri).*
☎ *Talking timetable 0756-795189. Other enquiries 0756-794727.*

Grassington

Grassington has an attractive cobbled market place that can be as packed as Trafalgar Square at peak holiday times. Numerous walks signposted in the area, including the Dales Way over the hill to Kettlewell, or beside the Wharfe at Grass Wood. The Upper Wharfedale Museum is in the market place, containing many collections of Dales farming implements, antiques, etc.
☛ *To Skipton bypass, taking B6265 north. The Museum is open Nov-Easter Sat & Sun only 2pm-4.30pm; Easter to Oct daily 2pm-4.30pm. Other times by arrangement.*
☎ *0756-752800.*

Kilnsey Park

This multi-activity centre in Upper Wharfedale has steadily expanded and now includes "all-weather" attractions like a Daleslife Visitor Centre, trout farm feeding area, plus farm shop, fly-fishing, garden centre with accent on herbal, alpine & aquatic plants, picnic area, pony trekking centre, and adventure playground. The Daleslife Centre is particularly interesting, illustrating dry-stone wall technique and other local themes. Nearby is Kilnsey Crag, where you can watch rock-climbers performing like spiders on coloured webs.
☛ *Take A65 to Skipton bypass, B6160 north. Between Threshfield and Kettlewell. Open daily, 9am-5.30pm (dusk in winter).*
☎ *0756-752861.*

Littondale

This off-shoot from Wharfedale is, as you would expect, quieter. The footpath along the glacial valley's deep floor from Arncliffe to Litton, following the musical River Skirfare, is one of the nicest walks in the Dales, and one of the least demanding. A more energetic ramble is up the eastern side to Old Cote Moor, signposted from Arncliffe. The latter village was the original Beckindale in "Emmerdale Farm" and its unspoilt pub the first Woolpack.

☞ *Take A65 to Skipton bypass, north on B6265 past Threshfield. Littondale road branches to left on narrow road.*

Parceval Hall

Originally a 15th century Dales farmhouse, in the 1920s it was bought by Sir William Milner, an Oxford-educated architect and brilliant landscape gardener. He turned the farmhouse into a classic Yorkshire gritstone residence, which is now used as a Bradford Diocesan retreat. The 16-acre woodland garden he created is open to the public and contains many beautiful plants, shrubs and trees which are seldom seen growing at such a height, or so far north. Especially interesting to birdwatchers and botanists. Streams, cascades, and pools abound and visitors can see Sir

William's private chapel, built on the scale of a Japanese Teahouse.

☞ *Via A65 to Addingham, taking the B6160 through Bolton Abbey, crossing Wharfe at Barden Tower, turning right past Appletreewick. The Gardens are open daily, Easter-Oct 10am-6pm.*

☎ *075672-311*

Skipton

The "Gateway to the Dales". Its name comes from the "Sheeptown" of the Angles but only herds squeezing through Skipton's streets today are tourists. Excellent shopping, especially on Saturday when there is a good market. The top attraction in the town is Skipton Castle, with its tranquil Conduit Court, shaded by an ancient yew tree. Over 900 years old, it is one of the best-preserved medieval castles in Britain. Most of the others were knocked down by Cromwell.

☞ *West on A65, or regular buses and trains from Leeds. Castle open every day 10-6pm (Sun open 2pm, closes 4pm Oct-Feb). Admission charge.*

☎ *0756-792442.*

The further west you go into the Dales, the more interesting the scenery becomes. The busiest honeypots are at Clapham, Horton-in-Ribblesdale and Dent. Elsewhere, it is possible to escape the crowds and enjoy some of the finest walking country in Britain. For this you will need OS Map 98 and Alfred Wainwright's brilliant little book "Walks in Limestone Country". See the area on the Settle-Carlisle railway line

Dentdale

For many, the greenest of all Dales. In summer, the centre of Dent village is surging with visitors, so go there early if you want to see the time-warp cobbled streets at their best. The best walks are beside the beautiful River Dee. Follow the Dales Way upstream for some interesting water-leaps and mini-gorges. Or down to Sedbergh (10 miles there and back) for some fine wooded sections, detouring to visit the signposted Brigflatts, birthplace of the Quaker movement.

☞ *To Skipton and west along A65, turning north at Settle on B6479, right at Ribblehead on B6255, then left for Dentdale a few miles on. Alternatively, use the Settle-Carlisle line. England's highest station is at Dent, although 4m. from the village.*

Falconry Centre

Falconry is one of the oldest sports, and this amazing new centre is where to come to learn all about it. Education and conservation are the keywords here. Many species of birds of prey can be seen, such as vultures, eagles, hawks, falcons and owls. Throughout the day, at regular intervals, free-flying demonstrations are given. Audience participation is encouraged, and you can be photographed holding one of these superb specimens. There is a tearoom and shop.

☞ *On the A65 on the western end of the Settle bypass. Open daily, ex. Xmas Day, from 10am until dusk.*

☎ *07292-5164.*

The green grass and dazzling limestone of Malham is one of the finest sights in the Dales. Centre of attraction is the 240ft. vertical cliff of **Malham Cove,** *pictured above. At the top is the now-dry valley along which the infant River Aire flowed before the Ice Age, plunging over the edge in what must have been a fantastic waterfall. Now, the stream runs underground, to appear at Aire Head Springs, on the Pennine Way half a mile south of the village. You can climb the staircase up one side and see the brain-like limestone pavement at the top. Walk further on to Malham Tarn, a large sheet of water trapped by a glacial moraine.*

☞ *Take A65 past Skipton, turning right in Gargrave. A National Park information centre, car park and plenty of refreshments .*

Ingleborough Caves

The subterranean world of the Yorkshire Dales is not the exclusive preserve of potholers. There are several ways in which visitors can see the extraordinary limestone structures fashioned by underground streams. The most dramatic is Gaping Gill, a cathedral-like hall to which you descend 340 feet on a winch. The gear is operated at the Spring Bank Holiday by Bradford Pothole Club, and at August Bank Holiday by Craven Pothole Club. On the walk up from Clapham, there is magnificent Ingleborough Cave, open to the public since 1837.

☛ *Clapham is a 90 min. drive west on A65. Check times with the Nationa Park Centre, Clapham.* ☎ *05242-51419.*

Ingleton Waterfalls

There is no short walk in Britain as exhilarating as the path round Ingleton's gorgeous waterfalls. Every step of the four-mile circuit reveals a new water-leap, bigger and more spectacular than before. Follow the River Doe up a narrow wooded gorge, past Pecca Falls to the majestic Thornton Force, a staple of Yorkshire calendars. The path cuts across the green hillside to the valley of the River Greta, where more watery ecstasies are presented in the form of Beezley Falls, Baxengill Gorge, Snow Falls and the grand finale of Cat Leap Fall.

☛ *About 50 miles west on the A65, via Skipton and Settle bypasses. The waterfalls are on private ground and an admission is charged. Car parking at the falls (signposted) or in Ingleton village centre.*

Kingdale

A delightful dale, and another place where the humble walker can see what actually lies under the limestone dales. The easiest way is the short walk to Yordas Cave, a large cavern with a thunderous waterfall, where you need a torch and wellies to appreciate its full splendour. This was once a showcase, but now anyone can enter free of charge. If you've brought your walking boots, continue west up the side of Gragareth

to the Turbary Road, once used for cutting peat but now one of the best walks in the Dales, especially for viewing the entrances to numerous potholes. It is possible to crawl through part of the Rowten system. But stay well clear of the great chasm of Rowten Pot itself, on the east side of the road.

☛ *As to Ingleton (above) but continue through village on road to Dent. Yordas Cave is at the foot of a plantation on the left approx. one mile beyond Braida Garth farm.*

Norber

This area is not well known, but those who discover it return often. Norber is a gently sloping hill littered with erratic boulders, described by Alfred Wainwright as "like a wrecked Stonehenge". Hundreds of huge rocks were left when the ice melted thousands of years ago, some of them left balancing in the most astonishing positions. They make good subjects for photographers.

☛ *Take A65 past Settle, branching right to park in the village of Austwick. Norber is a good three-hour return walk up the lane for Wharfe and Crummack.*

Settle

Since being bypassed in the 1980s, Settle has rediscovered its former charm. Visit for shopping, and discover streets like Shambles and Constitution Hill. The Museum of North Craven Life in Chapel Street displays the history of the Settle-Carlisle Line, and items from local doctors, pharmacists and shoemakers. The famous Victoria Cave, on the limestone scarp above the town, is reached by the fit via Banks Lane. Discoveries here include relics of Neolithic cave dwellers.

☛ *An hour's drive west on A65 road, via Skipton. The Museum is open Easter-June, Sat, Sun & Bank Hols 2-5pm; July Sep Tues-Sun & Bank Hols. Entrance fee.* ☎ *0279-822854.*

Settle-Carlisle Railway

Once compared with York Minster and Hadrian's Wall, the Settle-Carlisle railway line is indeed an extraordinary feat of engineering.

Built between 1869-76, it cuts right through the Pennines, using 325 bridges, 21 viaducts and 14 tunnels. The upkeep of the line was said to be so expensive that British Rail tried to close it in the 1980s, but fortunately backed down after a massive public outcry. Now you can travel to several reopened stations in the Dales: Horton-in-Ribblesdale, Ribblehead, Dent and Garsdale. Or continue through the lovely Eden Valley. One of the best days out is if you use the train from Leeds to visit the famous Appleby Horse Fair, the biggest event on the gipsy calendar. The main day is always the second Wednesday of June. Leaflets detailing special steam train excursions along the line are available at info. centres. There is a good programme of guided walks which use the stations along the line as the starting and finish points. If you would like to help maintain interest in this historic line, send an s.a.e. to: The Friends of the Settle-Carlisle Line, 16 Pickard Court, Leeds LS15 9AY.

☛ *Direct trains begin at Leeds, Shipley, Saltaire, Bingley, Keighley and Skipton. Best services for walkers are between May and October.*

The Three Peaks

The premier challenge walk in Northern England is the Three Peaks, a 26-mile circuit involving nearly 5,000 feet of ascent. It's easy walking mostly, but best on a fine spring day, when there's plenty of daylight. Begin at Horton-in-Ribblesdale, following the Pennine Way to the summit of Penyghent (2,273ft), past the great chasm of Hull Pot to Ribblehead, launching pad for Whernside (2,419ft). The climax is the tabletop summit of Ingleborough (2,373ft). Clock in at the Penyghent Café and qualify for the Three Peaks certificate and tie if you finish within 12 hours.

☛ *West on A65 to Settle, north on B6479 to Penyghent Cafe. Card-clock is free but book in advance. Start between 8am-9.15am (8.30am start in winter). Avoid last Sunday in April (fell race) and last Sun in Sept (Cyclo-cross race).* ☎ *072-96-333.*

Wensleydale

An unusually broad dale with an unusually broad range of things to see and do. For a start, there's all the James Herriot connections. Askrigg was Darrowby in the long-running "All Creatures Great and Small" and you can see Skeldale House and the pub across the road, just as they were in the TV series. There are good walks beside the River Ure, craft shops and galleries to browse through, and several stately homes, and fine markets at Hawes (Tuesday) and Leyburn (Friday). Wensleydale may be two hours' drive from Leeds, but there's enough to keep you interested for a week.

☛ *The scenic route is via Skipton and north through Wharfedale and Langstrathdale. A quicker way is north through Harrogate, Ripon, Masham and Leyburn.*

Bolton Castle

Bolton Castle, on the north side of the river near Leyburn, is a well preserved medieval fortress, where Mary Queen of Scots was once imprisoned. There are numerous halls and chambers, a monk's cell, armourer's forge, ale house, threshing floor, dungeon, battlements to walk along, historical tableaux, arms and suits of armour, tapestries, and a period nursery. And since most of it is under cover, it's a good place to take shelter when the rain comes on.

☛ *Signposted at Redmire, west of Leyburn on unclassified road running north of the A684. Open 10-5pm daily, March to Mid-Nov; Nov-Mar tours by arrangement. Admission charge.*

☎ *0969-23981.*

Hawes

Hawes is the "capital" of the area, the second highest town in England (Alston is higher). There's an excellent Dales Countryside Museum and Hawes National Park Centre at the old station, with the area's two famous industries well covered—cheesemaking and clockmaking. This is the famous Hartley/Ingilby collection, plus much more on today's scene in the Dales. Also in Hawes, see the candlemakers and the ropeworks. Walk the Pennine Way to Hardraw, to visit the 100ft. waterfall behind the Green Dragon pub. Down the dale are the picturesque Aysgarth Falls, three wide rocky river steps.

☛ *See Wensleydale introduction for directions. Hawes is on the A684, between Leyburn and Sedbergh. Museum open Easter-Oct inc. daily 10-5pm. Some winter opening (ring for details).*

☎ *0969-667450.*

Middleham

Once the capital of Wensleydale, Middleham has handed over its trade to Leyburn, but the sloping market place is perhaps the quaintest in Yorkshire. The hills rising above the town to Coverdale are a busy training ground for race-horses (Middleham is one of the key stables in England) but the main attraction is Middleham Castle. It was once known as the "Windsor of the North". Richard III lived here for many years.

☛ *On A6106 north of Ripon and Masham. Castle open daily Easter-end Sept, 10-6pm; winter Tues-Sun 10-4pm. Closed for lunch 1-2pm.*

☎ *0969-23899.*

Swaledale

The farthest of the Dales from Leeds, and the quietest. The Swale is the fastest flowing river in England, and grows from not much more than a beck up at Keld, to a raging torrent at the splendid Georgian town of Richmond. This reflects life in Swaledale itself, with a peaceful atmosphere at the head of the valley, and a bustling, noisy market downstream.

☛ *Scenic route is from Hawes (see above) over the Buttertubs Pass. Quickest approach is via Leyburn (Harrogate and Ripon road from Leeds) and taking Richmond and Reeth signposts from A6108.*

Reeth

Reeth was once much more prominent than it is today. Standing round the biggest green in Yorkshire, its prosperity was based on the extensive lead mining that took place in the nearby hills in the 17th and 18th centuries. Surrounded by high dale tops, and marking the confluence of the Swale with Arkle Beck, its situation makes it a great favourite with photographers. There are several excellent pubs, tearooms and craft shops. The main indoor attraction is the Swaledale Folk Museum, which tells the story of lead mining, farming and other Dales life over several centuries.

☛ *West of Richmond on the B6270. Museum open Good Friday-end Oct, daily 10.30-6pm.*

☎ *0748-84517.*

Richmond

One of England's most beautiful towns, Richmond stands high above the Swale. The big, sloping market place is the hub of activity, with a fine open market on Saturdays. The streets that lead off in all directions are mostly late 18th century and early 19th century, their façades well preserved. Among the many attractions are the Green Howards Regimental Museum in Trinity Church Square; the Richmondshire Museum in Ryders Wynd (includes the original Herriot surgery TV set); and the Theatre Royal (c.1788), one of only two Georgian theatres left (the other is at Bristol). The dramatic castle was built from 1071.

☛ *To Leyburn, and north on A6108. Allow up to two hours for drive. A Tourist Information Centre is in Friary Gardens, Queens Road.*

☎ *0748-850252.*

Upper Swaledale

For many, this corner of the Dales is the best, especially outside weekends and school holidays. Stone villages like Muker, Thwaite and Keld are altogether from another age, nestling on the valley floor. The walk up to the village from Muker has everything. A fine green dale without the accompaniment of noisy traffic, green fields, bracken-covered hillsides, fascinating old mine workings, a fine river, dramatic waterfalls and the cutest village in Yorkshire. Nothing but peace and quiet.

☛ *Continue west from Reeth on B6270.*

The York Area

A cathedral city full of museums. One Britain's most popular tourist destinations is right on the doorstep of Leeds

The history of York is the history of England. The hordes of tourists surging through the streets in summer are simply the latest invasion, and it has seen many. In A.D. 71, the Roman Ninth Legion marched in, established a garrison under Petilius Cerealis from which to keep control of the unruly Brigantes, and called it *Eboracum*. When the Romans left, the Angles were not far behind, making it in 634 the capital of Deira, their royal and ecclesiastical centre that spread to Northumbria. Next came the Danes in 867, burning it then rebuilding what they called Jorvik, from which York is derived. When the Normans arrived after 1066, they promptly burned it down again, then rebuilt the walls that you see today. Through the Middle Ages, York was allowed to grow into a magnificent city, with the great Minster at its heart. And today, the shape of York is basically the same 263 acres that the Normans developed almost 1000 years ago. It is the most perfectly preserved medieval city in Europe.

There are shops, good restaurants, pubs & wine bars, museums, churches and monuments galore. Whatever the weather, York can entertain. And should you finally think you've done everything, get out to surrounding districts.

☛ *York is 25 miles east of Leeds along the A64, and also served by regular bus and train services. But York has acute traffic problems, especially in summer, at weekends and in the Christmas period, so use public transport or the Park and Ride Schemes (a leaflet is available by post from the Tourist Information Centres De Grey Rooms, Exhibition Square, York, YO1 2HB.)*
☎ *0904-621756.*

York

York Minster

Europe's largest medieval cathedral (below) is also York's top attraction. Stepping through the door is the most humbling of experiences, and you will be awe-struck until the moment you leave. Built

of Tadcaster limestone between 1220 and 1472, there had been at least four other churches on that site. Don't miss the breathtaking great west window (the tracery stonework is heart-shaped); the choir screen (1475-1500) has statues of Kings of England from William the Conqueror to Henry VI; and find the ornate tomb of Archbishop Walter De Gray (1225) who was responsible for building the transept. Also, see The Crypt, The Undercroft & Treasury, the great museum of Minster archaeology, church plate and other valuables. Or climb the 198ft. Central Tower for stunning views of York and the surrounding countryside. And as you leave, don't forget your donation.
☛ *Entrance is off Deangate. Open daily from 7am to dusk.*
☎ *0904-624426.*

Jorvik

The incomparable Jorvik Viking Centre is one of the finest museums in Britain, a new concept in displaying and interpreting the past for present generations. Built on the site of the excavation of Coppergate, visitors sit in time-cars and are whisked back 1000 years to an exact reconstruction of the street, complete with people

The magnificent York Minster, Northern Europe's finest medieval cathedral

and even the authentic sounds and smells of the time. They pass through the "dig" then wander through an exhibition of thousands of artifacts of Viking York.

☛ *In Coppergate, York YO1 1NT Open daily Ap-Oct 9am-7pm; Nov-Mar 9am-5.30pm. Admission charge.*
☎ *0904-643211.*

The ARC

A brand new hands-on exploration of archaeology for visitors of all ages. Located in a restored medieval church near the Shambles, it allows visitors to sort and date authentic finds—Roman tiles, medieval pottery, bone fragments from Viking times etc. Sift through laboratory trays and see how the rubbish from the past reveal clues about how our ancestors lived. It's run by the Jorvik Centre.

☛ *ARC stands for Archaeological Resource Centre, and is in St. Saviourgate (round corner from The Shambles). Open, Ap-Oct inc. Mon-Fri 10-5pm, Sat & Sun 1-5pm. Nov, Feb & March Mon-Fri 10-5pm. Closed Good Fri. Admission charge.*
☎ *0904-654324.*

York Castle Museum

Another "must" is this museum of everyday life. Relive shopping as it used to be in time-warp streets, such as Victorian Kirkgate or Edwardian Half Moon Court. You can even smell the humbugs in Joseph Terry's sweet shop. See everything from a childrens' gallery to a 1943 kitchen, a 1953 sitting room complete with a nine-inch TV set. Displays of costumes and one of the best collections of arms and armour in Britain complete the museum's collection. While there, see Clifford's Tower, the keep of York Castle which has managed to survive the city's turbulent past. Here it was that a large number of Jews were massacred in 1190.

☛ *Off Tower Street, on south side of city centre. Open Ap-Oct, Mon-Sat 9.30-5.30pm, Sun 10-5.30pm; Nov-Mar Mon-Sat 9.30-4pm, Sun 10-4pm. Closed Xmas, Boxing & New Year's Day. Admission charge.*
☎ *0904-653611.*

National Railway Museum

Like the coming of the Romans and the Vikings, the coming of the railway had a profound effect on York. It became one of the country's greatest train building centres, thanks to one of its citizens, George Hudson, who became known as "The Railway King." Thus, York is the natural home of the magnificent National Railway Collection, ranging from a lock of Robert Stephenson's hair to the splendour of the Royal Train. Across the road from the Museum is the Great Railway Show, where visitors can walk down station platforms and imagine themselves as passengers on an Edwardian express, or a Boat Train to Paris. Locomotive footplates and carriages are open and there are timetabled working demonstrations and train rides. There is a shop, car park and restaurant. One of the top five museums in the UK.

☛ *The Museum is in Leeman Road, York Y2 4XJ, behind the British Rail station. Open, Mon-Sat 10-6pm, Sun, 11-6pm. Closed 24-26 Dec & 1 Jan. Admission charge.*
☎ *0904-621261.*

The Yorkshire Museum

Yet another top award for a York museum was won with this amazing collection. The displays include some of the finest Roman, Anglo Saxon, Viking and Medieval treasures ever discovered in Britain. In particular, the "Roman Life" galleries are stunning. See beautifully carved Roman statues, tombstones, wallpaintings, mosaics, a Roman kitchen, gold and silver jewellery and even the auburn hair of a Roman lady miraculously preserved. The New St. Mary's Galleries exhibit some of the finest medieval sculptures in Britain in an authentic setting. Also, there are displays of Anglo-Saxon and Viking Age sculpture, leatherwork, jewellery and medieval and later pottery.

☛ *In Museum Gardens, York YO1 2DR. Near York Minister. Open, Ap-Oct open daily, 10-5pm (Aug Mon-Sat 10-6.30pm, Sun 10-5pm); Nov-Mar, Mon-Sat 10-5pm, Sun 1-5pm. Closed Dec 24-26, Jan 1.*
☎ *0904-629745.*

Merchant Adventurers' Hall

A superb glimpse of medieval York, the Great Hall of the York merchants' Guild is one of the finest such places in Europe. Built in the 1350s, it is where the merchants transacted their business and held their feasts, just as their successors do today. Guild banners, merchant portraits, 500-year-old furniture—it's all absolutely intact.

☛ *In Fossgate, York YO1 2XD. Open, May-Nov, daily 8.30-5pm then Daily except Sun, 8.30-3pm. Closed 21 Dec to 6 Jan. Admission charge.*
☎ *0904-654818.*

Yorkshire Museum of Farming

On the outskirts of York is this eight-acre site in which the world of James Herriot is brought to life. Traditional farm implements, crops, craft demonstrations, reconstructed farm buildings from last century, and special events describe how life used to be down on the farm before they started spraying everything in sight. Part of the original Derwent Valley Light Railway operates at weekends and Bank Holidays

☛ *At Murton park, Murton, York. Just off the A64 at its junction with the A1079 (Hull) road. Open, end Mar-October, Tue-Fri 10.30-5.30pm; Sat & Sun 12-5.30pm. Closed Mon ex. Bank Hols. Admission charge.*
☎ *0904-489966.*

Marston Moor

On 2 July, 1644, the greatest and bloodiest battle of the entire Civil War was fought in these flat fields between Knaresborough and York. Here it was that the Parliamentary forces, led by the Fairfaxes of Yorkshire, and Cromwell, were finally victorious over the forces of Charles I. Of over 40,000 troops engaged in The Battle of Marston Moor, some 4,000 Royalists and 300 Parliamentarians were killed. Today, you will find peaceful fields and lanes, and a roadside obelisk commemorating the battle.

☛ *Quickest way from Leeds is via Wetherby, crossing A1 for Thorp Arch on B1224, turning left in Long Marston.*

Beningbrough Hall

On the Leeds side of York, standing in a wooded park close to the River Ouse, is this Baroque house. Unlike most other country mansions in the area, it has a significant art collection. There are over 100 portraits on loan from the National Portrait Gallery. One of the specialities is portraits of 18th century London society and Sir Charles Kneller's famous studies of The Kit-Cat Club, the influential group of Whig patriots who consumed mutton pie as the plotted to ensure the Protestant succession. And there is the usual fine furniture and porcelain. One of the most interesting features is the perfectly preserved Victorian Laundry outside. A wilderness play area, shop and cafe, and seven acres of beautiful gardens make Beningbrough a fine day out. Owned by the National Trust.

☛ *Take A64 for York, turning north on A19 to Shipton, then leftt. Open Ap-Nov daily ex. Mon & Fri and Bank Hols. Also Fri in July & Aug. 11-5pm.*
☎ *0904-470666.*

The Selby Area

Nearly 300 square miles between York and Leeds fall within the Selby District. In two towns, Selby and Tadcaster, and many villages there is a population of 95,000, many of whom commute to work each day in Leeds. Despite the opening of the most modern coalfield in Europe, the landscape has remained unspoiled, with traditional farmland and numerous beauty spots. It may not have the magnetic attractions of York or the Moors, but if you feel like a brief excursion out from Leeds the Selby area repays exploration.

Selby

Famous for its Abbey, and for its location on the tidal River Ouse, which allowed a thriving shipbuilding industry. The Abbey, reputed to be the birthplace of William the Conqueror's son, Henry I of England in 1100, is one of Yorkshire's most beautiful churches. Founded in 1069, it includes eight tall Norman arches and a 14th century "Washington Window" high up in the Choir. John de Washington, a Prior, stems from the same family tree as George Washington. The window bears the Washington Family arms, which you will see is the same as the present day American flag. Most Leeds folk go for the weekly market, held on Mondays, and which draws huge crowds on Bank Holidays.

☛ *The Selby District's western boundary is mainly the A1. For the town of Selby, take the A63 east from Leeds. There is a regular bus service; it lies on the Hull railway line. Selby Tourist Information Centre is in Park Street, Selby.*
☎ *0757-703263.*

Tadcaster

Three breweries dominate Tadcaster: John Smiths, Samuel Smiths and Bass Charringtons. They were established because of the availability of a consistent water supply from the River Wharfe, on which the town was founded by the Romans as an important bridge on the road to *Eboracum*, or York. After the Romans, quarrying was the big local industry and it was from Tadcaster limestone that York Minister and Selby Abbey were constructed. There are some excellent riverside walks, and some brewery tours but ring first for details. Bookings are essential.

☛ *Take the A64 York road. Or reached by regular York-Scarborough bus services from Leeds Central Bus Station.*
☎ *John Smiths 0937-832091; Samuel Smiths 0937-832225; Bass North Leeds 744444.*

Drax Power Station

Western Europe's largest coal burning power station stands on the banks of the River Ouse, south of Selby. A landmark for miles around, there is now public access on guided tours by prior arrangement only, and there is an information centre. See where more than ten per cent of all electricity in England and Wales is generated.

☛*Take A104 south from Selby and pick up left-hand sign in the village of Camblesforth. No casual visitors: ring for details.*
☎ *0757-618381.*

Skipwith Common

This area, a Yorkshire Wildlife Trust reserve, is one of the most important habitats for bird, plant and insect life in the Vale of York, and makes a splendid walk. In spring and summer, its 300 acres of dry and wet heaths, reed swamps, bogs and woodlands are the haunt of nightjar, all three woodpeckers, five species of owls, many species of warblers and a colony of black-headed gulls. In winter, it is good for wildfowl.

☛ *Best access to via the A64 York road, then south on A19 to Escrick and left onto the Skipwith road.*

Wheldrake

This flooded area next to the Yorkshire Derwent forms one of the best wetlands in the north. There several good hides for birdwatching (it is a Yorkshire Wildlife Trust reserve) and the best time is January to March, when hundreds of Bewick's swans fly in from Siberia. At other times, wigeon, teal, pintail, shoveler, pochard and goldeneye can be found. Also, short-eared-owls and sparrowhawks. It is worth motoring round the lanes to Aughton, Ellerton and East Cottingwith.

☛ *Access by private transport only. Take A64 to York bypass, south on A19 and fork left at Wheldrake sign. Through village on Thorganby road, turning sharp right and finding lane to left farther on, to small car park and bridge.*

York-Selby Cycleway

Since being completed in 1989, this marvelous route has attracted a growing number of Leeds cyclists. It follows part of the former main railway line between Selby and York, closed in 1983, and links two networks of quiet lanes. The route itself is around 15 miles long, with numerous access points as it runs north from the centre of Selby, through Riccall and Naburn and into the City of York. A leaflet is available from Selby TIC (see above)

☛ *Pick up the cycle route at the Ouse Bridge in Selby or at Terry Avenue, York. Work is underway on an extension south from Selby to Howden and Hull.*

Ryedale

A sprawling rural area to the east of York, centred on the Vale of Pickering and the River Rye after which it is named, Ryedale is most often seen by visitors on their way to the coast. But there are many beautiful villages to explore, the River Derwent to walk beside, and a number of interesting attractions to take in. The area includes Pickering, which is listed under the North York Moors (see page 179).

Malton

Since being bypassed in the 1970s, Malton's old streets are again a pleasant place to walk. The market place is one of the best preserved Georgian townscapes in Yorkshire. The open market is on Saturday. Malton Museum has a good collection of Roman artifacts gathered from local excavations. One of the nicest walks is beside the tranquil Derwent down to the ruins of Kirkham Priory, founded by Augustinian canons in 1125.

☛ *35 miles east of Leeds, past York on A64. On Leeds-Scarboro rail line. Museum open Easter-Oct, 10-4pm Mon-Sat, 2-4pm Sun. Nov & Dec. 1pm-3pm.*
☎ *0653-695136.*

Castle Howard

Sooner or later, Leeds residents end up at Castle Howard, setting for "Brideshead Revisited". Designed in 1699 by Sir John Vanbrugh, the house was not completed until 1737. Great arched windows, ballustrates, frieze and pilasters abound, and the mighty central cupola is unique in England. The rooms and galleries are filled with treasures and there is the largest collection of historical costumes in Britain. See paintings by Gainsborough, Holbein, Rubens and Van Dyke; furniture by Sheraton and Chippendale. In the 1,000-acre park there are many statues and obelisks and an amazing structure called The Temple of Four Winds.

☛ *15 miles east of York along A64 and well signposted off to the left. Open daily Mar-Nov, 10-5pm. Admission charge.*
☎ *065-384-333.*

Flamingo Land

An animal park, playground and multi-entertainment centre in the grounds of the Georgian Kirby Misperton Hall between Malton and Pickering. Claimed to be the world's largest privately owned zoo, there are chimps, baboons, black panthers, polar bears and brown bears, leopards, zebra, bison, lions and—of course—flamingos. There is a reptile house and an aquarium, too. Perhaps the biggest draw is an impressive funfair, with a big looping rollercoaster, cable car sky ride and much more. New attractions added all the time. There are camping/caravan facilities, bar and disco to encourage longer stays.

☛ *East on A64 York road to Malton bypass, turning left on A169 Picking road. Open Easter-Sept, 10am-late, depending on time of year. Dogs on leads.*
☎ *065-386-287.*

Eden Camp

A reconstructed World War II prisoner-of-war camp that once housed 1,500 Germans and Italians. Now it seeks to recreate civilian life in the 1939-45 war. The displays have moving "dummies" and sound and smell-generators to bring them to life. See what the black-out was like, or rationing, "Dad's Army", ARP wardens. Vera Lynn sings "The White Cliffs of Dover" in the music hall. See an original p.o.w. hut, complete with escape route. But there's no escape from the theme in the café, where you can eat Dambusters Stew and Dumplings, Rommel's Pie and Victory Roll. There's a Forces Reunion display to help old comrades find each other.

☛ *As to Flamingo Land above. The Camp is right on junction of A64 and A169. Open Mid-Feb to Dec 23, 10-4.30pm daily.*
☎ *0653-697777.*

Many villages disappeared in medieval times, their populations wiped out by the Black Death. The most famous deserted village in England is **Wharram Percy**, *on the northern fringe of the Yorkshire Wolds. It was built by Anglo-Saxon settlers in the beautifully tranquil Deep Dale, and for three centuries was a compact farming village of 30 households, a cemetery and around 150 inhabitants. In earlier times, there was an Iron Age house (c.100BC) as well as a Roman farm or villa. Its name is derived from the old Scandinavian hwerhamm, which means "at the bends" and from the Percies, who were Lords of the Manor in the 12th-14th centuries. A combination of the plague and a change from corn growing to less labour-intensive sheep rearing led to it being abandoned around the year 1500. Today, you can see earthworks and the results of numerous excavations on the hillside to the west and north of the church. There are the grassed-over foundations of peasant houses, a manor house and mill. St. Martin's Church (above) contains mostly the original 12th century materials. There is also a reconstructed pond.*
☛ *Between Malton & Driffield, signposted off the B1248. Access is a 10-minute walk from car park at Bella House Farm.*

The North York Moors

Another National Park within an hour's drive of Leeds. This one is famous for its heather moors and dark forests

A heather-clad wilderness of 553 square miles, created a National Park in 1952. A slightly longer journey from Leeds than the Dales, but the bonus is that the roads and landscape are less busy. Most of the Park lies above the 400 feet contour, rising to a maximum of 1,490 feet at Urra Moor, near Hasty Bank. It extends from the Vale of York to the coast, and from the Vale of Pickering to within sight of the chimneys of industrial Teesside. There are green valleys, prehistoric standing stones, Roman roads, mediaeval crosses and great monasteries, pantile-roofed villages, dark forests that are a labrynth of tracks, and windswept moors where visitors are unlikely to meet anything more than a curlew or red grouse.

Coxwold

Could be renamed "Cotswold" because it is more reminiscent of that area's honeystone villages than anything in Yorkshire. Picturesque main street, but the main attraction is Shandy Hall, the home of the local vicar and author Laurence Sterne from 1760 to 1768. Also in the village is a pottery workshop. And nearby see Byland Abbey, an imposing Cistercian Abbey noted for its glazed tiles. And since you've made the effort to drive this far, pop in at the workshops of Robert "Mouseman" Thompson, Kilburn. Every piece of oak furniture and ornament (some quite cheap to buy) carries the famous carved mouse.

☞ *A58 Wetherby road to A1 north then A168 for Thirsk, south on A19 for three miles, then left turn. Kilburn and Byland are signposted locally. Shandy Hall Open: Sun and Wed only, June-Sept 2-4.30pm or any other time by appointment.*

☎ *Coxwold (03476) 465.*

Thompsons workshops open 8-12 noon, 12.45-5pm Mon-Fri (3.45pm close Fri). 10-12 noon Sat. Closed Easter week and Xmas/New Year.

Helmsley

A pleasant market town with the gaunt ruin of a once-great castle containing "domestic" quarters of interest. There are some nice shops and pubs grouped around the wide square, dominated by the large memorial to William, 2nd Baron Feversham. The best day to visit is Friday, when there is an open-air market. Don't forget your boots for the fabulous Helmsley to Rievaulx Walk, three miles each way. Take the Cleveland Way from the old market cross, passing All Saints Church, turn right on the Stokesley Road (B1257) then follow Rievaulx signpost to the left.

☞ *Take A58 Wetherby road to A1, north on A168 Thirsk, then A170 up Sutton Bank. Castle open Weekdays 9.30-4.30 (winter) or 7.30pm (summer and Sundays).*

Rievaulx

Yorkshire's oldest Cistercian abbey is well preserved and has the most picturesque setting, dominating a wooded valley of the River Rye. Its original grandeur is at once obvious—the towering yellow shell seems to fill the valley. Over 600 monks and lay brothers were here in the late-12th century, the Rievaulx heyday. The famous Rievaulx Terrace overlooking the site belongs to the National Trust. Created in 1758, it curves for half a mile, with a temple at each end—one Ionic, the other Doric. Rievaulx is at its best early on a summer's morning. It also has a haunting atmosphere within.

☞ *As to Helmsley, but fork left two miles from top of Sutton Bank (signposted) to abbey car park & toilets. Open: all year in daylight hours. Terrace & Temples Easter-Oct each day ex. Good Fri., 10.30-5.30pm. Admission charges.*

☎ *Info Centre 04396-340.*

Sutton Bank

The steep road up is familiar to listeners of weather forecasts, since it is often one of the first victims of snow and ice. At the top is the busiest entrance to the North York Moors, an information centre, car park and toilets for the thousands of visitors who come to see the spectacular long-distance views to the west and south. From here, walk to the famous White Horse of Kilburn, measuring 314ft across and 228ft high, on Roulston Scar. Or to the allegedly bottomless Lake Gormire.

☞ *As to Helmsley. Info. Centre, café & toilets on the left at the top of the steep hill on the A170.*

Hutton-le-Hole

One of the cutest villages in Yorkshire, and loved by TV producers, it has wide greens, red-roofed stone cottages and the Hutton Beck gurgling picturesquely under little white bridges. Apart from soaking in the timeless atmosphere, visitors can visit the Ryedale Folk Museum, over two acres of open-air and indoor displays of farm implements, craftsmen's tools, rescued historic buildings, an Edwardian photographic studio and other antiques.

☞ *Take road to Helmsley, bypass Kirkbymoorside then left on minor road off A170. Museum open April-Oct inclusive, 10-5.30pm. Admission charge.*

☎ *Lastingham (07515) 367.*

Farndale

Once thirsted after by water engineers who wanted to dam it for a reservoir, Farndale survives as a classic moorland valley The singing River Dove flows south along the cultivated green floor, and it is for the sea of brilliant daffodils along its banks in April that Farndale is nationally famous.

☛ *As to Helmsley (above), then to Keldholme on A170, turning left on signposted minor road. Farndale circular walk leaflets available at shops in Kirkbymoorside shops.*

Rosedale

Little remains of the Cistercian priory dissolved by Henry VIII in the 16th century and most visitors come here for the fine walks and country inns. One of the most interesting walks in the entire National Park is a circuit of the famous Rosedale Ironstone Railway, an old railway line and kilns operated between 1850 and 1920 (access from Low Baring).

☛ *As to Pickering (below) but turn west on A170 to Wrelton, and right on minor road signposted Rosedale Abbey.*

Pickering

The sloping market place was once a village green, but now Pickering is a sizeable town with a busy market day each Monday. Among the numerous attractions are Pickering Castle, the impressive motte (mound) within being built at the time of William the Conqueror. Beck Isle Museum is a fine Regency building once owned by William Marshall, the farming pioneer. Interesting collections of local history and folk life.

☛ *A64 east to Malton, turning north on A169. Castle Open: Oct-Mar daily ex. Mon 10-4pm; Ap-Sept daily 10-6pm. Admission. Museum Open: Easter-end Oct daily 10-5pm. Admission.*

North York Moors Railway

At 18 miles, one of the longest private railways in Britain. It was among the earliest, built by George Stephenson in the 1830s to link Whitby with the important market centre of Pickering. A victim of the Beeching cuts in the sixties, it was reopened in 1973 and a variety of steam and diesel engines run back and forth to Grosmont, calling at Newtondale, Levisham and Goathland (location for the YTV series *Heartbeat*). The views are superb, and the line affords access to deep forests, high moors, waterfalls and good picnic sites.

☛ *Well signposted in Pickering (see above). Open daily between April & October.*

☎ *Talking timetable 0751-73535.Other info 0751-72508.*

Dalby Forest

The Forestry Commission's Dalby Forest Drive (toll road) is a 9-mile scenic ride between Thornton Dale and Hackness, passing through many different forest habitats. There are car parks, picnic sites, play areas forest walks and a good Visitor Centre. Of particular interest is The Bridestones, a sandstone outcrop, sculpted into fantastic shapes and sizes, three miles north of Low Dalby, forming a nature reserve. A circular nature trail combines oakwoods, gills, heather moors and Dovedale Griff, a marsh. On the hillside above is Thompson's Rigg, around 100 Bronze Age cairns.

☛ *As to Pickering (left) then east on A170 to Thornton Dale, taking forest road north. Leaflets at Visitor Centre. Open: April-Oct inclusive.*

☎ *0751-72771.*

Saltergate

High on Levisham Moor, this area was bought by the National park in 1976 because of the stunning views over the Hole of Horcum. This is a unique natural amphitheatre formed by the action of springs washing away the soft clay and leaving a rim of sandstone. There is a large car park, from which radiate a number of interesting walks over Levisham Moor. Popular with hang-gliders and radio-controlled aircraft enthusiasts.

☛ *As to Pickering (see left), then on Whitby road, A169. The Hole is seven miles north.*

Danby

On the far side of the National Park, beside the River Esk, Danby is the places to go to learn everything about the history, wildlife and work within the North York Moors. The Visitor Centre is in a former shooting lodge of the Lord of the Manor, and contains such facilities as a book and souvenir shop, brass rubbing room, and audio-visual display about the moors. There's a good playground and pathfinder course for children.

☛ *Signposted off the A171 out of Whitby. Open April-October every day, 10am-5pm; November-March weekends only, 11-4pm.*

☎ *0287-660654.*

*The Romans left Yorkshire in AD410 but their roads are still used today. See this original section on **Wheeldale Moor.** Wade's Causeway once linked Malton and Whitby. It is 16ft wide, constructed from flat stones on top of gravel, with side gutters and culverts.*
☛ *As to Saltergate (above) then branch off A169 for Goathland. The road can be seen 3 miles south-west. Go to hamlet of Hunt House to find signposted footpath.*

The East Coast

A day at the seaside means a choice of some of the best coastal scenery in Britain and you can make it as noisy or as peaceful as you like

Between the Tees and Humber, there is every single feature to be found elsewhere on the shores of Britain. Visitors can choose noisy seaside resorts with fish & chip shops and kiss-me-quick hats, or secluded bays, miles of sandy beaches and dramatic cliffs and headland. And if you've spotted the absence of an off-shore island, then stick around. The amazing spit of Spurn Head, which dangles like a fishing hook in the mouth of the Humber, is almost certainly going to become separated from the mainland by erosion in the next couple of decades. On a good day, it's possible to have a toe in the North Sea within 90 minutes of leaving your Leeds home. On summer Sundays and Bank Holidays, it will probably take longer. Everyone has their favourite resort or cove, and the following selection includes the most popular.

North Yorkshire Coast

Staithes
Once an important North Sea port with 400 fishing vessels, Staithes handed its glory to Whitby in Victorian times. But the old town, clinging to the cliffs, is well preserved, as much a time warp as it possible to find in the 1990s. Its greatest fame is that Captain Cook did a boyhood apprenticeship with a Staithes grocer. There's little to do other than enjoy the scene, drink at the fishermen's pubs, or browse in the craft shops.
☛ *As to Whitby, then north out of town on A174.*

Runswick Bay
Another jumble of red-roofed houses built in a seemingly impossible location, Runswick has one major advantage—its superb sandy beach, and a sheltered bay. There's even a small promenade, though the village is not a seaside resort.
☛ *As to Whitby, then north out of town on A174.*

Whitby
Unlike Scarborough and Bridlington, Whitby has managed to retain its fishing village character against the tide of tourism. Narrow 18th century streets huddle round the River Esk, with many good shops, pubs and bistros. Captain Cook sailed from here and lodged at Grape Lane, now the CC Memorial Museum. But fact is no match for fantasy. The busiest attraction in Whitby is the Dracula Experience, cashing in on the fact that Bram Stoker's famous novel was partly based here. There's also a Dracula Trail. Don't miss Whitby Abbey, gaunt 12th century remains perched on the headland.
☛ *Via A64 York bypass, A169 north from Malton bypass to Pickering, then over Fylingdales Moor. Tourist information centre is in New Quay Road.*
☎ *0947-602674.*

Robin Hood's Bay
Legend has it that this was where the famous outlaw made his escape to the Continent, and the name stuck. The village is a jumble of red roofs, presiding over a wide, if rocky, bay. The narrow streets have several good craft shops and are nice to wander, though the steepness of the hill is not for anyone who is unfit. The bay provides safe paddling for kiddies, and fossil hunting at low tide. It is worth checking with the National Trust Centre at Ravenscar as to the state of the tide before setting off. Local history, including much smuggling lore, is on display in the village museum. Walk the Cleveland Way to Ravenscar and back.
☛ *Via A64 to Scarborough, then north on A171 for about 10 miles. Car park at the top of hill, and gets full early at weekends and in summer. The museum is run by a local trust and open afternoons only, May-Sept.*
☎ *(NT Centre) 0723-870138.*

Ravenscar
This rocky promontory at the southern end of Robin Hood's Bay was once the site of a Roman signal station, part of a network along the coast and extending inland to warn York, then known as *Eboracum*, of invasion from the sea by Vikings. The modern equivalent, of course, can be seen at Fylingdales Early Warning Station up on the moors. Today, Ravenscar is all about peace, a restful place from which to watch the sea, or to potter around on the shore. The best views are from the Raven Hall Hotel gardens right at the edge of the cliffs. You can still see the remains of an attempt to turn Ravenscar into a holiday resort in Victorian times. The development company went bankrupt and work was abandoned. Take the Ravenscar Trail, a three-mile walk starting from the National Trust Coastal Centre.
☛ *North of Scarborough, signposted off the A165 Whitby road. National Trust centre open April-Oct inclusive.*
☎ *0723-870138.*

Scarborough
Scarborough developed out of a fashionable 18th century spa to become the premier holiday resort on the east coast of England. Despite the many thousands of visitors, Scarborough still manages to retain a sense of style. A Norman castle looms over the fine fishing port, and there are splendid Georgian terraces on the hillsides. Two bays, several good parks and miles of promenade make it an excellent place for walking when the weather's fine, or there are numerous indoor attractions, such as a Hologram exhibition, the Rotunda Museum, Lighthouse Tower, and a good aquarium at the Sea Life Centre, Scalby Mills. Of course, there are many amusement arcades and fish and chip shops, but then that's the English seaside. You can do the "kiss-me-quick" hat routine, or enjoy more cerebral activities.
☛ *Drive east along A64 from Leeds. Frequent bus and trains services, especially in summer. The Tourist Info. Centre is at St. Nicholas Cliff.*
☎ *0723-373333.*

Filey *is, for many, simply the best place on Yorkshire's coast. It has one of the biggest and sandiest bays in England. And to the north is the wonderful Filey Brigg (see page 155), almost a mile of black rock jutting out like an abandoned attempt at bridging the North Sea. To the south are the white chalk walls of Bempton. The town is not as noisy as other seaside resorts. The Coble Landing (above) has many coble fishing craft, a direct descendant of the Viking Longboat that was once a common sight here. The best part of town is the Queen Street area, still the centre of the fishing community. See the Folk Museum, where much old fishing and smuggling memorabilia is on display.*
☛ *Take A64 York-Scarborough road, branching right at Staxton roundabout on A1039. Or by train from Leeds via Scarborough, changing to the Hull line. The Tourist Information Centre is in John Street.*
☎ *0723-512204.*

North Humberside Coast

Bempton
Every spring, these 300-400ft chalk cliffs become a vertical city where tens of thousands of seabirds build their nests. It is the only mainland gannetry in England, and breeding place of puffins, guillemots, razorbills, kittiwakes, fulmars, shags, cormorants and several species of seagull. The eggs used to be collected by local men, called "climmers" on hemp ropes. The albumen (whites) of the eggs were used as a softener in the tanneries of Leeds. You can still see some of their rusting pulleys on the grassy clifftops. Several viewpoints allow excellent views of the birds, binoculars being an advantage. The cliffs are now an RSPB reserve. In season, there are boat trips from Bridlington to watch the birds from a different angle. The best time to visit Bempton is April-July. By August, most of the birds have gone.
☛ *By car, take A64 to Bridlington turn-off (A166), joining B1255 for Flamborough and B1229 north. Or by train, changing at Scarborough to Hull line. Check with Bridlington TIC for boat trips info in spring.*
☎ *0262-673474.*

Flamborough
This is the northernmost thrust of a seam of chalk that extends from Dorset, through the Marlborough and North Downs, the Lincolnshire and Yorkshire Wolds. The gleaming cliffs are now protected as a Heritage Coast. Since pre-historic times, the clifftop has been a coastal signal station. "Flam" is from "flame" beacons. Beacon Tower (c.1674) is an octagonal limestone predecessor of the lighthouse seen today, built in 1806 and one of the few still operated by Trinity House keepers. The sea erodes the chalk into strange caves and stacks, such as the King and Queen and Adam and Eve.
☛ *See directions for Bempton. There is a Flamborough Heritage Centre for information on the area and guided walks, events, etc.*
☎ *0262-678967.*

Sewerby
There are two attractions at this village on the cliffs above Bridlington. One is Sewerby Hall. It has an art gallery, a museum, an archaeological display and the Amy Johnson Collection, about the life of the pioneer airwoman from Hull. In the grounds is a formal garden, golf and putting, mini-zoo, aviary, herds of deer, wallabies and llamas and gardens. Down the road is Portminian Model Village.
☛ *Well signposted on the northern outskirts of Bridlington. Hall open daily, Easter-Oct; ring village for opening times.*
☎ *Hall: 0262-673769; Village 0262-606414.*

Bridlington
Bridlington has survived the decline of the English seaside resort for three reasons. One is that it still has a railway line. The second is the sophisticated modern attractions like Leisure World, four pools including a "surfpool" with waves breaking onto its "shore". And the third is Brid's appeal to young parents with prams and also for older people, because the town is mostly flat. There are boat trips and sea angling from the pier, walks along the north shore to Flamborough and countless pubs, cafés, shops and restaurants. The Bayle Gate Museum is a 14th century gatehouse full of local antiques and pictures. A huge number of amusement arcades, and several modern discos make it very popular with the young.
☛ *East on A64 to York bypass then follow A166 over the Wolds via Driffield. For up-to-date events programme ring the Tourist Information Centre.*
☎ *0262-673474.*

Hornsea
Hornsea is a quiet seaside town famous mainly for its pottery. It has been turned into a Retail & Lei-

sure Park. The famous tableware can be seen in production and you can buy new or bargain seconds. There's also a good aviary and a butterfly collection, a collection of vintage cars, mini farmyard, model village, funfair and adventure playground. One mile inland is Hornsea Mere, a 476-acre freshwater lake formed by glacial deposit. It is an RSPB reserve, having extensive reedbeds. But you can hire small dinghies.

☞ *Quickest way is by M62 eastbound, through Hull and east through Holderness on A165, B1243 & B1244. Pottery open daily March-Oct, from 10am.*
☎ *0964-534211.*

Withernsea

Withernsea is the holiday resort that time forgot, a pleasant place on a fine summer's day. Its high watermark of popularity was in the inter-war years, but its decline began when the railway line from Hull was closed in 1964. Its main custom comes from young families and the elderly from Hull. The most sophisticated attraction is the Pavilion Leisure Centre, full of waterslides, rollerskating, indoor bowls, etc. But mainly, people come for the walks along the substantial promenades, or the mile upon mile of clean, sandy beaches. There is a pleasure park, and numerous pubs and cafés.

☞ *Via M62, through Hull on Hedon road, then B1362.*

Spurn Point

If you haven't already visited this unique spit of land east of Hull, don't delay because it might soon be accessible only by ferry. The erosion on the seaward side of the three-mile peninsula has worsened in recent years, and some parts are not much wider than 100 feet. Spurn is a famous bird reserve, one of the best places in Britain for watching the spring and autumn migrations. At low tide, it is fun to explore the wide beaches, sand dunes and old wartime defences.

☞ *Two hour drive via M62, through Hull for Hedon on A1033 and Patrington on B1445. Access is informal but there's a car park charge at the bird warden's house. Some bird reserve restrictions.*

The County of Humberside

The brainchild of bureaucrats, a County of two different landscapes and people linked by a stunning bridge.

Within the shelf-life of this book, the actual County of Humberside could well disappear, with the north bank becoming known as East Yorkshire (probably not "Riding") and the south bank restoring its former links with Lincolnshire. Since being created on 1 April, 1974, Humberside has been a difficult concept to sell to many of its 850,000 population on either side of the mighty Humber. Old rivalries have continued, even after the opening of the great Humber Bridge, and the great industrial boom that was predicted for the south side of the river by and large did not materialise. Contrary to popular belief, the Humber is not a river, but an estuary—it actually drains one-fifth of England's land surface. Most of the great rivers of the Yorkshire Dales and West Yorkshire reach the sea here. The riverbank is a nice place to walk, with the ship and barge traffic providing constant interest, and there are some unusual towns and villages to explore on both banks.

The North Bank

Beverley

An attractive mix of Georgian and Victorian architecture dominates this market town eight miles north of Hull. It is a popular drive out for those Leeds residents, because of its good tea-rooms and pubs, up-market shops, others selling second-hand books, antiques and crafts, and its good market on Saturdays. From a distance, the town is dominated by the magnificent Beverley Minster, with its breathtaking pinnacled towers on the west front (c.1420). The newest attraction is the Museum of Army Transport, two-acres of road, rail, sea and air transport. There are two huge exhibition halls, one housing the last remaining Blackburn Beverley aircraft and "Monty's" Rolls-Royce.

☞ *Quickest route is east on M62 to A63, turning left on A1034 through South Cave and right on B1230 via Walkington. Transport Museum is in Flemingate. Open daily 10-5pm ex. 24-26 Dec. Admission charge.*
☎ *0482-860445.*

Burton Agnes

This haunted Elizabethan mansion near Bridlington is an outstanding example of 17th century architecture. The ghost is thought to be Anne Wickham-Boynton, murdered shortly after her father built the house. She wanted her head buried in the house but her whole body was laid in the churchyard. When her coffin was opened some years later, the head had gone! Ghostly sightings have been reported ever since. The more tangible features are paintings by Renoir, Pissaro, Gainsborough and others.

☞ *Take A64 east to York bypass, then A166 across the Wolds, through Driffield. Open Ap-Oct, 11-5pm daily. Admission charge.*
☎ *0262-89324.*

Hull

Those who know Hull keep going back. For a start, it is an excellent level shopping centre of which the most recent addition is Princes Quays, an enormous arcade built on stilts in what used to be Princes Dock. The old fish dock area has been turned into a vast retail and leisure park (clearly visible from the Clive Sullivan Way, the main drag into Hull from the M62). Another dock has been turned into a fancy marina, and most of the town's former glory is displayed in the old dock offices, now the Town Docks Museum, with galleries on fishing, whaling and shipping. In the Old Town, a well-preserved area of narrow streets missed by the Luftwaffe, you will find an excellent Archaeological Museum, with a 2,300-year-old

Bronze Age boat, once used on the Humber, and vintage cars in the Transport Museum. Nearby in the High Street is Wilberforce House, birthplace of the great anti-slave campaigner, who was born in Hull.

☛ *An hour's drive east along the M62. Or regular National Coaches and trains from Leeds. There is a Tourist Information Centre at 75-76 Carr Lane.*
☎ *0482-223559.*

Humber Bridge

This amazing structure five miles west of Hull (and pictured below) is the longest single-span suspension bridge in the world. It is just under 1.4 miles in length, carrying a dual two-lane carriageway 150 feet above the river. For centuries, the wide Humber was crossed only by ferry, the first regular crossing being established by the Romans at Brough. In Victorian times, there was a plan to dig a railway tunnel, but the House of Lords ruled against it on engineering grounds. And a bridge, looking similar to the Forth Railway Bridge, was designed in 1931. But the Bill that would have set things in motion was lost by the the fall of Ramsey MacDonald's government. The plan that finally made it is often said to have been a bribe to the voters of North Hull at a crucial by-election in 1965. Harold Wilson, the Labour Prime Minister at the time, had an overall majority of just three. Work started on July 27, 1972, and when the Queen opened it on July 17, 1981, it had cost £90 million. It has since run up interest debts four times as much. "The Bridge Too Far", as some people call it, is not widely used because of its high toll charges, and because it is too far away from the main north-south motorway network. But even when there's nothing on the bridge, visitors still gape in awe. To the immediate west of the north bank pier is the a large viewing area, with information centre, cafe, toilets, etc. There is also a good country park, formed from an old chalk quarry. The walk across the bridge to Barton-on-Humber (see page 184) is exhilarating, as is the cycle-ride. There are good walks, too, west along the Humber, using The Wolds Way, or east on the Hull Country Way.

☛ *Under an hour's drive east along the M62, which becomes the A63.*
☎ *Humber Bridge Information Centre 0482-640852.*

Rudston

This Wolds village on the Roman road from York to Bridlington, five miles from the coast, receives a steady stream of visitors for two reasons. One is the Rudston Stone, a 50ft. high and 15ft. wide block of gritstone. The tallest of Britain's ancient monoliths, it is thought to have been erected by sun-worshipping Bronze age people around 400 B.C. Early Christians put a cross on it, thus the village's name—"Rud" comes from "rood", old English for cross. It stands in the churchyard, where lies the second reason for Rudston's fame. Winifred Holtby, the novelist, is buried here, and a memorial to her is inside the church. She was born at nearby Rudston House. Her most famous work was *South Riding*.

☛ *A64 to York bypass, then east on A166 for Bridlington, taking signposted left turn at Burton Agnes.*

Sledmere House

This splendid Queen Anne house, built in 1787, is the ancestral home of the Sykes family, who were responsible for turning the Yorkshire Wolds from a grassy sheep-walk into some of the best

Dusk settles over The Humber Bridge, the world's longest single span suspension bridge

arable fields in the country. Today visitors can see some of the fine plasterwork by Joseph Rose, who worked with Robert Adam. One room is decorated with Turkish tiles, another is a magnificent 100ft. long library. There is furniture by Chippendale and Sheraton. The park was designed by Capability Brown. Sledmere itself is a lovely estate village. A spectacular 120ft. high monument to the fourth baronet, Sir Tatton Sykes is on the Garton to Sledmere road.

☛ *A64 to York bypass, then A161 for Bridlington. Open daily Easter-Sept inclusive. Ring for precise opening times.*
☎ *0377-86637.*

Yorkshire Wolds

Once described as "a piece of Southern England in the North" the Wolds are a sharp contrast to the bleak Pennine uplands or the wild North York Moors. These soothing chalk hills and embracing green valleys run in a crescent from the Humber to Flamborough Head. To begin your exploration, walk the Wolds Way from above Millington to Huggate, returning via the quiet road through the famous Millington Pastures. Or start from Thixendale, following any of several signposted rambles out of what is perhaps the most peaceful valley in the North. A good guide to the area, including circular walks, colour photographs and OS maps, is *The Wolds Way* (Aurum) by Roger Ratcliffe, the editor of *Leeds Fax.*

☛ *Millington is signposted from Pocklington, off the A1079 York road. Thixendale is signposted off the A161 York-Bridlington road.*

The South Bank

Barton-on-Humber

At the other end of the Humber Bridge is this interesting town, a network of narrow Victorian and Georgian streets that are enjoyable to wander through on a fine day. It was once *the* port on the Humber, when Hull was but a village. There is a bridge viewing area off Waterside road, and a new nature centre, the Barton Clay Pits project, which has public hides for

watching ducks and waders feeding in the mud along seven miles of the Humber. On the Caistor Road is Baysgarth Leisure Park, a Georgian House in 30 acres.

☛ *East on M62 and A63, south over Humber Bridge (toll). Baysgarth open day, ex. Dec 25-26 & Jan 1.*
☎ *Baysgarth 0652-32318; Clay Pits 33283.*

Brigg

This classic Lincolnshire market town (for the moment in South Humberside) exerts an extraordinary pull on the population of a wide area. From the outskirts of Grimsby to Scunthorpe and almost as far south as Lincoln, villagers prefer to come here to shop and find their entertainment, and the casual visitor can see why. It has a fine Georgian market place (open markets Thursday and Saturday), some quaint back alleys, picturesque walks along the River Ancholme, and more pubs than is probably good for it. A 40-mile scenic drive, The Brigg Round, starts here (pick up a leaflet from the Information Centre) and goes north to the Humber. Or travel south through the flat green fields to discover some beautiful villages, especially the award-winning Snitterby, off the A15.

☛ *East on M62, joining M18 at exit 35, and east on M180 to junction 4. Tourist Information Centre is in the Market Place.*
☎ *0652-57053.*

Goole

This strange, flat town 40 miles from the coast is the product of the 18th century canals system. Its prosperity was linked to the growing city of Leeds, being built in the 1820s as the eastern terminus of the Aire and Calder Navigation. And also to the Yorkshire coalfield, handling barges of coal from the South Yorkshire navigation. Here, two rivers—the Ouse and Don—are also joined by canal. It is the biggest inland port in the country, handling over a million tons of goods from ships arriving and departing by the Humber. The waterways history is displayed at the Sobriety Centre, where some of the last surviving coal carriers

are kept ("Tom Puddings" and "Codheads").

☛ *East on M62 to signposted junction 36. Sobriety Centre is at Dutch River Side. Open Mon-Fri, 9.30-3.30pm.*
☎ *0405-768730.*

Grimsby

Like all English towns that were based almost entirely on one industry then found it virtually wiped out by the 1990s, Grimsby has gone into the heritage business. Thus Grimsby is home to the National Fishing Heritage Centre, a new and expanding celebration of Grimsby's great days as one of Europe's biggest fishing ports. Come and see what conditions were like in a 1950s British steam trawler in the Arctic fishing grounds. Noises and smells bring the displays to life. If anyone had any doubts about who won the 1975-76 Cod War, see the Icelandic trawlers unloading their catches for the British market, while local vessels gather rust. The last Humber paddle ferry, the Lincoln Castle, it is moored beside the Heritage Centre.

☛ *M62 east to exit 35, then M18 and M180 east. Heritage Centre open daily Sept-June 10-6pm, (8pm close July & August). Admission charge.*
☎ *0472-344867.*

Sandtoft Transport Museum

Built on a former wartime airfield between Doncaster and Scunthorpe, the museum houses a collection of over 60 well-preserved public road transport vehicles from Britain and Europe. Among the exhibits is an old Leeds trolleybuses, six-wheeled double-deckers and a German one-and-a-half decker. You can still ride on some of the trolleybuses, when the museum's quarter of a mile of overhead cables (outdoors) is being used during working weekends.

☛ *Take M62 eastbound to junction 35 (for Scunthorpe), and M18 south, branching east on M180, exiting at junction 2 for the A161 south. Open 12-6pm weekends Easter-Sept inc, and often Sundays in winter.*
☎ *0724-711391.*

South Yorkshire

A late arrival in the tourism business, but catching up with heritage trails and a giant leisure complex

Twent years ago this county was in the old West Riding, with Leeds. But since they were split, West and South Yorkshire have become like different nations as far as leisure facilities are concerned. West Yorkshire's textile industry declined in the 1970s and much of what replaced it was geared to drawing visitors, helped by the lovely Pennine scenery. By contrast, South Yorkshire's coal and steel industries are recent casualties. Only now is it making a determined effort to draw tourists.

Barnsley

Barnsley's days as a tourist centre are just about to begin. For over a century, this hub of a 225,000 population has been too busy with the gritty business of earning a living to get involved in fancy heritage centres and the like. But a new attitude prevails since many of the local deep-mine collieries have closed in British Coal's programme of "rationalization". Already, there is a Yorkshire Mining Heritage Trail from the town (pick up at a leaflet at the Tourist Information Centre). On it, you see the Oaks Memorial, a reminder of the two disasters at Oaks Colliery in 1847 and 1866, the latter claiming the lives of 361 miners. Other mining disaster memorials are seen at Silkstone Churchyard, near Huskar Pit, where women and children were among 26 killed in 1838, and Darfield churchyard, near the site of the Lundhill Colliery Disaster of 1857. Barnsley itself has a very good market on Saturdays, and a distinctive Town Hall, built in 1933. Nearby, just at the start of Huddersfield Road, is the large building known by the news media as "Camelot", from where "King" Arthur Scargill led the once-militant Yorkshire Area of the National Union of Mineworkers. It was the scene of several mass rallies during the historic strikes of 1972, 1974 and 1984-85.

☛ *South on M1 to exit 35. Also Metro trains & buses. Tourist Information Centre is at 56 Eldon Street, Barnsley, S. Yorks. S70 2JL. Ask for info pack, including "Mining Heritage Trail" leaflet.*
☎ *0266-206757.*

Conisbrough Castle

This is the finest Norman castle in South Yorkshire, an enormous circular keep towering over the River Don mid-way between Doncaster and Rotherham. It was built in the 1170s by Hameline Plantagenet, the illegitimate half-brother of King Henry II. In the mid-14th century it passed into the hands of Edmund Langley, Duke of York, the son of Edward II. And on the accession of Edward IV in 1461, it became a royal castle. The 90ft. high circular keep is open to visitors with stairs right to the top, giving fine views through the Don Gorge. The keep contains a small chapel and vestry and living accommodation built into the buttresses. There is a good visitor centre within the castle grounds.
☛ *Not the shortest, but the no-fuss approach to Conisbrough is via the M1, M62 east, A1 south to its junction with the A630 Doncaster-Rotherham road and west into the town. Park by the war memorial. Open daily, summer 10-6pm; winter 10-4pm.*

Doncaster

Once an important coaching halt on the Great North Road, Doncaster is now bypassed by the A1 and gets fewer outside visitors, except during the St. Leger racing festival in early September. But this town of 100,000 is worth a visit for its Georgian High Street, which includes the impressive Mansion House, built in 1748. A few blocks east, on Chequer Road, is a good Museum and Art Gallery, housing the Regimental Collection of the Kings Own Yorkshire Light Infantry and Yorkshire Dragoons, plus a collection of St. Leger presentation cups from the early years of Britain's oldest classic race, which has been run since 1776. For shoppers, "Donny Market" is famous throughout South Yorkshire. With a staggering 650 stalls, it is held on Tuesday, Friday and Saturday, with a small curio market on Wednesday.
☛ *Allow 40 mins for drive south on M1, east on M62 and south on A1. Regular train and coach connections from Leeds. The Tourist Information Centre, which has a good visitor pack, is at the Central Library, Waterdale.*
☎ *0302-734309.*

Meadowhall

The green dome of this major shopping mall on the north-east side of Sheffield rears out of what was once the heart of the city's steelworks and attracts visitors from far and wide. It's the sort of place that delights in statistics, 230 stores on two levels, connecting five themed areas and occupying 1.5 millions square feet. Outside, there's 12,000 free car parking spaces. Inside, there's columns and galleries and palm trees and waterfalls and moving staircases and all the other decorations of indoor shopping centres. Except that this one just goes on . . . and on. The Oasis food court is said to be Europe's biggest, and you can eat French, American, Italian, Chinese, Olde English, etc. etc.
☛ *About 40 min. drive south on M1 to junction 34. Clearly signposted from motorway. Open 9am-8pm Mon-Thur, 9am-9pm Fri, 9am-7pm Sat, 11am-6pm Sun. Oasis open 9am-midnight Mon-Sat.*

Rother Valley Country Park

Clearing up the slag heaps and opencast scars left by more than a century of coal production seemed an impossible task a decade ago. Today what was once among the greatest eyesores of Yorkshire is now, astonishingly, a green valley where thousands go to spend their leisure time. The Country Park is over 700 acres of grass and trees, footpaths and cycleways, streams and lakes. Ongoing work will add a further 300 acres in the next few years. Among the recreational activities organised here are windsurfing, rowing, jet skiing, water skiing, model boating, canoeing, sailing, fishing, football, orienteering, rambling and birdwatching. There is also a grass-ski area, a Craft Centre containing a number of workshops (you can buy the results) and an excellent visitor centre.

☛ *South on M1 to exit 31, turning west on A57, south on A618.*
☎ *0742-471452; watersports enquiries 471453.*

Rotherham

Like Sheffield, Rotherham was built on the iron and steel industry. The town is the centre of a scattered population of 250,000 through the Rother Valley, and in the last few years has made a considerable effort to tidy its public face. "The Hanging Gardens of Rotherham" are not just a media gimmick. In a competition hitherto dominated by genteel spas like Cheltenham and Harrogate,

Rotherham has made a habit of winning the Britain in Bloom award (five times since 1977) with its vast flower show in spring and summer. There is the fine perpendicular All Saints Parish Church. Its pinnacled tower was built in 1409 and most of the building dates from the early 15th century. At the Clifton Park Museum (Clifton Lane) is a collection of items from the Rockingham Pottery. The York and Lancaster Regimental Museum in the Central Library in Drummond Street, has uniforms and Victoria Crosses.

☛ *South on M1 to exit 35. Or by train on Leeds-Sheffield line. Tourist Information Centre in Central Library, Walker Place.*
☎ *0709-823611.*

Sheffield

The prosperity of Yorkshire's second city was built on steel and the famous cutlery. Production of the latter began as early as the 14th century, and was built by Flemish immigrants in the 1500s. Old pho-

tographs show an extremely elegant city in Victorian times but the Luftwaffe made a mess in the last war and much of the centre is concrete and glass. Amongst several notable exceptions is the Town Hall, built in 1897 with a statue of Vulcan, the Roman God of fire and metalworking, on top. Sheffield now has a population of just under 550,000 but the steel and cutlery trade has contracted and the city has become mainly an education and commercial centre. For the visitor, Sheffield is still worth a visit for several reasons. One is the Abbeydale Industrial Hamlet (Abbeydale Road South, Sheffield 7) on the outskirts, where you can see a 200 year old crucible furnace, a water driven tilt forge and grinding wheel for cutlery, etc. Also connected with the cutlery business is The Shepherd Wheel (Whiteley Woods, Rustlings Road), a water-powered grinding works.

☛ *A 40-minute drive down the M1, or less than an hour by train or coach from Leeds. Sheffield Tourist Information Centre, Town Hall Extension, Union Street.*
☎ *0742-734671/2.*

Wentworth Woodhouse

A magnificent country house that you can look at but can't touch. Wentworth Woodhouse is two separate buildings, both built in the 18th century by William Watson Wentworth, Marquis of Rockingham, and facing in opposite directions. The west front was built in 1725-1734 in the Baroque style, and the east front was built later in Palladian style. At 606 feet in length, it is the longest frontage of any English county house. For many years after the war, the house was leased by the former West Riding County Council as a College of Physical Education, but since 1987 it has been in private ownership. Whilst public access is, therefore restricted it is possible to view the house and several notable "follies" from public footpaths.

☛ *South on M1 to exit 36, taking A6135 south, branching east on B6090 to Wentworth Village. The house can be used from the public footpath running from the village's main car park.*

Subtitled Doncaster Leisure Park, **The Dome** *is the country's largest multi-facility centre under one roof. Since it opened in the last gasp of the 1980s it has shot to the top five UK leisure attractions, and you can see why. It has a two-level ice rink, complete with a mock Alpine landscape, snow showers, special effects and lighting, and a custom-built disco on ice. Or if you prefer a hotter climate, there is The Lagoons, a six-pool swimming hall with flume rides, geysers, jacuzzi, tropical palms and ferns, under lights, and wild-water ride. Or relax beside an indoor village green, a bowls hall with a four-rink green. Squash courts, gymnasium, dance studio, snooker room, sports hall, indoor cricket arena, saunas and sunbeds, shops, bars and restaurnats (including what is claimed to be Britain's biggest fish restaurant) complete the impressive list.*

☛ *The Dome is next to Doncaster Race Course in Bawtry Road, Doncaster, DN4 7PD. Take M62 east, A1 south, A630 junction.*
☎ *0302-370888.*

Further Afield

From Hadrian's Wall to Robin Hood's Sherwood Forest, The Beatles in Liverpool to Beatrix Potter's house in the Lake District

The attractions of Yorkshire and Humberside, described in the previous pages, are many. But day-trippers from Leeds do not recognise county boundaries. Places like Alton Towers and Beamish are regular destinations for people from the Leeds area. And with the motorway system, destinations which would once have seemed too far are now well within reach. For example, Liverpool—right on the west coast of England—is actually around the same travelling time and distance from Leeds as Whitby. This final section details some of the attractions of national importance within a few hours' drive from Leeds.

Going South

Alton Towers

As theme parks go, this is among the best. The grounds of Alton Towers, once the Earl of Shrewsbury's seat, is now a magical fantasy land. There's an overhead railway, "skyride" gondolas, corkscrew rollercoaster, Aqualand, Grand Canyon rapids, 3D cinema, Black Hole, Kiddies Kingdom, landscaped gardens. And more attractions are added every year. Alton Street has interesting shops and a major Dolls Museum. There is no "off-season" - Christmas brings a winter wonderland, Ice Show, lights and Santa's Adventure.

☛ *South on M1 to exit 28, A38 to Derby, A52 to Ashbourne, B5417 to Oakamoor. Open Easter-Nov 10-7pm depending on season. Admission charge.*
☎ *0538-702200.*

American Experience

Ilkeston in Derbyshire is the unlikely home to over 100 acres of predominantly Wild West attractions, numbering almost 100. Ride the Santa Fe Railroad, the Thunder Canyon Runaway Train, the Yankee Clipper, and the High Si-

erra Wagon Train. You'll also meet Chief Sitting Bull and General Custer. There is an Indian canoe ride and if it all seems too false, a touch of authenticity is provided by the herd of North American Bison and some Apache ponies.

☛ *South on M1 to exit 26, following sign to theme park off the A6007 between Ilkeston and Heanor. Opens over Easter then weekends only to Spring B Hol. Daily to end Sept. 10am to dusk. Admission charge.*
☎ *0773-769931.*

Chatsworth

Chatsworth is the stately home of the Duke and Duchess of Devonshire and was built between 1686 and 1708. Inside there are rich furnishings and painted rooms, works by Van Dyck and Rembrandt and treasures in porcelain, silver and silk tapestry. The 100-acre gardens are what really set Chatsworth apart from the rest, however. Waterworks like the Sea Horse and Cascade Fountains and the astonishing 290ft. high Emperor Fountain keep the camera shutters clicking. There's a yew maze and serpentine beech hedge. And once you've explored the gardens, you still have 1000 acres of Capability Brown-designed parkland. For children, there's a farmyard and adventure playground plus all the usual shops and refreshments.

☛ *South on M1 to exit 29; A617 to Chesterfield, A619 to Baslow and south on B6012 (house is signposted). House and gardens open 27th Mar-30th Oct, 11.30-4.30pm. Farmyard and playground to 2nd Oct only. Admission charge.*
☎ *0246-582204*

Haddon Hall

This perfectly preserved medieval manor house near Bakewell in Derbyshire has been in the family of the Duke of Rutland for over 800 years. Although there are many country houses listed in

these pages, this one had to be included because—unlike the others—this one escaped wholesale alterations in the 18th and 19th centuries. It is the most complete medieval home in England. What you see today is exactly as it stood in the 14th and 15th centuries. See how the medieval lords lived, complete with the original furniture and decorations. The gardens were laid out in the 17th century, and extend down the steep hillside to the peaceful River Wye.

☛ *M1 south to exit 30, through Chesterfield and west on A619. Open from the end of March to early October, 11am-6pm. Closed Mondays in season, and Sundays in July and August. But open for Bank Hols except Xmas.*
☎ *0629-812855.*

Lincoln

Like York, Lincoln was founded by the Romans (and known as *Lindum*), developed by the Vikings and turned into an important city by the Norman invaders. Its location was an obvious place for a city—a limestone plateau rising 200ft. above the River Witham and providing long distance views over much of the flat Lincolnshire fen country. Star attraction is Lincoln Cathedral. It is England's third largest, being exceeded in size only by York Minster and St. Paul's. Begun in 1072, most of it was completed by 1092. Today's structure was altered after a fire and even an earthquake in medieval times. See its copy of Magna Carta, and the grotesque gargoyle called the Lincoln Imp. Next door is the original Norman Castle, and there are quaint streets winding down the steep hill to the modern city centre, where there is a new riverside shopping mall. Other attractions are the National Cycle Museum at Brayford Wharf North, with 200 years of cycling history on display, and the Usher Art Gallery in Lindum Road, full of clocks, watches and a collection devoted to the Lincolnshire poet, Tennyson.

☛ *Allow two hours for drive via M62 east, A1 south, to A57 east. Or by train, changing at Retford. Cathedral open from 7.15am daily. Other attractions from 10am.*

Lincolnshire Flower Fields

The fen country of South Lincolnshire, known as Holland, explodes every spring with dazzling sheets of coloured fields, a kind of Blackpool Illuminations of Bloom. First to burst through are the daffodils, turning the table landscape yellow as far as the eye can see. Then come the tulips of May. Much of the visitor activity is centred on the town of Spalding, which has a flower parade in the first week of May, and an organised attraction at Springfields Gardens, where over 2 million tourists have enjoyed the flowers. But the best way to see the blooms is by driving on a series of Rural Rides around the fields, some as long as 25 miles. New drives are being added every year. You can obtain maps from the Tourist Information Centre.

☛ *Allow two hours for drive, east on M62, south on A1, east on A151. Information Centre is in* *Churchgate, Spalding.*
☎ *0775-725468.*

National Tramway Museum

This open air working museum is near Matlock, Derbyshire, and is a collection of vintage trams. There are over 40 steam, horse-drawn and electric trams saved from the scrap heap and beautifully restored by enthusiasts. Visitors can ride on any of three trams in service, running every few minutes on a two-mile round trip starting off along the cobbled main street, which has been fitted with artefacts from a century ago, and running through shady woodland and across a hillside to give good views of the Derwent valley. There are picnic sites, and a shop.

☛ *At Crich, 15 miles north of Derby and only 8 miles from junction 28 on the M1. Signposted off the A6 and A38.*
☎ *0773-852565.*

Sherwood Forest

Since Hollywood discovered Robin Hood "The Prince of Thieves" this part of Nottinghamshire has become a favourite day out. Sherwood Forest, of course, is where the outlaw camped out with his loyal band of followers. There are 450 acres of ancient oak woodland and visitors can explore winding greenwood paths, shady glades and secret dells. Plenty of picnic sites, a café called Robin Hood's Larder, visitors' centre, and souvenir shop. Children love it but keep them from wandering off. Maps can be bought at the information centre.

☛ *Exit 30 off the M1 for the Sherwood Forest Visitor Centre, which is between the A616 and A6075 on B6034. Exhibitions, audio-visual displays, shop, refreshments and information. Ring for special events diary in season.*
☎ *0623-823202*

Going West

Blackpool

This is the place for champagne on draught, fish and chips on the end of the pier, the world's biggest sandcastle, and the gaudiest celebration of England's unique seaside culture. For the complete Blackpool experience, take the lift 518ft. to the top of the Tower, take a deckchair on the fine North Pier, swim or paddle on the seven miles of sandy beaches (the tide goes out half a mile), or if it's raining visit the "Inside Seaside" at the Sandcastle Leisure Complex, ride on Britain's oldest electric trams on their 12-mile runs along the promenade, enjoy the white-knuckle rides on the 40-acre Pleasure Beach, walk the incomparable Golden Mile and see the Blackpool Illuminations from September to early November.

☛ *By road, the quickest route is westbound on the M62, north on the M61 and M6 to junction 32, turning west on the M55. Ample car parking. There are also train connections and National Coach services from Leeds. For the complete tourist pack, ring or call in at the Tourist Information Centre, Clifton Street.*
☎ *0772-21623.*

Britain's first National Park was the **Peak District**, *designated in 1951, and it extends for 542-square miles between Sheffield in the east, Manchester in the west, Holmfirth in the North, and almost down to the Birmingham conurbation in the south. The landscape ranges from bleak peat moorlands and gritstone edges, like Stanage Edge (see above) to gentle limestone dales, green river valleys and pretty stone villages. Among numerous attractions, see Arbor Low, the "Stonehenge of the North", a ring of stones 6ft. high and 250ft. in diameter. Castleton has Peak Cavern, the largest limestone cave in Britain. At Speedwell, there is a disused lead mine visitors explore by an illuminated canal. Near Edale is Mam Tor, known as "the shivering mountain" because of its unstable shales. Near Buxton is the beautiful wooded Goyt Valley, with some of the nicest walks in the National Park. The list of attractions is endless. Fortunately, the National Park compiles a detailed information pack each year. Write or call for your copy.*
☛ *South on M1 the exit depending on your specific destination, or over Holme Moss from Holmfirth on A6024. For information, write to Peak National Park, Baslow Road, Bakewell, Derbyshire DE4 1AE.*
☎ *0629-814321.*

British Commercial Vehicle Museum

By far Europe's biggest museum of its kind, this is a fascinating collection of vintage vans, trucks, buses, steam wagons, fire engines and many classes of heavy goods delivery vehicles dating back to the late-19th century. Over 40 vehicles and engines are on show at any one time, with "guests" joining the permanent exhibits. Among the favourite attractions are a gleaming red 1920s fire engine and the "Popemobile" used by Pope John Paul II during his visit to Britain a decade ago. Visitors can stand where he did, waving to the crowds.

☛ *In King Street, Leyland, near Preston, Lancs. Take M62 westbound, north on M61 to junction 8 and pick up signpost in Leyland. Open: April-Sept daily (ex. Mon) 10am-5pm; Oct-Nov weekends only 10-5pm.*
☎ *0772-451011.*

Carnforth Steamtown

Carnforth was one of the biggest junctions in the days of steam but its 37-acre engine shed was closed in 1968. Now it houses the biggest collection in Europe of British and Continental locomotives. This is the permanent home of the famous Flying Scotsman and other great express engines; tough freight locos and even the tiny tank engines, the latter pulling trains down the one-mile branch in Steamtown. Look at the apple green of the Loch Eil Saloon, the chocolate and cream of the Great Western, and opulent interior of an Edwardian Directors' Saloon. There's a huge coaling plant and a Midland signal-box, which you can see in operation.

☛ *Just north of Lancaster. Drive west on A65 to M6 then south to exit 35 and join A6 for signpost. Open daily Easter-Oct 9-6pm (8pm close Jul-Aug); 11-4pm in winter). Admission covers everything. Many special excursions so ring for advance notice.*
☎ *0524-732100.*

Chester

Similar to York, but with the notable absence of a Minster (the Cathedral, although interesting, is not in the same league). Chester still has much to see and do. Evidence of the Roman occupation of *Deva*, as they called it, is visible in the city walls and an amphitheatre which seated 7000 people. See the medieval Rows (two-tier galleries of shops) in Watergate, Eastgate and Bridge Streets. Shopping is excellent in streets lined with Elizabethan half-timbered buildings. Combine a shopping trip with visit to Chester Zoo, largest outside London.

☛ *M62 westbound to M6. Turn south to M56 and take westbound route signposted for Chester. Tourist Information at the Town Hall.*
☎ *0244-324324.*

Granada Studios Tour

You can walk across the hallowed cobbles of the outdoor "Coronation Street" set, and see a special "Street" museum with everything from Hilda Ogden's "muriel" to Bet's wedding dress. Or have your photograph taken outside 10 Downing Street or walk round the House of Commons (used in Jeffrey Archer's "First Among Equals"), and go behind the scenes to see indoor studios, control rooms, wardrobes, etc. Round it off with a drink in the Rover's Return and buy Newton & Ridley beermats.

☛ *In Water Street, Manchester, (off Quay St). Opening times vary according to season and day of week. Ring for details. Admission charge.*
☎ *061-833-0880.*

Jodrell Bank

This 250ft. high radiotelescope was opened in 1957 just in time to track the Russians' Sputnik One, the first artificial earth satellite. Its main role is astronomy, providing the first lunar surface pictures in 1966 and today its vision reaches ever further. Visitors see a three-dimensional planetarium and feel like they're hitchhiking through the galaxy. At Christmas there is a special "Star Watch." The site was originally a botanical garden and today this has been turned into a 35-acre tree park with specimens from all around the world.

☛ *M62 westbound to M6 and turn south to exit 18. Take left turning (A535) through village of Holmes Chapel and Jodrell Bank is signposted to left 4 miles along this road. Open daily Easter to late-October. 10.30-5.30pm. Planetarium show every three-quarters of an hour. Nov-Easter weekends only 2-5pm.*
☎ *0477-71339*

Lake District National Park

The biggest and most dramatic of all National Parks in England and Wales, the Lakes are now a two-hour drive from Leeds. But where do you start, when there's 16 lakes and almost 300 separate mountain summits? Try the National Park Visitor Centre at Brockhole, between Windermere and Ambleside. It has displays explaining the Park's landscape and facilities, and loads of free leaflets. For the complete Lake District experience, climb England's highest mountain, Scafell Pike (3,210 feet) signposted from Wasdale Head, or Helvellyn (3,118 feet) from Patterdale. Cruise Coniston Water on the restored steam yacht Gondola. Visit William Wordsworth's Dove Cottage at Grasmere. Take the kids to Beatrix Potter's Hill Top house, and see her original watercolours. Ride on the Ravenglass-Eskdale Railway, a seven-mile journey by Lilliputian engine and coaches.

☛ *West along A65 from Leeds, following Kendal sign. For a complete information pack, including "Where to Stay", contact the Cumbria Tourist Board, Ashleigh, Holly Road, Windermere, Cumbria. LA23 2AQ. Don't go walking without the Wainwright guidebooks, which are available at all bookshops.*
☎ *Brockhole: 05394-46601; Teletourist (What's On service): 05394-46363; Lakes Weather Service: 05394-45151.*

Liverpool

Increasingly, Liverpool's destiny is as a massive heritage park devoted to the city's—and Britain's—glorious past. At its heart is the 150-year-old Albert Dock, where the Merseyside Maritime Museum is located. This contains historic ships exhibits, working displays and highlights like the "emigrants to a New World" display. There is a northern Tate Gallery, with 20th century art by famous artists, and The Beatles Story, a wonderful collection of Fab Four memorabilia and a reconstructed Cavern Club. The rest of the dock is filled with speciality shops, good cafés, bars and bistros. If you have time, walk west to the Pierhead and take a ferry across the Mersey.

☛ *Allow up to two hours for drive west on M62. Tourist Information Centre is in the Atlantic Pavilion, Albert Dock. Good parking.*
☎ *051-708-8854.*

Manchester Museum of Science & Technology

Winner of the "Museum of the Year" award, it is based on the site of the world's oldest passenger railway station (1830), has the biggest collection of working steam engines anywhere. The Air & Space Gallery has historic planes and tells the story of flight from Spitfire to Space Shuttle. You can even walk down a real Victorian sewer. A highly modern approach is the hands-on "Xperiment", the interactive science centre where you can shake hands with yourself and walk away from your own shadow.

☛ *M62 west to exit 18. Hourly trains (journey approx. one hour) from Leeds City. Also National Express coaches. The museum is at the corner of Liverpool Road and Lower Byrom Street. Open daily, 10-5pm. Car park on site. Admission charge.*
☎ *061-832-2244.*

Morecambe

If you find Blackpool too noisy, try this more traditional seaside resort, where there are still some old-fashioned cafés on the seafront. Modern attractions include the "Bubbles" Leisure Park, swimming pools with waterslides, tropical ponds and wave machine. Frontierland is a Wild West theme park/funfair And the famous Marineland Oceanarium has dolphins and sea lions performing stunts and a range of alligators, tropical fish, etc. The walk across

the sands at low tide is a memorable experience (ask for guided tours at info centre). Morecambe pioneered seaside illuminations in 1919 and there are nearly five miles of them each autumn.

☛ *Trains via Skipton & Settle. Or two-hour drive via Skipton and A65 Dales route forking left near Clapham through High Bentham and Lancaster. Tourist Info Centre is in Marine Road.*
☎ *0524-414110.*

Sellafield

Through the 1970s and the early 1980s, the nuclear plant at Windscale on the Cumbrian coast took a hammering. Documentaries about radioactive pollution and its effects were a stable of TV schedules. Then the plant's owners, British Nuclear Fuels, decided to fight back. Changing its name to the more pastoral Sellafield, it opened its gates to tourists and is now one of the top attractions in the northwest. You can see how the uranium rods are handled, and have the whole process of atomic power generation explained.

☛ *Off the A595 West Cumbria road, between Barrow-in-Furness and Whitehaven. Before going, ask for a free guide, explaining visiting arrangements. Write to Sellafield Visitors Centre, Sellafield, Seascale, Cumbria CA20 1PG.*
☎ *09467-27027.*

Wigan Pier

This quay on the Leeds-Liverpool Canal was made famous by George Orwell, who made a celebrated trip through the North of England in 1936 to describe poverty among the working-classes and published the results in The Road to Wigan Pier. Some of the book, incidentally, was written while staying at his sister's house in Headingley, Leeds. Today, the pier is a busy heritage attraction, with warehouses full of displays. There's an exhibition centre for schools, a steam engine/working machinery hall, concert hall, shops and pub-restaurant ("The Orwell"). A unique exhibition is called The Way We Were, brought to life by actors trained to "humanize" scenes of everyday 19th century

industrial and domestic activity.
☛ *M62 east, then north on M61 to exit 6, following Wigan sign. Pier is well signposted and there is ample parking.*
☎ *24 hour recorded info (opening times, events etc) on 0942-44888. General inquiries 323666.*

Going North

City of Durham

On a sandstone bluff high above an enormous loop of the River Wear stand the great Norman cathedral and castle, which together are acknowledged as a World Heritage site. They dominate a lovely city of narrow, mostly pedestrianised streets. Many people cite the cathedral as their favourite building in Britain. Constructed between 1093 and 1133, it has hardly been altered since then. Inside are the tombs of St. Cuthbert, one of the most revered of the early Northern saints, and the Venerable Bede, author of the earliest English History. Next door at the castle, see the beautiful Norman chapel and 13th century great hall. The most dramatic views are from one of the hired rowing boats on the river in season.

☛ *Frequent train service from Leeds, via York. Or allow 90 mins. north on A1. Plenty of parking. The Tourist Information Centre is in the Market Place.*
☎ *091-384-3720.*

Hadrian's Wall

The most famous Roman remains in Britain extend for almost 75 miles from Wallsend on the east coast to the Solway Firth in the west. Built by Emperor Hadrian in AD 122 to keep out the unruly Picts, it eventually included 17 forts, garrisoned by 13,000 infantry and 6,000 cavalry. When it was completed, the wall stood 20ft high and 10ft broad, but today—even at the best-preserved stretch, between the Tyne and Gilsland—it does not exceed 10 feet in height. For your first visit, go to Housesteads, where the wall traverses a dramatic series of crags. Also here is a five-acre fort, the best surviving example of all the forts, where 1000 infantry were encamped. A good footpath leads over the fields from the car park, and the cliff on which the fort stands makes an impressive photograph. You can still see the foundations of the granary, hospital and barracks. Most interesting of all are the officers' baths, which were fed by rainwater. There is a small museum.

☛ *Housesteads is well signposted off the B6318. Quickest way from Leeds is north on A1, branching left on A68 near Darlington, and west on A69 at Corbridge. Museum open Oct-Mar daily from 10-4pm; Ap-Sept 10-6pm.*
☎ *0434-344363.*

Metro Centre

Europe's largest out of town shopping and leisure "city" is at Gateshead, just south of Newcastle. Let's get the statistics out of the way: over 350 shops, 12,000 parking places, 10-screen cinema, 28-lane bowling centre, 650-seater food-court containing more than 50 different places to eat and drink. There's also a creche, antique village, fantasyland fairground, and many retail hypermarkets. The Metro Centre draws shoppers, and browsers from all over Britain.

☛ *Three miles south of Newcastle, easily found off the A1. It has its own bus and railway stations, for connections from Newcastle city centre. Shopping hours Mon, Tue, Wed & Fri 10-8pm; Thur 10-9pm; Sat 9-7pm.*
☎ *091-460-5299.*

Newcastle

Any Georgian-Victorian city with a large waterfront area is worth a visit and you will find the Tyne's Quayside packed with things to see and do, from staring at the six great bridges to the hectic Sunday market, old pubs and river cruises. In the city centre, your priority should be to visit the excellent Grainger Market. It was Europe's largest under-cover shopping area when opened in the 1830s to sell meat and vegetables and the model on which many others, including Leeds's Kirkgate Market, were based. It still has its Marks and Spencer Penny Bazaar, while the original—in Leeds—no longer ex-

ists. Of the many Newcastle museums, best is the Museum of Science and Engineering in West Blandford Street, detailing the city's shipbuilding and coalmining history with startling displays.

☛ *Regular trains from Leeds via York, or 90 min. drive north on A1. For the city's excellent tourist brochure, contact the City Information Service, Central Library, Princess Square, Newcastle-upon-Tyne NE99 1DX.*
☎ *091-261-0691.*

Teesdale

Much of Upper Teesdale was stolen from Yorkshire in 1974. Start at the cobblestoned Barnard Castle, high above the Tees, where Charles Dickens wrote part of Nicholas Nickleby. Nearby, Bowes Museum is called the "Treasurehouse of the North" because has much priceless European art. But the best of Teesdale is west up the dale, past High Force waterfall, England's most dramatic, where the Tees leaps 50ft over a cliff. Continue past Langdon Beck up to Cow Green Reservoir, famous for Alpine flowers, and take the Pennine Way to Cross Fell, at 2,591ft. once known as "Yorkshire's Everest".

☛ *North on A1 to Scotch Corner, then west on A66. Barnard Castle is right on B6277. The Tourist Information Centre will provide a pack of leaflets. It is at 43 Galgate.*
☎ *0833-690909.*

Weardale

The least discovered of all the Pennine dales, Weardale happens to be one of the most interesting. It was an important lead mining area until Victorian times, and there is no better example of what was for centuries the main industry of the North Pennines than Killhope, a perfectly restored lead crushing mill and mine. The site is dominated by its huge water wheel, and there are many displays for visitors. The valley floor has numerous interesting villages, yet to become "holiday let" ghosts, like Nend Head and St. John's Chapel, where there is good walking beside the Wear.

☛ *North on A1, forking right on A68 and wst on A689.*

The 200-acre **Beamish Industrial Museum** *is an open-air working reproduction of a north-eastern industrial village at the turn of the century. Real houses, shops and traditional tradesmen's premises were rebuilt on-site. You can go inside the homes of miners to see their tin baths in front of the bread-oven fire, and see a Co-op long before supermarket check-outs. Ride on the tramcars, visit Victoria Park to hear a brass band or ride on the steam-driven carousel, see the colliery workings or the home farm, or the forge, pigsty and henhouse from times when free-range was taken for granted. See the bakery, dentist, railway station. Great nostalgia for pensioners but a good day out for everyone.*
☛ *By car north on A1, leaving at Chester-le-Street/Beamish sign on A1(M), and west along the A693 to Stanley. Open 10-6pm daily Apr-Oct, 10-5pm in winter but closed Mon. Admission charge.*
☎ *0207-231811.*

Leeds Lifelines

A handy list of phone numbers and contacts for
emergencies, advice and important information

For Fire, Police & Ambulance Emergencies
Call 999

GENERAL

Police. Enquiries and non-emergencies—
Leeds centre and suburbs ☎ Leeds 435353.
Garforth Police (East of Leeds & Wetherby) ☎ Leeds
868616.
Horsforth Police (North of Leeds & Otley) ☎ Leeds
585065
Morley Police (South and South West of Leeds) ☎
Leeds 533531.
Pudsey Police (West of Leeds) ☎ Leeds 552222.
Electricity. ☎ Leeds 415000. (24 hour service for
emergency calls and supply failure. In event of a pro-
longed supply emergency, customers should listen
to local radio stations on battery-operated radio).
Gas. If you suspect an escape of gas call the emer-
gency number (24-hour service) for your area
West and North West Leeds ☎ Leeds 590761
East and North East Leeds ☎ Leeds 737555
South Leeds ☎ Leeds 440244.
Water Services. For day to day enquiries, including
emergencies, in the Leeds area ☎ Leeds 492291
Morley Area ☎ Wakefield (0924) 372101
Otley Area ☎ Bradford (0274) 691111.
Lost Property. The lost property office for Leeds is
at Milgarth Police Station. Open Mon-Thur 9am-5pm,
Fri 9am-4.30pm. Closed Sat & Sun. ☎ Leeds 435353.
BBC Radio Leeds Helpline (Community help/advice)
☎ 0422-349407.

COUNCIL

Leeds City Council. General enquiries about the vast
range of services offered by the council. Tell them
your problem/query and they'll pin-point who can help.
Open Mon-Thur 8.30am-5pm, Fri 8.30am-4.30pm. ☎
Leeds 474024.
Housing. (Council properties, landlord problems,
homelessness, etc). ☎ Leeds 476919.
Social Services. Help for elderly, children support,
disabled, family problems. General Enquiries ☎ Leeds
478630. After-hours emergencies ☎ Leeds 696198.
Poll Tax/Council Charge. Office depends on your
area of Leeds. ☎ Leeds 474024 for advice.
School Education. Enquiries about any aspect of
your child's education. ☎ Leeds 475678.
Pest/Rodent Control. ☎ Leeds 493781.

TRAVEL

Yorkshire Rider (Leeds area buses) ☎ Leeds 429614
Metro bus & train services ☎ Leeds 457676.
British Rail General Enquiries ☎ Leeds 448133.
National Coaches ☎ Leeds 460011.
Leeds-Bradford Airport Information ☎ Leeds
509696.

PLACES/EVENTS INFORMATION

Leeds Tourist Info Centre ☎ Leeds 478301/2/3.
Otley Tourist Info Centre ☎ Leeds 477705.
Wetherby Tourist Info Centre ☎ Leeds 477253.

HEALTH

Late Chemists. A list of late-opening chemists in the
suburbs is published nightly in the Evening Post. In
Central Leeds, Peels Chemists, 83 Briggate, opens
weekdays 9am-9pm, Sat 9am-6pm and Sun 12-4pm.
☎ Leeds 431589.
Blood Donations. Leeds Blood Donor Centre ☎
Leeds 645091.
Leeds General Infirmary ☎ Leeds 432799.
St. James' Hospital ☎ Leeds 433144.
Wharfedale General Hospital ☎ 0943-465522.
Emergency Dental Treatment. Woodsley Road
Health Centre, Woodsley Road, Leeds LS6. Opens
Sun and Bank Hols 9am-11.30am. ☎ Leeds 444526.
Disabled Help. DIAL (Disablement Information and
Advice Line) ☎ Leeds 795583.
AIDS. Body Positive Yorkshire (Helpline/support) ☎
0924-456667.
Sexually Transmitted Diseases. For appointments
☎ Leeds 437124 (men) and 437125 (women).

ADDICTION

Leeds Addiction Unit. ☎ Leeds 316940.
Leeds Drugs Project. ☎ Leeds 423182.
Alcoholics Anonymous. ☎ Leeds 434567.

HELPLINES/COUNSELLING

Samaritans. (24-hour confidential support for suicidal,
depressed, people with problems) ☎ Leeds 456789.
Relate. (Marriage/relationship guidance) ☎ Leeds
452595.
Victims Support. (Sympathetic/practical help for vic-
tims of crime). North East Leeds ☎ 485028; North
West Leeds ☎ 756928; South Leeds ☎ 713558.
Careline. Help with emotional problems, stress, etc.
for families & young persons ☎ Leeds 456456.
Touchline. For children & adults with problems of
sexual abuse ☎ Leeds 457777.
Women's Counselling. ☎ Leeds 455725.
Leeds Rape Crisis. ☎ Leeds 440058.
Student Nightline. Confidential help for all Leeds stu-
dents, 8pm-8am term-time. ☎ Leeds 442602.
Leeds Gay Switchboard. Information & help 7pm-
10pm nightly ex. Tues. ☎ Leeds 453588.
Leeds Lesbian Line. Information & help 7.30pm-
9.30pm every Tues. ☎ Leeds 453588.

ANIMALS/WILDLIFE

**Royal Society for the Protection of Cruelty to Ani-
mals.** (RSPCA) Inspectors (for reports of cruelty)
☎ Leeds 342144.
RSPCA (Animal home and clinic) ☎ Leeds 455132.
West Yorkshire Raptor Rehabilitation Centre. (Help
for injured birds of prey, ducks, geese & swans. Can't
take smaller birds). ☎ Leeds 777347.
Royal Society for the Protection of Birds. North of
England Office (for reports/tips about offences against
protected species, eggs and young). ☎ 091-232-4148.